SANTA BARBARA

& THE CENTRAL COAST

California's Riviera

Help Us Keep This Guide Up to Date

Every effort has been made by the authors and editors to make this guide as accurate and useful as possible. However, many things can change after a guide is published—establishments close, phone numbers change, facilities come under new management, etc.

We would love to hear from you concerning your experiences with this guide and how you feel it could be made better and be kept up to date. While we may not be able to respond to all comments and suggestions, we'll take them to heart and we'll also make certain to share them with the authors. Please send your comments and suggestions to the following address:

The Globe Pequot Press
Reader Response/Editorial Department
P.O. Box 480
Guilford, CT 06437

Or you may e-mail us at:

editorial@globe-pequot.com

Thanks for your input, and happy travels!

HILL GUIDES™ SERIES

SANTA BARBARA & THE CENTRAL COAST

California's Riviera

by Kathleen Thompson Hill
&
Gerald Hill

The Globe Pequot Press

Guilford, Connecticut

Cover painting entitled "Santa Barbara: California's Riviera" by Judy Theo Lehner, M.F.A. Studio address: 134 Church Street, Sonoma, CA 95476; (707) 996–5111. Medium: monotype.
Cover and text design by Lana Mullen
Maps by Lisa Reneson
Illustrations by Mauro Magellan
Photos by Kathleen & Gerald Hill unless otherwise noted

Library of Congress Cataloging-in-Publication Data
Hill, Kathleen
    Santa Barbara & the Central Coast : California's Riviera / by
  Kathleen Thompson Hill & Gerald Hill.
      p.   cm.   -- (Hill guides series)
    Includes index.
    ISBN 0-7627-0555-8
    1. Santa Barbara Region (Calif.) Guidebooks.   2. Pacific Coast
  (Calif.) Guidebooks.   3. San Luis Obispo Region (Calif.) Guidebooks.
  I. Hill, Gerald N.   II. Title.   III. Title: Santa Barbara and the
  Central Coast.   IV. Series: Hill, Kathleen. Hill guides.
  F869.S45H595   1999
  917.94'7--dc21   99–41724
                                                                CIP

Manufactured in the United States of America
First Edition/First Printing

CONTENTS

PREFACE

The Central Coast of California is a treasure trove of discoveries, all too often neglected by travelers who race along the highway between Los Angeles and the San Francisco Bay Area. To fully appreciate California's Riviera, we ask you to pause with us long enough to come to know the charming towns, the varied menus, the new wave of wines, and the pleasant and interesting people of this under-discovered scenic wonderland.

We take you through historic Santa Barbara, which has established a Mediterranean style of architecture and living with a climate to match, newly beautified and surprisingly sophisticated San Luis Obispo, and the coastal and wine country villages and valleys in both counties. Solvang has managed to create a slice of Denmark-in-America without phony glitz, Santa Maria has become synonymous with scrumptious barbecue, and Paso Robles has much more to offer than just horse country.

The recently acclaimed wines of the central coast are demonstrating the wisdom shown by pioneering experts who believed San Luis Obispo and Santa Barbara counties could be some of the world's ideal wine-producing regions. Follow us to the vineyards in the hills above San Luis Obispo, on the roads fanning out from Paso Robles, the lanes of Edna Valley, and the old frontier towns of Santa Ynez Valley. Grapes are growing everywhere and we guide you to tasting rooms of every size and style. The hosts include the rich and famous, descendants of early settlers, enologists from UC Davis, and families who decided to give up the fast track of downtown Los Angeles.

Five sensitively restored missions, the remarkable Hearst Castle and dozens of tempting restaurants await your visit. The beaches call out to you: Morro Bay, Avila Beach, Pismo Beach, Goleta, Carpinteria, and Santa Barbara, as well as hidden coves in between, with clear white sand, easy access, pleasant accommodations, and summer sun from spring to fall.

We urge you to explore the California Riviera in depth. You may never leave.

—Kathleen Hill
—Gerald Hill

ACKNOWLEDGMENTS

*A*s is true for all our books our work was made possible by the assistance and cooperation of many people and organizations.

We were given fabulous help by the staffs of the Santa Barbara Visitors Bureau, the San Luis Obispo County Visitors and Conference Bureau, the San Luis Obispo Downtown Association, the San Luis Obispo Chamber of Commerce, the Santa Barbara Historical Society, the Paso Robles Vintners & Growers Association, the Santa Barbara County Vintners' Association, and the Santa Barbara Public Library among others.

Several friends served as reporting scouts including Gordon Phillips, Marie Hicklin, Gig and Mel Owen, Sue Holman, Susan Weeks, and Kathleen's Santa Barbara cousin, Deborah Baker. Charming and knowledgeable local guides to people and places were Susan Dickenson, Laura Kath Fraser, and Peter Fraser. Karen Kyle of the San Luis Obispo Art Center steered us toward valuable information and contacts. Our ever patient, always helpful, and often hilarious editor Gail Gavert helped make it fun.

The store proprietors, chefs, winery owners, winemakers and staffs, and hotel and motel operators we met in our travels were generous with their help and willingness to share their secrets and recipes. Thank you very much.

And a special thanks to Julia Child for her encouragement.

INTRODUCTION

The first time we went to Santa Barbara together was on our honeymoon. We were slowly making our way down the Pacific coast from San Francisco, with one criterion for places to stay: we had to be able to hear the ocean's waves from our hotel room. Bliss! Eventually we arrived in Santa Barbara—a gorgeous and welcoming place for singles, couples, partners, and families of all sizes and most income levels.

For this book we treat everything from Hearst Castle at San Simeon in the north to south of Carpinteria near the Santa Barbara–Ventura County line as central coast. Some people would include Monterey County, but you can enjoy that information in our *Hill Guide to Monterey and Carmel* for complete details ranging from natural wonders to galleries, shops, museums, wineries, and restaurants.

Santa Barbara, Santa Barbara County, San Luis Obispo, and the rest of San Luis Obispo County are all so beautiful and rich in California history, varied climates (coastal to arid), beautiful beaches, waving palm trees, little-known wineries and restaurants, and natural flora that we almost hesitate to spread the word. But since these areas are well accustomed to visitors from throughout the world, our consciences are clear. So here we go.

SANTA BARBARA

Santa Barbara is simply one of the most beautiful and romantic places in North America. Plain and simple. It is at once quiet and exciting, flat and mountainous, small-town and big-city, progressive and conservative, and elegant and casual.

You can visit a western guest ranch a la President Ronald Reagan and Fess Parker, or go whale watching, wine tasting, mountain biking, sailing, parasailing, sunbathing, Jet Skiing, surfing, and beachcombing along nine beaches stretching 20 miles; you can play volleyball, try in-line skating, go shopping-shopping-shopping, visit art galleries galore, and enjoy theatrical and musical performances year-round. To say nothing of celebrity spotting.

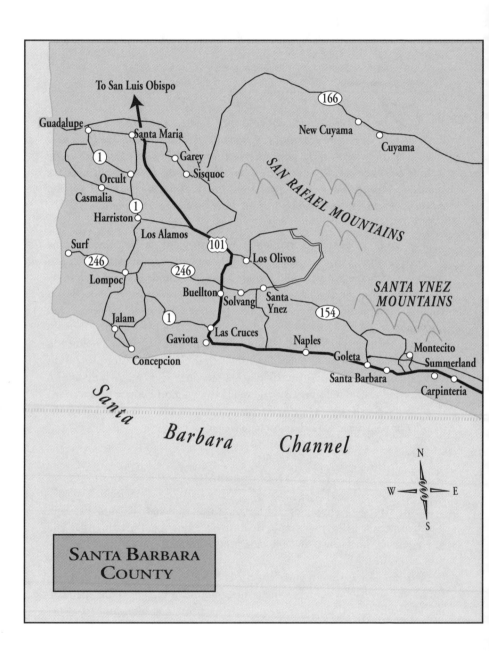

To San Luis Obispo

Guadalupe

166

New Cuyama

Cuyama

Santa Maria

1

Garey

Orcutt

Sisquoc

SAN RAFAEL MOUNTAINS

Casmalia

1

Harriston

Los Alamos

101

Surf

246

Los Olivos

Lompoc

246

SANTA YNEZ
MOUNTAINS

Buellton

Solvang

Santa
Ynez

Jalam

1

154

Las Cruces

Gaviota

Naples

Concepcion

Goleta

Montecito

Summerland

Santa Barbara

Carpinteria

Santa Barbara Channel

N

W   E

S

**SANTA BARBARA
COUNTY**

Hollywood stars flock here to find a unique privacy of togetherness in breathtaking surroundings, and many live here at least part-time, knowing that Santa Barbarans won't reveal their secret hideaways. In the early 1900s Santa Barbara became the film capital of the world before Hollywood developed as movie capital. In a ten-year period twelve hundred movies (lots of Westerns) were made here, and you will recognize the scenery as you visit the wineries throughout Santa Barbara and San Luis Obispo Counties.

Santa Barbara County sits 90 miles north of Los Angeles and borders on Ventura County to the south. It's an easy 90 minute drive from Los Angeles, but a good eight hours from San Francisco, which is 332 miles north. Traveling from San Francisco, we recommend a luxurious stop in Cambria or in the San Luis Obispo wine country to split the drive into two days and allow for a visit to Hearst Castle at San Simeon. But you can just barrel on down in one day if you wish.

The county includes the cities of Carpinteria, Goleta, Montecito, Summerland, Santa Barbara, and the five Channel Islands. Ballard, Buellton, Lompoc, Los Alamos, Los Olivos, Santa Maria, Santa Ynez, and Solvang are all in northern Santa Barbara county and have their own interesting and distinct reasons for you to visit.

You will find Santa Barbara's Mediterranean climate to be possibly the best you have ever experienced: sunny 300 days over twelve months of the year. Newscasters refer to drizzle or a temperature drop to about 55° as a "storm." The temperature averages in the 60s and 70s, with surprisingly low humidity, considering Santa Barbara's proximity to the Pacific Ocean.

Santa Barbara's mixed population results in marvelously diverse ethnic foods and markets, with restaurants ranging from local Mexicans' favorite Mexican to northern outposts of some of Los Angeles' finest. Population totals for Santa Barbara reach around 95,000—nearly 400,000 for the county.

SAN LUIS OBISPO

San Luis Obispo may be one of your great West Coast travel discoveries. The county stretches from the Monterey County line south to Santa Barbara County with exciting cliffs and beaches along the Pacific Ocean, and interesting towns such as San Simeon (and the Hearst Castle), Cambria, Morro Bay, San Luis Obispo, Pismo Beach, Guadalupe, Arroyo Grande, Nipomo, Avila Beach, Atascadero, Templeton, and Paso Robles with its wine country.

Located 200 miles north of Los Angeles and 230 miles south of the San Francisco Bay area, the city of San Luis Obispo feels small and intimate, with tree-lined streets, small boutiques as well as large chain coffee and book stores, innovative and comfort food restaurants, reasonable prices, Mission San Luis Obispo de Toloso, a mission plaza with library and historic museum, art center and galleries, California Polytechnic State University (Cal Poly), a children's museum, a modern performing arts center, and its own path of history walking tour. San Luis Obispo's Thursday evening farmers' market is a classic with abundant local growers' fruits of labor, entertainment, and shops staying open late.

Paso Robles and its neighbor to the south, tiny Templeton, are both Western movie-style towns where it's hot and dusty in summer, lovely in winter. Both are growing as food and wine centers and are worth rediscovering.

The climate in San Luis Obispo County varies, with mild days (50° to 70°) year-round on the coast to cool 55° nights and hot 109° days in the summer inland near and east of San Luis Obispo.

Lake Nacimiento, Lopez Lake, Laguna Lake, Santa Margarita Lake, and Atascadero Lake afford boating, water sports, and lake fishing. Hiking, kayaking, golf, miniature golf, horseback riding, specialty farms, museums, whale watching, a monarch butterfly grove at Pismo State Beach, sailing, windsurfing, and the Charles Paddock Zoo in Atascadero all offer plenty to do and see for the whole family. And then there are the wonderful wineries.

HOW TO GET HERE

Santa Barbara and most of the central coast are easily reachable via California Highway 101 or Highway 1, which occasionally merge and become one. Highway 101 is a scenic and relatively peaceful freeway route that runs the length of California slightly inland from the ocean, while Highway 1 runs along the Pacific Ocean, at times seeming to hang over it. You can also ride Amtrak's Coast Starlight to and through this gorgeous terrain, sometimes getting even closer views of the ocean than from the highway. Several airlines land at Santa Barbara Airport just outside of nearby Goleta, and the Santa Barbara Airbus transports visitors to and from Los Angeles area airports.

Getting Here by Car

From Los Angeles: Either take the Ventura Freeway (Highway 101) straight out of town heading north to Santa Barbara through Thousand Oaks, Oxnard, Ventura, and Carpinteria to Summerland, Montecito, and Santa Barbara, or take the scenic route along Highway 1 from Newport Beach or Santa Monica along the coast through Malibu. Highway 1 and Highway 101 join near

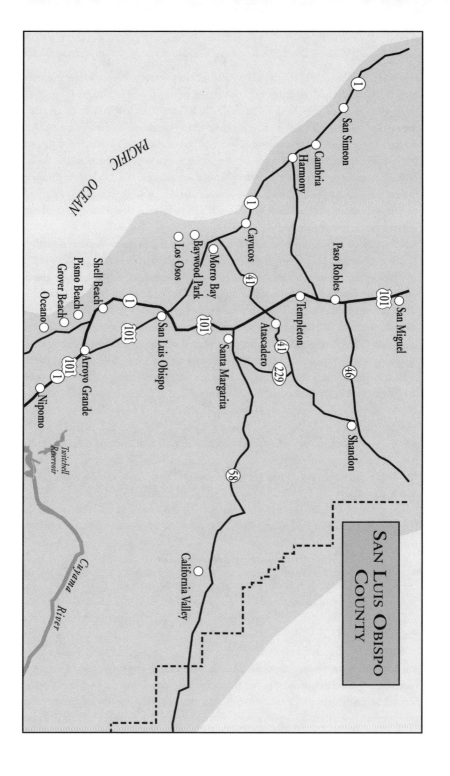

Oxnard and run northwestward along the water through Carpinteria, Summerland, and Montecito to Santa Barbara.

To reach San Luis Obispo you basically follow Highway 101 or Highway 1 when they are one and the same or when they separate and then follow our directions to specific destinations. North of Santa Barbara Highway 1 splits off from 101 near Las Cruces and takes you to Lompoc, Vandenberg Air Force Base, Guadalupe, and Grover Beach, and then rejoins 101 at Arroyo Grande, heading north to Pismo Beach, Avila Beach, and San Luis Obispo. It splits off to the west again at San Luis Obispo and goes to Morro Bay, Cambria, and San Simeon and Hearst Castle.

From Bakersfield and Fresno, take Highway 46 to Paso Robles, and then 101 south to San Luis Obispo and Santa Barbara.

From San Francisco and San Jose: Your two choices are to take Highway 101 on the east side of the Coast Range and Santa Lucia Mountains (excellent wine tasting along the way) or to take Highway 1 down the Pacific Ocean for the dramatically scenic and occasionally breathtaking route through Carmel, Big Sur, San Simeon and Hearst Castle, Cambria, and Morro Bay, where Highway 1 turns inland to meet Highway 101 at San Luis Obispo. You can also cross the Santa Lucia Mountains on Highway 46 from Cambria to Paso Robles on Highway 101.

Then you follow Highway 101 south from Paso Robles to Templeton, Santa Margarita, and San Luis Obispo, where it joins Highway 1, and proceed southward on Highway 1 to Avila Beach, Pismo Beach, and Arroyo Grande. From here Highway 1 splits oceanward through Guadalupe, to Orcutt, Vandenberg Air Force Base, Lompoc, Las Cruces, Gaviota, Isla Vista, Goleta, and finally Santa Barbara.

San Luis Obispo is about four hours from Los Angeles and San Francisco (five hours from San Francisco via scenic, winding Highway 1).

Getting Here by Air

Major airlines: American Eagle and American Airlines (800) 433–7300; America West and America West Express (800) 235–9292; Skywest/Delta Connection (800) 453–9417 or (805) 683–1780; United Airlines, United Express, and United Shuttle (800) 241–6522; and U.S. Air Express (800) 428–4322 all land at Santa Barbara Airport (805) 683–4011, the most elegant and charming small airport we have ever seen. The airport's architecture and landscaping give first-time visitors their first glimpse of the agreed-upon architecture and ambience of the Santa Barbara area. The only slight negative is that the car rental offices are a good walk from the landing tarmac, which is sometimes a problem wheeling loaded luggage carts.

Santa Barbara Airbus (805–964–7759 or 800–733–6354) provides transportation to and from Los Angeles Airport (LAX), picking passengers up close to their airlines if they reserve ahead. Fares are $35 for one person, $62 for two people together, and $78 for three people traveling together for about a two-hour trip. Airbus also offers tours from Santa Barbara to the Los Angeles County Museum, L.A. Dodgers games, and to the J. Paul Getty Museum, as well as limousine service.

American Eagle (800–433–7300) serves San Luis Obispo County Airport, 3 miles from downtown San Luis Obispo, as do Reno Air, United Express, Alaska Airlines, Canadian Airlines, and Hawaiian Airlines, for a total of forty flights a day.

Air charters: The Santa Barbara area's unique residential and visiting populations often prefer to charter their own air transportation. In case you fit into that category, we offer the most prominent of those services. Call them for personalized specifics: Above All Aviation (805) 967–2116; Air Trails (805) 683–4595; Cabaco Aviation (805) 693–9777; Hunter Charters of Santa Barbara (805) 681–9161; Mercury Aviation (805) 964–6733; Pacific Aviation (805) 967–0429; Signature Flight Support (805) 967–5608; and Sunwest Aviation (800) 293–2437.

Getting Here by Amtrak

Amtrak stops in both Santa Barbara and San Luis Obispo with convenient safe stations. Santa Barbara's train station has just undergone an earthquake retrofit and renovation restoring it to its historic glory.

Getting Here by Bus

Greyhound Bus Lines (800–231–2222) stops regularly in both Santa Barbara and San Luis Obispo. The Santa Barbara bus station is modern, well-lighted, and centrally located just a block from State Street at 34 West Carrillo Street (805–965–7551). In San Luis Obispo Greyhound stops at 150 South Street (805–543–2121).

GETTING AROUND ONCE YOU'RE HERE

By Bus in Santa Barbara

Santa Barbara Metropolitan Transit District provides bus transportation in and between Goleta, Santa Barbara, and Carpinteria. Essential for visitors, it also offers an electric downtown/waterfront shuttle up and down State Street, along Cabrillo and the beach, and to Coast Village Road in Montecito. Cost: twenty-five cents. The Santa Barbara Trolley runs between hotels, historic sites, shopping areas, and cultural attractions.

Santa Barbara's electric downtown shuttle departs from Stearns Wharf every ten minutes from 10:15 A.M. to 6:00 P.M. It departs every thirty minutes weekdays from 7:45 to 10:00 A.M., Friday and Saturday from 6:30 to 9:00 P.M.; Saturday from 8:15 to 10:00 A.M.; and Sunday from 9:30 to 10:00 A.M. There is no evening service in winter. Watch for the turquoise blue signs for shuttle stops.

Both Santa Barbara and San Luis Obispo have excellent public transportation systems, but in case you need private alternatives, here they are.

By Taxi in Santa Barbara

Several transportation entities offer taxi service in Santa Barbara: Airbus Express (805) 864–7759 or (800) 733–6354; Orange Cab (805) 964–2800; Rose Cab (805) 564–2600; SuperRide Airport Shuttle (805) 683–9636; and Yellow Cab (805) 965–5111 or (800) 549–TAXI (from California phones only).

Limousine Service in Santa Barbara

Limo services that cater to locals, visitors, and celebrities include Ambassador Limousine Service (805) 648–7104; Celebrity Limo Service (805) 683–1613; Classic Limousine Service (800) 243–5466; Executive Limousine Service (805) 969 5525 or (800) 247 6980; Home James Limousine Service (805) 647–1739; Mammoth Limousine Service (805) 683–4807; Ocean Cities Limousine Service (805) 962–0507; Personal Tours Ltd. (805) 685–0552; Santa Barbara Professional Limousine Service and Final Detail (805) 967–9831 or 964–5466; Santa Ynez Valley Limousine Service (805) 688–6532; Sunset Limousine Service (805) 963–0419; and Walter's Limo Service (805) 964–7759.

Rental Car Agencies in Santa Barbara

The usual are available and generally well kept up: Avis Rent-A-Car (805) 965–1079 downtown and (805) 964–4848 at the airport; Budget Rent-A-Car & Truck (805) 963–6651 downtown and (805) 964–6791 reservation center; Dollar Rent-A-Car (805) 683–1468; Enterprise Rent-A-Car (805) 966–3097 downtown and (805) 683–0067 in Goleta; Ford Rent-A-Car (805) 682–2444; Hertz Rent-A-Car (805) 967–0411 at the airport;

National Car Rental (805) 967–1202; and U-Save Auto Rental (805) 963–3499.

By Bus in San Luis Obispo

A free and open trolley runs in a loop around San Luis Obispo's downtown area, a wonderful convenience. SLO Transit (which is an abbreviation, not a comment) provides bus service throughout the city of San Luis Obispo and to Cal Poly. CCAT (Central Coast Area Transit) runs buses outside the city of San Luis Obispo to communities from San Simeon to Santa Maria.

PARKING

Parking in Santa Barbara is easiest if you plant your car before lunchtime in a public parking lot or garage where the rates are reasonable enough to encourage you to come downtown. Ten parking lots and garages are available behind the shops on State Street, with entrances from the cross streets or from Chapala Street on the west side and Anacapa Street on the east. Chapala runs one-way up (north) and Anacapa runs one-way down (south). (See map p. 12) There is no parking on State Street, which lack definitely contributes to its visual beauty.

Downtown parking in San Luis Obispo is available on many streets or in several parking lots. Try the lots at: Higuera Street between Broad and Garden Streets; Higuera and Morro Streets; a block west of the mission on Nipomo Street between Higuera and Monterey Streets; east of the mission on Chorro Street between Monterey and Palm Streets; behind the post office on Pacific Street; and on Palm Street between Chorro and Morro Streets, just east of the Ah Louie store.

HOW TO BE A VISITOR AND NOT A TOURIST IN CALIFORNIA'S RIVIERA

Both Santa Barbara and San Luis Obispo have wildly contrasting populations, integrating college students and professors and all their support staff with winemakers and winemaking investors, extremely wealthy southern Californians, and retired and still active dignitaries and celebrities. So they're nice to everybody, because, being so close to Hollywood, who knows who you might really be!

Do yourself a favor and don't criticize the slow pace, lack of big-city influences, and minor disdain for smaller cities. It is OK, though, to complain about gas prices, which are high here. Might as well be honest and say you're visiting, because you will never be able to fake it—you have to live here at least a decade to even pretend to be local. If you're from a big city, just make it clear you're only passing through. Locals here want their place to stay just the way it is, thank you very much, and actually fear it becoming more big-cityish even though they like big-city-quality restaurants and amenities.

Try to master correct pronunciation of street names. Don't flash money or gold cards. Santa Barbarans are impressed only with how long you've lived here. Restaurant, hotel, and shop staffs are slightly impressed with celebrity and like to mention that Geena Davis or Julia Child "shops here all the time."

Walking down the street talking on your cell phone will give you away, probably. You see more and more of it, but old-timers don't even own one. So will lots of gold jewelry and earrings on men or a flashy gold-trimmed new car. Do not ask a movie star or celebrity for an autograph.

Rearrange your perspectives: Think of everything in terms of its distance from Santa Barbara, a place most residents don't want to leave. Everything south of Carpinteria is practically L.A.

Both Santa Barbara and San Luis Obispo Counties are full of both working ranchers and gentlemen ranchers (who may or may not be gentlemen) who hire others to do the work.

If you go out in the (infrequent) rain, you must be a tourist, because locals hide safely at home so they won't dissolve. It actually has rained when we've visited Santa Barbara and it is indeed lonely in restaurants, but who cares—the service is great.

Learn to like tri-tip barbecues. Tri-tip has become a regional source of pride, competition, and celebration. Restaurants specialize in it, individuals and service organizations set up barbecues in parking lots on weekends, and locals kibitz about marinades versus flavored-salt coatings.

Go in knowing significant dates about Santa Barbara: the 1925 earthquake, the 1970 burning of the Bank of America, and the 1995 floods will do for starters. The seasons all seem to occur later here than in most places, but for Easterners, Northerners, and almost everyone else, it seems to be mild summer here all the time.

Take a sweater or light jacket with you in case the temperature drops to 55°—a near freeze in these here parts. Locals complain if it's below 60°, and outsiders call them sissies when they do. But it does cool off at night year-round.

For an all-too-clear insight into the real Santa Barbara, consult the *Society Lady's Guide on How to Santa Barbara,* a hilarious exposé of how to fit in if you move to Santa Barbara. Author Erin Graffy de Garcia is "society lady" for the *Santa Barbara Independent* newspaper. Jeanne Graffy, Santa Barbara County supervisor, says, "The author was raised by gypsies and I never heard of her."

So now that we've filled you with hang-ups and uncertainties, relax and enjoy one of the most beautiful developed places on earth: California's Riviera.

MONTECITO, SUMMERLAND, CARPINTERIA, AND GOLETA

n the greater Santa Barbara area are these communities to the southeast: luxurious Montecito, the seashore settlement of Summerland, and the town of Carpinteria. Also in Santa Barbara's orbit is Goleta, a peninsula that juts into the ocean northwest of the city, and home to University of California Santa Barbara and the airport.

MONTECITO

Nestled in the lower slopes of the San Ysidro Mountains and adjoining Santa Barbara's southern edge, Montecito ("little mountain") is home or second home to some of the most famous and wealthy stars and families of the world. Is Montecito a suburb of Santa Barbara, or is it the other way around?

Directions: Take Highway 101 south of Santa Barbara to the San Ysidro Road exit. The Miramar Hotel is on the west side of the highway, and Montecito Village is on the east side. Turn east on San Ysidro to East Valley Road to the village, which will be to your left (north) at the intersection, while the Plaza del Sol is to your right (south).

While you see little of Montecito's plushness from the road (except the Montecito Country Club as a backdrop to the Andree Clark Bird Refuge), lush gardens and enormous spend-whatever-it-takes mansions dot the hillside among the trees. Montecito is also home to the fine Music Academy of the West and the Brooks Institute of Photography, the San Ysidro Ranch and Trailhead, La Casa de Maria Immaculate Heart Community, and the Boescke Adobe off San Leandro Lane.

As early as the 1890s wealthy Easterners flocked here because of the Santa Barbara area's sheer beauty and perfect climate, ideal to cure physical and emotional ills developed on the East Coast and in the Midwest. Since then the rich and famous have flocked to Montecito, bringing with them friends, the ability to spend to create beautiful and dramatic surroundings, and a small community to cater to their tastes.

Charlie Chaplin built the Montecito Inn to attract and cater to Hollywood stars of various kinds, and they have been coming here ever since. For a while actor Ronald Colman owned the San Ysidro Ranch, which then attracted stars such as Jean Harlow and William Powell.

The Miramar Hotel, built by Josiah Doulton, a member of a British porcelain-making family, is now a bit decrepit but boasts a still-popular bar/institution with Al Reese drawing the crowds after 9:30 P.M. Thursdays–Saturdays. Visit the hotel with its train car cafe, train station, and train tracks that run right through the resort's beachfront cottages.

BEACHFRONT HOMES FROM MIRAMAR HOTEL BEACH,
MONTECITO

The spectacular Biltmore Hotel (1927) overlooks Butterfly Beach, where monarch and other butterflies make a brief stop in the eucalyptus trees.

Drive into the village of Montecito and walk around. It is small and won't take long (elegant, small strip malls offer interesting shops beyond the community's center). Be sure to check out the legendary Montecito Inn and the

Montecito Cafe on Coast Village Road. Montecito's principal newer shopping centers are Montecito Village Shopping Center on the west side of East Valley and San Ysidro Roads, and the Old Village Shopping Center on the east side of East Valley Road.

The extremely popular **MONTECITO CAFÉ** in the historic Montecito Inn offers a casually elegant atmosphere right off the small hotel lobby in a dining room whose walls have heard it all. Movie and political romances have matured here, as may yours. And the food is good, featuring imaginative California cuisine based on chicken breasts, lamb, pasta, and that wonderful flank steak, which is definitely okay, all under $15.00, unusual for the neighborhood and atmosphere.

Montecito Café, 1295 Coast Village Road, Montecito 93150; (805) 969–3392. Open 11:30 A.M.–9:30 P.M. No lunch reservations. Full bar. Visa, MasterCard, American Express. Wheelchair accessible.

La Marina and the Patio Restaurants are the more and the less expensive dining rooms of the Santa Barbara Four Seasons Biltmore. **LA MARINA** is elegant and makes you feel very special, while the **PATIO** is more casual and slightly more reasonable. Locals come here for special occasions, while movie stars have been known to request catered lunches from the restaurants. From the Patio you can hang over the beach and enjoy the glorious Thursday through Sunday buffet that changes each evening.

La Marina and Patio Restaurants, 1260 Channel Drive, Montecito 93150; (805) 969–2261. La Marina: open for dinner from 5:30 P.M. Tuesday–Saturday; Patio Restaurant: 8:00 A.M.–9:00 P.M., Sunday brunch. Full bar. Visa, MasterCard, American Express. Wheelchair accessible.

PIERRE LAFOND'S superb delicatessen and gourmet special foods and cafe are a local hangout for the famous and infamous nearby residents. The low-fat muffins balance out the hand-dipped chocolate truffles and cheesecakes and pumpkin breads. Try the open-faced Scottish salmon sandwich, the thick, rich lasagna, the popular vegetarian Montecito burrito, or the veggie or chicken enchiladas. Fresh-off-the-farm produce is interspersed with a fabulous selection of local wines, the salad bar salves the conscience, and you can enjoy all this at outside cafe tables near the sparkling fountain or in the nearby park dubbed "Corner Green."

You will also want to visit their market and the Lafonds' Wendy Foster home shop and dress boutique.

Pierre Lafond, 516 San Ysidro Road, Montecito 93150; (805) 565–1502. Open 6:30 A.M.–8:00 P.M. daily, with the market open 9:00 A.M.–8:00 P.M. daily. Beer and wine. Visa, MasterCard, American Express. Wheelchair accessible.

MONTECITO VILLAGE GROCERY is worth finding for gourmet foods and meats, as well as picnic delicacies, fine liquors, and local as well as imported wines. Montecito Village Grocery also delivers free to your home or hotel Monday–Saturday.

🐝 *Montecito Village Grocery, 1482 East Valley Road, Montecito 93150; (805) 969–1112 or for deliveries (805) 969–7845. Full license. Open 8:30 A.M.–7:00 P.M. Monday–Saturday, 9:00 A.M.–7:00 P.M. Sunday. Visa, MasterCard, American Express. Wheelchair accessible.*

If you are looking for a dining experience more formal than your lap and not as formal as the Biltmore, you might try Palazzio with its two-drink bar, Cava for Spanish/Mexican food, or Via Vai and its sister Pane e Vino.

PALAZZIO is decorated with murals of Venice and Tuscany by Irene Roderick, and while it has a full liquor license, it serves only Italian margaritas and Italian martinis (Absolut vodka in which garlic has swum for at least three hours and kept pre-made in the freezer for you). Its twin (of the same name) is at 1026 State Street, downtown Santa Barbara.

🐝 *Palazzio Trattoria Italiano, 1151 Coast Village Road, Montecito 93150, (805) 969–8565; Web site: www.palazzios.com; open for lunch 11:30 A.M.–2:30 P.M. Monday–Saturday, dinner 5:30 P.M.–11:00 P.M. Sunday–Thursday, 5:30 P.M.–midnight, Friday–Saturday. Visa, MasterCard, American Express. Wheelchair accessible.*

CAVA features regional Latin cuisine and is between the Cabrillo Boulevard and San Ysidro Road exits from Highway 101 on Coast Village Road, which runs east of and parallel to Highway 101. Here you can lounge on Cava's patio while tasting tapas, sipping margaritas, and listening to soothing guitars. Cigars are encouraged.

The wide variety of tapas and appetizers range from shrimp sautéed with garlic ($8.95) to nachos, grilled pork, chicken, or veggie ($8.95) carnitas, or a tortilla española, a traditional Spanish potato and onion frittata with chimichurri sauce ($5.96). But there's much more than tapas.

The salads are healthy and exciting, like the grilled scallop and shrimp salad with mango, jícama, red pepper, mesclun greens, and lime vinaigrette ($14.95), or the grilled vegetable, chicken, or steak tostada ($10.95–$11.95). Besides the usual hamburgers and grilled chicken sandwiches with spanishized names, venture into the posole (a hearty Mexican soup with pork or chicken) ($9.95), mahimahi fajitas platter ($13.95), or the grilled skirt steak torta ($8.95).

Dinner offers many of the same selections, plus paella Valenciana ($17.95); spicy baby back ribs with guava chili sauce, chipotle mashed potatoes and grilled veggies ($14.95); grilled lamb chops with mango-mint salsa ($16.95); and grilled fresh salmon with papaya salsa ($15.95).

Cava, 1212 Coast Village Road, Montecito 93150; (805) 969–8500. Open 10:00 A.M.–10:00 P.M. Monday–Thursday, 10:00 A.M.–10:30 P.M. Friday, 8:00 A.M.–10:30 P.M. Saturday–Sunday. Full bar. Visa, MasterCard, American Express, Discover. Wheelchair accessible.

VIA VAI is an informal Italian restaurant in the Montecito Village Shopping Center featuring excellent specialized pizzas under $10, terrific bruschetta con pomodoro (Tuscan garlic bread topped with fresh tomato, basil, and garlic) ($5.75), fried calamari with spicy tomato sauce ($6.95), and a great roasted chicken salad ($6.50) outdone only by the spinach salad with warm pancetta, egg, and balsamic vinegar and olive oil dressing ($6.50). But try the antipasto della casa for an assortment of Via Vai's special appetizers ($8.50).

Main courses include loads of pastas and lasagnas, all under $10, and an excellent grilled Italian sausage with polenta and spinach ($9.95), rotisseried game and fowl, and choices of lamb or pork chops and steaks ($9.95–$16.95).

Via Vai, 1483 East Valley Road, No. 20, Montecito 93150; (805) 565–9393. Open 11:00 A.M.–10:00 P.M. daily. Beer and wine. Visa, MasterCard, American Express. Wheelchair accessible.

Just across East Valley Road in the Old Village Shopping Center is PANE E VINO, the trattoria offering of the two Italian restaurants with slightly more interesting and complicated food than Via Vai. Antipasti here include vitello tonnato (sliced roasted veal with capers and a lemony tuna sauce) ($8.95), an excellent stuffed cold artichoke ($6.95), grilled polenta with sautéed scallops ($9.75), and dry cured beef with arugula, sweet onions, and vinaigrette ($7.75).

Pastas range from the usuals to flat, curly, or round noodles with smoked mussels, capers, smoked mozzarella and eggplant. There is pancetta with fontina and peas, fresh tuna cubes, or porcini mushrooms, as well as a risotto (all under $10). Large veal chops, grilled rib-eye steak, and an excellent garlicky grilled rack of lamb (all $17.95) top the grilled meats list, with grilled polenta, stewed tomatoes, and Italian sausages ($9.95) a real treat.

Tiramisu and crème caramel fans will be happy (both under $5.00), but try the chocolate terrine tort with fresh berries sauce (Valentino con passata di fracole e lamponi) ($5.75) or the almond dipping cookies with aged Trebbiano wine ($6.75). Oh my!

Pane e Vino, 1482 East Valley Road, Montecito 93150; (805) 969–9274. Open 11:30 A.M.–9:30 P.M. Monday–Saturday, 5:00–9:00 P.M. Sunday. Beer and wine. Visa, MasterCard, American Express. Wheelchair accessible.

SUMMERLAND

Both Summerland, just south of Montecito, and Carpinteria are antiques collectors paradises, with antiques shops scattered along the main streets of both small towns. Explore and browse for yourself.

Once known to Santa Barbarans as "Spooksville" for the mind-expanding spiritualistic events that supposedly went on here, Summerland went through a period as surfer heaven, when it was filled with tan blond kids who hung out in the shabby bungalows along the coast, followed by a period as an oil boomtown, when, after oil was discovered offshore, rigs were installed to take away the oil— and the natural view. It now enjoys being a slightly offbeat fashionable attraction for the rich and famous.

Even President Bill and Hillary Rodham Clinton have "dined" at the NUGGET, always famous for its juicy hamburgers, crisp fries, and cocktails, and now famous for its famous customers. Great patio seating for people watching and sunbathing, if you still do that.

Nugget, 2318 Lillie Avenue, Summerland 93067; (805) 969–6135, fax (805) 969–0143. Open 11:00 A.M.–10:00 P.M. daily. Full bar. Visa, MasterCard, American Express. Wheelchair accessible.

Summerland's largest business is the Bikini Factory, which prides itself on having the largest stock of bikinis anywhere and for making custom bikinis (we can hardly wait!). One of the town's best views (of the ocean, that is) is from Lookout Park with stunningly clear lookouts to the Channel Islands, secluded beaches, and good surf fishing.

CARPINTERIA

Twelve miles south of Santa Barbara is the small, spread-out burg of Carpinteria, whose main draw is the gorgeous, 4,000 feet of ocean frontage and the forty-eight acres of Carpinteria State Beach Park. Here you can camp overnight, surf-fish, and observe (but don't you dare disturb) tide pools, rare phenomena in these parts. The visitor center has interesting natural history exhibits. To make camping reservations call (800) 444–PARK. Some of the best surfing in this part of California is off Rincon Point.

Main Street parallels the beach, and Linden Avenue, which leads to and from the beach, is lined with palm trees, rather than lindens. The best hamburgers and milkshakes in town are clearly at The Spot, which has outdoor tables right on Linden Avenue.

For a nostalgic dining experience reminiscent of an era you may not have known, drop in on THE PALMS, in the once famous Palms Hotel building, where you select and cook your own steak, shrimp, scallops, crab, and lobster just one block from the ocean. You can just imagine the sticky Manhattans and billows of Lucky Strike smoke of decades ago.

The Palms, 701 Linden Avenue, Carpinteria 93013; (805) 684–3811. Bar opens 1:00 P.M., dinner 5:00–10:00 P.M. daily. Full bar. Visa, MasterCard, American Express. Wheelchair accessible.

To continue in the extremely local place theme, you might also want to try out CLEMENTINE'S, another steak place—where *they* cook it and serve you— and where you will never forget the mouthwatering pies, that all-American sweet indulgence. Clementine's claims to be "Santa Barbara's Best Kept Secret," maybe because it's in Carpinteria instead of Santa Barbara! Great local atmosphere and gossip here, too.

Clementine's, 4631 Carpinteria Avenue, Carpinteria 93013; (805) 684–5119. Open 5:00–9:00 P.M. Tuesday–Sunday. Full bar. Visa, MasterCard, American Express. Wheelchair accessible.

Carpinteria's name comes from Spanish for "carpenter's shop," a reference to the Chumash Indian practice of using tar (natural asphaltum) that came up out of the ground to hold their canoes and baskets together. Later the Spaniards used the Indians to use the tar to hold the presidio roof together after they had the Indians clear the land. Early arrivals grew crops by trial and error (lima beans worked), and eventually commercial tar companies opened the pits to extract all they could. You can still see the remains of the pits by following Concha Loma Avenue to Calle Ocho. Park at the end of Calle Ocho and walk across the railroad track to the lookout point for fabulous views of the coast and the Channel Islands.

The CARPINTERIA VALLEY MUSEUM OF HISTORY is worth a visit if you're down this way. Exhibits of clothing and furniture contributed by Carpinteria's pioneer families depict turn-of-the-century life and create the ambience of the period. Newish exhibits include Chumash Indian artifacts, the replica of an early school classroom, traditional agricultural tools, and, what do you know, an oil boom, the current industrial artifact of the region.

Carpinteria Valley Museum of History, 956 Maple Avenue, Carpinteria 93013; (805) 684–3112. Open 1:30–4:00 P.M. Tuesday–Saturday. Admission free. Wheelchair accessible.

Orchid and gardening aficionados should stop at STEWART ORCHIDS to view (and maybe take home a wee part of) 80,000 square feet of greenhouses containing thousands of orchid and other exotic plant varieties. A gorgeous experience that's best February to May.

❧ *Stewart Orchids, 3376 Foothill Road, Carpinteria 93013; (805) 684–5448. Open 8:00 A.M.–5:00 P.M. Monday–Friday, 9:00 A.M.–5:00 P.M. Saturday, 10:00 A.M.–5:00 P.M. Sunday. Visa and MasterCard. Mostly wheelchair accessible.*

SANTA BARBARA POLO & RACQUET CLUB is actually here in Carpinteria. The elite group opens its field so visitors can watch polo matches from the grandstands and partake of the snack bar's substantial offerings. You're welcome to watch polo games Sunday afternoons from April to October. If you've never seen polo, it is an amazingly daring game of horse and player wielding what look like golf clubs to hit a ball on the ground toward the goal. The horses work the hardest and suffer the most.

❧ *Santa Barbara Polo & Racquet Club, 3375 Foothill Road, Carpinteria 93013; (805) 684–8668 or 684–6683 for game times. Mostly wheelchair accessible.*

One mile west of Carpinteria off Highway 101 is SANTA CLAUS LANE, a rather fun year-round Christmas haven, despite its unabashed commercialism. Loads of stuff with a Christmas theme, ornaments, an art gallery, toy stores, gift and dried fruit specialty shops, a bakery, candy kitchen, rock shop, and a casual restaurant facing the water all make this place attractive to thousands of visitors annually.

❧ *Santa Claus Lane, off Highway 101 ½ mile west of Carpinteria, 93101. No phone for center.*

Be sure to make it to Carpinteria's California Avocado Festival the first weekend in October (805–684–0038) and the annual flower show during the festival, as well as the monthly flea market (last Saturday) at the Carpinteria Valley Historical Museum.

And don't miss the farmers' market on Thursdays, in the 800 block of Linden Avenue (4:00–7:00 P.M. spring and summer; 3:00–6:00 P.M. fall and winter).

GOLETA

The main attraction in Goleta is the University of California, Santa Barbara, which is not actually in Santa Barbara, nor in Goleta, where it is usually thought to be. The university is really in Isla Vista, just west of Santa Barbara and Goleta; although it is in Santa Barbara County. Actually Goleta and Isla Vista run together and are not really distinguishable.

Locals and visitors all enjoy biking on designated trails, bird watching on Goleta Beach, golf, picnics, and hiking. Visit Santa Barbara Shores, a new county park next to Sandpiper Golf Course. Stow Grove Park and Lake Los Carneros Park are next to Stow House and the South Coast Railroad Museum.

STOW HOUSE was the central Stow family home when they were prominent lemon growers in Goleta, which once produced one-tenth of the nation's lemons. The orchards around the house are still owned by the Stow family's descendants, although the 5,000-square-foot 1872 Victorian home itself was donated to Santa Barbara County in 1967. Today you can walk through and enjoy its antiques and the excellent restoration job overseen by the Goleta Valley Historical Society. If you visit in October, plan to attend the lemon festival at Stow House with lemon foods, games, arts, crafts, and entertainment for the whole family.

Don't miss the Horace Sexton Memorial Museum of farm tools and machinery next door in the old red barn or the South Coast Railroad Museum. ❧ *Stow House, 304 North Los Carneros Road, Goleta 93116; (805) 964–4407. Open 2:00–4:00 P.M. Saturday–Sunday, tours when visitors show up. Partly wheelchair accessible. To get to Stow House, Horace Sexton Museum, and South Coast Railroad Museum, take Highway 101 north of Santa Barbara and take the Los Carneros Road exit. Turn right (north) on North Los Carneros Road (train station on the right).*

The SOUTH COAST RAILROAD MUSEUM offers miniature steam train rides in this county park to which the train station was moved in 1981. The park surrounding the railroad museum is true California: tall eucalyptus trees, mustard, and grasses. Enjoy the caboose and picnic areas, as well as the old freight office with the oh-so-sensible Morse code equipment, the passenger waiting room, a slide show, railroad films, a terrific shop and bookstore with nostalgic train posters and rare Santa Barbara books.

If you fly into Santa Barbara, check out the Air Heritage Museum at Santa Barbara Airport, which is also in Goleta.

Venture beyond Goleta's superficial appearance, which offers little to attract, to find its most natural beauty of beach, cliffs, dunes, and unusual wild birds, all below the plateau that supports UC/Santa Barbara. You will share our amazement at this beauty so close to tract homes and cement-box shopping. Park at the Goleta Beach lot or on the campus, although it's a bit of a walk or bike ride either way.

Goleta is not known for its fine cuisine, but you might try WOODY'S BODACIOUS BARBECUE, which until 1998 was known as Woody's Beach Club & Cantina. Sandwiches and burgers come with fries and beans, slaw, or tossed salad, and range from one-third pound ($5.45) to the One Pound Behemoth! ($7.95). And then there's the Triple Double Burger ($6.95) or a Texas brisket sandwich ($6.95). You'll also find oak-roasted rotisserie chicken dinner ($6.95), smoked half-duckling ($9.95), big combos of beef and ribs, Santa Maria-style tri-tip, baby backs, half-chicken, hot links, duck in various arrangements ($8.95–$15.45), and a BBQ Orgy ($21.95). Turkey and grilled tuna burgers also creep onto the lunch menu, along with big, cheap salads. Kathleen likes Woody's Caesar salad with oak-smoked chicken, grilled tuna, or tri-tip ($6.95). Kids will like the special kids' menu, and grown-up kids will enjoy the very local microbrews.

Most local media rate Woody's the best BBQ around.

Woody's Bodacious Barbecue, 5112 Hollister Avenue, Goleta 93116; (805) 967-3775. Open 11:00 A.M.–9:00 P.M. Monday–Thursday, 11:00 A.M.–11:00 P.M. Friday–Saturday, 11:00 A.M.–10:00 P.M. Sunday. Beer and wine. Visa, MasterCard, American Express, Discover, Diners. Wheelchair accessible.

CHAPTER 2

SANTA BARBARA ITSELF

*W*e call Santa Barbara *"California's Riviera" because it is. Towering Santa Ynez Mountains drop dramatically to sea level and light-colored, sand-covered beaches. Gently swaying palm trees line the beaches, lightly shade joggers and volleyball players, and create a stunning outline against the mountains. Santa Barbara's beach—the only beach between Alaska and Cape Horn to run east–west—faces south, as does France's Riviera, an unusual orientation along the north–south running Pacific Coast. For left-coast folks it is truly odd to wake up in a Santa Barbara coastside hotel room and see the sun rise over the ocean. We usually see it set over the water. There aren't quite as many sidewalk cafes in Santa Barbara as there are on the other Riviera, and beach lovers generally wear bathing suits here.*

As you wander around town and explore the rest of Santa Barbara County and its wineries, the scenery might just look familiar to you, and for good reason. Thousands of Western movies were filmed here, which helps us understand why Nancy and Ronald Reagan had a ranch here for decades. We still can visualize President Reagan in his cowboy boots and hat mending fences—at the ranch, that is.

Other early film stars, including Douglas Fairbanks, Mary Pickford, and Charlie Chaplin, used Santa Barbara as their favorite retreat. Rockefellers, Vanderbilts, Carnegies, and DuPonts used to arrive by private railcar. Now celebrities such as Michael Jackson (Neverland), Julia Child, Diane Keaton, Michael Douglas, Sylvester Stallone, Geena Davis, Julia Louis-Dreyfus, Bill Cosby, Jonathan Winters, James Brolin (Barbra Streisand), Kevin Costner, Kenny Loggins, and Jane Seymour spend part of their year here. Well, actually many of them live in Montecito, Santa Barbara's rarefied suburb to the south. (See Chapter 1.)

Besides its historic California architecture, Santa Barbara boasts 900 different plant species, the basis for which were brought here in the late 1880s by the grandfather of horticulture, Francesco Franceschi. Forty-eight public parks and 22,000 public trees, blooming exotic gardens, manicured private gardens, and

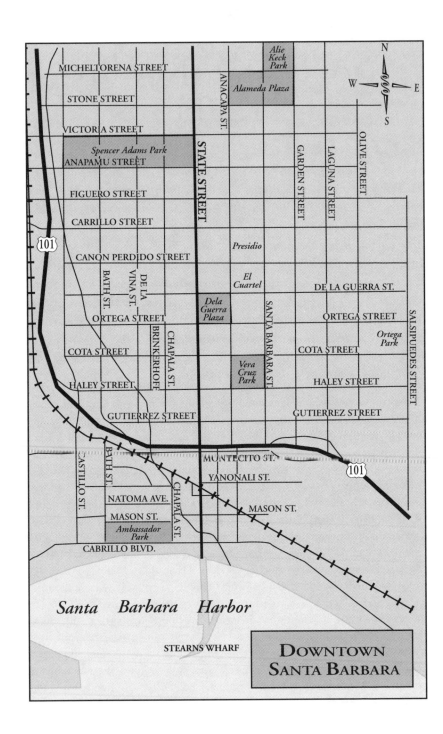

million-dollar estates all contribute to Santa Barbara's once-in-a-lifetime beauty. An orchid lover's paradise, Santa Barbara has 3 million square feet of orchid greenhouses and a spring international orchid show of more than one hundred varieties.

Santa Barbara has had the rare opportunity to redo itself following natural disasters. After the 1925 earthquake destroyed or severely damaged most of the public buildings (including the mission) and private residences, the town took advantage of a miserable situation and established an architectural board of review that developed guidelines for what you now see as Santa Barbara's facade. Floods, fires, and more earthquakes serve to jolt the locals ever so slightly into the reality that all is not always beautiful and perfect. But again and again Santa Barbarans resurrect themselves and their facades (edifices, that is) for all to enjoy.

Santa Barbara's architecture reflects its and California's history from the early days of the Chumash Indians 9,000 years ago, through landings by Spaniards, up to the late-eighteenth-century arrival of Franciscan friars. Residents and architects made a conscious effort to blend and enhance varied design influences—Mediterranean, Spanish, early California/Mexican, Moorish, and English country. As a result, Santa Barbara buildings often have low-pitched, reddish tile roofs, earth-tone plaster walls, arched entryways, enclosed garden courtyards, and occasional wrought-iron gates.

Notice that no cars are parked on downtown State Street, enabling all to enjoy the architecture and celebratory atmosphere. But don't worry; there's plenty of parking in lots behind the shops on State Street.

To help you find your way around Santa Barbara using this Hill Guide, we first take you up and down State Street, Santa Barbara's main shopping paradise, and to highlights on its cross streets, then to factory outlet stores (these are actually outlets selling stuff made in Santa Barbara). Then we'll go to what we call "significant others," by which we mean attractions and restaurants outside the State Street area that you should try to visit.

STATE STREET

State Street is the ultimate mix of elegant boutiques, upscale ethnic restaurants, funky-to-fine art galleries, local and chain cafes, and strut-your-stuff promenade mixed with historic malls, local offices, and necessary stores like Long's and Rite-Aid. Thus State Street is meant for locals as well as visitors, and both groups mingle comfortably.

We start our walking tour near the top of State Street's core of fine restaurants

ARLINGTON THEATRE, SANTA
BARBARA, DURING FILM
FESTIVAL, 1999

and shops at the corner of Anapamu and State Streets, across from the Santa Barbara Museum of Art. There is excellent parking in the blocks west and east of this part of State Street. We take you down the west side of the street, and then back up the east side, ending at the museum.

Just 1½ blocks up State Street from the corner of Anapamu Street are three significant must experiences: Arlington Theatre, Brigitte's restaurant, and Downey's restaurant.

The elegant Arlington Hotel was destroyed by a disastrous 1909 fire, and the second Arlington Hotel was destroyed by the subsequent 1925 earthquake. Fox West Coast Theatres subsequently commissioned Santa Barbaran Joseph Plunkett and his partner, William A. Edwards, to design the ARLINGTON THEATRE. This Spanish revival motion picture palace, restored in 1976, serves as the Arlington Center for the Performing Arts (where the Santa Barbara Symphony and visiting orchestras perform), and as an outstanding movie theater that is a major venue of the Santa Barbara Film Festival. Notice the Spanish village feeling to the architecture, as well as the star-studded ceiling, the dramatic arches, and courtyard entry.

On the sidewalk outside the entrance is a sign marking the spot as Old Stage Coach Route I, where stagecoaches stopped from 1861 to 1901. Gasoline-free public transportation!

❧ *Arlington Theatre, 1217 State Street, Santa Barbara 93101; (805) 963–4408. Hours vary. Visa and MasterCard for some events. Wheelchair accessible.*

In the same block of State Street as the Arlington are two of Santa Barbara's finest restaurants, Brigitte's and Downey's.

BRIGITTE'S, a couple doors up from the theater, is extremely popular with locals, and you will instantly know why. Surrounded by fun French art posters, try the hearts of romaine with anchovy croutons ($5.95), the pesto sautéed bay scallops on spinach ($8.95), or the warm seafood salad ($11.50) for starters. Superb value pizzas range from prawn to smoked chicken for $10. Entrees may include red chili-crusted filet mignon with cheese-filled pasilla and sweet potato gratin ($16.25) or pan-roasted venison medallions with sun-dried cherry wild rice, roast veggies, and a green pepper sauce ($18.95).

Brigitte's is a reasonably priced outstanding restaurant. Be sure to read owner Bergitta Guehr's prizewinning local wine list for the very best of central coast wines. One of our favorites.

Bergitta is, thank heavens, heavily involved in local environmental fundraising causes. Recently she purchased and renovated the delightful Meadowlark

---

BRIGITTE'S PAELLA
from Bergitta Guehr, Brigitte's Restaurant Cafe, Santa Barbara

12 Manilla clams	6 Roma tomatoes, peeled, seeded,
12 black mussels	and chopped
12 medium prawns	2½ cups basmati rice
½ lb. chorizo sausage,	¼ cup dry white wine
cut into ½-inch slices	3 cups chicken stock
⅓ lb. chicken breast,	3 Tbs. butter
cut into ½-inch cubes	2 Tbs. olive oil
½ lb. bay scallops	1 tsp. ground cumin
½ lb. rock shrimp	1 tsp. ground coriander
1 medium onion, diced	1 tsp. oregano
4 cloves garlic, sliced	1 tsp. saffron threads
1 large red bell pepper,	salt and pepper to taste
roasted and sliced	few stems of cilantro for garnish
2 Anaheim peppers, roasted and sliced	

In a large heavy saucepan, heat butter and olive oil. Sauté chicken and chorizo until golden brown. Add garlic and onion, and cook until tender. Stir in tomatoes and spices. Stir in rice and roasted peppers. Add wine and stock.

Cook covered for about 15 minutes. Salt and pepper to taste. Uncover and add shellfish, clams, and mussels. Cook until shells just open. *(Do not eat clams or mussels whose shells do not open in the cooking process.—Kathleen Hill)*

Cook until opaque. Transfer to large serving dish. Garnish with chopped cilantro and enjoy. Serves four.

Inn with its expansive gardens and twenty rooms, 1.6 miles east of Solvang, a perfect place to stay to host parties in the wine country.

❧ *Brigitte's, 1325 State Street, Santa Barbara 93101; (805) 996–9676. Open lunch Monday–Saturday from 11:30 A.M., dinner from 5:30 P.M. daily. Full bar. Visa, MasterCard, American Express, Discover, Diners. Wheelchair accessible.*

Santa Barbara's most reviewed and highly rated restaurant is DOWNEY'S, the creation of John and Liz Downey and chef Christian Hill (unfortunately, no relation to us). Since they are not open for lunch, make your dinner reservations in advance to assure a table for this culinary experience.

For starters, we highly recommend the Santa Barbara mussels with chili vinaigrette ($9.95), the gravlax and avocado ($9.95), or the porcini mushroom soup with crème fraîche. Tom Shepherd's greens with English Stilton cheese dressing or garlic dressing ($6.95) are superb.

Entrees range from fresh king salmon with tomato tarragon sauce or grilled swordfish (each $22.95) to navarin of spring lamb with French chanterelle mushrooms ($23.95) or boneless veal chop ($27.95). Desserts and the wine list are impeccable. You are bound to at least see, if not mix with, some of Santa Barbara's most interesting celebrities here.

❧ *Downey's, 1305 State Street, Santa Barbara 93101; (805) 966–5006. Open for dinner from 5:30 P.M. Tuesday–Sunday. Visa, MasterCard, American Express, Discover. Wheelchair accessible.*

In the fast food block between Downey's and Anapamu Street, WINE TIME is a terrific wine shop without attitude where you can sample sixty Central Coast wines, including twenty dessert wines, and purchase local as well as "imported" wines from Napa and Sonoma valleys, Washington, Oregon, Europe, Australia, New Zealand, South Africa, and South America. Enjoy sidewalk table seating, cheeses and a few specialty foods. If you can't visit the wineries, stop in here to try and/or purchase different wines to take with you or ship home. Get on the mailing list to receive owner Scooter Treen's hilariously informative *Wine Times.*

❧ *Wine Time, 1227 State Street in Victoria Court, Santa Barbara 93101; (805) 568–0010 or (800) 264–3844, fax (805) 568–1102. Open 10:00 A.M.–7:00 P.M. Sunday–Thursday, 10:00 A.M.–9:00 P.M. Friday–Saturday. Tasting fee: $1.00 per taste, $3.50 per glass. Visa, MasterCard, American Express, Discover. Wheelchair accessible.*

Anapamu Street crosses State Street and sports several establishments worth visiting. On West Anapamu, which means to your left facing up State Street, we take you first to the KARPELES MANUSCRIPT LIBRARY MUSEUM, other branches of which are located in Jacksonville, Florida; Tacoma, Washington; Duluth, Minnesota; Montecito, California; Buffalo, New York; and Charleston, South Carolina. Dedicated to the preservation of the original handwritten letters and documents of the great men and women of the past who have changed and shaped history, this underknown treasure of original manuscripts and documents is a literary and documentary heaven. Together, the Karpeles Manuscript Library Museums constitute the world's largest private holding of important original documents and manuscripts.

The Montecito museum is reserved for scholars to do research, but at the Santa Barbara Karpeles you might see original papers of George Bernard Shaw, Enrico Fermi, President Harry S Truman, Glenn Seaborg, and President Dwight D. Eisenhower. The Karpeles holdings—covering history, music, science, literature, and art—rotate through its other museums. Each showing focuses on no more than twenty-five documents at any one time.

Exhibits have included the original proposal draft of the Bill of Rights, the Emancipation Proclamation signed by Abraham Lincoln, the Thanksgiving Proclamation signed by George Washington, and the original autograph drafts of the national constitutions of France, Spain, Mexico, Ireland, and the Confederate States of America. Music manuscripts exhibited have included pages of Beethoven, Mozart, Wagner, Handel, and Puccini; scientific manuscripts have included those of Galileo, Descartes, Kepler, Newton, Einstein, Freud, and Darwin. And you might see the Surrender Agreement of World War II.

Do not miss this. And it's free! One of our favorites.

❧ *Karpeles Manuscript Library Museum, 21 West Anapamu Street, Santa Barbara 93101; (805) 962–5322. Open 10:00 A.M.–4:00 P.M. daily. Admission free. Partly wheelchair accessible.*

You might want to have a look into SANTA BARBARA HEMP CO. for its eco products and no marijuana. Based on the environmental theory that hemp provides sound alternatives to cotton and lumber products, Steve Levine and Jessica Norris offer Hempy's bags, hemp Adidas, clothes, bags, and Cannabis Creations lotions. Worth checking out.

❧ *Santa Barbara Hemp Co., 15 West Anapamu Street, Santa Barbara 93101; (805) 965–7170, e-mail: sbhempco@gte.net. Open 11:00 A.M.–6:00 P.M. Tuesday–Saturday, noon–5:00 P.M. Sunday. Visa, MasterCard, American Express. Wheelchair accessible.*

Now cross Anapamu to four fun shops, including Crispin Leather, Santa Barbara Hobbies, Pacific Travellers Supply, and Metro Comics, Games & Toys.

CRISPIN LEATHER SHOP smells as if leather scent is sprayed through the air conditioning! Yum. Crispin has two storefronts offering leather hats, bags, wallets, jewelry, belts, and a few clothes, plus Birkenstocks, Clarks shoes and sandals, Santana boots from Canada, UGG from Australia, Aussi togs and moccasins, and even Dr. Scholls shoes and Teva sandals.

꙳ↄ *Crispin Leather Shop, 18 West Anapamu Street, Santa Barbara 93101; (805) 966–2510. Open 10:00 A.M.–5:30 P.M. Monday–Saturday, 11:00 A.M.–5:00 P.M. Sunday. Visa, MasterCard, American Express. Wheelchair accessible.*

Vern Morseman's SANTA BARBARA HOBBIES is a hobbyist's delight. Here you will find plastic models, air brush equipment, model rockets, X-ACTO tools, model trains such as Marklin Z, HO and N train supplies, g gauge trains, Screaming/Horizon vinyl figures, how-to books, Dremel tools, finishing supplies, military aircraft models, and a rare kit corner. One of Jerry's favorites.

꙳ↄ *Santa Barbara Hobbies, 14 West Anapamu Street, Santa Barbara 93101; (805) 965–8433. Open noon–6:00 P.M. Monday, 10:00 A.M.–6:00 P.M. Tuesday–Saturday. Visa, MasterCard, American Express. Wheelchair accessible.*

PACIFIC TRAVELLERS SUPPLY sells a fabulous range of travel guides, camping accessories and equipment, globes, adventure-travel gear, luggage (including TravelPro, Kelty Kids, and Eagle Creek), walking sticks, and hundreds of handy accessories for travel. Everything you could possibly need. Watch for guest programs. One of our favorites.

꙳ↄ *Pacific Travellers Supply, 12 West Anapamu Street, Santa Barbara 93101; (805) 963–4438. Open 10:00 A.M.–6:00 P.M. Monday–Wednesday and Saturday; 10:00 A.M.–8:00 P.M. Thursday–Friday; 11:00 A.M.–6:00 P.M. Sunday. Visa, MasterCard, American Express, Discover. Wheelchair accessible.*

METRO COMICS, GAMES & TOYS is a big and little kid's paradise where Pokemon seminars go on at a sidewalk table out front. Often voted Santa Barbara's Best Comic Store, Metro, which occasionally has a free comic day Saturday, is where you get Star Wars everythings, Beanie Babies, South Park and X-Files paraphernalia, magic supplies, games, collectibles, and television and movie memorabilia. One of Jerry's favorites.

꙳ↄ *Metro Comics, Games & Toys, 6 West Anapamu Street, Santa Barbara 93101; (805) 963–2168; e-mail: metrocomix@aol.com; Web site: www.the-keep.com/metro/. Open 10:00 A.M.–7:00 P.M. Sunday–Monday, 10:00 A.M.–8:00 P.M. Tuesday–Saturday. Visa, MasterCard, American Express, Discover. Wheelchair accessible.*

We encourage you to walk across State Street on Anapamu to visit a classic bookstore and cafe, SULLIVAN & GOSS BOOKS & PRINTS LTD., one of the largest art bookstores in the world, and its cafe, the ARTS & LETTERS CAFE. Just walking in here is like walking into a book museum. What a treat to enjoy such reverence!

Sullivan & Goss features elegant rare books, prints, monographs, and paintings, and caters to artists, collectors, galleries, and art lovers. Among the artists whose original work is exhibited are Robin Gowen and Don Freeman.

To get to the Arts & Letters Cafe gallery dining room, walk or wheel through Sullivan & Goss and through the exquisite flower-framed patio where you can dine and occasionally listen to live opera and Broadway musicals.

The menu is as appealing as the surroundings. Try their famous pumpkin soup served hot or chilled (even praised by *The New York Times* as well as the Hills) ($4.25); the prosciutto and persimmon topped with arugula and hazelnut vinaigrette ($7.95); or the charcutière, a plate of duck and truffle pâté, cornichons, black olives, Jarlsberg cheese, mustard, and baguette and rye breads ($8.95). The salads are all excellent, but standouts include roasted chicken with wild rice ($8.95), duck breast and prosciutto with baby spinach ($10.95), and the kasseri spinach pasta salad ($8.95). Sandwiches, with choice of soup, include the French country with duck and truffle pâté, creamy Brie, cornichons, and Dijon mustard ($8.95). Memorable!

At lunch the Eastern blue crab cakes ($9.95) are grand treats, particularly for Westerners. Dinner delicacies include pan-roasted salmon with merlot and fennel and potato hash ($13.95), and roasted vegetable and polenta lasagna ($9.95). Or you may want to try the prix fixe Menu des Artistes ($14.95), which includes a choice of soup and entree, the chef's dessert selection, and coffee or tea. The courtyard dining is especially popular with locals.

ꝑ *Sullivan & Goss Books & Prints Ltd., 7 East Anapamu Street, Santa Barbara 93101; (805) 730–1460. Open: bookstore: 10:00 A.M.–5:30 P.M. Sunday–Thursday, 8:00 A.M.–5:30 P.M. Friday–Saturday; cafe: lunch 11:00 A.M.–3:30 P.M., breakfast 8:00 A.M.–3:30 P.M., dinner from 5:30 P.M. Tuesday–Sunday. Visa and MasterCard. Wheelchair accessible.*

The typical something-for-almost-everyone COPELAND'S sports is right at the southwest corner of State Street and Anapamu. While residual resentment for tearing down older stores still exists here, some people are grateful that Copeland's moved in, bringing local and visiting customers to the downtown. Small sports stores worry Copeland's convenience and inventory will hurt their business—classic dilemma.

ꝑ *Copeland's, 1137 State Street, Santa Barbara 93101; (805) 963–4474. Open 10:00 A.M.–7:00 P.M. Monday–Thursday, 10:00 A.M.–8:00 P.M. Friday–Saturday,*

11:00 A.M.–6:00 P.M. Sunday. Visa, MasterCard, American Express. Wheelchair accessible.

LA SALSA FRESH MEXICAN GRILL is part of a refreshingly good, healthy-if-you-order-right, vast southern California chain rated highly by *Zagat Guide* readers, calling it "Mexican at its very best." *Los Angeles Magazine* rates the chain Best Mexican Overall, and it's worth a try for a cheap, quick meal.

Although an occasional taco wrapper blows around in the small front patio, you can sit at the four outdoor tables and watch the strutters and strollers parade by. Go inside to order at the counter, then take a seat at the French-style high tables and watch the cooks grilling fresh vegetables, skinless chicken, or extra-lean steak to go with the fun salsa bar and your hot-off-the-press tortillas. You can actually order nearly fat-free burritos and tacos if you so choose.

Soft taco baskets may include two flour tortillas filled with grilled mahimahi, lettuce, tomatoes, and cheese, topped with Sonora sauce and a squeeze of lime, served with chips and trips to the salsa bar for $5.45. Add rice and black beans for $1.00. Classic quesadillas with melted cheeses, guacamole, and sour cream ($3.50) can acquire chicken or steak for just $1.25. Gourmet burritos range from bean and cheese ($2.85) to a fajita burrito ($4.75).

The best deal in town for kids is the choice of a chicken taco, nachos, quesadilla or bean and cheese burrito with rice or beans, and a small drink for a whopping $1.95!

La Salsa Fresh Mexican Grill, 1131 State Street, Santa Barbara 93101; (805) 963–1001; Web site: www.lasalsa.com. Open 10:00 A.M.–10:00 P.M. Visa, MasterCard, Discover. Wheelchair accessible.

Just beyond La Salsa is BISTRO MED—follow the walkway toward the tables covered with white linen tablecloths and umbrellas in the protected sandstone courtyard. The owners' proclamation that Bistro Med is "Europe in the Heart of Santa Barbara" is close to true, and some locals do like to linger over lunch among the bright-colored flowers here on a nice day.

Try the pomegranate chicken with basmati rice and fresh vegetables ($11.95), New York sirloin steak ($11.95), vegetable musaka ($8.95), or mixed mezes of dolmathes, baba ghanoush, hummus, and buekkas ($8.95). You might also enjoy the occasional subtle live music.

Bistro Med, 1129 State Street, Santa Barbara 93101; (805) 965–1500. Open 11:00 A.M.–10:00 P.M. Full bar. Visa, MasterCard, American Express, Diners, Discover. Wheelchair accessible.

Next door to the walkway to Bistro Med and in stark naked contrast to its dignity is CANYON BEACHWEAR, which features tiny ladies' bathing suits and bikinis (both tiny bathing suits and tiny ladies). Those in need will find the best of Esprit and Raisins, perfect for covering the bare minimum at Santa Barbara's seductive beaches.

➳ *Canyon Beachwear, 1127 State Street, Santa Barbara 93101; (805) 899–1117. Open 11:00 A.M.–7:00 P.M. Monday–Friday, 11:00 A.M.–8:00 P.M. Friday–Saturday, 11:00 A.M.–6:00 P.M. Sunday. Visa, MasterCard, American Express. Wheelchair accessible.*

ALPHA THRIFT STORE helps finance the Alpha Resource Center for people with developmental disabilities and for their families. You will know it by the restful benches on the sidewalk and its enormous selection of kitchen equipment and utensils along the left wall. You will find slightly-better-than-usual dolls, antique jeans, furniture, and clothing for all sizes and tastes. If you are into used and collectible stuff, check this one out. Your purchase contributes to a good cause.

➳ *Alpha Thrift Store, 1123 State Street, Santa Barbara 93101; (805) 963–1123. Open 10:00 A.M.–6:00 P.M. Visa, MasterCard, Discover. Wheelchair accessible.*

Next down State Street is RUGS & MORE, an imported rug company actually voted Best Rug Store in Santa Barbara by locals. Here you will find handmade elegant Native American rugs, African kilims, needlepoints, tapestries, and Oriental carpets ranging in price from $29 to $1 million. Both the setting and the rugs are striking, and you can actually find something affordable, as well as oversized carpets. Rugs & More offers ninety minutes of free parking in the lot behind the store on Chapala Street.

➳ *Rugs & More, 1119 State Street, Santa Barbara 93101; (805) 962–2166. Open 10:00 A.M.–6:30 P.M. Monday–Saturday, noon–5:00 P.M. Sunday. Visa, MasterCard, American Express, Discover. Wheelchair accessible.*

Just down from the rugs is YUCATAN FRESH MEXICAN GRILL AND CANTINA, one of State Street's louder dance bars and restaurants, happily frequented by swinging, dancing UC/Santa Barbara students, locals, and visitors alike. Local workers also stop by at lunchtime for some Mexican food and sit at high tables in front. There is a $5.00 cover charge on Thursday night, which is college student night with entertainment by popular DJs, and on Saturday night, which features salsa music with dance lessons at 7:00 and 8:00 P.M. Women pay no cover on Saturdays before 10:00 P.M.

🎵 *Yucatan Fresh Mexican Grill and Cantina,* *1117 State Street, Santa Barbara 93101; (805) 564–1889. Full bar. Open 11:00 A.M.–12:30 A.M. Sunday–Wednesday, 11:00 A.M.–1:30 A.M. Thursday–Saturday. Visa and MasterCard. Wheelchair accessible.*

CAMILLE, next along the street from Yucatan, is a day spa, salon, and retail store selling natural beauty supplies and scents. The entrance is through the shop; the day spa and salon are downstairs toward the back. The spa uses "only the purest products from the South of France" and offers a "menu" of French therapies and treatments in a casual and relaxed atmosphere.

Camille offers French hydrotherapy treatments with seaweed and algae ($45–$90), sea mud body wraps ($40–$65), body exfoliants ($45–$120), body massage from Swedish to shiatsu, aromatherapy, and anticellulite ($40–$120), facials and skin treatments ($40–$75), waxing, hands and feet treatments, make-up services including on location ($100 per hour), spa packages ($105–$240), wedding packages for some or all wedding participants ($45–$280 for five and one-half hours for the groom), and even couples specials!

🎵 *Camille, 1115 State Street, Santa Barbara 93101; (805) 899–4883. Open 10:00 A.M.–6:00 P.M. Monday, Wednesday, Friday; 10:00 A.M.–7:00 P.M. Tuesday, Thursday; 9:00 A.M.–5:00 P.M. Saturday; noon–5:00 P.M. Sunday. Visa and MasterCard. Shop is wheelchair accessible.*

Next door good old LONG'S DRUGS, a seemingly local chain pharmacy and other essentials store, headquartered in Walnut Creek, California, has a little extra feature a Dreyers ice cream counter that also sells pizza under the front window inside. This is a great stop on a warm day, and you can take your cone outside if the stools are filled. Long's is handy for Santa Barbara souvenirs (along the left wall) and generally all the usual things you forgot to bring.

🎵 *Long's Drugs, 1109 State Street, Santa Barbara 93101; (805) 564–0079 (twenty-four-hour refills 564–6948); Web site: www.Longs.com. Open 7:00 A.M.–10:00 P.M. Monday–Saturday, 8:00 A.M.–8:00 P.M. Sunday. Visa and MasterCard. Wheelchair accessible.*

Hanging out at COPELAND'S GOLF is such a pleasant experience that we were nearly converted to playing golf. Local ladies and gentlemen come in for the latest in Ralph Lauren Polo golf clothes, shoe sales, golf clubs and balls, and everything else one could imagine needing on the links or even putting in the living room.

🎵 *Copeland's Golf, 1107 State Street, Santa Barbara 93101; (805) 963–4474. Open 10:00 A.M.–7:00 P.M. Monday–Thursday, 10:00 A.M.–8:00 P.M.*

Friday–Saturday, 11:00 A.M.–6:00 P.M. Sunday. Visa, MasterCard, American Express. Wheelchair accessible.

Walking into TIENDA HO', one of Kathleen's favorites, is like walking into another continent. Pressed mud hut–looking dressing rooms, a waterfall, rugs, sarongs, and soothing and sexy music combine to create an alluring atmosphere few women and brave men can resist. Fabulous leather and brass belts with enormous buckles, flowing scarves, sale racks, and loads of feminine clothes from Morocco, Indonesia, and India render most women weak. Enjoy!

Tienda Ho', 1105 State Street, Santa Barbara 93101; (805) 962–3643, fax (805) 564–7030. Open 10:00 A.M.–8:00 P.M. except when they close at 7:00. Visa, MasterCard, American Express. Mostly wheelchair accessible.

GILLIO buys and sells fine jewelry, rare coins, antiques, and collectibles, and helps you connect to Jim O'Mahoney who appraises all of the above. They even make house calls if you would like to sell or buy art objects, old paintings, vintage photographs, bronze and silver sculptures, Asian works of art, movie memorabilia, Indian artifacts, old Western and cowboy items, and old sterling silver and stock certificates. Se habla español.

Gillio, 1103 State Street, Santa Barbara 93101; (805) 963–1345. Open for antiques and collectibles 11:00 A.M.–4:00 P.M. Wednesday–Saturday, and for coins and jewelry 9:30 A.M.–5:30 P.M. Monday–Friday. Visa, MasterCard, American Express, Discover. Wheelchair accessible.

CAFE SIENA, a popular non-Starbucks local cafe, occupies the corner of State Street and Figueroa. Locals stop in for the breakfast special, a double espresso drink with fresh baked pastry for $4.00, great sandwiches and bagels, and healthy fruit cups. Interesting people hang out here day and night.

Cafe Siena, 1101 State Street, Santa Barbara 93101; no phone. Open 6:00 A.M.–11:00 P.M. Monday–Thursday, 6:00 A.M.–1:00 A.M. Friday–Sunday. Visa and MasterCard. Wheelchair accessible.

At the corner of Figueroa and State, turn west for three special businesses, including MRS. WEINSTEIN'S TOFFEE KITCHEN, the brainchild and love product of Lotte Weinstein, and an excellent place to find a special gift or allow yourself a little self-indulgence.

As a young girl in Copenhagen, Denmark, Lotte watched her mother make toffee. Immigrating to the United States in 1964, she later became Mrs. Weinstein, gave birth to two children, and pursued her chosen career as a psychotherapist and consultant. Remembering her mother's recipe, Lotte began making toffee at home for her family, adding her own unique touches.

One holiday season she gave some away as presents to friends and neighbors. The next year those same friends and neighbors asked if she could make a little extra so they could give some away themselves, and then people from all over the country called begging to be considered "friends" and "neighbors." That was four years ago, and now Mrs. Weinstein has this attractive, immaculately clean little toffee factory, where you can sample and buy blue-and-white tins of her scrumptious treats. In a record rapid success story, Mrs. Weinstein's Toffee is now sold at Neiman-Marcus, Bergdorf Goodman, and Saks Fifth Avenue.

Toffee lovers and temptees can indulge in milk chocolate toffees such as almond, almond dark chocolate, pistachio, Irish coffee, hazelnut, and pecan, plus daily specials, all sold by the pound and portable in bags or handsome tins. ⚭ *Mrs. Weinstein's Toffee Kitchen, 14 West Figueroa, Santa Barbara 93101; (805) 965-0422 or (800) 682-0978; fax (805) 965-8123; Web site: www.mwtoffee.com. Open 10:00 A.M.–6:00 P.M. daily. Visa, MasterCard, American Express, Discover. Wheelchair accessible.*

PING PONG PIZZERIA does not sell pizza that bounces, but good pizza that brings you back. Popular with locals for a quick lunch, Ping Pong's pizza menu is pretty standard, and the decor is primarily red-and-white checked tablecloths. ⚭ *Ping Pong Pizzeria, 12 West Figueroa, Santa Barbara 93101; (805) 962-9442. Open noon–2:00 P.M. Monday–Friday, 5:00–10:00 P.M. Monday–Saturday. Visa and MasterCard. Wheelchair accessible.*

Back toward State Street from Mrs. Weinstein's and Ping Pong is SANTA BARBARA CIGAR & TOBACCO, an elegant cigar boutique owned by tobacconists Matthew Lanford and Tom Georgouses. Dark and solid looking, the shop has a humidified cigar room and a smoking lounge in the back, where cigar aficionados gather to talk cigars and world problems, puff, and inhale each others' smoke. While we do not encourage any form of smoking, this is an excellent shop for cigars, pipes, tobaccos, and rare imported cigarettes, if you must. ⚭ *Santa Barbara Cigar & Tobacco, 10 West Figueroa, Santa Barbara 93101; (805) 963-1979; fax (805) 963-8780. Open 10:00 A.M.–6:00 P.M. Monday–Saturday, 11:00 A.M.–4:00 P.M. Sunday. Visa, MasterCard, American Express. Mostly wheelchair accessible.*

Back to the southwest corner of Figueroa and State Street to TOM'S TOYS, a fun browsing treasure for kids of all ages. Almost everything in the Gone With the Wind and Beatrix Potter lines can be found here (even lunch boxes), as well as crayons (most essential on a trip), tea sets, wooden yo-yos from $2.99, Madame Alexander dolls, Gund and Steiff bears, Legos, and most other major toys for preschoolers on up.

🐾 *Tom's Toys, 1035 State Street, Santa Barbara 93101; (805) 564–6622. Open 10:00 A.M.–6:00 P.M. Monday–Thursday, 9:30 A.M.–7:00 P.M. Friday–Saturday, 11:00 A.M.–5:00 P.M. Sunday. Visa, MasterCard, American Express, Discover. Wheelchair accessible.*

Just down State Street from Tom's is ALDO'S ITALIAN RESTAURANT, with a highly Italian ambience and outdoor tables and umbrellas under a huge maple tree. Many locals say this is their favorite Italian restaurant in town.

Italian and French posters wind their way around interior poles and arches, and flamenco guitarists set a romantic tone nightly. All of Aldo's entrees cost $1.00–$2.00 more at dinner than at lunch, and salads and soups come in small and large servings. Vegetarian entrees are marked with a "v" on the menu.

You might want to try the swordfish alla Grecca ($9.95) or the gnocchi cilantro pesto with Caesar salad ($8.95). Antipasti include roasted garlic and olive oil ($3.95), bruschetta ($3.95), and baked artichoke hearts, local mussels, and prosciutto and melon, each $7.95. Salads range from Greek and salmon to seafood spinach salad and Aldo's chicken Caesar ($3.50–7.95). Lunchtime sandwiches include eggplant parmigiana, BLT, or meatball ($6.95), and include soup or salad. Yummy pizzas are all under $10, and twenty pastas range from $6.05 a plate at lunch to $11.95 at dinner, including soup or salad; additions of meatballs, sausage, or chicken are an extra $1.50–$2.00.

Enjoy a wide variety of eggplant and chicken breast and seafood dishes, especially snapper piccata or "provincial" ($8.95/$10.50), shrimp piccata or salmon cilantro ($9.95–$14.95), and cioppino ($15.95). Carnivores might try the half-pound pork chop all'agrodolce, which is oven-roasted with sweet and sour cherry sauce, rosemary, and pine nuts and served with fettucine alfredo—the cholesterol special! Good filet mignon and New York steaks are also available ($16.25), and veal almost any way is $14.95 at dinner.

Aldo serves brunch Saturday and Sunday with specialty egg dishes ($4.95–$10.95), scrambles ($5.95), and huevos rancheros or chicken machaca ($7.95). Various eggs Benedict range from hollandaise sauce with Black Forest ham ($7.95) to the Aldo with blackened filet mignon and the Poseidon with poached salmon ($9.95).

🐾 *Aldo's Italian Restaurant, 1031 State Street, Santa Barbara 93101; (805) 963–6687. Open 11:00 A.M.–9:30 P.M. Monday–Thursday, 11:00 A.M.–10:30 P.M. Friday–Saturday, 10:00 A.M.–9:30 P.M. Sunday. Visa, MasterCard, American Express, Discover. Wheelchair accessible.*

Just south of Aldo's pleasant fountain and courtyard is, of all things, the aptly named CHUBBIES HAMBURGERS, which we would all become if we "dined" here very often. Chubbies is actually a very pleasant chain fast-food joint, with comfortable seating and lamps hanging from the roof inside and out. Thick milk shakes are only $1.69, while hamburger alternatives range from a garden veggie burger at $2.89 to a chicken breast sandwich for $3.29. You can easily feed the troops here for around $3.00 a person.

& *Chubbies Hamburgers, 1027 State Street, Santa Barbara 93101; (805) 965–6004. Open 11:00 A.M.–8:00 P.M. daily. No credit cards. Wheelchair accessible.*

RUSS' CAMERA AND VIDEO has often been voted Best Camera Store by Santa Barbara residents, and we agree. Russ' offers everything from postcards to huge telescopes for viewing passing whales and ships from your rancho. Cameras, film, frames, how-to books, and batteries are all available.

& *Russ' Camera and Video, 1025 State Street, Santa Barbara 93101; (805) 963–9558, fax (805) 966-4947; Web site: www.russcamera.com. Open 9:00 A.M.–5:30 P.M. Monday–Saturday, noon–4:00 P.M. Sunday. Visa and MasterCard. Wheelchair accessible.*

Patrick and Brian Milligan and their brother-in-law Ken Sterling left Scotland in 1989 and established P. J. MILLIGAN, the interesting and lovely home furnishings store next to Russ' Camera. Right here in Santa Barbara they make French country, British country, Scottish farmhouse, and Shaker-style furniture, all with dovetail joinery. P. J. Milligan also features home and garden accessories, miniature ships, and subtle chandeliers. Prices range from $69 to $5 million for exquisite designs and handwork.

& *P.J. Milligan, 1023 State Street, Santa Barbara 93101; (805) 966–1188; Web site: www.pjmilligan.com. Open 10:00 A.M.–6:00 P.M. Monday–Saturday, 11:00 A.M.–5:00 P.M. Sunday. Visa, MasterCard, American Express. Wheelchair accessible.*

Sunglass Hut sells sunglasses, and we move on to take you just down the street to DAY DREAMS, until recently known as Play It Again Sam. Owner Jeanne Ward changed the name because she has moved from specializing in recycled clothing to stocking 90 percent new clothing and 10 percent recently recycled trendy fun clothes and accessories, hair accessories, watches and sterling. Bargain boxes in the back have $3.00 to $7.00 stuff for the young-minded of all ages.

& *Day Dreams, 1021 State Street, Santa Barbara 93101; (805) 966–9989. Open 10:00 A.M.–6:00 P.M. Sunday–Thursday, 10:00 A.M.–7:00 P.M.*

Friday–Saturday. Visa, MasterCard, American Express, Discover. Wheelchair accessible.

Just down from Day Dreams, the LUGGAGE HOUSE has adapted itself to current travel trends and carries popular bags and packs made by Olympia, TravelPro, Timberland, Jansport, Force Ten, and various sizes and shapes of leather bags. Just in case you need to carry all those Santa Barbara purchases back home.

❧ *Luggage House, 1017A State Street, Santa Barbara 93101; (805) 965–1036. Open 10:00 A.M.–7:00 Monday–Saturday, 11:00 A.M.–6:00 P.M. Sunday. Visa, MasterCard, American Express, Discover. Wheelchair accessible.*

FROMEX PHOTO SYSTEMS next to the Luggage House specializes in one-hour film developing, but also prints from slides and passport photos, restores digital photos, and does digital imaging right on the premises. Passport photos too. You can also get postcards, frames, batteries, film, and albums. Handy if you need those photos now!

❧ *Fromex Photo Systems, 1017 State Street, Santa Barbara 93101; (805) 966–2269. Open 8:30 A.M.–7:00 P.M. Monday–Friday, 9:00 A.M.–7:00 P.M. Saturday, 10:00 A.M.–7:00 P.M. Sunday. Visa and MasterCard. Wheelchair accessible.*

Next door CHURCHILL'S JEWELERS is Santa Barbara's oldest jewelry firm, and it feels like it. The "since 1918" company sells estate and fine jewelry, fine diamonds, colored gems, Rolex watches, and antique jewelry amid a substantial and calm ambience. You can also have jewelry of your dreams designed and created here.

❧ *Churchill's Jewelers, 1015-1015A State Street, Santa Barbara 93101; (805) 962–5815, fax (805) 962–6168. Open 9:30 A.M.–5:00 P.M. Monday–Saturday. Visa, MasterCard, American Express. Wheelchair accessible.*

MACDUFF'S GOLF & FLYFISHING has a completely local and slightly folksy feel compared to Copeland's Golf up the street. In addition to a green blackboard on the wall listing fishing conditions in surrounding waters, MacDuff has flytying materials, hand-tied flies, and fishing outfits galore. Both men and women can also find the best in golf equipment and clothes, including custom-fit golf clubs, Taylor Made, Top Flite, Orvis clothing, jeans, and nearly all pertinent books. Don't miss the hat hook that says, "If my hat's missing I've gone fishing."

❧ *MacDuff's Golf & Flyfishing, 1013 State Street, Santa Barbara 93101; (805) 963–1776. Open 10:00 A.M.–6:00 P.M. Monday–Saturday, noon–5:00 P.M. Sunday. Visa, MasterCard, American Express. Wheelchair accessible.*

Holding down the northwest corner of State Street and Carrillo is a SAKS FIFTH AVENUE, with several floors of elegance and perfect clothes for Santa Barbara, as well as the usual perfume and makeup counters as you enter. But explore further.

✣✣ *Saks Fifth Avenue, 1001 State Street, Santa Barbara 93101; (805) 884–5200. Open 10:00 A.M.–6:00 P.M. Monday–Thursday and Saturday, 10:00 A.M.–9:00 P.M. Friday, noon–6:00 P.M. Sunday. Visa, MasterCard, American Express. Wheelchair accessible via elevators.*

One of our favorite restaurants is around the corner and across the street on Carrillo.

We hereby "discover" **ROY** for the outside world. Roy used to have the extremely popular Espressway Cafe local hangout on Chapala Street and grew to this fabulous funky bistro and bar. Catch the local art exhibit the minute you pass through the door, along with turquoise vinyl banquets, swivel chairs, and old diner parts such as tables and lamps.

Roy Gandy, a native of Buffalo, New York, virtually grew up in his parents' and grandparents' fish house, which the family has had for a mere sixty-three years. Roy "chased a woman out here" and never went back, although she did. We are all lucky he never left.

This is down-to-earth, creative good food. If you want nouvelle, we will take you to other restaurants. Every entree at Roy's comes with subtle soup, a house salad of mixed organic greens from the Santa Barbara farmers' market, and warm melt-in-your-mouth homemade wheat bread.

We especially recommend the charbroiled king salmon with lemon hollandaise and a fresh fruit salsa, or the charbroiled filet mignon, perfectly cooked medium rare unless you ask otherwise. You might prefer the chicken breast stuffed with spinach and Swiss cheese and homemade chicken gravy, chicken marsala with sliced mushrooms, pork tenderloin sautéed with port, ginger, and brown sugar, or the New York steak with whipped fresh herb butter (all $15). There is always a vegetarian pasta at $10. For us the portions are perfect: a smallish meat serving with plenty of veggie accompaniments. For a $6.50 charge, you can split an entree and get an extra bowl of soup and an extra salad. Deal!

Desserts are beyond belief. Our favorite is the espresso chocolate chip cheesecake, which consists of a wedge of the cheesecake with chocolate chip crust, a pile of delicate chocolate chips, and whipped cream, all resting in a pool of chocolate sauce. Oh my!

Roy's wine list is carefully selected from among the central coast's finest, with Ravenswood Zinfandel and a Trefethen Cabernet Sauvignon thrown in, all under

$35. Beer fans can also try local Firestone Ale and San Luis Obispo Brewery's Amberale, in addition to several Irish, British, and German brews.

A local favorite, Roy is an absolute must on your culinary itinerary.

❧ *Roy, 7 West Carrillo Street, Santa Barbara 93101; (805) 966–5636. Open lunch 11:30 A.M.–2:30 P.M. Monday–Friday, dinner 6:00 P.M.–midnight nightly. Full bar (great martinis). Visa, MasterCard, American Express. Wheelchair accessible.*

Back to State Street. Right at the southwest corner of Carrillo and State is GAME KEEPER, a heavenly store for grown-up kids, except for maybe the Koosh toys. Hundreds of puzzles, chess sets, play stations, Nintendo games, darts, and gambling supplies combine to attract even men inside this store.

❧ *Game Keeper, 939 State Street,* Santa Barbara 93101; (805) 965–8383. Open 10:00 A.M.–7:00 P.M. Tuesday–Saturday, 11:00 A.M.–6:00 P.M. Sunday, 10:00 A.M.–6:00 P.M. Monday. Visa, MasterCard, American Express. Mostly wheelchair accessible.*

> ### FAMOUS TOMATO BISQUE
> ### *from Roy Gandy of Roy, Santa Barbara*
>
> ---
>
> *3 lbs. organic vine-ripened tomatoes, cored and quartered*
> *¼ cup sugar*
> *½ pint heavy whipping cream*
> *1 cube (4 oz.) sweet butter*
> *salt and pepper*
> *just about any fresh herbs*
>
> ---
>
> Simmer tomatoes over low heat for 30 minutes. Puree cooked tomatoes and run through a strainer, discarding skins and seeds.
>
> Reheat the tomato sauce to a simmer, then add sugar and heavy whipping cream, and then whisk in butter. Add salt and pepper to taste. Just about any fresh herb or herbs may be added to suit your taste as well as for making a nice garnish.

Just down from the corner is DIANE'S OF CALIFORNIA LADIES SWIMWEAR featuring possibly the smallest bikinis and thong bathing suits in the West. Labels include Sunsets, Jay, AM, Cole, Esprit, and Roxie. And then there are the high platform thong sandals. Perfect figures required, seemingly, at their ten southern California locations.

❧ *Diane's of California Ladies Swimwear, 933 State Street, Santa Barbara 93101; (805) 957–2070. Open 10:00 A.M.–6:00 P.M. Monday–Saturday, 11:00 A.M.–6:00 P.M. Sunday. Visa, MasterCard, American Express. Wheelchair accessible.*

In total contrast to Diane's is ENCHANTED FOREST next door, a "wildlife gallery and gifts" with Jenny Allio's handpainted canvases, mood music tapes, animal everythings, elegant walking sticks and canes, floral scents, chimes and weather vanes, and wildlife sketches and stationery. A stuffed brown bunny sits in a chair and goes home with you for $163. Tsunami sterling jewelry even comes in animal motifs.

❧ *Enchanted Forest, 931 State Street, Santa Barbara 93101; (805) 957–0051. Open 10:00 A.M.–6:00 P.M. Monday–Friday, 10:00 A.M.–7:00 P.M. Saturday, 11:00 A.M.–6:00 P.M. Sunday. Visa, MasterCard, American Express, Discover. Wheelchair accessible.*

SHOE PHORIA specializes in competitive pricing of ladies' casual comfort and fashion shoes such as Esprit, Zodiac, Sam & Libby, Report, Destroy, Unlisted, and Nicole Griffin. Styles are very with-it, as are the young employees.

❧ *Shoe Phoria, 927 State Street, Santa Barbara 93101; (805) 962–6263. Open 10:00 A.M.–7:00 P.M. daily. Visa, MasterCard, American Express, Discover. Wheelchair accessible.*

In case you are weakening from all this walking and shopping, BASKIN ROBBINS comes to the rescue just in the nick of time. Dozens of flavors of ice cream and yogurt, ice cream cakes and pies, and a few novelties refresh all ages.

❧ *Baskin Robbins, 925 State Street, Santa Barbara 93101; (805) 957–0031. Open 11:00 A.M.–9:00 P.M. Sunday–Thursday, 11:00 A.M.–10:00 P.M. Friday–Saturday. No credit cards. Wheelchair accessible.*

UDDER MADNESS is headquarters for souvenirs such as golf balls imprinted with "Santa Barbara," shirts, tote bags, glasses, and Dilbert and South Park stuff galore.

❧ *Udder Madness, 923 State Street, Santa Barbara 93101; (805) 966–4140. Open 10:00 A.M.–7:00 P.M. weekdays, 10:00 A.M.–8:00 or 9:00 P.M. weekends. Visa, MasterCard, American Express. Wheelchair accessible.*

At the CANDY STATION one door down from Udder Madness, Susan Peterson serves as conductor and Pete Peterson is the engineer on their train to candyland. And it's full of chocolates, saltwater taffy, licorice, novelties, Violet Crumbles, and jelly beans. You can actually purchase whole packs of Black Jack, Clove, and Beemans chewing gum here.

❧ *Candy Station, 921 State Street, Santa Barbara 93101; (805) 899–9182. Open 11:00 A.M.–8:00 P.M. Sunday–Thursday, 10:30 A.M.–9:00 P.M. Friday–Saturday. Visa and MasterCard with a $15 minimum purchase. Wheelchair accessible.*

Z GALLERIE moved here from down State Street in July 1999, only to make available more of their always interesting home accessories, ranging from abstract and classical picture frames and furniture to wild lamps, candlesticks, and loads of European and American poster art, usually bargains framed or unframed. At all their locations in California, Z Gallerie is an excellent place to find accoutrements for your new apartment or hip room.

Z Gallerie, 917 State Street, Santa Barbara 93101; (805) 564–1974. Open 10:00 A.M.–9:00 P.M. daily. Visa, MasterCard, American Express, Discover. Wheelchair accessible.

Just down from the new Z Gallerie is BOON MEE DECOR & GIFTS, a fascinating devotion of Robert Adkins where he features "eclectic collections" of things spiritual and beautiful. Boon Mee means good karma, which Robert creates and exudes through his home furnishings, incense, music, spiritual jewelry, cards, and gifts. This is a sights-and-sounds experience.

Boon Mee Decor & Gifts, 915 State Street, Santa Barbara 93101; (805) 966–7369. Open 10:00 A.M.–6:00 P.M. Monday–Thursday, 10:00 A.M.–9:00 P.M. Friday–Saturday, 11:00 A.M.–6:00 P.M. Sunday. Visa, MasterCard, American Express, Discover. Wheelchair accessible.

EL PASO IMPORT COMPANY is one of our favorites, specializing in "originals from Mexico," meaning furniture, not people (shucks!). Be sure to browse through the old and cleaned-up (as well as reproductions of) heavy wood and metal Mexican furniture, all with new hardware made by El Paso that holds it together so you can actually use it. Many of the new pieces are made from old or recycled wood. Notice the rich, naturally vibrant colors, the Tara Humara pots, and the below-retail prices. El Paso claims to offer "America's largest selection of original vintage Mexican country furniture" at its eleven stores, and you can order the fascinating catalogue for $4.00.

El Paso Import Company, 913 State Street, Santa Barbara 93101; (805) 963–7530. Open 10:00 A.M.–6:00 P.M. Monday–Saturday, noon–5:00 P.M. Sunday. Visa and MasterCard. Wheelchair accessible, although a little tight in places.

Just south of El Paso, the GREEN AND YELLOW BASKET (where's the tisket and tasket?) is a complex emporium of washable linen clothes, hats, gifts, collectibles, big Polonaise Christmas ornaments, storybooks, movies, baskets, cookie cutters, Ty stuffed animals and Beanie Babies, postcards, and the deal of the street: colorful Mexican blankets for $9.98 (normally around $20.00 elsewhere). Do not let the pouty young staff deter you.

✣ *Green and Yellow Basket, 911 State Street, Santa Barbara 93101; (805) 965–7777. Open 10:00 A.M.–6:00 P.M. Monday–Thursday, 10:00 A.M.–9:00 P.M. Friday–Saturday and daily in summer. Visa, MasterCard, American Express. Wheelchair accessible but tight.*

Leather lovers: here it is! LEATHER DEPOT, new to Santa Barbara in 1999, is possibly the most elegant and pleasant leather boutique we have seen. And Kathleen knows them all. Here you will find fabulous quality at excellent prices, as well as friendly and informative hosts. Touch and feel the leather clothing, bags of all sizes, belts, travel gear, jewelry, wallets, shoes and slippers, and Southwest clothing. Don't miss!

✣ *Leather Depot, 909 State Street, Santa Barbara 93101; (805) 564–4161. Open 10:00 A.M.–6:00 P.M. Monday–Friday, 10:00 A.M.–9:00 P.M. Saturday, 11:00 A.M.–7:00 P.M. Sunday. Visa, MasterCard, American Express, Discover. Wheelchair accessible.*

Just down from leather, the NAKED WALL suggests they offer things with which to cover that wall, and they do, primarily posters and paintings of local Santa Barbara scenes. Many are the work of Santa Barbara artist Marcia Burtt.

✣ *Naked Wall, 907 State Street, Santa Barbara 93101; (805) 965–4223. Open 10:00 A.M.–5:30 P.M. Monday–Saturday. Visa, MasterCard, American Express, Discover. Wheelchair accessible.*

Finally, a restaurant! And right across State Street convenient to Borders Books and Fiesta 5 Theatres and just up and across Canon Perdido from Barnes & Noble.

BACCIO touts "the healthy sun-drenched flavors of Santa Barbara" at both lunch and dinner. Starters range from Baccio bread, a toasted baguette with garlic butter, fontina, and mozzarella ($3.50), and Baccio's six bean soup ($3.00–$5.00), to Tigrati tiger shrimp sautéed in garlic butter with capers, mushrooms, and artichoke hearts ($8.25). Salads range from local greens ($4.25) to the Medina with grilled tiger shrimp, kalamata olives, and feta cheese ($8.95).

Pizzas are all $7.95 and include pepperoni with kalamata olives, one with sliced eggplant, and one featuring roasted chicken. Three calzones are $8.95 each, while all pasta entrees are $8.95. Try the mushroom ravioli, or the Florentino—giant Florentine ravioli with a sausage tomato sauce, roasted bell peppers, and feta cheese. Chicken every which way is $9.95, and seafood with pastas are all $11.95, but indulge in the paella Valencia ($13.95) or the Sinatra buco lamb shank simmered in tomato sauce with fresh veggies and garlic mashed potatoes ($13.95).

❧ *Baccio, 905 State Street, Santa Barbara 93101; (805) 564–8280. Open 11:30 A.M.–10:00 P.M. daily. Beer and wine. Visa, MasterCard, American Express. Mostly wheelchair accessible.*

ANTHROPOLOGIE reminds us of another chain, Urban Outfitters, although Anthropologie emphasizes slightly more elegant accessories for your home, with many tempting reproductions of European iceboxes, mailboxes, candelabra, kitchen utensils and equipment, and lots of attractive little stuff.
❧ *Anthropologie, 901 State Street, Santa Barbara 93101; (805) 962–5461, (800) 309–2500; fax (805) 962–2613; Web site: www.anthropologie.com. Open 10:00 A.M.–8:00 P.M. Monday–Saturday, 11:00 A.M.–6:00 P.M. Sunday. Visa, MasterCard, American Express. Wheelchair accessible.*

At the southwest corner of State Street and Canon Perdido street is the PIERRE LAFOND–WENDY FOSTER boutique, one of the offspring of entrepreneur Pierre Lafond and his wife. They also have a Wendy Foster women's clothing shop in Montecito.

Actually in the Paseo Nuevo complex, this shop specializes in casual, sophisticated clothing of natural fibers and soft colors from designers Lisa Jasso, Diesel, Industry, Curiositees, Oh Boy!, Lucky, Big Star, and allen allen usa.
❧ *Pierre Lafond–Wendy Foster, 833 State Street, Santa Barbara 93101; (805) 996–2276. Open 10:00 A.M.–6:00 P.M. Monday–Thursday, 10:00 A.M.–8:00 P.M. Friday–Saturday, 11:00 A.M.–6:00 P.M. Sunday. Visa, MasterCard, American Express. Wheelchair accessible.*

BARNES & NOBLE bookstore is a comfort zone for some people with best-sellers discounted (which is why they remain best-sellers?) and a Starbucks cafe inside. Wide range of books with excellent hours for late night browsing.
❧ *Barnes & Noble, 829 State Street, Santa Barbara 93101; (805) 962–8509. Open 9:00 A.M.–11:00 P.M. daily. Visa, MasterCard, American Express, Discover, Diners. Wheelchair accessible with elevator to upper floors.*

Just south of Barnes & Noble is another handy chain store, RITE-AID PHARMACY, which, most places, used to be Payless Drugs. Everything you forgot to bring along is here, from Band-Aids and aspirin to beach balls, writing materials, flashlights, and more personal supplies including pharmaceuticals.
❧ *Rite-Aid Pharmacy, 825 State Street, Santa Barbara 93101; (805) 965–5227 store, (805) 966–2760 pharmacy. Open 8:00 A.M.–9:00 P.M. Monday–Saturday, 10:00 A.M.–7:00 P.M. Sunday. Visa and MasterCard. Wheelchair accessible.*

BETTY'S FABRICS is primarily frequented by locals because they are the ones with the sewing machines. It's worth a browse though, because you might find everything from period fabrics to elegant bolts that you or your handy-dandy tailor can craft into something wearable for you or yours.

❧ *Betty's Fabrics, 821 State Street, Santa Barbara 93101; (805) 963–0311. Open 9:30 A.M.–5:30 P.M. Monday–Saturday, noon–5:00 P.M. Sunday. Visa and MasterCard. Wheelchair accessible.*

Take the next walkway to the massive **PASEO NUEVO** mall, which is lined with fifty light- and medium-fast-food restaurants and small shops, such as California Pasta and a Häagen-Dazs ice cream shop. Heavens! You will also find People's Pottery, Rudy's Mexican Restaurant, Santa Barbara Candy Co., Banana Republic, Nine West, Victoria's Secret, Nordstrom, Macy's Lucky Brand Dungarees, the Warner Brothers Studio Store, Limited, Gap, Chile's, Eddie Bauer Home Collection, and the Center State Theater. If familiar shopping is your thing, this is where you find the shops you will recognize from home.

Paseo Nuevo offers ninety minutes' free parking in its garage, which you reach from Chapala Street.

❧ *Paseo Nuevo, State and De la Guerra Streets, Santa Barbara 93101; (805) 963–2202. Open 10:00 A.M.–9:00 P.M. Monday–Friday, 10:00 A.M.–8:00 P.M. Saturday, 11:00 A.M.–6:00 P.M. Sunday. Visa, MasterCard, American Express. Wheelchair accessible.*

Back on State Street at the entrance to Paseo Nuevo is the **COFFEE BEAN AND TEA LEAF**, a favorite tea and coffee stop for locals. The only problem here is limited seating, but you can sit at tables in the Nuevo Paseo walkway. Feast your eyes and salivary glands on their fruit cheesecakes, carrot cake, and Death by Chocolate cake, and be sure to take home one of their handsome black glass jars filled with their own teas.

❧ *Coffee Bean and Tea Leaf, 811A State Street, Santa Barbara 93101; (805) 966–2442. Open 7:00 A.M.–10:00 P.M. Sunday–Thursday, 7:00 A.M.–11:00 P.M. Friday–Saturday. Visa and MasterCard. Wheelchair accessible.*

SUNDANCE BEACH is slightly more appealing to families than the two swimwear shops farther up State Street. Check out the beachwear for men, women, and kids, including Reef sandals, Point Conception bathing suits, Noes on the Nose shirts, UGG boots. You'll know you're here by the plastic parasols and flowers in big clay pots on the sidewalk.

❧ *Sundance Beach, 809 State Street, Santa Barbara 93101; (805) 966–2474. Visa, MasterCard, American Express, Discover. Wheelchair accessible.*

LEFT AT ALBUQUERQUE, truly one of our favorites, has both terrific New Mexican food and a wildly fun ambience. We have sat at the sidewalk tables for a late lunch of lime chicken fajitas with sensational beans and piles of fresh condiments ($7.95), and also dined inside with the full bar atmosphere, music, and people meeting people. One caution: do not accept the inside table near the sliding glass door to the sidewalk tables unless it's in warm weather. The wind the door sucks in can blow the napkins off your lap! Lunch and dinner prices are the same.

This Mobil Travel Guide–recommended restaurant has the longest list of gourmet tequilas we have ever seen, red and white corn tortilla chips with fresh, fresh salsas, lip-smacking tortilla soup ($3.95), enormous nachos, and a variety of meat, seafood, and vegetarian dishes. Of the quesadillas, try the tequila lime rock shrimp ($6.99).

House favorites include "hot-off-the-griddle" corn cakes with tequila lime butter and sun-dried tomato corn salsa ($3.99); chopped chicken salad with feta cheese and a basil pesto dressing ($8.99); Dixon apple and blue cheese salad with candied pecans and ancho chili balsamic dressing ($6.99); an unbelievable towering tostada that varies in price for vegetarian, chicken, or steak; and a green monster enchilada with poblano chicken topped with roasted green chili sauce, jack and cheddar cheeses, sour cream, and green rice ($8.88).

The pan-roasted BBQ salmon served with tequila lime butter sauce, sun-dried tomato-corn salsa and green rice ($11.99) and the roadhouse fajitas (price also varies by choice) are also fun. To accompany your pastas, enchiladas, pork tamales, or grilled chicken breasts, you can choose your own sauces: New Mexican red sauce or roasted green chili sauce or both. Enjoy!

❧ *Left at Albuquerque, 803 State Street, Santa Barbara 93101; (805) 564–5040. Open 11:00 A.M.–11:00 P.M. Full bar. Visa, MasterCard, American Express. Wheelchair accessible.*

One door down the street from Left at Albuquerque is ROCKS RESTAURANT & LOUNGE, a two-level restaurant with a cafe/bar atmosphere downstairs that includes computer plug-ins and window tables, great viewing metal tables on the sidewalk facing State Street, and a big entrance to Paseo Nuevo.

Rocks has great prices—salads and burgers (including tuna carpaccio or sashimi) at lunch are $6.95, with offerings ranging from a warm spinach scallop salad with pesto, pine nuts, and goat cheese ($6.95) to Rocks' half-pound burger that comes with choice of French fries, green salad, or pasta salad and a mere fifty cents extra for cheddar or blue cheese ($4.95). We like the blackened mahimahi sandwich ($5.95) or grilled salmon sandwich ($6.95). Entrees may include roasted Chilean sea bass, macadamia crusted halibut (each $6.95), or eggplant Parmesan ($4.95). Plus a variety of pastas, all under $7.00. No wonder it's packed!

Evening selections are both similar and more extensive, with additions including seared tuna tataki ($16), pepper-crusted filet mignon with baby bok choy and crispy polenta ($16), braised lamb shank with scalloped potatoes and root veggies ($15) or spicy Korean-style ribs ($13).

Rocks' wine list is short but good, offering Domain Chandon, Schramsberg, Veuve Cliquot, and Moet & Chandon sparkling wines, as well as excellent Santa Barbara, Monterey, Napa, and Sonoma Chardonnays, Sauvignon Blancs, and Cabernet Sauvignons.

➳ *Rocks Restaurant & Lounge, 801 State Street, Santa Barbara 93101; (805) 884–1190. Full bar. Open 11:30 A.M.–10:00 P.M. Monday–Thursday, 11:30 A.M.–11:00 P.M. Friday–Saturday. Visa, MasterCard, American Express, Discover. Downstairs and sidewalk are wheelchair accessible.*

On the other side of the pathway to Paseo Nuevo is ONE BEACH ROAD, another home accessories shop full of elegant reproductions of French, British, Mexican, and plantation furniture, lamps, armoires, wall sconces, and even garden lanterns. And really nice people. Check out the clever magnifying glasses and Picasso pottery.

➳ *One Beach Road, 725 State Street, Santa Barbara 93101; (805) 962–9379. Open 10:00 A.M.–7:00 P.M. Monday–Saturday, 11:00 A.M.–6:00 P.M. Sunday. Visa, MasterCard, American Express. Wheelchair accessible.*

We are about to do another disservice to Santa Barbarans. We hereby "discover" PASCUCCI for the outside world. When you ask almost anyone working on State Street what their favorite restaurant is, they say "Pascucci's." The name combines parts of "pasta and cappuccino," with some good wine poured in.

Think about this: mosaic and iron tables in front, opera playing in the background, brick and mustard walls, large colorful paintings, an open curved kitchen, a big tiled fireplace, and fabulous garlic smells wafting throughout the restaurant at all times of the day—even when the restaurant is closed!

Pascucci's is a happening hangout where you can enjoy extremely tasty food at reasonable prices. For antipasti, try the carciofi tre formaggio, which is artichoke hearts and prosciutto baked with fontina, Gorgonzola, and Parmesan cheeses ($5.25), or the bruschetta of fresh Roma tomatoes, fresh basil, roasted garlic, herbs, and balsamic vinegar on toasted rosemary bread ($5.25). Oh yes, be sure to sample the breads brought to your table.

The soups of the day ($2.25–$3.25) are excellent, as are the salads, which come in small or large. We often share a large Caesar ($5.00–$7.00) and one of their thick and aromatic pizzas. At lunch the panini (sandwiches) are mostly $6.96 and are made on garlic-cheese bread and served with mixed green or Caesar salad. The Amalfi includes prosciutto, herbed mushrooms, and smoked mozzarella; the San Remo features grilled garlic and herb marinated tri-tip steak, spicy marinara, and avocado; the Como is grilled shrimp, marinated artichoke hearts, and pesto. You can also get roasted eggplant, and children's pizza or spaghetti for under $4.00.

The pastas are equally exciting and even more varied, and range from $4.75 to $6.95 at lunch and up to $10.00 at dinner. Head for the "specialita" at the end of the menu for grilled vegetable plates, tiger shrimp stuffed with pesto and wrapped in prosciutto, grilled salmon filet with capellini, and boneless chicken breasts several inventive ways.

❧ *Pascucci, 729 State Street, Santa Barbara 93101; (805) 963–8123. Open 11:30 A.M.–9:00 P.M. Monday–Friday, 11:30 A.M.–10:00 P.M. Friday–Saturday. Full bar. Visa, MasterCard, American Express. Wheelchair accessible.*

One door down the street from Pascucci is the WARNER BROS. STUDIO STORE, a hit with kids of all ages featuring souvenirs of Warner Bros. movies and cartoons. You'll find clothes and hats for babies, little kids, and large adults depicting Tom & Jerry and loads of other cartoon and movie favorites. Collectors will love the Bean Bag character dolls.

❧ *Warner Bros. Studio Store, 721 State Street, Santa Barbara 93101; (805) 966–3348. Open 10:00 A.M.–9:00 P.M. Monday–Friday, 10:00 A.M.–8:00 P.M. Saturday, 11:00 A.M.–6:00 P.M. Sunday. Visa, MasterCard, American Express, Discover. Wheelchair accessible.*

George Zimmer's MEN'S WAREHOUSE occupies the next storefront down State Street, with his usual men's clothing from casual to designer work and dress suits. He guarantees it!

❧ *Men's Warehouse, 719 State Street, Santa Barbara 93101; (805) 962–2694; Web site: www.menswarehouse.com. Open 10:00 A.M.–9:00 P.M. Monday–Friday, 10:00 A.M.–9:00 P.M. Saturday, 11:00 A.M.–5:00 P.M. Sunday. Visa, MasterCard, American Express, Discover. Wheelchair accessible.*

And here comes MACY'S, our all-American, bicoastal favorite at the corner of State and Ortega Streets. Expect the usual and reliable designer merchandise from makeup and perfume on the first floor to shoes and all sorts of clothing.

❧ *Macy's, 701 State Street, Santa Barbara 93101; (805) 963–4566. Open 10:00 A.M.–9:00 P.M. Monday–Friday, 10:00 A.M.–8:00 P.M. Saturday, 11:00 A.M.–6:00 P.M. Sunday. Visa, MasterCard, American Express. Wheelchair accessible.*

It's worth crossing Ortega Street to go to the **TRAILHEAD,** known to be the friendliest outfitting store in town. We agree. In a building originally the site of the Gutierrez Drug Store (1855), the Trailhead now offers lots of information, as well as active clothing and shoes by Osprey, Arcteryx, Siena Design, Woolrich, La Sportiva, Ecco, and Timberland, as well as Swiss Army knives, Walrus tents, hiking accessories, a great selection of pertinent books, and backpacks of all sizes and shapes. Manager Christopher Gaines says he will "match any deal or beat it." So beat it down there.

✺✣ *Trailhead, 635 State Street, Santa Barbara 93101; (805) 963–9308. Open 10:00 A.M.–6:00 P.M. Monday–Saturday, 10:00 A.M.–5:00 P.M. Sunday. Visa, MasterCard, American Express, ATM, no personal checks. Wheelchair accessible.*

Cyclists will want to be sure to drop in at **VELO PRO BICYCLES,** either for repairs or new equipment and bikes. Two mechanics work full time behind the counter, while you check out the bike parts, mountain bikes, cruisers, and helmets. Bike brands include Raleigh, GT, Kona, Gary Fisher, Klein, Santa Cruz, Redline, Mongoose, Powerlite, Haro, Robinson, and Bontrager. Rentals vary by bike, and helmets are extra.

✺✣ *Velo Pro Bicycles, 633 State Street, Santa Barbara 93101; (805) 963–7775. Open 10:00 A.M.–6:00 P.M. Monday–Thursday and Saturday, 10:00 A.M.–7:00 P.M. Friday, 11:00 A.M.–4:00 P.M. Sunday. Visa, MasterCard, American Express, Discover, ATM. Wheelchair accessible.*

SUPPLY SERGEANT, a preparedness store next to the bike shop, has a load of military surplus or reproduction clothing, military patches, badges and medals, hats, pith helmets, dog tags made while you wait, just in case the war—any war—is coming to your neighborhood. You'll also find a few handy things, like Swiss army knives and camping supplies.

✺✣ *Supply Sergeant, 631 State Street, Santa Barbara 93101; (805) 963–3868. Open 10:00 A.M.–6:30 P.M. Monday–Saturday, noon–6:00 P.M. Sunday. Visa and MasterCard. Wheelchair accessible but crowded.*

The next two shops down the street sell shoes by the seashore. Actually **PAYLESS SHOES** and **PURE GOLD SHOES** offer good selections—knockoffs at Payless and the real Doc Martens, Skechers, and vintage clothing and linen tablecloths at Pure Gold.

While there are lots more shops further down State Street, the truly interesting ones are spread out over several blocks. You may want to venture down to Santa Barbara Brewing Company brewery and pub and Something's Fishy Asian seafood and veggie restaurant, both popular with college students and young locals.

We recommend that you cross State Street right here and work your way back up the east side to complete your shop walk.

Don't get overly excited over the name SANTA BARBARA GRILL unless you are looking for (a) decent hamburgers, tacos, carne asada, wraps, and smoothies (all under $5.00) that you order at the counter—and (b) rest rooms. This place actually advertises that its rest rooms are open to visitors from 8:00 A.M. to 8:00 P.M., a welcome sight in tourist areas that usually allow rest room use only by customers. The rest rooms are behind the building and not exactly luxurious, nor are they wheelchair accessible.

❧ *Santa Barbara Grill, 628 State Street, Santa Barbara 93101; no phone. Open 11:30 A.M.–2:00 P.M., 3:30–8:30 P.M. Sunday–Wednesday, and until 2:00 A.M. Friday–Saturday. Restaurant is wheelchair accessible; rest rooms are not.*

Next door to the hamburger joint, ZELO RESTAURANT presents a much more enticing ambience with the grill right in front of the dining room, brick walls, stepped terraces inside, large bright paintings, and a substantial bar. At lunch Zelo offers quesadillas with chicken or shrimp ($4.95), and pastas including salmon capellini ($6.95), mustard chicken fettucine ($4.95), and Thai beef ($5.50) with side salads for $1.50 extra. Easterners can enjoy a Philly steak sandwich ($5.50), Zelo's Killer Pastrami ($5.50), and half-sandwich specials with soup or salad ($3.95). All sandwiches come with salad, soup, or fries. Deal.

At dinner you might try baked artichoke hearts with fennel and Gorgonzola cream ($7.50); Zelo vera pasta with veggies, sun-dried tomatoes, garlic, and olive oil ($8.95); mustard spinach fettucine with chicken or tiger prawns ($9.95); or spicy Thai beef noodles ($9.95). Specialties range from paella ($13.95) and sesame seared ahi tuna ($12.95) to grilled filet mignon with caramelized shallots in pink peppercorn brandy ($14.95) and crab-stuffed salmon with dill beurre blanc ($15.95). All entrees come with soup or salad. Sandwiches are available. Salads, from blackened shark ($7.95) to Caesar ($5.95), are good, and the kids' menu for pastas or cheeseburgers is just $4.95.

Zelo boasts a list of special vodkas, rums, tequilas, and liqueurs, and a short wine list of Napa, Monterey, and central coast wines.

❧ *Zelo Restaurant, 630 State Street, Santa Barbara 93101; (805) 966–5792, fax (805) 966–5034. Open lunch 11:30 A.M.–3:00 P.M. Wednesday–Sunday, dinner from 5:30 P.M. Tuesday–Sunday. Visa and MasterCard. Not wheelchair accessible.*

Don't miss the ITALIAN GREEK MARKET at the corner of State Street and Ortega. A local favorite for decades, this place has been voted Best Deli & Sandwiches for fourteen years in a row by Santa Barbarans. Pay attention!

As you walk in, the deli case on the right makes it clear that this is the place for light lunches and sandwiches: huge marinated artichoke salad, macaroni salads like you've never seen, a large selection of meats, and comics taped to the deli counter's glass. You can sit on stools along the Ortega Street side window or at red-and-white-checked tableclothed tables in the back room. Italian soccer matches play on the television, and Italian basketball team photos line the walls. This is a great place to collect your picnic if you're heading off to the wineries.

The store area sells everything from the *Complete Armenian Cookbook* and Italian vinegars and oils to Genova tonno (tuna), Indo-European grains, Medaglia D'Oro Instant Espresso, small to large tins of anchovies and sardines, and even halvah at $5.40 per pound. Cafe Bustelo, Lavazza, and Kimbo coffees are all available next to blue bottles of Brioschi for upset stomachs! This is the place if you are looking for Greek wines and retsina.

⁊ॐ *Italian Greek Market, 636 State Street, Santa Barbara 93101; (805) 962–6815. Open 8:00 A.M.–6:00 P.M. daily. Beer and wine. No credit cards, but ATM in store. Wheelchair accessible.*

As you cross Ortega heading up State Street, you come to MA DOLCE VITA, an unusual combination of restaurant and coffee roastery.

Burgundy and pink seem to be the mood colors du jour at Ma Dolce Vita, where you enter the corner restaurant through its enclosed front patio adorned with burgundy print seat cushions, sponge pink walls, and pink and white azaleas. The restaurant's name translates to "My Sweet Life," the sweet of which definitely translates into the pastries, breads, and ice cream made here—all of which can be enjoyed with fresh espresso from beans roasted in their Diedrich coffee roaster toward the back of the dining room and bar.

Chef Porfirio A. Lemus concocts decent panini (sandwiches) of grilled vegetables, chicken melt, turkey clubs, tuna salad, and a portobello mushroom burger (all under $9.00). Various made-here pastas range from vegetarian penne primavera tossed in olive-garlic tapenade, sun-dried tomatoes, seasonal vegetables and Parmesan cheese ($7.95) to several with sautéed seafood and orchette picante, a spicy-chili tomato sauce with sautéed ground filet mignon, oregano, and Parmesan cheese ($8.95).

Minestrone soup is always on the menu ($3.25–$4.25), along with seared rare tuna salad ($9.25), grilled salmon salad ($9.25), and homemade pizzas or pizza and salad combo ($8.25). The dessert tray is decorated with flowers, making the desserts even more attractive than they need to be.

⁊ॐ *Ma Dolce Vita, 700 State Street, Santa Barbara 93101; (805) 965–3535, reservations (805) 965–3895, fax (805) 965–3654, E-mail: Jean.Moreau@gte.net. Open 11:30 A.M.–10:30 P.M. Tuesday–Friday, ˙9:00*

A.M. breakfast–10:30 P.M. Saturday–Sunday. Full bar. Visa and MasterCard. Front patio is wheelchair accessible.

Just up State Street from Ma Dolce Vita are two of our favorite shops to check into whenever we visit: Antique Alley and the State Street Antique Mall. We encourage you to browse at both places for little historic pieces of Santa Barbara history.

ANTIQUE ALLEY is the smaller of the two, although we find that its fifteen dealers sell well-selected antiques and collectibles more to our particular tastes. Alan Howard personally selects his dealers and oversees the whole place, willing to bargain within limits set by each dealer. We have found prize kitchen utensils, rare Viewmaster reels, and other gems we and our twentysomething kids collect at the moment.

❧ *Antique Alley, 706 State Street, Santa Barbara 93101; (805) 962–3944. Open 11:00 A.M.–6:00 P.M. Monday–Thursday, 11:00 A.M.–10:00 P.M. Friday–Saturday, noon–5:00 P.M. Sunday. Visa and MasterCard. Wheelchair accessible.*

STATE STREET ANTIQUE MALL is the larger of the two adjacent shops with eighty dealers and a lot more stuff. You have to look very carefully here to not miss some goodies and you have to go back and back if you are looking for something specific.

❧ *State Street Antique Mall, 710 State Street, Santa Barbara 93101; (805) 965–2575. Open 10:00 A.M.–6:00 P.M. Monday–Thursday and Sunday, 10:00 A.M.–10:00 P.M. Friday–Saturday. Visa and MasterCard. Wheelchair accessible but tight.*

For healthy refreshment after a morning or afternoon of antiques browsing, you might want to stop into PIRANHA RESTAURANT AND SUSHI BAR for sushi or robata-grilled beef, eggplant, Chilean sea bass, or Norwegian salmon ($16.50). And of course teriyaki galore.

❧ *Piranha Restaurant and Sushi Bar, 714 State Street, Santa Barbara 93101; (805) 965–2980. Open for lunch 11:30 A.M.–2:00 P.M. Tuesday–Sunday, dinner 5:30–10:00 P.M. Tuesday–Thursday, Saturday, Sunday, and until 11:00 P.M. Friday. Beer, wine, and sake. MasterCard and Visa. Wheelchair accessible.*

The rest of this block has a series of light-fastish-food cafes from which you can choose, including Fat Burger (how inspiring!) with smoothies; Espresso Roma Cafe, which boasts of offering "liquid culture"; Presto Pasta, often voted Best Dinner Under $10 in Santa Barbara; every mall's alternative food chain,

Fresh Choice, featuring soups, salads, and pastas; and Jamba Juice, with fresh juice drinks at the corner across from Starbucks.

MINGEI ORIENTAL IMPORTS sits in the middle of these food stops with its gorgeous Japanese chests, pottery, and wall hangings. Mingei specializes in Edo and Meiji furniture, art, and "objects of merit." A must see.

✣ *Mingei Oriental Imports, 736 State Street, Santa Barbara 93101; (805) 963–3257. Open 11:00 A.M.–5:00 P.M. Monday–Saturday, noon–6:00 P.M. Sunday. Visa, MasterCard, American Express. Wheelchair accessible.*

Practically tucked into a doorway of the De la Guerra Building between Fresh Choice and Jamba Juice is H & M EMBROIDERY, where Harvey Banick performs embroidery on hats, caps, shirts, and almost anything else while you wait. His prices are reasonable, and he also gives discounts on volume orders, doing lots of local logo business at his more formal locations. A great place to create your own souvenir.

✣ *H & M Embroidery, 742 State Street, Santa Barbara 93101; (805) 963–9220, fax (805) 564–3432. Open when he's there. Visa, MasterCard, American Express. One step up, but he easily comes to sidewalk.*

Here comes STARBUCKS, a home base essential in some people's lives. This one has the usual good coffee, scones and muffins, a few cozy tables inside, some seats at a counter along the De la Guerra Street window, and a few in front on State Street where smokers hang out. The outdoor tables are shady and cool in the morning, and great for sunbathing in the afternoon if you are so inclined (but don't incline or recline). Get a token at the counter to use the rest room.

✣ *Starbucks, 800 State Street, Santa Barbara 93101; (805) 962–0173. Open 7:00 A.M.–10:00 P.M. daily. Wheelchair accessible.*

As a pleasing alternative, try the local NAPOLEON PATISSERIE BOULANGERIE right next door to Starbucks. As you walk in you don't even see the people at tables to the right because your eyes dart straight for the long, curved case of napoleons, gorgeous fruit-covered tarts, gooey creamy éclairs, elegant sandwiches and panini, quiches, and pasta salads. Napoleon Patisserie Boulangerie also has a full menu of light meals, including breakfasts up to $7.50.

✣ *Napoleon Patisserie Boulangerie, 808 State Street, Santa Barbara 93101; (805) 899–1183. Open 8:00 A.M.–9:00 P.M. Monday–Thursday, 8:00 A.M.–10:00 P.M. Friday–Saturday, 8:30 A.M.–9:00 P.M. Sunday. Visa and MasterCard; wheelchair accessible.*

BRYANT & SONS JEWELERS LTD. deals in the finest jewelry there is, including Piaget, Cartier, Ebel, and Baume & Mercier diamonds, Mikimoto pearls, and colored gemstones. Bryant & Sons is also a Tiffany & Company authorized jeweler and has full time gemologists, appraisers, and a master goldsmith on the premises. This exquisite shop bends around the corner into El Paseo, one of Santa Barbara's older courtyards.

❧ *Bryant & Sons Jewelers Ltd., 812 State Street, Santa Barbara 93101; (805) 966–9187; Web site: www.sbweb.com/bryants. Open 10:00 A.M.–5:30 P.M. Monday–Saturday. Visa, MasterCard, American Express. Wheelchair accessible.*

We'll get to El Paseo in a minute but first want to tell you about A. GOLD E., which features "clothing for all curious Americans," which seems to mean sportswear, sweats, comfortable casual clothing, and denim (particularly featuring Tencel).

❧ *A. Gold E., 814 State Street, Santa Barbara 93101; (805) 564–1218. Open 10:00 A.M.–6:00 P.M. Monday–Saturday, noon–5:00 P.M. Sunday. Visa, MasterCard, American Express. Wheelchair accessible.*

EL PASEO itself is worth exploring, particularly if you wander into El Cuartel and make it all the way to the back at Anacapa Street to one of our favorite restaurants anywhere, the WINE CASK RESTAURANT AND WINE STORE. Doug Margerum presides over his culinary empire right here with Santa Barbara's major restaurant, the Wine Cask. The Wine Store is the finest on the central coast and features the best of local wines, as well as interesting and unusual imports. Do not miss Intermezzo, the new wine bar/cafe, and the Happy Hour with complimentary appetizers from 4:00 to 6:00 P.M. And on Sunday and Monday evenings you can enjoy a special five-course tasting menu, as well as a brunch-lunch Saturday and Sunday.

Doug and his fabulous crew prepare lunches for two of Santa Barbara's most prestigious private clubs, the University Club and the Polo Club, and also cater affairs for Michael Jackson (at his Neverland estate), Michelle Pfeiffer, and President Bill Clinton when he's in town.

At lunch you might want to try starters such as the shrimp tamale stuffed with black bean salad or the duck ravioli (each $8.00), or the wild mushroom risotto ($12) or the best sides of garlic-rosemary fries you will ever encounter. As a surveyor of ahi tuna sandwiches, I can tell you that the Wine Cask's tops them all with the addition of smoked bacon arugula and tomato with wasabi aioli on toasted levain ($11). Heaven!

The Hudson Valley foie gras at lunch or dinner is a standout, served at dinner with French lentils, sautéed apples, and onion marmalade, and a red wine reduction with dry cherries and ginger ($18). If uncooked fish doesn't bother you, try the tuna tartare with cucumber-potato salad, pineapple ponzu sauce with plum, and wasabi ($11).

SEARED AHI WITH SECHWAN PEPPERCORN CRUST, PONZU SAUCE, AND GINGER RISOTTO
from Doug Margerum of the Wine Cask, Santa Barbara

FOR THE SEARED AHI:
  6-6 oz. *portions of fresh ahi tuna,*
    cut 1½ inch thick
  ⅓ *cup each of crushed white,*
    black, green, and red peppercorns
    mixed together
  2 *Tbs. olive oil*

FOR THE PONZU SAUCE:
  ¼ *cup light soy sauce*
  ¼ *cup rice vinegar*
  ⅓ *cup water*
  1 *Tbs. dry white wine*
    or sherry

FOR THE RISOTTO:
  ½ *onion, finely chopped*
  1 *Tbs. butter, melted*
  2 *cups Arborio rice*
  8 *cups chicken stock or water*

FOR THE CHAMPAGNE GINGER BEURRE BLANC
  2 *large shallots, chopped*
  1 *cup dry champagne*
  4 *cups cream*
  4 *Tbs. freshly grated ginger*
  1 *Tbs. butter*
  salt and pepper to taste

SEARED AHI TUNA: Coat ahi with crushed peppercorns. Sear over medium heat in heavy fry pan until just medium rare.

PONZU SAUCE: Combine all ingredients for ponzu sauce and set aside.

RISOTTO: Sauté onion in butter over low heat just until transparent. Add the rice and 2 cups of the stock. Continue to cook over low heat until the rice absorbs the liquid, stirring continuously. Add the rest of the stock and cook the liquid down until the rice is al dente. Do not overcook.

CHAMPAGNE GINGER BEURRE BLANC: Sauté shallots and ginger in the butter over low heat. Add the champagne and continue to cook until reduced to syrup consistency. Add the cream and reduce until sauce coats the back of a spoon. Season with salt and pepper. Blend and strain through a sieve.

TO ASSEMBLE: Place the rice in a large saucepan over medium heat. Gradually stir in the sauce (approximately ⅓ cup at a time), being sure to let the rice absorb the liquid before adding more. Once all of the sauce is incorporated and the mixture is piping hot, stir in the Parmesan cheese and serve. Top with seared peppercorn crusted ahi. Drizzle plate with ponzu sauce. Serve with stir-fried vegetables. Serves six.

Everything here is outstanding, so it is always hard to select an entree. Kathleen likes the Chilean sea bass with saffron risotto and roasted veggies ($25), the peppercorn-crusted ahi tuna ($24), and the potato wrapped white-fish ($25), while Jerry goes for the Colorado lamb sirloin with red wine mush-room risotto and veggie ratatouille ($26). The Wine Cask's menu varies week-ly, so these delights may be replaced with others. One of our favorites.

Wine Cask, 813 Anacapa Street, Santa Barbara 93101; (805) 966–9463 or (800) 436-9463, fax (805) 568–0664; e-mail: winecask@winecask.com; Web site: www.winecask.com. Open for lunch 11:30 A.M.–3:00 P.M. Monday–Friday, brunch 10:00 A.M.–3:00 P.M. Saturday–Sunday, dinner 5:30–10:00 P.M. daily. Full bar. Visa, MasterCard, American Express, Diners. Wheelchair accessible.

Within El Paseo's courtyard, wander also to Europa Antiques, which aren't all from Europe; the Cat & Mouse House for patchwork quilts, gifts, and antiques; Old Towne Cafe, where you can get sandwiches and salads to eat at tables around the courtyard fountain; and El Paseo Restaurant, an average Mexican restaurant that features a huge buffet for about $7.00.

Parking alert! There's an excellent parking lot just north of El Paseo. Its entrance is on Anacapa Street, which is one-way (toward the ocean).

BORDER'S BOOKS, with its high-columned entryway, fills the northwest cor-ner of the intersection. Border's Cafe is just to your left as you walk in, and excellent discounts on best-sellers or well-financed wannabees are close to the door. The staff is very friendly here, and this particular Border's borders on the pleasant funk of an independent bookstore. In good weather, you can sit at round tables in front reading and sipping your Border's coffee.

Border's Books, Music & Cafe, 900 State Street, Santa Barbara 93101; (805) 899–3668. Open 9:00 A.M.–11:00 P.M. Monday–Thursday, 9:00 A.M.–midnight Friday–Saturday, 9:00 A.M.–10:00 P.M. Sunday. Visa, MasterCard, American Express. Wheelchair accessible.

FIESTA FIVE THEATRE, a multiscreen movie house with papers blowing around even during the Santa Barbara Film Festival, shows five films at a time for downtown moviegoers.

Fiesta Five Theatre, 916 State Street, Santa Barbara 93101; (805) 963–0454. Open 1:00–11:00 P.M. Monday–Thursday, 2:15 P.M.–midnight Friday–Sunday. No credit cards. Not wheelchair accessible.

SHE FASHION BOUTIQUE, one of the most fun clothing shops in town, spe-cializes in casually elegant wash-and-wear, easy-to-pack, contemporary clothing. So there! But it's true. Ladies, this is a great spot for well-made, feminine resort clothes.

❧ *She Fashion Boutique,* 916 State Street, Santa Barbara 93101; (805) 965–5593, fax (805) 965–0454. Open 10:00 A.M.–6:00 P.M. Monday–Thursday, 10:00 A.M.–10:00 P.M. Friday–Saturday, noon–6:00 P.M. Sunday. Visa, MasterCard, American Express. Wheelchair accessible.

Just up the street SPORTS FAN caters to—guess what—sports fans, and will sell you/them everything from team hats and jackets, cards, and watches to all sorts of sports memorabilia such as signed photos. The owner seems not to like people asking questions, but will deliver worldwide.

❧ *Sports Fan,* 916 State Street, Santa Barbara 93101; (805) 965–8106. Open from 10:00 A.M. Monday–Saturday and from 11:00 A.M. Sunday. Visa and MasterCard. Wheelchair accessible.

Advertising "visitors rest rooms in the back," R. G.'S GIANT HAMBURGERS basically puts out popular, greasy hamburgers and all that goes with them: French fries, cokes and other drinks, other sandwiches, and light breakfasts.

❧ *R. G.'s Giant Hamburgers,* 922 State Street, Santa Barbara 93101; (805) 963–1654. Open 9:00 A.M.–9:00 P.M. Monday–Thursday, 9:00 A.M.–10:00 P.M. Friday–Saturday, 9:00 A.M.–8:00 P.M. Sunday. No credit cards. Wheelchair accessible.

Probably the most visually exciting experience on State Street is 3D STUDIO GALLERY, which exclusively features the work of Fazzino, whose serigraphs are shown in 400 galleries throughout the world. Fazzino's three-dimensional images are eye-catching, colorful, communicative, and attractive in a slightly far-out sort of way. He has created special pieces for Disney, Rosie O'Donnell's fund, the Special Olympics, the New York Yankees, the National Football League, and opera star Marilyn Horne at the Music Academy of the West in Montecito.

Walk by 3D in the evening when neon and other bright lights make these works pulsate!

❧ *3D Studio Gallery,* 922½ State Street, Santa Barbara 93101; (805) 730–9109, fax (805) 730–9147. Open 11:00 A.M.–6:00 P.M. Monday–Thursday, 11:00 A.M.–9:00 P.M. Friday-Saturday, 11:00 A.M.–6:00 P.M. Sunday. Visa, MasterCard, American Express, and no-interest layaway for five months. Wheelchair accessible.

Right next door, ROOMS & GARDENS presents a lifestyle many of us wished we lived. Plush furniture, feather beds, lamps, and scents galore abound here, along with idyllic garden decor and equipment. This is definitely an upscale version of what you will find one store up the street at Pier 1 Imports.

❧ *Rooms & Gardens, 924 State Street, Santa Barbara 93101; (805) 965–2424. Open 10:00 A.M.–5:30 P.M. Monday-Saturday, noon–5:00 P.M. Sunday. Visa, MasterCard, American Express. Wheelchair accessible.*

PIER 1 IMPORTS is what it is throughout the United States: a fun, average-priced home accessories store that specializes in colorful imported fabrics, furniture, door mats, pillows and cushions, bedspreads, and lots of other fun stuff to decorate your apartment or home.

❧ *Pier 1 Imports, 928 State Street, Santa Barbara 93101; (805) 965–0118. Open 10:00 A.M.–9:00 P.M. Monday–Friday, 10:00 A.M.–8:00 P.M. Saturday, 10:00 A.M.–7:00 P.M. Sunday. Visa, MasterCard, American Express. Discover. Wheelchair accessible.*

One store up from Pier 1 Imports is the locally popular PAPER STAR, a shop selling cards, pillows, beans, stickers, wrapping supplies, and wedding invitations, just in case you develop sudden plans! The occasionally brusque owner insists that part-time Santa Barbara resident Julia Child shops here often.

❧ *Paper Star, 930 State Street, Santa Barbara 93101; (805) 965–5509. Open 10:00 A.M.–6:00 P.M. Monday–Saturday, 11:00 A.M.–5:00 P.M. Sunday. Visa, MasterCard, American Express, Discover. Wheelchair accessible.*

At the corner of State and Cabrillo, SHOOZ is a wonderful true shoe boutique with staff to actually serve you and help you try on shoes, the old-fashioned way! Owner Elie Entezari offers Anne Klein, Charles David, Martines Valro, Moda Spana, Seychelles, and Misa, as well as gorgeous Dalya Collection sweaters. Worth a look, anyway, just for service nostalgia sake.

❧ *Shooz, 936 State Street, Santa Barbara 93101; (805) 962–3121. Open 10:00 A.M.–7:00 P.M. Sunday–Thursday, 10:00 A.M.–8:00 P.M. Friday–Saturday. Visa, MasterCard, American Express, Discover. Wheelchair accessible.*

The huge attractive building on the northeast corner of State and Carrillo is Montecito Bank and Trust, beyond which you will find the always crowded CHASE BAR & GRILL, which boasts "East Coast Italian-style food."

As far as we can tell "East Coast" seems to mean waiters in white jackets with towels over their arms. Dinner starters include yummy pesto bread ($3.75), steamed clams ($7.95), or large Caesar salad ($5.95). All dinner entrees include soup, such as housemade minestrone, Venetian fish chowder, or the soup of the day, or salad with choice of dressings. Pastas range from spaghetti with broccoli and garlic ($8.95) to handmade ravioli with choice of sauces ($9.50) and fettucine Alfredo with chicken ($11.95).

All house specialties come with fettucine or spaghetti, and you get sauce choices—piccata (lemon, wine, and capers) and Provençal (sherry and garlic)—for your chicken, red snapper, halibut, calamari, jumbo shrimp, or hand-trimmed veal ($10.75–$14.75). Of course there are steak choices too, and cioppino ($16.95), and scampi ($17.50).

꙰ *Chase Bar & Grill, 1012 State Street, Santa Barbara 93101; (805) 965–4351. Open for lunch 11:00 A.M.–2:30 P.M. Monday–Friday, dinner 5:00 P.M.–midnight daily. Full bar. Visa, MasterCard, American Express, Discover. Wheelchair accessible.*

MORNING GLORY MUSIC is a great and crowded place to find interesting new and used CDs if you don't mind an occasional punk. We don't. morning glory (that lower-case self-image problem) has lots of rock and roll, heavy metal, rap, etc.

꙰ *morning glory music, 1014 State Street, Santa Barbara 93101; (805) 966–0266. Open 10:00 A.M.–10:00 P.M. Monday–Saturday, 10:00 A.M.–8:00 P.M. Sunday. Visa, MasterCard, American Express, Discover. Wheelchair accessible.*

To complete the Italian dining choices in this block of State Street, PALAZZIO TRATTORIA ITALIANA is interesting as well as good. While the trattoria's accurate motto is "People generally don't leave here hungry," it also shows its dedication to and appreciation for the arts. Besides, locals voted Palazzio Best Service and Best Italian Restaurant in Santa Barbara every year from 1993 to 1998. Palazzio boasts that its food is ready for takeout in fifteen minutes or less.

Be sure to check out Palazzio's "Sistine Chapel ceiling," begun by local artist Irene Roderick March 2, 1998, and completed January 11, 1999. Read placards on the wall as you enter to get the full impression of this very different restaurant.

All menu selections are available in half-order/full-order portions and prices. An excellent pizza lunch combo with salad or soup is $8.75, and half orders of pastas at lunch are only $6.00.

Antipasti include chopped black olive spread (how well Kathleen remembers chopped olive sandwiches at her aunt Dorothy McKelligon's—not exactly Italian!) ($2.50); fried calamari ($6.75/$8.95); Caprese fresh Italian mozzarella, fresh Roma tomato, and sweet basil ($6.75/$8.75); antipasti Palazzio of sun-dried tomatoes, artichoke hearts, mozzarella, prosciutto, roasted peppers, mushrooms, and epiu ($9.75/$11.75); and baked artichoke hearts ($6.75).

Spinach, Caesar, and green salads are available, but try the Gorgonzola salad topped with roasted walnuts ($8.25/$10.25).

This is the only Italian restaurant we have ever seen that translates pastas to plain English for guests who are unfamiliar with pasta shapes and sizes—for example, *penne*, thin short tubes; *fettucine*, long flat; *fusilli*, corkscrew. A real plus!

Many of the standards are here, but specialties include penne brandy chicken with wild mushrooms, caramelized onions, Roma tomatoes, and brandy cream sauce ($10.75/15.25); Mama Pearl's spaghettini with meatballs, tomato sauce, bell peppers, garlic, chili peppers, fennel, mushrooms, and basil ($10.75/15.75); Papa Ruby's rigatoni grilled chicken with artichoke hearts and sun-dried tomatoes, sautéed in roasted red bell pepper cream sauce ($10.50/15.50).

The oven-roasted rosemary chicken is excellent ($10.95/15.95), as are the roasted eggplant lasagna ($11.95) and cannelloni made with ricotta, smoked mozzarella, prosciutto, fresh mushrooms, caramelized onions, spinach, and marinara sauce ($10.75/ 15.75). One of our favorites.

✣✣ *Palazzio Trattoria Italiana, 1026 State Street, Santa Barbara 93101; (805) 564–1985; Open for lunch 11:30 A.M.–3:00 P.M., dinner 5:30–11:00 P.M. Sunday–Thursday, 1:30 P.M.–midnight Friday–Saturday. Full bar. Visa, MasterCard, American Express. Wheelchair accessible.*

OVEN-ROASTED ROSEMARY CHICKEN
from Ken Brown, Palazzio Trattoria Italiana, Santa Barbara and Montecito

1 cup garlic, minced (chopped)
1 bunch Italian parsley, chopped
3 Tbs. fresh rosemary, chopped
salt and pepper to taste
6 whole chicken breasts, boneless with the skin on
1 cup unsalted butter
2 Tbs. white wine
juice of 1 whole lemon

Combine garlic, parsley, rosemary, butter, lemon juice, white wine, salt, and pepper. Stuff the mixture underneath the skins of the chicken breasts. Roast the chicken breasts at 350° F for 30–40 minutes. Serve with steamed seasonal vegetables. Serves six.

Ever-present Kinko's completes this block to State Street's intersection with Figueroa Street.

What you are about to encounter is the beautifully preserved and developed LA ARCADA complex, which was restored with storefronts on State Street as integral parts of the project, with the Santa Barbara Museum of Art up the street at the other end of the block.

At the northeast corner of State and Figueroa you first encounter P.S. LTD., an elegant home accessories boutique that features the Santa Barbara lap robe, Nicholas Mosse pottery from Ireland, French Heritage pottery from Brittany, Rochard Limoges, Churchill weavers, Les Etains pewter, Nancy Thomas folk art, Simon Pearce glass, Woodbury Woodenware, and Gien faience. You will also find Vera Bradley bags, elegant cards, and the best of Beanie Babies, which the owner's husband, Hugh Petersen, La Arcada restorer and developer, collects.

Be sure to visit Marge Petersen's back room, which is actually the dining room from the home of Theodore Willard (1902), owner of Willard Electric Barry Company in Cleveland, once America's largest automobile battery company and builder of the Willard electric car. The bench outside on the sidewalk welcomes bored men.

What is a Santa Barbara lap robe? It is really a quilt designed by Seddon Ryan Wylde, who has filled commissions for private label designs from the Boston Symphony Orchestra to the Historic Charleston Foundation and the Metropolitan Museum of Art in New York. She also creates private-label lap robes for the Boston Museum of Fine Arts, resorts, and cities from Nantucket to Catalina.

The Santa Barbara lap robe design depicts significant events and buildings in Santa Barbara's history, including the Santa Barbara Courthouse, Santa Barbara Mission, Santa Barbara Museum of Art, La Arcada, Arlington Theatre, the 1836 visit of the ship *Alert*, the Dolphin Fountain at Stearns Wharf, Lobero Community Theater, Old Mission Santa Ines, and fiesta time in Santa Barbara. This is truly a uniquely useful souvenir of your stay in Santa Barbara ($68). Wander through the store slowly so you don't miss anything. One of our favorites. ✷❧ *P. S. Ltd., 1100 State Street, Santa Barbara 93101; (805) 963–6808. Open 10:00 A.M.–5:30 P.M. Monday–Saturday. Visa, MasterCard, American Express, Discover. Downstairs is wheelchair accessible.*

Before you reach the actual entrance to La Arcada, two tempting restaurant/cafes present themselves. ANDERSEN'S DANISH BAKERY & RESTAURANT produces remarkably large and refreshing fruit plates served with Havarti cheese, Danish bread, ice cream, and a "surprise" all for $6.95. You will also enjoy their salads, "crispy" omelettes, sandwiches, smoked Scottish salmon with dill sauce, capers, Havarti cheese, cream cheese, bread and "surprise" ($11.95) and with a side of eggs for $13.95.

Daily hot specials may include port schnitzel ($8.95), Hungarian goulash ($8.95), or New York steak ($11.95). Andersen's Good Morning Breakfast includes bacon, eggs, ham, cheese, fruit, and potatoes for a whopping and notable $4.95, with no deductions for subtracting the meats or the eggs. Steak and eggs is $9.95. You also may want to check out the smorrebrod, an open-face decorated sandwich on pumpernickel served with fresh fruit and the day's salad ($6.95–$8.95; soup $1.00 extra).

Andersen's bakery always has warm Danish, strudels, croissants, and wonderful marzipan pastries, éclairs, napoleons, Sarah Bernhardts, Danish layer cake, Danish marzipan layer cake, and butter cookies. Just a sample. And then there's the homemade vanilla ice cream with whipped cream, fruit, and meringue ($4.95)!

❧

᛭᛬ *Andersen's Danish Bakery &*
Restaurant, 1106 State Street,
Santa Barbara 93101; (805)
962–5085. Open 8:00 A.M.–8:00
P.M. daily. Visa and MasterCard.
Wheelchair accessible.

Assuming you haven't enlarged
yourself by a full size, you might
check out **SOCORRO**, a relaxed resort
clothing store with the lovely loose,
natural fiber dresses of Mishi, Kiko,
and M.A.C. A few hats to protect
you from the summer sun, too.
᛭᛬ *Socorro,* 1106A State Street,
Santa Barbara 93101; (805)
966–5779. Open 10:00 A.M.–6:00
P.M. daily. Visa and MasterCard.
Wheelchair accessible.

Right at the corner of State
Street and the entrance to La
Arcada is **BARCLIFF & BAIR**, a
favorite of locals, and a favorite of
ours, too. We love to sit at the sidewalk tables, which face both State
Street and the occasionally cooler
La Arcada pathway, and enjoy a
sumptuous salad and excellent iced
tea. The people watching is primo
Santa Barbara. So is the food. And
so is the ambience in the dining
room to your right as you enter, if
you can pass the pastry counter.
We are ecstatic to be able to share
with you Connie Barcliff and
Alicia Bair's sought-after recipe for
their sour cream chocolate cake.

Barcliff & Bair makes a point
of offering interesting vegetarian

SOUR CREAM CHOCOLATE CAKE
from Connie Barcliff and Alicia Bair, Barcliff & Bair, Santa Barbara

FOR THE CAKE:
  2 cups flour, unsifted
  2 cups sugar
  1 cup water
  ¾ cup sour cream
  ¼ cup butter, softened
  ¼ tsp. baking soda
  1 tsp. salt
  1 tsp. vanilla
  ½ tsp. baking powder
  2 eggs
  4 oz. unsweetened baking chocolate, melted

FOR THE FROSTING:
  ½ cup butter
  4 oz. baking chocolate, unsweetened
  4 cups powdered sugar, sifted
  1 cup sour cream
  2 tsp. vanilla

CAKE: Preheat oven to 350° F.
Measure all ingredients into a bowl and
beat with a mixer at low speed 3–4 minutes. Pour into two 9-inch-round greased
and floured baking pans. Bake 20–25
minutes.

FROSTING: Melt butter and chocolate
over boiling water. Cool. Add powdered
sugar, then blend in sour cream and vanilla. Beat until smooth. After cake is cool,
frost cake in between layers and on top.
Enjoy!

alternatives to roast beef tri-tip with cheddar cheese sandwiches ($6.95/$8.95), all of which are available by the half or whole. The grilled eggplant and roasted bell pepper with mozzarella and feta cheeses, tomato, fresh basil, and Bermuda onion ($6.95/$8.95) melts in your mouth, soups and chicken chili ditto, and Kathleen loves the salads of the day, which are always excellent. Or try the low-fat or regular twice-baked potato with green salad or soup ($5.95) and the chicken quesadilla with Asiago cheese and roasted red bell peppers ($7.95). The children's menu is just right with half peanut butter and jelly or ham and cheese, tuna, turkey, and tri-tip sandwiches with sliced apple and chips for $3.95. Don't miss the espresso drinks.

Since tea service is unusual for Santa Barbara, we highly recommend a relaxing Friday Afternoon Tea from 2:30 to 5:00 P.M. Reservations are a must.

ᴥ *Barcliff & Bair, 1114 State Street, Santa Barbara 93101; (805) 965-5742. Open 8:00 A.M.–3:00 P.M. Monday–Thursday, 8:00 A.M.–5:00 P.M. Friday– Saturday, 9:00 A.M.–5:00 P.M. Sunday. Beer and wine. Visa, MasterCard and personal checks. Wheelchair accessible.*

Now we enter LA ARCADA for a rare experience, both cultural and commercial. On the sight of a Catholic church demolished during the 1925 earthquake, La Arcada was designed and constructed in 1926 under the supervision of Myron Hunt. Hunt also designed several other important buildings in southern California, including Pasadena's Rose Bowl, San Marino's Huntington Library and Huntington Hotel, Occidental College in Los Angeles, and Pomona College in Claremont.

Hugh Petersen rescued the slightly dilapidated complex and restored it slowly and accurately, with a handworking wood shop and full time woodworkers still practicing their craft in the basement. Petersen took Kathleen and a friend into the third-floor men's room to see the green marble fixtures and the mural of Hawaii's Kunai Peninsula. What a treat!

Petersen has peppered this marvelous development with humorous and rare sculpture and his varied collections, so pay attention to labels as you go. Individual local shops are even adorned with his treasures, including an eighteenth-century mission bell, and it's worth browsing just to see them. Petersen is a particular fan of J. Seward Johnson Jr., who created the whimsical "Nice to See You" window washer (known locally as "Bob") in front of the Lewis & Clark shop, as well as "Who's In Charge." You will also find sculptured fountains by famed James "Bud" Bottoms, who did the 8-foot bronze dolphins in the court and the sea lion in the main lobby. The Mozart Trio Fountain in front of Ingrid's was designed by Bonifatius Stirnberg, Germany's foremost sculptor of interactive public art.

Ingrid's is a charming gourmet kitchen and dining boutique. Further into La Arcada be sure to check out Gallery 113, a cooperative of the Santa Barbara Art Association, and Waterhouse Gallery, featuring quality local talent. Restaurants

LA ARCADA, STATE STREET,
SANTA BARBARA

include the colorful and lively Acapulco Mexican Restaurant, Bogart's Café and wine bar with a Bogey theme, and the Whale Tail Deli, whose jolly hosts serve terrific breakfasts and lunches wolfed down by locals. Clothing boutiques include Montana Mercantile and W. A. King for men—both worth a look and possibly a fitting. Browse at In Stitches for fabulous yarns and classes, Santa Barbara Luggage Company for high quality leather goods and a mouth-watering scent, and the Santa Barbara Nutrition Center, a natural juice bar and a pharmacy. Check out The Barbershop with its classic chairs and clocks.

❧ *La Arcada, 1100 block of State Street at Figueroa, Santa Barbara 93101; no general phone. Credit cards vary by store. Wheelchair accessible.*

LEWIS & CLARK ANTIQUES AND FINE THINGS does not reflect the American Northwest as Westerners might expect. It actually presents the elegant best from estate sales; French prints; imports from India, Thailand, Morocco, and France; and Spode china from England. Notice the lovely table in the middle of the store and the tapestry (from $20) and needlepoint ($60–$200) pillows. Mother and daughter Elizabeth and Lisa Reifel moved their shop here from Victoria Court in 1997. Don't miss.

❧ *Lewis & Clark Antiques and Fine Things, 1116 State Street, Santa Barbara 93101; (805) 962–6034. Open 10:00 A.M.–5:30 P.M. Monday–Saturday, noon–5:00 P.M. Sunday. Visa and MasterCard. Wheelchair accessible.*

At the corner of State Street and Anapamu Street is the renowned SANTA BARBARA MUSEUM OF ART in all its glory. From its transformation from an empty post office into a major regional museum, the Santa Barbara Museum has always emphasized renewal and expansion of services to the community. Hence it now offers audio tours of the permanent collection, a new exciting children's gallery to encourage family visits, an ongoing youth mural project, a large new store, and excellent snacks and refreshments at Zal's Cafe. The galleries are arranged so that visitors can view the museum's collection in chronological order to show the exchange of ideas and influences among period artists.

The museum's Ridley-Tree Education Center at McCormick House, 1600 Santa Barbara Street (805-962-1661), is a remarkable center for hands-on art education, offering studio art classes for children, teens, and adults in painting, drawing, ceramics, sculpture, puppetry, mask-making, and cartooning. There are also educational exhibitions, including special Rainy Day Saturdays of fun-filled classes and drop-in sessions. The museum also offers bus tours to significant showings in Los Angeles, extremely popular worldwide tours, and even culinary classes, most of which are open to the public for a fee.

Santa Barbara Museum benefits from the area's wealthy and generous residents, such as Lord and Lady Ridley-Tree, Mr. and (the late) Mrs. Austin H. Peck Jr., and the late Suzette Morton Davidson. The museum's ten galleries showcase 4,500 years of art from classic Greco-Roman figures to modernism's masterpieces. The Asian collection fills a whole floor.

Permanent collection pieces include works of Raoul Dufy, John Singleton Copley, Hans Hofmann, Javier Marin, Auguste Rodin, Frederic Lord Leighton, Marc Chagall, Joaquin Torres-Garcia, Childe Hassam, and Lan Ying.

♣ *Santa Barbara Museum of Art, 1130 State Street, Santa Barbara 93101; (805) 963-4364, fax (805) 966 6840, Web site: www.sbmuseart.org. Open. museum: 11:00 A.M.–5:00 P.M. Tuesday–Saturday, 11:00 A.M.–9:00 P.M. Friday, noon–5:00 P.M. Sunday; cafe: 11:00 A.M.–5:00 P.M. Tuesday–Saturday, 11:00 A.M.–8:00 P.M. Friday, noon–4:00 P.M. Sunday. Admission: adults $5.00, seniors (sixty-two and over) $3.00, students with ID and ages six to seventeen $2.00, under six and members free. Admission is free each Thursday and the first Sunday of each month. Visa, MasterCard, American Express. Wheelchair accessible.*

SIGNIFICANT OTHERS

Significant Others, in this case, refers to restaurants and other places of interest not located on State Street that we highly recommend you check out. We save really important historical stops for *Things You Really Should See,* which follows immediately after this section.

BOUCHON is Santa Barbara's newest, hottest restaurant and the baby of Culinary Institute of America–Hyde Park (NY) graduate Charles Frederick. A Santa Barbara native, Charles has honed his art at both local and East Coast restaurants. His wife Jennifer is publicity director at very local Santa Barbara Winery. He concentrates on using local produce and creating a "Santa Barbara wine country cuisine with French-California influences." You can sample more than fifty wines by the glass, a truly unusual offering anywhere. The menu is fairly simple but exquisite; entrees range from $18-$29. This Bouchon is related to no others.

❧ *Bouchon, 9 West Victoria Street near State Street, Santa Barbara 93101; (805) 730–1160. Open from 5:30 P.M. daily. Beer and wine. Visa, MasterCard, American Express. Wheelchair accessible.*

LOUIE'S CALIFORNIA BISTRO at The Upham Hotel, Santa Barbara's oldest hotel recently and lovingly restored. Louie's is small and worth the trip, with terrific food and extremely reasonable prices. Kathleen tries everyone's Caesar salads, and this one is excellent. Also try the grilled ahi tuna with tomatoes or the perfect potato-crusted sea bass, a melt-in-your-mouth experience. Lots of locals enjoy lunch or dinner here, and The Upham has lots of convenient meeting or party rooms to suit your needs.

Louie's California Bistro, 1404 de la Vina Street, Santa Barbara 93101; (805) 963–7003. Open for lunch 11:30 A.M.–3:00 P.M. Monday–Friday, dinner from 5:30 P.M. daily. Full bar. Visa, MasterCard, American Express. Wheelchair accessible.

PARADISE CAFE is one of most Santa Barbarans' favorite restaurants, although hardly anyone from out of town has even heard of it. We're almost hesitant to tell you about it because it's such an unspoiled prize.

Located one block east of State Street at the corner of Anacapa and Ortega Streets, Paradise Cafe occupies what looks like a former bar/storefront on the corner, as well as a houselike building next door. The umbrellaed patio is especially fun in good weather, and locals young and old hang out here most hours. Soft green walls in the dining room complement the light hardwood floors and make the whole experience breezy and fun. Birthday kids love to come here for their free slice of Paradise Pie.

While lunchtime appetizers such as grilled mussels with basil vinaigrette and oysters on the half shell are available (each $7.95), the salads are large and fresh and range from Cobb ($7.25) to rock shrimp and spinach ($7.95). Omelettes are served through the lunch hour. Kathleen likes the grilled ahi tuna sandwich when it's available ($8.95), and Jerry loves the half-pound bacon burger with crispy shoestring potatoes and pasta or green salad. Drooling good. A tender calamari steak sandwich completes our favorites. Vegetarian selections are always available.

The dinner menu expands to include oak-grill specialties that come with soup or salad, and rice or shoestring or roasted potatoes; sautéed mushrooms are seventy-five cents extra. Try the mouthwatering lamb chops ($20.95), the large or small New York steaks ($19.95/$16.95), or the oak-grilled shark, swordfish, ahi tuna, or salmon ($14.95/$19.95). Several pastas ($10.95–$14.95) are available, too. Wonderful fresh berries and cream ($4.25), and espresso drinks. Good local wine list. One of our favorites.

❧ *Paradise Cafe, 702 Anacapa Street, Santa Barbara 93101; (805) 962–4416. Open 11:00 A.M.–11:00 P.M. Monday–Saturday, 9:00 A.M. brunch–11:00 P.M. Full bar. Visa, MasterCard, American Express. Wheelchair accessible.*

We encourage you to stroll east on Cota Street from State Street for what might be Santa Barbara's version of a gourmet ghetto. Here you can taste several cultures, including New Orleans/Cajun at the Palace Grill, Indian at Jag's India Restaurant, and French at Mousse Odile. Wedged in between all this is a great store, Miss Daisy's Boutique Antique, to browse in. Excellent parking is available in the lot across from the restaurants.

Movie stars and local residents all stand in line on the sidewalk outside the PALACE GRILL, a self-described Cajun-Creole-Italian restaurant called Best on the West Coast by *Los Angeles Magazine.* You have to come here several times to get the full experience. It's simply impossible to try all the goodies (or even a few) in one visit. Everyone must order the Cajun crawfish popcorn—Louisiana crawfish tails dipped in cornmeal buttermilk batter and flash-fried to a mouthwatering crispiness ($7.75 but varies with availability).

Lunch salads include plantation fried chicken salad ($6.25)—fried like the "popcorn," and a fresh crab and asparagus salad ($8.95). Then there's the Santa Barbara salad with fresh grilled Norwegian salmon with Creole vinaigrette ($10.95). If you want to go to heaven right on the spot, try the soft-shelled crab po'boy with garlic mayonnaise ($9.25). The Creole crawfish crab cakes are $9.95 at lunch and $15.95 at dinner.

Dinner also offers the Palace's signature steaks, thick thick thick and served from the grill or blackened with a side of browned garlic butter. Étouffées and chicken marsala, piccata, or Atchafalaya are all intriguing, but be sure to save room for the Palace's famous Louisiana bread pudding soufflé ($3.95 at lunch, $6.00 at dinner). Order it anyway, even if you have indulged in one of the bar's wild martinis.

The Palace Grill is full all the time, and the neon lights in the back proclaiming THE RAJIN CAJUN CATERING CO. set the upbeat tempo. Service is surprisingly impeccable, and locals have voted it Best Service in Santa Barbara every year since 1988. Monday is locals night (meaning locals with cards get discounts), and a magician entertains Saturdays. The staff will gladly store your farmers' market goodies while you relax and dine. It's wise to make reservations. One of our favorites.

᷍ᴥ *Palace Grill, 8 East Cota Street, Santa Barbara 93101; (805) 963–5000, Web site: www.palacegrill.com. Open for lunch 11:00 A.M.–3:00 P.M., dinner from 5:30 P.M. daily. Limited reservations are available Friday–Saturday. Full bar. Visa, MasterCard, American Express. Wheelchair accessible.*

Next door be sure to browse in George and Daisy Scott's MISS DAISY'S BOUTIQUE ANTIQUE while waiting. George and his collectibles are worth a trip of their own, with humorous and serious antiques, dolls, trays, and everything else imaginable.

᷍ᴥ *Miss Daisy's Boutique Antique, 12 East Cota Street, Santa Barbara 93101; (805) 730–9155. Open 10:00 A.M.–10:00 P.M. daily. Visa, MasterCard, American Express. Wheelchair accessible.*

JAG'S INDIA RESTAURANT serves the best of Indian cuisine, including curries, lots of vegetarian selections, and chicken and meats. The staff is extremely helpful in advising those of us who are not terribly knowledgeable about the cuisines of India.

᷍ᴥ *Jag's India Restaurant, 14 East Cota Street, Santa Barbara 93101; (805) 884–1988. Open Tuesday–Sunday from 5:30 P.M. Full bar. Visa and MasterCard. Wheelchair accessible.*

MOUSSE ODILE occupies two storefronts and has a charming small bar, lots of colorful French (Gauguin) posters and paintings on the walls, and mood-setting blue tablecloths. The bistro serves *spécialités françaises,* including breakfast with fabulous egg dishes, three-egg-omelettes served with French bread, applesauce, and potatoes au gratin ($5.45–$7.25), and real espresso drinks. Lunch offers foot-long Parisian sandwiches of cold roast lamb, cold roast chicken or turkey, barbecued ham and Swiss cheese, egg salad, and smoked salmon ($5.75–$8.25).

Lunchtime specials may be pasta, bouchée a la reine (light flaky pastry with chicken and mushrooms), chef/owner Yvonne's Fisherman Soup with halibut, mussels, shrimp, and scallops, and a real salade niçoise (prices vary by special and availability). Grilled boudin blanc (white pork and veal sausage) is $8.75, petit filet mignon $11.95, quiche of the day $6.95, and eggplant au Parmesan $7.25.

Dinner offers an excellent pâté maison, escargots de Bourgogne, or smoked salmon (all under $7.00), escalope de veau with sweet basil cream ($16.95), gigot Provençale, which is leg of lamb roasted with garlic and herbs and served with flageolet beans ($15.75), North African couscous ($15.45), and always a vegetarian entree ($14.45). Duck, fresh fish, and veal aux chanterelles are occasionally available also. We particularly enjoy the light and fragrant poached Norwegian salmon and the game hen with garlic, green beans, carrots and rice, both at $15, including soup or salad.

The list of wines by the glass is the best at bargain prices we have seen. You can enjoy local Firestone Cabernet Sauvignon or French Beaujolais Villages for $3.95 a glass, and Gilles Noblet Pouilly-Fuisse at $6.00. Joseph Drouhin's Laforêt Bourgogne Pinot Noir is only $16 per bottle. Several excellent ales are under $4.00.

Mousse Odile, 18 East Cota Street, Santa Barbara 93101; (805) 962–5393. Open for breakfast 8:00 A.M.–11:30 P.M., lunch 11:30 A.M.–2:30 P.M., dinner 5:30–9:00 P.M. Monday–Saturday. Full bar. Visa, MasterCard, American Express, Discover. Wheelchair accessible.

Another door along Cota is the BLUE AGAVE cafe/bar, a pleasantly relaxing restaurant and bar that also sells fine cigars and has a smoking balcony on the second floor facing Cota Street from which rocking music blasts weekend nights. It's casual enough that you can come in alone and feel good about it. Blue Agave uses organic produce when possible, their eggs come from free-range chickens, and their meats and poultry are naturally fed and hormone-, preservative-, and nitrate-free.

Try the black tiger shrimp sautéed in garlic and butter ($6.50) or the tortilla soup ($5.95) as appetizers, or the great Caesar salads ($5.75/$9.50), the grilled lamb burger with homemade mint mayonnaise and roasted potatoes or salad ($8.50), or a Lingurian fish stew ($12.95). A bargain Cowboy Plate features natural turkey sausage poached in Sierra Nevada ale and then grilled, with mashed yams, poblano chili rice, black beans, and butterleaf salad ($9.95). Kathleen likes the slightly sexist Cowgirl Plate of mashed yams instead of the Cowboy's sausage, plus the other yummies ($8.75). Veggie fans can also select grilled vegetables ($12.75). The duck carnitas relleño features a fire roasted poblano chili stuffed with tender duck and veggies, baked and served on avocado-lime crema with poblano chili rice, black beans, and butterleaf salad ($15.95).

Don't miss the whiskey bread pudding with comfort sauce ($4.75) or the Mexican wedding cake cookies ($3.50). Add flan to the cookies ($4.75). Reservations for six or more.

❧ *Blue Agave, 20 East Cota Street, Santa Barbara 93101; (805) 899–4694. Open 4:30 P.M.–2:00 A.M., dinner 5:00–10:30 P.M., light menu until 11:30 P.M. daily. Full bar. Visa and MasterCard. Partly wheelchair accessible.*

A little further away but worth the trip (in alphabetical order):

ANDRIA'S HARBORSIDE RESTAURANT is rated by local critics as serving the best seafood in town. Not to be confused with the more casual Harbor Restaurant on Stearns Wharf, the Harborside has a stunning view of the beach, ocean, and both the yacht harbor and Stearns Wharf. It also has an oyster bar and a piano bar, featuring singer/songwriter and co-owner Peter Clark.

In addition to its classic breakfasts, midday lunch specialties include a fisherman's sandwich ($7.50), lots of seafood pastas, fried jumbo scallops, and great shrimp Louie salads ($7.95; add $5.00 for crab) and whitefish ($8.95).

SANTA BARBARA FROM STEARNS WHARF

The oyster bar features a true shellfish orgy of oysters on the half shell, oysters Rockefeller, shrimp, shrimp cocktails, mussels, clams, calamari, all served with their remarkable cheese bread. Signature entrees include carnivore specials such as Jack Daniel's BBQ baby-back pork ribs ($16.95), mesquite-broiled spring lamb chops with herbed mashed potatoes ($19.95), certified Angus sirloin steak ($14.95), pistachio nut-crusted snapper with potato soufflé ($13.95), New England sea scallops wrapped in bacon, mesquite-broiled and topped with crab, asparagus, and béarnaise sauce served over risotto ($17.95) and rich rich rich!

You can choose the preparation of your fish from pistachio nut-crusted and skillet blackened to mesquite-broiled or mimosa (poached in Chardonnay wine and topped with artichoke hearts, Roma tomatoes, herb caper vinaigrette, and Parmesan cheese. Whew!). And there are a couple of pizzas for the kids (under $7.00). Good selection of local and other California wines.

❧ *Andria's Harborside Restaurant, 336 West Cabrillo Boulevard (along the beach), Santa Barbara 93101; (805) 966–3000, fax (805) 962–8902. Open for breakfast 8:00–11:00 A.M. Monday–Friday, 8:00 A.M.–1:00 P.M. Sunday; lunch 11:00 A.M.–3:00 P.M. Monday–Friday, 10:00 A.M.–3:00 P.M. Sunday; dinner 5:00–9:00 or 10:00 P.M. Monday–Friday, 5:00–9:00 P.M. Sunday; oyster bar and bar open between meals also; happy hour with hors d'oeuvres 4:00–7:00 P.M. Monday–Friday. Full bar. Visa, MasterCard, American Express, Diners, Discover. Wheelchair accessible.*

South of Santa Barbara off 101 in Summerland, you might want to try the BIG YELLOW HOUSE, well-known for its weekend brunches, breakfasts, fried chicken, and other dressed-up comfort foods. The house's first version was built in 1884 in the town of Ortega, which was purchased by Easterner and spiritualist Henry L. Williams in 1883 and renamed Summerland. Williams built a house overlooking the ocean for his new wife.

After his death sixteen years later, his widow remodeled the house to resemble a San Francisco Victorian to please her new husband, George F. Becker. Becker's extravagant taste included imported Australian gum wood pillars, staircases and paneling, tile from the Santa Barbara Channel Islands, satin wallpaper with twenty-four-karat trim, heavy oak furniture, and green velvet upholstery.

Usual breakfasts are offered, plus corned beef hash ($6.75); usual sandwiches and salads are offered at lunch, plus fried chicken and a sirloin steak sandwich ($10.50); and at dinner the famous fried chicken ($9.95), old-fashioned pot roast ($10.95), Auntie's pork roast ($11.95), and steaks come with soup or salad and choice of potatoes. Light dinners and kids' specials also abound, in addition to seafood specials such as coconut fried shrimp ($10.95), seafood sampler tempura ($13.95), fresh thrasher shark ($11.95), halibut, salmon, and scampi, all under $15. Traditionalists might enjoy the holiday-style turkey dinner ($12.95).

❧ *Big Yellow House, 108 Pierpont Avenue, Summerland 93067; (805) 969–4140. Open for breakfast 8:00 A.M.–noon Monday–Friday, brunch 8:00 A.M.–2:30 P.M. Saturday–Sunday, lunch 11:00 A.M.–4:00 P.M. Monday–Friday, dinner from 4:00 P.M. Monday–Thursday, from 3:00 P.M. Saturday–Sunday. Full bar. Visa, MasterCard, American Express. Mostly wheelchair accessible.*

The BROWN PELICAN, located truly on the beach just north of Santa Barbara proper below a cliff, is another of those wonderful finds we hesitate to reveal to the outside world. The ambience here is casual, rustic, fun, and romantic whether it's pouring rain or pouring sun. Locals walk their dogs down the rocks and on the beach, and you can walk off your dining room splurges either while you wait for a table or all day or evening afterward. History fans will enjoy the historic photos in the rest room's waiting room at the far end of the bar.

The best way to get here is to take Highway 101 north of Santa Barbara and take the Las Positas Road exit. Then turn right (north) on Cliff Drive and follow it to Arroyo Burro State Beach. Just beyond the Beach sign is the parking lot you can use for the Brown Pelican.

At breakfast, Belgian waffles or French toast can come with one egg and two strips of bacon ($7.95); pancakes come with strawberry butter (!) ($4.50–$7.50); eggs plus range from $4.50 to $5.50; and breakfast specials include ocean hash of sautéed potatoes with crab cakes and poached eggs ($8.75, and well worth it), an open-faced breakfast sandwich of ratatouille and Black Forest ham on toasted focaccia and potatoes ($8.25), salmon plate with bagel etc. ($8.95), and omelettes ranging from $6.50 to $8.25. Kids get two choices, including chocolate chip pancakes ($3.25).

At lunch or dinner do not pass go without trying the New England-style clam chowder which *Gourmet* has called "clam chowder that may be the best on the entire coast." All salads and the pâté, cheese, and fruit plate ($8.50) are excellent, as are the grilled Black Forest ham sandwich ($8.50), the half-pound hamburger, ahi tuna burger, and crab cake sandwich, all under $10. Fish and chips in Bass ale batter are greasy-great ($8.95).

At dinner you may want to try the fabulous fresh fish, such as seafood linguine, salmon fillet baked in red wine sauce, Mediterranean fish soup, roasted halibut, grilled portobello mushroom with polenta, or grilled ahi tuna ($10.95–$14.25). Carnivores will enjoy half a free-range chicken, New York steak, or half-pound hamburgers ($8.95–$18.95). Excellent local wine list. One of our favorites.

❧ *Brown Pelican, 2981½ Cliff Drive, Santa Barbara 93109; (805) 687–4550, fax (805) 569–0188. Open 7:00 A.M.–8:30 P.M. daily. Full bar. Visa, MasterCard, American Express. Wheelchair accessible.*

CA'DARIO RISTORANTE ITALIANO is a true Italian restaurant, not the California-ized version we are used to. Some of the menu selections may seem downright exotic, particularly in Italian. Thankfully, the translations are simple.

For instance, the carpaccio con grana e capperi ($7.50) is thinly sliced raw beef topped with Parmesan, capers, and cold-pressed olive oil; and grigiata d'asparagi ($8.50) is grilled asparagus wrapped with pancetta, Parmesan cheese, and balsamic vinegar. Yum. Or try the lamelle di spada, thin slices of smoked swordfish with fennel, radicchio, and arugula ($8.50). For a different taste experience we suggest the bocconcini trevisani, a gratin of homemade crepes filled with ricotta cheese and radicchio ($12.50), or the vegetarian bigoletti al ragu di olive e capperi, featuring a thin spaghetti with a ragout of olives, capers, fresh tomato, and pecorino cheese ($8.75). The osso buco with saffron Arborio rice ($18.50) and the daily specials are usually excellent.

Lunch is equally good, although selections are slightly lighter, including lots of salads, pastas, polenta, and steaks and chicken. For a more delicate lunch try the ciabatta Tirolese, which consists of warm ciabatta bread filled with Gorgonzola and smoked prosciutto and served with a house salad ($6.75). Ca'Dario is related to Bucatini Trattoria & Pizzeria at 436 State Street, Santa Barbara; (805) 957–4177.

☙ *Ca'Dario Ristorante Italiano, 37 East Victoria Street, Santa Barbara 93101; (805) 884–9419; Web site: www.bucatini.com. Wine and beer. Open for lunch 11:30 A.M.–2:00 P.M. Monday–Friday, dinner 5:30–10:00 P.M. Monday–Friday, 5:00–10:00 P.M. Saturday–Sunday. Visa, MasterCard, American Express. Wheelchair accessible.*

CHAD'S REGIONAL AMERICAN CUISINE is the pride and joy of Michelle and Chad Stevens. Chad also owns the first and last Sambo's on Cabrillo and is the grandson of Sambo's founder.

Chad's menu is brief and well planned, adhering to the adage "Do a few things and do them well." For a different experience try the blackened halibut salad, in which the fresh halibut is dusted in Cajun spices, blackened, and placed atop a bed of organic lettuces and tossed with tomatoes, Cajun pecans, sweet red onions, and feta cheese in the house vinaigrette ($12.75). The chicken Brie pasta is Jerry's undoing, with mouthwatering fettucine tossed with tender pieces of chicken breast, tomatoes, onions, garlic, toasted almonds, melted Brie, and a touch of cream ($14.95).

You can enjoy fresh salmon or ahi tuna either broiled or blackened ($17.95), Texas-barbecued shrimp wrapped in hickory-smoked bacon and cooked over an open flame ($18.95), a regional pride favorite pan-seared tri-tip crusted in coarse ground pepper ($15.95), or Chad's sampler platter for two, which includes a Caesar salad, filet mignon, Texas-barbecued shrimp, and chicken Tchopitoulas, plus Chad's sinfully delicious chocolate Jack Daniel's soufflé ($4.95). In any case, you must try the soufflé!

❧ *Chad's Regional American Cuisine, 625 Chapala Street, Santa Barbara 93101; (805) 568–1876. Open 5:30 P.M. till closing daily. Full bar. Visa, MasterCard, American Express, Discover. Wheelchair accessible.*

A spin-off of Michel Richard's Citron of Los Angeles, CITRONELLE is said by many to be the finest restaurant in Santa Barbara. *Gourmet,* the *Los Angeles Times,* and *Condé Nast Traveler* magazine readers all say Citronelle is the best, and even one of the most "perfect" in the country.

Citronelle serves breakfast throughout the week and a very special Sunday brunch, pleasant lunch, and elegant dinner daily. Located atop the Santa Barbara Inn on Cabrillo Boulevard, the restaurant offers one of the best views on the central coast, encompassing all of Santa Barbara and seemingly everything between here and Hawaii!

Breakfast is fairly basic, offering both egg, meat, and healthy choices, with a special chicken hash with eggs ($7.50). Sunday brunch is exceptional, with soup or salad, juice, champagne or mimosa, and melt-in-your-mouth breads to go with everything from a chicken Caesar salad, chicken hash and eggs, Citronelle eggs Benedict, and shiitake mushroom omelette (all $17) to sautéed scallops with saffron sauce and mashed potatoes ($19), baby salmon ($19), and braised lamb shank ($21).

A rare treat at lunch is the duck prosciutto with frisée salad ($8.00), as are the mini cheese raviolis with pesto sauce ($8.50), the roasted chicken sandwich with grilled eggplant ($11), the chicken hash with poached eggs ($14), and the crispy sand dabs with New Mexico chili sauce ($14). Small steaks, lamb shanks, and specially tender pork with daily specialties complete the menu. Some locals find the menu repetitious, but you might enjoy a few visits.

We repeat, everything is exceptional here and the service is impeccable, so expect the sky at dinner. For a rare experience, try the chilled tomato fennel soup ($6.00) or shiitake feuilletée with garlic cream ($10) for starters. Kathleen is partial to the Lake Superior whitefish with calamari sauce and mashed potatoes ($23)—the only sweeter whitefish she ever tasted was out of a lake in Mexico long enough ago that the lakes there weren't polluted!—and the tournedo of ahi tuna with black pepper and basil aoili ($26). Jerry is a real fan of the braised lamb shank with flageolet beans (perfectly French!) and garlic sauce ($24). You simply can't miss with the asparagus crusted chicken ($23). Exceptional imported, domestic, and local wine list.

❧ *Citronelle*, *Santa Barbara Inn, 901 Cabrillo Boulevard, Santa Barbara 93101; (805) 963–0111. Open for breakfast 7:00–10:00 A.M. Monday–Saturday, brunch 12:30–2:30 P.M. Sunday; lunch noon–2:30 P.M. Monday–Saturday; dinner 6:00–9:00 P.M. Monday–Thursday and Sunday, 6:00–9:30 P.M. Friday, 6:00–10:00 P.M. Saturday. Full bar. Visa, MasterCard, American Express, Diners, Discover. Wheelchair accessible via elevator.*

The SAMBO'S on Cabrillo Boulevard is the first and last Sambo's restaurant in the world. This Sambo's opened on June 17, 1957, and still has some of the original wooden walls and counter and loads of Sambo's memorabilia.

In the 1960s many of us boycotted Sambo's for its apparent belittling of African-Americans. Little did we know that the name Sambo was actually a combination of its founders' names, "Sam" from Italian-American Sam Battistone, and "Bo" from his partner, Newell F. Bohnett. At one time there were thirty-nine Sambo "stores" (when did they cease to be "restaurants"?), but boycotts and mismanagement eventually destroyed the empire.

Two generations later, grand-son Chad Stevens bought back the original at this site and now also owns Chad's on Chapala Street.

SAMBO'S FIRST AND LAST
RESTAURANT, SANTA BARBARA

Much to our surprise, Sambo's still serves one of the best breakfasts in town, especially for the money. The minute you sit down, a basket of mini muffins arrives (Kathleen's favorite is chocolate chip and Jerry's is peanut butter) with soft butter. Coffee follows almost immediately, and soon you wonder if you ought to order anything else!

All egg selections arrive with real potatoes, choice of toast, and strawberries and wedges of melon; a larger serving of fruit can be substituted for potatoes. A real waker-upper is the Polish sausage and eggs ($6.95), and the imitation crab and real avocado omelette ($7.49) is better than we expected. Real carnivores can indulge in pork chops and eggs ($7.25), which ought to load one up for a day or two. The grilled halibut ($7.95) is light, and the grilled veggie sandwich is quite good and refreshing ($6.39). Of course there are hamburgers, chicken, and fish strips, and all the other deep-fried favorites. Tables on the front sidewalk are perfect for people watching across Cabrillo Boulevard from the beach and Santa Barbara Yacht Harbor.

❧ *Sambo's, 216 West Cabrillo Boulevard, Santa Barbara 93101; (805) 965–3269. Open 6:00 A.M.–3:00 P.M. daily. Beer and wine. Visa, MasterCard, American Express, Discover. Wheelchair accessible.*

If you want to explore truly Mexican restaurants, drive along Milpas Street and choose the one that appeals to you. The Mexican bakeries along here are also authentic and tempting.

THINGS YOU REALLY SHOULD SEE

Here we tell you about all the important historic sites and museums that are not on State Street and which we think you should see to complete your cultural experience of Santa Barbara. For us the purpose of traveling is to experience the sites/sights, cultures, and languages of a new place. To us the culture includes the foods grown, cooked, and served in a region, as well as the wines, history, art, and architecture.

Tours

Santa Barbara has three kinds of tours that provide an overview of the city. The SANTA BARBARA TROLLEY offers a ninety-minute open-air guided trolley tour, which is well worth the price. We picked it up at Santa Barbara Mission, which we highly recommend since there is lots of parking in its lot.

Santa Barbara Trolley starts at the mission at 11:00 A.M. and at 12:30 and 2:00 P.M. and goes past a variety of colorful history and current gossip. It takes you by the Crocker cottages, the Atcheson House (as in the Atcheson, Topeka & Santa Fe), down Anacapa Street past the five-star Simpson House Inn bed-and-breakfast, the Ellis Keck Memorial Gardens with its South American blooms, Alameda Park, the Santa Barbara County Courthouse, the Orena Adobe, and Casa de la Guerra. It stops at the beach for a ten-minute stretch near Stearns Wharf, then continues on to Chase Palm Park, Cabrillo Arts Center and the East Beach Grill, and along Coast Villages Road, where many of Hollywood's stars have homes or at least frequent other peoples'. Take in the Biltmore Hotel, Montecito and the Montecito Inn and Cafe, Butterfly Beach, Santa Barbara Zoo, Santa Barbara Zoological Gardens, the first Motel 6, Santa Barbara Harbor, and State Street.

❧ *Santa Barbara Trolley, (805) 965–0353 for information and charters. Tickets: $5.00 adults, $3.00 under twelve years. Not wheelchair accessible.*

The RED TILE TOUR enables you to walk or wheel your way through 12 blocks of downtown to view some of Santa Barbara's most important historical buildings. [The sidewalks are being replaced with red bricks as this book goes to press, which makes the tiles harder to see. Follow our directions carefully.] Begin at the Santa Barbara County Courthouse and cross Anacapa Street to the elegant Spanish-style public library. Go west on Anapamu Street to the Santa Barbara Museum of Art, then down State Street and turn east on Carrillo Street to the Hill-Carillo Adobe. Head back to State Street and go south two blocks to El Paseo's arcade or keep going to De la Guerra Street, turn left and visit Casa de la Guerra. Now go across De la Guerra to De la Guerra Plaza, the setting for several movie scenes. The Orena Adobes are in the same block of De la Guerra.

Cross Anacapa Street to Presidio Avenue, the oldest street in Santa Barbara, and then into the Presidio Gardens where the Presidio parade grounds used to be. Back on De la Guerra Street, visit the Santiago de la Guerra Adobe and the Lugo Adobe/Meridian Studios next door. Continue on De la Guerra to the next intersection, Santa Barbara Street, and visit the Santa Barbara Historical Museum. Heading up Santa Barbara Street, you come to the Casa Covarrubias adobe and then the Rochin Adobe. Continuing up Santa Barbara to the corner of Canon Perdido, you arrive at El Presidio de Santa Barbara State Historic Park. Head west on Canon Perdido and check out the Presidio Chapel, the Caneda Adobe, and El Cuartel next door to the Spanish deco-style main post office at the corner of Anacapa Street. Notice the Lobero Theatre diagonally across Anacapa Street. Now walk up Anacapa to the courthouse to complete the Red Tile Tour, take a rest, and take the courthouse tour!

SANTA BARBARA'S SCENIC DRIVE takes you to sixteen points of interest in a continuous loop that requires about one hour by car. Great way to get oriented!

Begin, of course, at the Santa Barbara County Courthouse on Anacapa Street (one-way heading toward water) between Anapamu and Figueroa Streets. Just follow the turquoise Scenic Drive signs with an ocean wave and an arrow, and they will lead you (hopefully) to El Presidio de Santa Barbara State Historic Park, Santa Barbara Historical Museum, El Paseo, Santa Barbara Museum of Art, La Arcada, Mission Santa Barbara, Santa Barbara Museum of Natural History, Santa Barbara Botanic Garden, Andree Clark Bird Refuge, Santa Barbara Zoological Gardens, Stearns Wharf, Moreton Bay Fig Tree, Fernald Mansion and Trussell-Winchester Adobe, the Yacht Harbor and Breakwater, and the luxurious Hope Ranch residential community.

Details

Once you've experienced an overview via a tour, you may want to visit some of the sites in detail. They are in alphabetical order starting on the next page.

ANDREE CLARK BIRD REFUGE near Cabrillo Boulevard. Directions: Exit from Highway 101 to parking lot on Los Patos Way. Go west toward the water to this scenic lagoon with hundreds of water birds, fabulous gardens, a lake, footpath, and bikeway. Or take Cabrillo Boulevard along the beach to it. Ms. Clark still has servants turn down the beds and set the dinner table every night in her twenty-six-room mansion even though she's never there—she's lived in Hawaii for years. (SANTA BARBARA ZOO AND ZOOLOGICAL GARDENS are right next door. See p. 75.)

ARTS & CRAFTS SHOW, along a 1-mile stretch of Cabrillo Boulevard east of Stearns Wharf, is reputedly the longest running (thirty-five years) weekly outdoor art show in the United States, a rather finite claim. Everything is created and made in Santa Barbara.

❧ *Arts & Crafts Show, Cabrillo Boulevard east of Stearns Wharf, Santa Barbara 93101; (805) 962–8956. Open 10:00 A.M.–sunset every Sunday, Memorial Day, July Fourth, Saturday of Fiesta Week, and Labor Day. Admission free. Credit cards vary by artist. Wheelchair accessible.*

BRINKERHOFF AVENUE off Cota Street between De la Vina and Chapala Streets has a rare collection of unique Victorian homes all in one block. Imagine living here in classic nineteenth-century Santa Barbara. Now you can enter many of them and browse among the antiques, collectibles, and art galleries. Most of the shops are open 11:00 A.M.–5:00 P.M. Tuesday–Sunday.

SANTA BARBARA BOTANIC GARDEN features more than 1,000 species of rare and indigenous native California plants. You can walk or wheel along 5 ½ miles of paths through sixty-five acres of landscaped meadows, canyons, a redwood forest, across historic Mission Dam, and along the ridge. You'll get spectacular views, on good days, of the central coast and the Channel Islands.

Directions: Take State Street to Mission Street, go up (east) on Mission, left on Garden Street, right on Los Olivos past Santa Barbara Mission, the museum of natural history, and Rocky Nook Park. Turn right on Foothill Road (Highway 192), follow signs to Botanic Garden, take first left up Mission Canyon Road, and bear right at fork ½ mile to garden entrance on left.

The botanic garden is a private, nonprofit institution dedicated to increasing the public's awareness of plant life, with active research and education programs going on all the time. Gardeners, don't miss the garden growers nursery selling native California and Mediterranean plants or the garden shop with great books, crafts, cards, gifts, and posters.

❧ *Santa Barbara Botanic Garden, 1212 Mission Canyon Road, Santa Barbara 93105; (805) 682–4726, Web site: www.sbbg.org. Open November–February weekdays 9:00 A.M.–4:00 P.M., weekends 9:00 A.M.–5:00 P.M.; March–October* *weekdays 9:00 A.M.–5:00 P.M., weekends 9:00 A.M.–6:00 P.M. Specific topic tours 2:00 P.M. daily, 10:30 A.M. Thursday, Saturday–Sunday. Visa and MasterCard. Admission: adults $3.00, seniors and teens $2.00, children five and up $1.00, five and under free. Partly wheelchair accessible.*

CABRILLO PAVILION ARTS CENTER, above the East Beach bathhouse across from the Radisson Hotel, features rotating exhibits of local artists' work, providing a bright and energetic insight into Santa Barbara's artistic community. The arts center was built and given to the city by Mrs. and Mrs. David Gray Sr. in 1925. Stop for lunch at the East Beach Grill, right here on the beach in the same building. Excellent views and food.

☙ *Cabrillo Pavilion Arts Center, 1118 East Cabrillo Boulevard, Santa Barbara 93101; (805) 962–8956. Open 9:00 A.M.–5:00 P.M. Monday-Friday. Wheelchair accessible.*

CARRIAGE AND WESTERN ARTS MUSEUM has a unique collection of horse-drawn vehicles and stagecoaches used by early Santa Barbara families and those just arriving. Check out the army wagons, a fire truck (a bright red steam pumper), and an electric hearse (we should have paid attention to these gasoline-free vehicles!). Kathleen loves the display of historic saddles and bridles, which, along with the artwork and other memorabilia, take you back to the original Western life the movies depicted. Many of these carriages come out for August Fiesta Week.

☙ *Carriage and Western Arts Museum, 129 Castillo Street, Santa Barbara 93101; (805) 962–2353. Open 8:00 A.M.–3:00 P.M. Monday–Friday, 1:00–4:00 P.M. Sunday. Admission by donation. Wheelchair accessible.*

CASA DE LA GUERRA is the home Jose de la Guerra y Noriega, the fifth comandante of the Santa Barbara Presidio, who began building for his family in 1818. Don Jose and his wife, Dona Maria Antonia, had twelve (yes, a full dozen) children. Their home became the social and commercial center in Santa Barbara and even Alta (upper, as opposed to Baja) California. Richard Henry Dana (for whom Jerry's sister, Dana, is named) made the home famous in his *Two Years Before the Mast* (1840). Be sure to visit Plaza de la Guerra, right across De la Guerra Street, where the first city council met in 1850 and where the first city hall was built in 1875. It was torn down in 1924 after the current city hall was built. Fiesta Week brings wildly colorful celebrations here in August.

☙ *Casa de la Guerra, 15 East De la Guerra Street, Santa Barbara 93101; (805) 965–0093. Open noon–4:00 P.M. Thursday–Sunday. Wheelchair accessible.*

CHASE PALM PARK refers to a 2-mile stretch of Santa Barbara's beach that is lined with palm trees. Pearl Chase (who had a B.A. and an honorary doctorate from the University of California, Berkeley) planted the palms as just one of her efforts to preserve, protect, and beautify Santa Barbara.

Through Chase Palm Park you will find a well-maintained paved recreation path for wheeling, skating, walking, running, or whatever you can think of, as well as a view of some large metal objects sticking up out of the water offshore. Those are oil well drilling rigs, folks, and what we in California call "offshore oil drilling." In 1969 a huge oil spill occurred on one of the oil platforms 5 miles offshore, and the oil drifted for miles. Chase sued the oil companies, which resulted in safety tanks being added to the rigs to prevent such spillage. Thank you, Dr. Chase! You definitely left the world a better place.

Along this part of the beach, you will see volleyball net after volleyball net. This is where many of the televised beach volleyball tournaments in Southern California take place, with sponsors such as Jose Cuervo, Big Bud, and Bud Lite. Play ball!

CONTEMPORARY ARTS FORUM in Paseo Nuevo mall off State Street is a terrific gallery of contemporary local art. Get their schedule for year-round exhibits, performances, and lectures.

ভ *Contemporary Arts Forum, 653 Paseo Nuevo, second floor, Santa Barbara 93101; (805) 966–5373. Open 11:00 A.M.–5:00 P.M. Tuesday–Saturday, noon–5:00 P.M. Sunday. Admission free. Wheelchair accessible.*

DOLPHIN FOUNTAIN, the creation of local sculptor Bud Bottoms, is more formally known as the Bicentennial Friendship Fountain. It's located at the entrance to Stearns Wharf at Cabrillo Boulevard at the bottom of State Street. Through the cosponsorship of the Santa Barbara/Puerto Vallarta Sister City Committee (what a pairing!), dolphins were also installed on Puerto Vallarta's waterfront, in Toba, Japan; Yalta, Ukraine; and in Santa Barbara's other sister cities.

EL PRESIDIO DE SANTA BARBARA STATE HISTORIC PARK is where the first forty-two Spanish soldiers and their families arrived in April 1782 and built this large permanent presidio (fort). The presidio's military function ceased with the American invasion, and much of it fell down due to earthquakes and neglect, all to be rescued in 1974 by the Santa Barbara Trust for Historic Preservation, which began reconstruction of the presidio as a state historic park. You can now visit the chapel, the padres' and comandante's quarters, and watch a fifteen-minute slide show.

EL PRESIDIO DE SANTA BARBARA, SANTA BARBARA

❧ *El Presidio de Santa Barbara, 123 East Canon Perdido Street, Santa Barbara 93101; (805) 965–0093. Open 10:30 A.M.–4:30 P.M. daily. Admission free, donations accepted. Wheelchair accessible.*

FERNALD MANSION and TRUSSELL-WINCHESTER ADOBE are must-sees for antiques aficionados. The Fernald Mansion is an 1862 fourteen-room Queen Anne-style Victorian with carved wood stairway and luxurious wood decoration. Next door walk through the 1854 Trussell-Winchester Adobe, a "Yankee adobe" typical of Santa Barbara architecture, a hybrid somewhere between American and Mexican styles and covered with wood siding and a roof made of timbers from a ship wrecked off Anacapa Island.

❧ *Fernald Mansion & Trussell-Winchester Adobe, 414 West Montecito Street, Santa Barbara 93101; (805) 966–1601. Open only 2:00–4:00 P.M. first Sunday of every month. Admission free, donations accepted. Group tours $3.00 per person for twenty or more by advance reservation. Partly wheelchair accessible.*

FARMERS' MARKET is one of the most beautiful we have seen, but then so is Santa Barbara. Local restaurateurs, Julia Child when she's in residence, and home cooks all come to gather their organic foods and socialize, as is true in every good market in the world. Plan to visit, even if you can't cook in your hotel room.

❧ *Farmers' Market, corner of Cota and Santa Barbara Streets, Santa Barbara 93101; (805) 962–5354. Open 8:30 A.M.–12:30 P.M. Saturdays, rain or shine. At the 500–600 blocks of State Street: open 4:00–7:30 P.M. summer and 3:00–6:30 P.M. winter, Tuesdays.*

SANTA BARBARA HISTORICAL MUSEUM is a modern adobe constructed in 1965 next to the 1817 Casa Covarrubias and the 1836 Historic Adobe by the Santa Barbara Historical Society and since has exhibited artifacts from Santa Barbara's rich multicultural heritage of the Chumash, Spanish, Mexican, "Yankee," and Chinese cultures. You can see photos, furniture, and the Gledhill Library with rare literary and visual documents, including 30,000 historic photographs. Don't miss the fabulously interesting museum shop with handcrafted artifacts and a great selection of books, cards, and jewelry.

➳ *Santa Barbara Historical Museum, 136 East De la Guerra Street, Santa Barbara 93101; (805) 966–1601, fax (805) 966–1603. Open 10:00 A.M.–5:00 P.M. Tuesday–Saturday, noon–5:00 P.M. Sunday. Guided tours at 1:30 P.M. Wednesday, Saturday–Sunday. Admission free, donations appreciated.*

HOPE RANCH is one of the U.S.' most luxurious and expensive residential communities, with miles of bridle trails; polo, soccer, and baseball fields; a golf course and tennis courts; and huge wistful old palm trees, many of which line the main street, Las Palmas Drive (funny thing!). It's fun to drive through and see how some people live. Don't if it will make you cry.

LOBERO THEATRE is in a wonderful old building opened originally as an opera house in 1873 by Jose Lobero, an Italian entertainer. Lobero's original theater was demolished in 1923, and local citizens built the current Spanish-style building designed by George Washington Smith and Lutah Maria Riggs. It now houses the Santa Barbara Chamber Orchestra, the Santa Barbara Grand Opera, the Sings Like Hell concert series, concerts by the faculty (including Marilyn Horne) and students of the Music Academy of the West, and the Mind/Supermind lecture series. Call ahead for Lobero's schedule if you are coming to visit.

➳ *Lobero Theatre, 33 East Canon Perdido, Santa Barbara 93101; (805) 963–0761. Box office open 10:00 A.M.–6:00 P.M. Monday–Saturday and two hours prior to performances. Visa and MasterCard. Wheelchair accessible.*

LOTUSLAND in Montecito is the wild fantasy of the late Madame Ganna Walska, who supposedly created the very special and huge cycad collection by cashing in her vast emerald and diamond jewelry. Such passion! You can only get in by reservation (a year in advance), but it's worth it if you want to see rare plantings of lovely Japanese, aloe, blue, and lotus gardens.

MISSION SANTA BARBARA

✣ *Lotusland, address given at time of reservation, Montecito 93150; (805) 969–9000. Office open 9:00 A.M.–noon Monday–Friday; tours 10:00 A.M. and 3:00 P.M. Wednesday–Saturday February–November. Partly wheelchair accessible.*

MISSION SANTA BARBARA, the tenth of the California missions, is known throughout California as the "Queen of the Missions," even though it's not in its original form. The first Mission Santa Barbara was built by Chumash Indians for the Franciscan friars and formally established here on December 4, 1786. The original adobe buildings were badly damaged by the 1812 earthquake. The present stone church was begun in 1815 and completed with a second tower in 1833, but it was damaged again, by the 1925 earthquake. A citizens committee raised funds to repair and rebuild the main facade in the 1950s.

Now a Catholic parish, the church is open to the public, and you can visit the mission on a self-guided tour for $3.00. We highly recommend the tour of the mission, its lovely gardens, historic cemetery (respect the hundreds of unmarked Chumash Indian graves here, please), and the historically accurate exhibits. The museum shop is small and packed with great books and church and historic memorabilia. Rest rooms and soft drink and Naya water machines are down the ramp to the left of the tour/shop entrance. Excellent parking lot.

✣ *Mission Santa Barbara, 2201 Laguna Street, Santa Barbara 93105; (805) 682–4713. Open 9:00 A.M.–5:00 P.M. daily except major holidays. Masses at 7:30, 9:00, and 10:30 A.M. Sunday, 8:00 A.M. Monday–Saturday. Self-guided tour $3.00, children under fifteen free; gift shop admission free. Visa and MasterCard. Mostly wheelchair accessible.*

MORETON BAY FIG TREE is the famous Australian fig tree replanted here in 1877 and reputed to be the largest tree of its kind in the United States. Its 160-foot arm span offers approximately 21,000 square feet of shade. It is huge! Dr. Pearl Chase prevented Standard Oil from taking the tree down.
✣ *Moreton Bay Fig Tree, bottom of Chapala Street on the south side of Highway 101. You have to take State Street under 101 to reach it.*

RAINBOW ARCH and FESS PARKER'S DOUBLETREE INN have a curious story attached. Fess Parker wanted to add rooms to his sprawling hotel on Cabrillo Boulevard, so the city said he could but he would have to dedicate and develop a huge piece of land as a park. And he did it. And did he ever. The star of Daniel Boone and Davy Crockett movies imported and installed a lovely merry-go-round/carousel and commissioned a sculpture. The sculpture had no name, and, many people think, no meaning or purpose. It is also painted rainbow colors, which to some people signifies gayness. So popular vernacular now deems it to be the "Rainbow Arch" because that's exactly what it is.

SANTA BARBARA COUNTY COURTHOUSE is an absolute Don't Miss in your visit to Santa Barbara. After the 1925 earthquake, Santa Barbara turned an intense negative to a positive and took the opportunity to rebuild and reinvent itself. Hence the city built a bold new courthouse designed by William Mooser III after he had lived in Spain for many years. The steel frame building was completed in two years at a cost of $1.5 million. Today it is priceless.

Be sure to check out the bell tower well at the ceiling inspired by El Transito fourteenth-century synagogue in Toledo, Spain; the Moorish mosaic tiled stairway to the second floor; the rose window; the board of supervisors assembly room with murals by Dan Sayre Groesbeck depicting Santa Barbara County history; the jail wing; the bridge of sighs connecting the jail at the third floor with the main building; the leather-covered brass-studded doors; the great doors; and the law library with its sculptured sword of justice over the entrance.

Outside the Santa Barbara Street exit look up at the sheriff's tower, the tall wooden gates at the jail entrance, the stage and the sunken garden where the

SANTA BARBARA COUNTY
COURTHOUSE, SANTA BARBARA

1873 courthouse stood. Live concerts and Fiesta Week performances are held here. Don't miss the relief map in the main entrance lobby, and the fountain, *Spirit of the Ocean*.

At the docent desk, pick up a brochure describing the botanical richness of the sunken garden.

❧ *Santa Barbara County Courthouse, 1100 Anacapa Street between Anapamu and Figueroa Streets, Santa Barbara 93101; (805) 962–6464. Open 8:00 A.M.–5:00 P.M. daily. Tours 10:30 A.M. Monday–Tuesday, Friday, 2:00 P.M. Monday–Saturday or by reservation. Partly wheelchair accessible.*

SANTA BARBARA MARITIME MUSEUM is at the entrance to the harbor right on Cabrillo Boulevard at the west end of the beach (which seems like the north end of the beach). Here you can almost experience the Santa Barbara area's rich maritime history with exhibits including Chumash culture and navigation, submarine periscopes (they're not Chumash), a radio-controlled boat, and a flying submarine. Browse around the pier. This is where whale-watching boats take off from, too.

❧ *Santa Barbara Maritime Museum, 132 Harbor Way, Santa Barbara 93101; (805) 962–8404. Open 10:00 A.M.–4:00 P.M. daily. Admission free. Wheelchair accessible.*

SANTA BARBARA MUSEUM OF NATURAL HISTORY is a nationally respected center for education and research in California and North American West Coast natural history. Visit Chumash Hall with its diorama of prehistoric native life in the Santa Barbara area, see a giant blue whale's giant skeleton, the area's only planetarium, regional and marine exhibits, bird, mammal, and insect habitat displays, and enjoy interactive computers and hands-on displays, a space lab and observatory, fossils, American Indian artifacts, and an intriguing museum store.

Directions: From State Street take Los Olivos or Mission Streets to Mission Santa Barbara and turn right up Mission Canyon Road. The Museum of Natural History will be on the left. Pass Puesta del Sol and enter via Las Encinas Road to the parking lot.

❧ *Santa Barbara Museum of Natural History, 2559 Puesta del Sol Road, Santa Barbara 93105; (805) 682–4711. Open 9:00 A.M.–5:00 P.M. Monday–Saturday, 10:00 A.M.–5:00 P.M. Sunday. Closed major holidays. Admission adults $5.00, students and seniors $4.00, children under twelve $3.00; free first Sunday of each month. Visa and MasterCard. Mostly wheelchair accessible.*

SANTA BARBARA ORCHID ESTATE is sheer heaven to orchid lovers, home gardeners, and general lovers of colors. While we have never succeeded in getting an orchid to bloom after it came to live with us, we know many people are perfectly capable of nurturing and cajoling them. But we do promise that you will enjoy a visit to this orchid farm where the Gripp family has grown classic prized orchids since 1957.

You can stroll through greenhouses to see more than 2,000 varieties of orchids and visit the shop to take home house plants. They will also ship anywhere.

The best times to visit are from February to May in normal weather years, whatever those are, and during their orchid fair during the third week of July. Real devotees might want to tie in a trip to the annual orchid show (March or April) with a special event at the orchid estate the same weekend.

❧ *Santa Barbara Orchid Estate, 1250 Orchid Drive, Santa Barbara 93101; (805) 967–1284. Open 8:00 A.M.–4:30 P.M. Monday–Saturday, 11:00 A.M.–4:00 P.M. Sunday. Visa, MasterCard, American Express, Discover. Mostly wheelchair accessible.*

SANTA BARBARA ZOO AND ZOOLOGICAL GARDENS occupy the former Child Estate (not Julia) and offer 700 animals living in imitation natural habitats, thirty teemingly lush acres of botanical gardens atop a knoll with the Santa Ynez Mountains as a backdrop, and the blue Pacific Ocean as a view. Can't beat it. Bring your picnic or book. Kids of all ages will enjoy the narrow-gauge miniature railroad, carousel, and snack bar. The Santa Barbara Zoo is about conservation, species survival, and education. The Ridley-Treehouse Restaurant overlooks Swan Lake and offers excellent menu selections for discerning palates and kids. The gift stores are something else! The Andree Clark Bird Refuge is practically next door. Directions: Take Cabrillo Boulevard along the beach and turn north on Ninos Drive, or take Bus 14 or the downtown-waterfront shuttle.

❧ *Santa Barbara Zoo and Zoological Gardens, 500 Ninos Drive, Santa*

Barbara 93103; (805) 962–5339, Web site: zooinfo@santabarbarazoo.org. Open 10:00 A.M.–5:00 P.M. daily except Thanksgiving and Christmas; tickets sold until 4:00 P.M. Admission adults (thirteen to fifty-nine) $6.00, children and seniors $4.00, children under one free. Visa and MasterCard. Wheelchair accessible.

SEA CENTER on Stearns Wharf, which is operated by the Santa Barbara Museum of Natural History and the Channel Islands National Marine Sanctuary, majors in touchy-feely learning about living marine creatures with a touch tank that you can dip your arm into to touch live sea creatures, loads of aquariums of native local sea species, historic Indian peoples displays, life-size models of dolphins and whales, shipwreck artifacts, special Santa Barbara Channel ecological exhibits, a marine art gallery, and, of course, a museum gift shop to take home some of those treasures from the deep blue.

❧ *Sea Center, 211 Stearns Wharf, Santa Barbara 93101; (805) 962–0885. Open 10:00 A.M.–5:00 P.M. daily June 1–Labor Day; noon–5:00 P.M. Monday–Friday, 10:00 A.M.–5:00 P.M. Saturday–Sunday September–May. Visa and MasterCard. Wheelchair accessible.*

STEARNS WHARF is supposedly the oldest operating wooden wharf on the West Coast. Built in 1872 by John Peck Stearns, the wharf was partly owned by Jimmy Cagney and his brothers in the 1940s. Here you can visit the Sea Center; the Harbor Restaurant with fresh fish, prime rib, steak, chicken, and Sunday brunch; or Longboard's Grill, a real beach bar and grill with casual food and attire, exotic drinks with umbrellas, outdoor dining where you can smell the fresh air and water, a large screen television in case you're afraid to miss the game, and breakfast Saturday and Sunday. Souvenir shops, art galleries, wine tasting, and espresso bars are available.

One of the best reasons to visit Stearns Wharf is to look back at Santa Barbara from the pier. Unbelievable view! Despite broad media coverage of a 1998 fire at Stearns Wharf, rest assured that all of the above enterprises are still there.

SANTA BARBARA YACHT HARBOR & BREAKWATER combine for one of our favorite sunrise strolls among more than 1,000 work and pleasure craft, rowing and canoeing teams practicing, whale-watching boats, and supply stores. Launch facilities, boats for rent, and charters are all at the north end of the harbor.

❧ *Santa Barbara Yacht Harbor, Breakwater, Santa Barbara 93101; (805) 965–8112. Wheelchair accessible.*

CHAPTER 3

SANTA YNEZ VALLEY TOWNS

he Santa Ynez Valley and the Foxen Canyon area north of Santa Barbara hold most of Santa Barbara County's best wineries and some charming small towns, such as Lompoc, Buellton, Solvang, Santa Ynez, Ballard, and Los Olivos.

First we tell you about the towns and their individual assets, and believe us, they all truly have something to offer. Then in Chapter 4 we take you on a tour of the wineries, working our way northward toward Santa Maria. (We mention a few wineries and several tasting rooms here because of their proximity to these towns.)

LOMPOC

Most Californians would wonder why anyone would want to go to Lompoc (LAHM poke). The six reasons we can think of are to: experience the spectacular flower fields (seas of sweet peas, asters, lavender, marigolds, larkspur, lobelia, and calendula) in bloom from early June to mid-July; tour the forty-one colorful historical and cultural murals on building walls depicting the vastly diverse cultures of the Lompoc Valley; visit a prisoner at the Lompoc Federal Penitentiary, known as the country club of prisons (Watergate conspirators served their time here); visit Jalama Beach; visit La Purisima Mission State Historic Park; and tour Vandenberg Air Force Base.

Lompoc is actually becoming slightly fashionable because it offers some of the most reasonable new housing on the central coast in a mild and seductive climate.

You can get maps of the murals and a 19-mile tour of hundreds of acres of flowers from the Lompoc Valley Chamber of Commerce (805) 736–4567. There are clusters of murals on blocks near the intersection of Ocean Avenue and North Street. You might plan your visit around the annual Lompoc Flower Festival the last weekend in June, which features a two-hour downtown parade with floral floats, marching bands, and equestrian units from all over California. The festival also offers bus tours of the flower fields, a carnival, flower show (duh!), arts and crafts fair, food booths, and entertainment.

Take Highway 1 or Highway 246 west to Lompoc from Highway 101 at Buellton. If you approach Lompoc on Highway 246, 3 miles northeast of town you can visit one of California's best restored and preserved missions, LA PURISIMA CONCEPCION in La Purisima Mission State Historic Park. La Purisima is one of only three missions preserved within the state park system.

All major buildings have been rebuilt and furnished as they were in 1820, and the grounds have been planted to reflect the period, including livestock of the correct genetic types, such as four-horn churro sheep, horses, longhorn cattle, goats, swine, turkeys, and geese. The original aqueduct and pond system are maintained, and more than 900 surrounding acres provide a buffer against modern developments and intrusions. Kathleen particularly likes the weaving room and kitchen, as well as the *lavanderias* in the garden, where Chumash Indians washed the missionaries' clothes.

❧ *La Purisima Mission State Historic Park, 2295 Purisima Road, Lompoc 93436; (805) 733–3713. Open 9:00 A.M.–5:00 P.M., tours Wednesdays. Mostly wheelchair accessible.*

The turnoff from Highway 1 to Jalama Beach is 4 miles south of Lompoc on Highway 1. Follow Jalama Road for 15 miles through lush forest and ranches to the twenty-eight-acre park donated to Santa Barbara County in 1943 by Richfield Oil Company. World famous for windsurfing, Jalama Beach is wildly gorgeous but somewhat dangerous for swimmers because of a strong undertow. Be careful! Campsites have picnic tables and barbecue pits, and RV travelers will appreciate the hookup facilities. If you forgot the essentials, you can get them and fishing tackle and bait (possibly in the essential category). You'll also find a survivable snack bar. Call (805) 736–6316 for campsite availability.

Ocean Park's rugged shoreline is fifteen minutes from downtown and is great for blustery walks and surf fishing, but officials warn against swimming due to the swiftly swirling currents.

VANDENBERG AIR FORCE BASE occupies only 2 percent of its 99,000 acres of gorgeous California coastal terrain. It is occasionally praised for its ecological efforts to maintain a physical buffer between its rocket launchers and the outside world with undeveloped land that harbors 270 endangered species of flora and fauna as well as a new wildlife sanctuary.

From Vandenberg the Air Force launches toward the South Pacific both government and commercial unarmed test missiles that pass 4,200 miles in twenty-five minutes. Many launches are announced forty-eight hours ahead so visitors can watch, but weather conditions can force delays or postponements. For launch and Wednesday tour information call (805) 734–9232, ext. 63595.

If you are hungry, make your way to H Street, where there's a plethora of Thai, Mexican, seafood, and Italian restaurants, steak houses with bars, and coffeehouses.

To get to Buellton, Solvang, Santa Ynez, Ballard and Los Olivos, take Highway 246 east from Lompoc.

Right on Highway 246, wine lovers must stop at **BABCOCK VINEYARDS**, whose owner/winemaker Bryan Babcock was rated in 1995 by the James Beard Foundation as one of the "ten best small production winemakers in the world." The other nine were in Europe.

RISOTTO WITH GORGONZOLA AND SPINACH
from Mona Babcock, Babcock Vineyards, Lompoc

---

3 Tbs. olive oil

1 medium onion, finely diced

2 cups Arborio rice

6 cups chicken stock

½ cup dry white wine

1 small bunch fresh spinach leaves, (well washed and) coarsely chopped

salt and pepper to taste

1 cup pieces of cooked chicken

½ cup Gorgonzola cheese

¼ cup half-and-half

¾ cup grated Parmesan cheese

Heat oil in heavy 2-quart saucepan. Add the onion and cook slowly over low heat until tender. Add rice and, stirring constantly, sauté until the grains of rice are opaque, about 2 to 3 minutes.

Meanwhile heat the chicken stock until it is very hot, then keep it warm over low heat. Add the wine to the rice and cook slowly, stirring constantly, until wine is completely absorbed. Add the spinach to the rice and stir until well mixed. Add the chicken stock to the rice mixture, one large spoonful at a time, stirring frequently. Cook the rice very slowly over low heat. When the liquid is absorbed, add the next spoonful. Halfway through cooking, add salt and pepper to taste. Then add the chicken.

When the rice is just barely tender, add the Gorgonzola cheese and cream, and cook until the cheese is softened. Turn off the heat, add the Parmesan cheese, and stir until the cheese and cream are absorbed. Pass additional grated Parmesan when serving. Serves four. Serve with Babcock's Eleven Oaks Sauvignon Blanc.

Babcock Vineyards and its owners are modest and their winery is grossly underhyped, which is definitely a blessing and possibly results in their ability to concentrate on making some of the country's best wines. And it is right here between Lompoc and Buellton, and not in the Napa Valley!

Bryan Babcock has quickly risen to quiet prominence and respect in the winemaking business by simply producing excellent wines. First Bryan earned his B.S. in biology and chemistry from Occidental College in 1982, and then got his M.S. in food science, specializing in enology at the University of California, Davis. In 1984 his very first harvest brought a double gold medal for Babcock's estate Sauvignon Blanc.

Using only estate-grown or Santa Barbara County fruit, Bryan has made some daring moves. When his estate Riesling "wasn't hitting the benchmark he was aiming for," he pulled out the vines and planted Pinot Gris. He produced Sauvignon Blanc when it was out of fashion and criticized for its "herbal character" and converted it to a highly acclaimed wine that sells out every year under Babcock's Eleven Oaks label. And now he's trying to make Gewürztraminer "as good as the best Alsatians."

Bryan Babcock is also helping to spearhead introductions of Spanish Albarino and Tempranillo varieties and Italian Pignolo, which he predicts "will be California's next frontier in winemaking."

SAFFRON PARMESAN SHORTBREAD
from Mona Babcock, Babcock Vineyards, Lompoc
(fabulous with the risotto or Alex Trebek's Almond Soup—see p. 198)

---

1 cup Parmesan cheese, finely grated
¾ cup white flour
¼ cup masa harina
½ cup butter, room temperature
dash salt
dash white pepper
½ tsp. saffron

Preheat oven to 375° F. Mix ingredients together until thoroughly incorporated (really fast in a food processor!). The texture will be of cookie dough. Shape into a long log about 1½ inches in diameter. Cover with plastic wrap and refrigerate 1 hour or until ready to use. Bring to room temperature and slice into cookies about 1½ inches thick. Place on an ungreased cookie sheet and bake 10–12 minutes. They will be barely golden. Do not overbake. Serve warm.

Bryan has taken one slightly wild step. He formed a partnership with Anne Rice, author of *Interview with the Vampire* and other such spectacularly success-ful novels, to create a Cuvee Lestat Syrah, named for one of her leading charac-ters. The wine was so popular that a second series was launched. That one includes a Syrah, a Chardonnay, and a Claret, and a blend of Cabernet Franc, Cabernet Sauvignon, and Merlot.

Babcock is truly a family operation. Bryan serves as vice president, general manager and winemaker; his parents Mona and Walt are co-owners; his wife Lisa handles marketing (and their son Sean); his sister Brenda Via is the finan-cial officer; and her husband Mikael is company lawyer.

Fine points: Featured wines: Babcock, Cuvee Lestat, Mt. Carmel, Grand Cuvee, Fathom and Eleven Oaks labels, including Cuvee Lestat Chardonnay, Claret, and Syrah; Grand Cuvee Chardonnay and Pinot Noir; Mt. Carmel Chardonnay and Pinot Noir; Eleven Oaks Sauvignon Blanc; and Babcock Chardonnay, Gewürztraminer, Pinot Gris, and Pinot Noir. Owners: Mona, Walt, and Bryan Babcock. Winemaker: Bryan Babcock. Cases: 15,000. Acres: 70.

🍇 *Babcock Vineyards 5175 Highway 246, Lompoc 93436; (805) 736–1455, fax (805) 736–3886; e-mail: babcock@silcom.com; Web site: www.wineaccess.com/bab-cock. Open 10:30 A.M.–4:00 P.M. Friday–Sunday, by appointment during the week. Tasting fee: $2.00 refundable with wine purchase. Visa, MasterCard, American Express. Wheelchair accessible.*

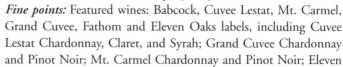

BUELLTON

Twenty miles north of Santa Barbara on Highway 101 you come to exits to El Capitan State Beach and then Refugio State Beach with its romantic palm trees and turquoise water, and Lake Cachuma County Park (805–688–4658), full of bass, catfish, trout, bluegill, and crappie. Impulse fishers or potential fish-ers can get licenses at the local bait and tackle shop, and you can even rent boats if you wish. Enjoy the snack bar, general store, service station, camping sites, and picnic sites galore.

Another 7 miles north is San Onofre Beach with two ugly oil well drilling platforms besmirching the ocean. Another couple of miles brings you into the city limits of Gaviota, best known for its flower farms. If you travel by Amtrak, the tracks follow the water even more closely than the road does at this point. Gaviota Beach State Park is a highly accessible, right-down-to-the-beach camp-ground and parking lot. Watch for the speed bumps on the road.

Three miles north of Gaviota Beach at Las Cruces, Highway 101 turns northeast, while Highway 1 heads northwest to Lompoc. Buellton is just 3 miles north of the intersection if you stick with Highway 101.

If you are coming from the north, you will first pass through Santa Maria on Highway 101, or Lompoc via Highways 1 and 246.

Buellton's primary attraction is Andersen's Pea Soup, which has renamed itself **PEA SOUP ANDERSEN'S**, based on people's main goal in getting there. And is it worth it! Anton and Juliette Andersen opened the restaurant in 1924 as Andersen's Electrical Cafe, a name they chose to celebrate their prized new electric stove! Since then, Juliette's pea soup has attracted millions of comfort pea soup fans to sample the original. We are most fortunate to be able to offer you their original pea soup recipe.

The building's trim is pea-soup green, the doors are pea-soup green, and even the Best Western motel next door has pea-soup green trim. There seems to be a theme here.

Here you can buy Pea Soup Andersen's cookbook, flatish mugs for soup, soup bowls, canned pea soup (surprise!), preserves, soup and fried chicken spices, and Solvang Bakery's breads and pastries. Andersen's Pea Soup wines are actually made by Honeywood Winery, Salem, Oregon's champion fruit wine producer. They come in pomegranate, cherry, raspberry, plum/cranberry, and

PEA SOUP ANDERSEN'S, BUELLTON

ORIGINAL PEA SOUP
from Pea Soup Andersen's

1 qt. soft water
2 cups Andersen's specially selected green split peas
1 branch of celery, coarsely chopped
1 small onion, chopped
¼ tsp. ground thyme
1 pinch cayenne pepper
1 bay leaf
salt and pepper

Boil hard (all ingredients) for 20 minutes, then slowly until peas are tender. Strain though fine sieve and reheat to boiling point. "You are in for a treat! The one that made Andersen's nationally famous." Makes eight bowls of Andersen's Famous Split Pea Soup.

---

orange flavors. Sample the local cheeses cut in cubes and placed in trays on a wine barrel. All this between the restaurant shop and its doll and curio shop, where you will also find fabulous historic photos of the Andersen family and the restaurant, on the way to the rest rooms.

➤ *Pea Soup Andersen's, 376 Avenue of the Flags, Buellton 93427; (805) 688–5581. Open 6:30 A.M.–10:00 P.M. daily. Full bar. Visa and MasterCard. Wheelchair accessible.*

Pea Soup Andersen's has spawned some good nearby motels, golf courses, special events, a magic show theater, and a farmers' market, so you can actually stay there if you wish. Another choice is the Danish village of Solvang on the other side of Highway 101.

Nojoqui Park, on Alisal Road between Highway 101 and Solvang, has the only waterfall in Santa Barbara County. This is a true community park for day use only and features great picnic areas, softball diamonds, volleyball courts, horseshoe pitches, and playgrounds among California live oaks and birds worth watching. A short but steep trail leads to the waterfall.

From Highway 101 take the Highway 246 east exit (toward Solvang). In less than a mile you come to a shopping center with Long's Drugs and other familiar large stores, plus a delightful local espresso joint cleverly called Thanks a Latte.

Within the next half mile you have arrived! That is, at two of the central coast's most renowned steak houses: A.J. Spurs, a small chain, and the locally famous and infamous Hitching Post.

The **Hitching Post**, which looks like an Old West bar and hangout—which it is—is a must-try if you eat meat or just want to experience what the locals look like or like to eat on occasion. Along with good, stiff drinks, great oak-fire barbecued steaks and French fries, you can indulge in fabulous grilled artichokes and mushrooms, seafood and chicken, lamb, turkey, ostrich, pork, ribs, and smoked duck. The *New York Times* has said "A must stop for beef and Pinot lovers"; the *Los Angeles Times* says "perfect steaks and fires and a daring Pinot Noir"; and *Gourmet* said "We'd drive anywhere for steaks like these." Got the message?

The Hitching Post also has a wine tasting room for its own label wines. The secret to these great Pinot Noirs is that in 1984 Gray Hartley and Frank Ostini began making wines for the Hitching Post, and in 1991 they moved on to Qupe/Au Bon Climat, where they make limited bottlings of Pinot Noir and Syrah and an even better reputation for themselves. Here you can taste both.

Now you can even order cooked steaks and ribs by phone and have them shipped around California. The meat is seasoned and grilled (rare is recommended so you can reheat according to instructions), chilled, packed, and shipped overnight. Be sure to have them include their special artichokes and

---

Herb Marinated Ostrich Steak
from Colin and Rosi Cooper, Ostrich Land, Buellton

---

2 lbs. tender ostrich steaks, approximately 1 ½ inches thick
Marinade:
⅔ cup balsamic vinegar
¼ cup olive oil
2 Tbs. garlic, finely chopped
1 Tbs. fresh rosemary, crushed
1 Tbs. fresh thyme leaves
1 tsp. freshly ground black pepper

Combine marinade ingredients in plastic bag. Add meat, turning to coat. Close bag securely and marinate in refrigerator 1 hour, turning occasionally.

Remove meat from marinade; discard marinade. Place meat on rack in broiler pan so that meat is 3–4 inches from heat. Broil 26–31 minutes for medium rare to medium doneness, turning once. Carve into slices. Serves six to eight.

smoked tomato mayo. Steaks from $15–$30 for two, artichokes $20 for four, plus sales tax and $14 shipping. Order two days ahead at (888) 429–6300.
✥ *Hitching Post, 406 East Highway 246, Buellton 93427; (805) 688–0676, (888) 429–6300. Open bar at 4:00 P.M., dinner 5:00–9:00 P.M. daily. Full bar. Visa, MasterCard, American Express. Wheelchair accessible.*

OSTRICH LAND is the pride and joy of Colin and Rosi Cooper, whose first Ostrich Land was in South Africa twenty years ago. Now you can visit their unique thirty-three acres of ostriches and emus, a ranch based upon the original 1,000 African black ostrich eggs they imported to California. Here you can feed the friendly emus, gaze at their green eggs that look like avocados, and see ostrich products such as eggshell lamps, ostrich feather dusters, and leather (highly valued by some people for Western boots). Most of Ostrich Land's eggs and birds are exported to Japan, Korea, China, Taiwan, Equador, Brazil, and the Philippines, although you can also buy meat here. Ostrich meat is reputed to be the one of the highest-protein, lowest-fat meats available. We have tried ostrich jerky, and while slightly chewy, it is quite tasty. Bon appétit!
✥ *Ostrich Land, 610 Highway 246 east, PO Box 490, Buellton 93427; (805) 686–9696; e-mail: ostri@earthlink.net; Web site: www.ostrichland.com. Open 9:00 A.M.–5:00 P.M. Saturday–Sunday. Visa and MasterCard. Wheelchair accessible.*

SOLVANG
("MAKE MINE DANISH")

A half mile east of Ostrich Land on Highway 246 you arrive in Solvang. (In Solvang Highway 246 becomes Mission Drive, just to unconfuse you.)

Solvang is a consciously constructed Danish village plunked down in the Santa Ynez Valley by Danes and Danish-Americans who plunked themselves here by choice to establish a Danish community in California. It was simply too cold in the Midwest from which most of them came.

Suddenly as you drive along Highway 246, you have been transported to an eighteenth-century Danish village—authentic except for such modern touches as cement curbs, a neon sign here and there, and automobiles. How did this seeming miracle come about?

Back in 1910, not far from the then crumbling Santa Ines Mission, this area was a bean field owned by the Santa Ynez Valley Development Company. The only building was the one-room Ynez School, which served the children of the valley farms.

Meanwhile in Michigan the Danish Lutheran Church Convention adopted a proposal to develop a Danish colony and a Danish "folk school," patterned after the Grundtvigian folk school movement in Denmark, in a suitable location in the west. In 1911 a committee of two Lutheran ministers (Benedict Nordenstoft and J. M. Gregersen) and Professor P. P. Hornsyld found the valley, bought 9,000 acres of the Rancho San Carlos de Jonata, and named the colony Solvang ("sunny field").

Within a few months the first wave of Danes arrived, including lumber dealer Hans Skytt. Soon there arose the Solvang Hotel, the Bethania Lutheran Church, several homes, a bank, a bakery, and other shops. The folk school, Atterdag ("another day") College, was erected in 1914. Classes on Danish culture and trades for young men were given there until 1937.

The town buildings' only variations on plain were the Spanish arcade on Copenhagen Drive and the one true Danish-style building, the new Bethania Lutheran Church, designed and completed by pioneer Hans Skytt in 1928. Solvang's twenty-fifth anniversary celebration in June 1936 gave birth to "Danish Days," which grew each year until it became overwhelming for the town, which rescheduled it to September after kids return to school to limit attendance at the festival.

Solvang's transformation into an old Danish village began in 1945 after World War II. Home builder Fred Sorensen returned from a visit to Denmark with plans for a home in the Danish provincial style, and he built it, including

LINTON'S RESTAURANT AND WINDMILL, SOLVANG

a windmill—the Mill on the Hill (*Mollenbakken*). This induced Ray Paaske, himself just home from a German prison camp, to hire Sorensen to design commercial establishments in the Danish style where Copenhagen Drive meets Alisal Drive (now Copenhagen Square).

In the early 1950s a couple of new buildings on Copenhagen Drive were built in the same style (gingerbread along the eaves, visible wood forms like the Tudors, multipaned windows, meticulous attention to detail, sharply peaked roofs, lots of dormers). Then the Spanish arcade went Danish in 1958.

Architect and developer Earl Petersen designed the Royal Copenhagen Motel on Mission Drive (Highway 246) to recreate a street in Hans Christian Andersen's home town of Odense. Then across the street Petersen developed an entire city block, called Petersen's Village Square, with a hotel, bakery, and several shops, using varied facades, Danish style. Meanwhile more windmills were built—joining the original Paaske Mill on Alisal—the Blue Windmill in Hamlet Square at Second and Copenhagen and one as part of the Danish Inn on Mission Drive.

The rush was on. Old buildings were converted to Danish provincial by merchants eager to do their part and attract tourist business. The postal service got the message and the new post office grew up Danish, as did several gas stations and motels. A series of shopping and dining squares in the medieval format and carved signs came into vogue. Among other structures Earl Petersen designed the outdoor 720-seat Solvang Festival Theater with its old-world stage house which opened in 1974. Solvangans planted the Hans Christian Andersen Park.

Saleswomen and waitresses wear attractive Danish costumes every day, whether they are of Danish heritage or not. Many women bleach their hair to match someone's notion of female Danes. *Honen*—horse-drawn pre-1900 streetcars (built by local artisans)—clop through town daily in summer and on weekends the rest of the year (adults $3.50, seniors $3.00, children $2.50). The wind harp from the Danish exhibit at the 1915 Pan-Pacific Exposition plays its siren song in the breezy afternoon. There is an imported model of the famed Copenhagen mermaid statue. The mouth-watering aromas of Danish baked goods draw visitors into the multitudinous bakeries and restaurants. Warm hospitality completes the picture.

Local historian Elaine Revelle calls Solvang "a Danish-American jewel set in a wealth of cultures and blessed by the California sun." We agree.

While cranky critics have called Solvang the "Denmark Disneyland" and a town "more Danish than Denmark," we think you should take time to have a look, give it a chance, enjoy it for what it is, and draw your own conclusions. Besides, in the process you can sample more pastries than you will see in the whole rest of your life, try more smorgasbords than you should, and shop till your feet fall off. Everything is close together along a 4-block stretch of Mission Street and within a couple of blocks to the south.

Walking maps are available at most hotels, motels, and businesses.

Among the most popular bakeries are Mortensen's Danish Bakery (an almond custard ring to die for), Olsen's Danish Village Bakery, and Solvang Bakery up Alisal Road, which bakes breads for lots of local restaurants. Walk around the few blocks and check out menus and compare smorgasbords if you want to sample Danish specialties. Within a block or two of most hotels and motels you can also find Mexican, Italian, and fast foods, if you must. Another popular favorite is the River Grill at the Alisal Golf Course just up Alisal Road from Mission Street. (Great views.)

Two new restaurants have opened to raves from Santa Barbara restaurateurs, and we suggest you try them: Brothers Restaurant and the Santa Ynez Feed & Grill, the former a somewhat formal dining room, the latter a casual bistro where Norbert Schulz, former partner in Brigitte's in Santa Barbara, presides as chef. Brigitte's owner Bergitta Guehr recently purchased and began substantial improvements to the Meadowlark Inn, so watch for an even better casually elegant inn with twenty rooms, some with kitchenettes, and two acres of lush gardens perfect for weddings and parties.

Other than the village of Solvang itself, its architecture, and its food, special attractions include the Hans Christian Andersen Museum, the Elverhoj Museum of History and Art, and the Solvang Antique Center.

The HANS CHRISTIAN ANDERSEN MUSEUM is operated by the Ugly Duckling Foundation, dedicated to increasing enjoyment and understanding of Andersen and his work. You get to the museum either through our favorite Solvang bookstore, the Book Loft, or through the adjoining Kaffe Hus.

Exhibits and displays depict Jenny Lind, a singer beloved throughout the world (and Andersen's unrequited love); a model of Andersen's childhood home; a model of "The Princess and the Pea" by local artist Carl Jacobsen; antique tools for making wooden shoes; hundreds of volumes of Andersen's tales, including many first and early editions, as well as illustrated editions (many in the Danish language); and original letters and photographs. This is a great place for adults and kids, even if they can't read yet.

❧ *Hans Christian Andersen Museum, 1680 Mission Drive, Solvang 93463; (805) 688–2052. Open 10:00 A.M.–5:00 P.M. daily. Admission free. Wheelchair accessible.*

The ELVERHOJ MUSEUM OF HISTORY AND ART specializes in the history of Solvang and the heritage of Denmark. It is one of the few museums outside Denmark devoted solely to Danish culture and the Danish-American experience.

The museum is located in the former residence of one of Solvang's most artistic families, the Viggo Brandt-Erichsens. Built in 1950, the structure was built to mirror the large farmhouses of eighteenth-century Jutland in northern Denmark. The name Elverhoj (pronounced Elverhoy and meaning "elves on a hill") was taken from Denmark's most famous folk play, *Elverhoj,* written in 1828 and still performed. The story involves a king's visit to the night world of dancing female wood spirits.

Don't miss the terrific gift shop and a diorama depicting Solvang before the Danish village was created. As usual, Kathleen is fascinated with the brightly painted kitchen with typical Danish farmhouse folk paintings. Docents in Danish folk costumes take you on personal tours.

❧ *Elverhoj Museum of History and Art, 1624 Elverhoj Way, PO Box 769, Solvang 93463; (805) 686–1211. Open 1:00–4:00 P.M. Wednesday–Sunday. Admission is free, donation box near door. Visa and MasterCard. Wheelchair accessible.*

SOLVANG ANTIQUE CENTER offers unusually high quality antiques in fifty well-lit galleries and showcases. You will find the most elegant of European carved furniture, American oak, porcelain, cut glass, estate jewelry, pianos, Wedgwood, Majolica, clocks and music boxes, Japanese antiques, scales and tools, and collectibles. Right off Mission Drive on First Street at the eastern end of town, the antique center ships anywhere in the world and offers in-house restorations.

❧ *Solvang Antique Center, 486 First Street, Solvang 93463; (805) 686–2322, fax (805) 686–4044. Open 10:00 A.M.–6:00 P.M. daily. Visa, MasterCard, American Express. Partly wheelchair accessible.*

Another draw to Solvang is its outstanding PACIFIC CONSERVATORY OF THE PERFORMING ARTS (known in local secret code as PCPA), an outdoor theater designed by Earl Petersen seating 720 guests and featuring rotating repertory. Director Donovan Marley, now in Denver, built the PCPA's reputation. Call (805) 922–8313 for performance schedule June–October and information.

Solvang stages festivals throughout the year, among them the Flying Leap Storytelling Festival the third weekend in February (805–688–8823); the Taste of Solvang annual food festival, the theme of which changes each year, the third weekend in March (800–468–6765, ext. 520); the Old Mission Santa Ines Fiesta the second weekend in August; Danish Days with folk dancing, music, parades, and food the third weekend in September (805–688–6144); and the giant Winterfest celebration from Thanksgiving to Christmas with millions of white lights, pageantry, and special events (read shopping).

OLD MISSION SANTA INES is one of the gems of the California missions, founded in 1804 by Padre Estevan Tapis and built for the Franciscans by Indians whom the Franciscans planned to colonize and convert to Catholicism. It is currently run by the Capuchin Franciscans. Although much of the mission was destroyed by the 1812 earthquake, half the original twenty-two arches and over one-third of the original mission quad still stand. The mission functioned as a self-sustaining village with tanning, threshing, wool pulling, weaving, carpentry, grist and olive milling, wine making, metal and ironworks, and full scale farm and ranching operations. Mission Santa Ines was also the first college and seminary in California.

The church, which was rebuilt in 1817, is one of the few chapels of the California missions that has been in continuous use since 1817. In the museum

OLD MISSION SANTA INES, SOLVANG

you will see artifacts from the Spanish, Indian, Mexican, and early American civilizations, including arrowheads, adobe bricks and tiles, pestles and mortars, pottery, musical instruments, tools, silver, firearms, and ironwork produced on the mission's grounds, as well as priceless seventeenth- and eighteenth-century European and Indian art.

Don't miss the preserved vestment collection dating from the sixteenth century, including one worn by Padre Junipero Serra, founder of the California missions. Be sure to visit the semiformal garden with its boxwood hedge sculpted in the shape of a Celtic cross, flowers, a California pepper tree brought by Father Serra—a quiet oasis from rushing society. Mission bells still toll daily to tell the valley what time it is.

The mission cemetery has 1,700 unmarked Indian graves, as well as those of seventy-five early California settlers of Spanish, Portuguese, German, and Irish descent, with engraved gravestones, of course. Please especially respect the unmarked Indian graves.

❧ Old Mission Santa Ines, 1760 Mission Drive, PO Box 408, Solvang 93463; (805) 688–4815. Open 9:00 A.M.–5:30 P.M. daily winter, 9:00 A.M.–7:00 P.M. summer; masses 8:00 A.M. daily, Saturday 5:00 P.M. in English, 7:00 P.M. in Spanish, Sunday 8:00, 9:30, 11:00 A.M. in English, 12:30 P.M. in Spanish. Admission to the museum and gardens: $3.00 donation accepted but not compulsory, children under sixteen free. Wheelchair accessible.

SANTA YNEZ

Possibly the biggest, newest attraction in Santa Ynez is the CHUMASH INDIAN CASINO, right on Highway 246. How convenient!

This place is about as wild, fun, and exciting as you would expect, taking advantage of U.S. government laws allowing gambling on Indian reservation property that is not allowed elsewhere. You are now on the Santa Ynez Indian Reservation, so please respect it and its territories south and east of here.

If it's your inclination, you can take your chances on a variety of casino thrills such as slot machines, video gaming, poker, Chumash 21, and boxing.

❧ Chumash Indian Casino, 3400 Highway 246 east, Santa Ynez 93464; (805) 686–0855. Open 10:00 A.M.–2:00 A.M. Monday–Thursday, twenty-four hours Friday–Sunday. Full bar. Visa, MasterCard, American Express. Wheelchair accessible.

Another popular attraction in Santa Ynez is the SANTA YNEZ VALLEY HISTORICAL MUSEUM and the nearby carriage museum. One of the most interesting exhibits at this charming small museum is the room dedicated to the Chumash Indian culture, including a diorama, tools, and a fabulous basket collection. The carriage museum has a surprisingly wonderful collection of stagecoaches, wagons, and other horse-drawn vehicles that set the tone for your winery tour into the Santa Ynez Valley where thousands of Western movies were filmed.

✦ *Santa Ynez Valley Historical Museum,* *3596 Sagunto Street, Santa Ynez 93464; (805) 688–7889. Open: museum: 1:00–4:00 P.M. Friday–Sunday; carriage house: 10:00 A.M.–4:00 P.M. Tuesday–Sunday. Admission free.*

BALLARD

Ballard is one of the smallest and most intensely cute communities anywhere. It's so small that it doesn't have a post office, so the official address is Solvang. All of Ballard is on Baseline Road, an old Wells Fargo stagecoach route just east of Alamo Pintado Road. One of the town's most charming buildings is the white-trimmed, red-steepled Ballard School, which is still used for kindergarten classes. Conveniently located now within tenths of a mile of Buttonwood, Rideau, Foley, and Beckmen wineries, Ballard's two premier restaurants offer perfect stops on your search for perfect wines.

BALLARD STORE RESTAURANT AND WINE BAR has been a mainstay of sophisticated travelers' dining choices since 1970. Chef John and Alice Elliott bought it then and turned it into a small and extremely fashionable emporium of French and American food (including an oyster bar) greatly praised by *Gourmet, Bon Appétit,* and *Zagat.*

Brooklyn native John Elliott graduated from New York City Culinary Arts College and served his apprenticeship at the "21" Club in Manhattan. Eventually he worked as Executive Chef at the original Neiman Marcus Zodiac Room in Dallas, where he met his now wife, Alice Flynn, who was born and raised on the Orella Ranch and attended schools in Santa Ynez Valley.

In 1970 the Elliotts bought the 1939 Ballard Store and Gas Station and opened the restaurant May 14, 1970. Now it includes a larger kitchen, pantry, the Chandler Dining Room, Chelsea's Pub, and the André Tchelistcheff Wine Cellar.

Don't miss the bouillabaisse ($18.95) or the perfect filet mignon ($22.95). The garden pasta is also superb ($13.95), and all dinners include choice of appetizer. Should you want to try the dramatic Flambé Pheasant Dinner for Two ($50), call one day in advance.

Call the day before also for their gourmet picnic boxes, four selections at $15 with a minimum order of two. Sunday brunch is excellent and pricey, with eggs Benedict ($23.95), huevos rancheros ($22.95), Monte Cristo Sandwich ($19.95), two large eggs any way ($19.95), flambé banana pancakes ($20.95), although all include champagne or ramos fizzes, fresh fruit, pastries, meats, and potatoes.

✻✧ *Ballard Store, Restaurant and Wine Bar,* 2449 *Baseline Avenue, Solvang* 93463; (805) 688–5319. *Open for dinner 5:30–9:30* P.M. *Wednesday–Friday,* 6:00–9:30 P.M. *Saturday, from 5:00* P.M. *Sunday, brunch 10:30* A.M.–2:00 P.M. *Sunday. Full bar. Visa, MasterCard, American Express. Wheelchair accessible.*

Across Baseline from the Ballard Store is the Ballard Inn and its CAFE CHARDONNAY serving "creative wine country cuisine." Be sure to mentally "save room" for Chef Martin Schneider's famous desserts.

At dinner main courses come with either soup or Shepherd's Mix salad. One of Martin's specialties is his Dungeness crab ravioli with lemon butter sauce, which come with spring vegetable slaw ($15.95) or as a smaller a la carte version ($8.95). Or try the roasted and grilled prime rib of pork with caramelized shallots and port wine sauce ($17.95), the classic red wine and rosemary braised lamb shank on garlic mashed potatoes ($17.95), seared rare ahi tuna (you can have it cooked more—just ask) with sesame pepper crust on snow pea and red onion slaw ($18.95 or $9.95), or certified Angus filet mignon with pancetta and balsamic vinegar sauce ($21.95).

And those desserts. Our favorite is Martin's homemade ice cream sandwich (it redefines the ice cream sandwich), with chocolate cake layers filled with vanilla bean ice cream and raspberry and chocolate sauces ($5.50). See what we mean? Also enjoy the excellent local wine list.

✻✧ *Cafe Chardonnay at the Ballard Inn,* 2436 *Baseline Avenue, Solvang* 93463; (805) 688–7770 *or* (800) 638–2466. *Open 6:00–9:00* P.M. *Wednesday–Saturday, 5:30–9:00* P.M. *Sunday. Full bar. Visa, MasterCard, American Express. Wheelchair accessible.*

CAFE CHARDONNAY AT THE BALLARD INN, SOLVANG

LOS OLIVOS

Los Olivos (the olives) is definitely one of our favorite little places. Surrounded by large ranches and vineyards unabashedly owned by the rich and famous, Los Olivos is a marvelous cross between elegant sophistication and country funk. And besides, the surrounding hills and dales look like scenes in all those Westerns you grew up on—because they are. Los Olivos is ultimate Santa Ynez Valley.

Nancy and President Ronald Reagan, Cheryl Ladd, Bo Derek, John Forsythe, Doc Severinsen, Ray Stark, Rona Barrett, James Stewart, Dean Martin, Johnny Mathis, Michael Jackson, Jimmy Connors, Bruce Jenner, Efrem Zimbalist Jr., David Crosby, and Whoopi Goldberg have all chosen the Los Olivos area of the Santa Ynez Valley as their hangout or home. Greta Garbo used to live here. And cowboy movie star residents Leo Carrillo, Gene Autry, Noah Berry Jr., Will Rogers, and Tom Mix first came here on the springtime treks made by Ranchero Visitadores in the 1930s.

Los Olivos itself began in 1860 when a stagecoach stop was established. Several years later Felix Mattei foresaw that the Pacific Coast Railway would stop here, too, and built a hotel to accommodate rail and stage passengers making connections. It did. Ballard became the railroad's terminus in November 1887, and two expected booming land sales were rained out. Stage service to Los Olivos terminated in 1901, and train service terminated in 1934, so progress and life slowed down tremendously.

Felix Mattei's hotel and eatery are still in business and still frequented by old-timers, travelers, and newcomers. Be sure to drop in for a sample of the Old West on Railway Avenue a block west of Grand Avenue.

The center of town is the Los Olivos flagpole in the middle of the Grand Avenue–Alamo Pintado intersection, the first version of which stood east of this one and had a thirty-gallon Schilling's Best coffee can as a base. The current pole was erected in 1918 to honor World War I veterans.

Most everything you'll want to see is on Grand Avenue or in the first blocks off it on Alamo Pintado, Jonata, or Railway cross streets.

We start at the bottom of the east side of Grand at what is now Fess Parker's Wine Country Inn & Spa, until recently the Grand Hotel and Remington Restaurant. The hotel was once the Lige Campbell Livery Stable (1910) from which Lige carried mail and passengers to Gaviota in a mud wagon stage until 1914. The west wing occupies what was once the Irv Henning Tent House (1886). An artesian well on the property furnished water for the dairy and a Chinese laundry.

Just up from Fess Parker's is the Cody Gallery, the first art gallery in Los Olivos, and then the Judith Hale Gallery. If the yellow flag is out, Judith Hale is open. This property has been a general store, barber shop, post office, and town library.

Across Alamo Pintado at the corner is perhaps the most familiar site in Los Olivos, the Los Olivos Garage (1903), made famous as Goober's garage in "Return to Mayberry." Until it closed January 1, 1990, because of a new California contamination law, the garage was the oldest continuously operating gas station in California.

Behind the garage (down the Alamo Pintado side) is an excellent deli, PANINO, the perfect place to select a salad or panino sandwich and dine in front at the round, umbrellaed tables or pick up the perfect picnic to enjoy at a winery. Eighteen meaty sandwich varieties and eight yummy vegetarian kinds make decisions difficult. One of the most popular is a smoked turkey/Genoa salami combo ($6.50). Or try the Italian combo of layered ham, Genoa salami, and imported provolone cheese and fresh basil ($7.00), or the smoked turkey with sliced Brie and fresh basil ($7.00). All on freshly baked bread.

Vegetarian choices include English Cotswold and tomato ($6.50), English Stilton and Asian pear ($6.50), mixed veggies ($6.00), and a kalamata olive tapenade with fresh mozzarella, organic greens, and basil ($6.00). Several of the sandwiches are made in salad form. Specials, and they are, are posted on the slate boards.

You can also get special picnic box lunches ($12.50) with a sandwich, salad, and cookie, as well as smoothies, fabulous carrot cake, and espresso drinks. Check out the attractive splash-painted metal bowls and dishes.

❧ *Panino, 2900 Grand Avenue (around the corner), Los Olivos 93441; (805) 688–9304, fax (805) 688–2552. Open 9:00 A.M.–5:00 P.M. daily. No credit cards. Wheelchair accessible.*

On the west side of Grand Avenue, you will find a series of wine tasting rooms representing small, excellent wineries that don't have tasting rooms at their wineries. Walk down the street to the tasting room of RICHARD LONGORIA WINES in the former D. D. Davis' Warehouse and Welding shop where Davis' brother Bernard ran a steam barley roller.

Rick Longoria served full-time as cellar foreman at Firestone Vineyard, Rancho Sisquoc, J. Carey Cellars, and, since 1985 at Gainey Vineyard, until he finally took the plunge in 1997 to make his own label wines full-time. Rick strives for perfection and makes only four wines, to maximize the potential of the character of grapes and vineyards he selects.

Check out Rick's Blues Cuvees, a tribute to his first blues song experience at age seventeen and to the soul of the music and his wines.

Longoria's wines have been highly praised by the *Wine Spectator*, the *Wine Advocate,* and by Dan Berger in the *Los Angeles Times.*

Fine points: Featured wines: Chardonnay, Pinot Noir, Merlot, Cabernet Franc, Blues Cuvee Litho. Owners: Rick and Diana Longoria. Winemaker: Rick Longoria. Cases: 3,000. Acres: 8 and buy locally.

ᎷᏝ *Richard Longoria Wines, 2935 Grand Avenue, Los Olivos 93441; (805) 688–0305, fax (805) 688–2676. Open noon–4:30 P.M., Monday, Wednesday– Thursday, 11:00 A.M.–4:30 P.M. Friday–Sunday. Visa and MasterCard. Wheelchair accessible.*

Next door **Los Olivos Vintners** specializes in small quantities of a few wines, including Chardonnay, Sauvignon Blanc, white wine blends, Pinot Noir, Cabernet Sauvignon, Merlot, Cabernet Franc, red wine blends, Riesling, and Muscat Canelli. (The site once housed the D. D. Davis General Store, the Bucket O'Blood Saloon, and the valley's first theater, the Liberty, which opened in 1916.)

ᎷᏝ *Los Olivos Vintners, 2923 Grand Avenue, Los Olivos 93441; (805) 688–9665 or (800) 824–8584, fax (805) 686–1690. Open 11:00 A.M.–6:00 P.M. daily. Visa, MasterCard, Discover. Wheelchair accessible.*

Next is the new tasting room of **Arthur Earl**, which moved here in the summer of 1999 from near the crossing of Highways 101 and 246 in Buellton. Arthur White and Earl Brockelsby converted a warehouse into a full-function winery and tasting room at their "city" winery in Buellton. Focusing on dry whites, dry reds, and sweet wines, Art and Earl are delighted to be able to offer their wines in these pleasant surroundings honoring the arts of various disciplines.

The owner of the Stonebarger Foundry and shop (1906) in this historic building shaded by a large old oak tree put together Los Olivos' first water system and erected the flagpole (1918).

Fine points: Featured wines: Rousanne, Nebbiolo, Merlot, Syrah. Owners: Arthur White and Earl Brockelsby. Winemaker: Art White. Cases: 3,000. Acres: none, buy locally.

ᎷᏝ *Arthur Earl, 2921 Grand Avenue, Los Olivos 93441; (805) 693–1771 or (800) 646–3275. Open 11:00 A.M.–6:00 P.M. daily. Visa, MasterCard, American Express. Wheelchair accessible.*

Chris Benzinger's (not Benziger) LOS OLIVOS TASTING ROOM & WINE SHOP offers tastes, representing small wineries that don't have their own tasting rooms or other wineries Benzinger simply likes. This is a truly fun place where you can learn lots about a variety of wines. This building was first Henry Lewis' barbershop, then "Uncle Tom" Davis ran a small grocery store here until 1935, and then it was used as the post office with combination lockboxes outside.

Here you can sample the finest from Au Bon Climat (Pinot Noir), Qupe, and Vita Nova, whose label reads "Incestuous products from like minds," as well as Claiborne & Churchill (which now has its own new tasting room), Brophy Clark, Brucher, Daniel Gehrs, Foxen Vineyards, Hitching Post, Il Podere Dell Olivos, Laetitia, Lane Tanner, Makor, Nichols, Ojai, Bonny Doon dessert wines, and Kalyra (Australia).

☙ *Los Olivos Tasting Room & Wine Shop, 2905 Grand Avenue, Los Olivos 93441; (805) 688–7406. Open 11:00 A.M.–5:30 daily. Visa, MasterCard, Discover. Wheelchair accessible.*

Back at the corner of Grand Avenue and Alamo Pintado, you can enjoy (if you're still sampling) fine ANDREW MURRAY VINEYARDS wines in a bright and airy, beautifully appointed tasting room in a new 1998 building called the Corners. The winery itself is above Foxen Canyon Road. Andrew Murray is Santa Barbara County's only exclusively Rhone estate.

Andrew Murray, the person and the winery, are devoted to Rhone varietals and to the production of unfiltered wines from estate-grown grapes. This is a family enterprise with Andrew's parents, Jim and Fran, pitching in at all levels from picking to pouring. Andrew and his wife Kristen basically run the winery. Andrew fell in love with Rhones at age fifteen while tasting them with his parents in Condrieu, France, where Viognier is made. He and his father were the first people to plant on hillsides in Santa Barbara County, and on steep hillsides at that, rising quickly from 1,200 feet to over 1,500 feet.

Kristen is a fabulous cook who loves to entertain (good thing!) in the winery and keeps her cuisine simple so she can enjoy her guests. Many thanks for the recipes. The winery itself looks like a French country manor, complete with aromatic Provençal gardens and terraces with breathtaking views of the hillside vineyards and surrounding mountains. Kristen's love of food and things kitchen shows in the books and other gifts available.

Fine points: Featured wines: Syrah, Viognier, Rousanne, Grenache, Mourvedre. Owners: Andrew, Kristen, Frances, and James Murray. Winemaker: Andrew Murray. Cases: 5,000. Acres: 35.

☙ *Andrew Murray Vineyards, 2901 Grand Avenue, PO Box 718,*

Los Olivos 93441; (805) 693–9644, fax (805) 693–9664. Open 11:00
A.M.–6:00 P.M. Wednesday–Monday. Tasting fee: $4.00 includes logo glass. Visa and
MasterCard. Wheelchair accessible.

LOS OLIVOS PARK occupies the southwest corner of Grand and Alamo
Pintado, and Los Olivos' version of punks occupy lots of the park in the afternoons. It and they are all interesting to look at. Fear not! They are just enjoying
the sunshine as you are. Lavinia Campbell gave the land for a park following its
historical uses as a blacksmith shop, garage, drayage, and welding shop.

At the site of Frank and Charlie Whitcher's blacksmith shop, JEDLICKA'S
SADDLERY takes you right into the Western movies, old and new. Reminiscent
of Los Olivos' role in the older Wild West, Jedlicka's has everything horse fans
could need and caters to many of the gorgeous horse ranches in the Santa Ynez
Valley. Whitcher's old ledger listed seventy-seven customers, and Jedlicka's probably has seventy-seven browsers a day in tourist time. Huge red wagons, huge
cowboy hats, a wide range of boots for men and women, and gorgeous ranch
wear are all pampered and sold here. Enjoy!

❧ *Jedlicka's Saddlery, 2883 Grand Avenue, Los Olivos 93441; (805)*
688–2626. Open 9:30 A.M.–5:30 P.M. Monday–Saturday, 10:00 A.M.–4:30 P.M.
Sunday. Visa, MasterCard, American Express, Discover. Wheelchair accessible.

The must-stop restaurant in Los Olivos is the LOS OLIVOS CAFE, with LIN
RICH ANTIQUES in the same building. The simple decor is also very clever:
sponge-painted cement-block walls with functioning pipes hanging from the
ceiling and natural cotton fabric swooping between the pipes, and varied
Mexican iron light fixtures—all in stark contrast to the original store destroyed
here in 1914 when two robbers tried to blow up the safe. Today the deck in
front is a superb place to enjoy lunch or dinner after the sun has passed and
watch Los Olivos society and visitors stroll by.

Los Olivos Cafe is truly the gathering place in Los Olivos, and for good reasons. It features lots of local wines by the glass, such as Rusack, Sunstone, and
Bedford Thompson. Kathleen also enjoyed the passion fruit iced tea.

Lunch excites the taste buds, even if they've been dulled by wine tasting (!),
with a whole menu of selections under $10. Perfect Caesar salads, roasted veg-
gie plates, Greek or Chinese salads, curry chicken, and a special salade niçoise
that comes with fish of the day all can acquire a grilled chicken breast for just
$2.00. The Los Olivos burger is a half pound of lean beef with sautéed onions
and mushrooms ($6.75); the roasted veggie sandwich has zucchini, eggplant,
red peppers, onions, oven-dried tomatoes, and smoked mozzarella with pesto

($6.50); there's a great meatball sandwich ($6.50), the Reuben is perfect ($6.50), and the grilled ham, Swiss cheese, and roasted eggplant sandwich ($6.95) is exceptional, as are the large servings of aromatic pasta specials. Gourmet pizzas are well planned and can have tomato or light pesto sauces. Don't miss the homemade ice cream ($2.50) and espresso drinks.

Be sure to walk right back to the bar and sample Los Olivos' breads with their dipping oils, available in the cozy little deli back by the kitchen. Here you can get Italian pastas, large tins of sardines and anchovies, imported cheeses, French bread, Best from Oregon Jams, and menu goodies to go, including picnic and gift baskets.

*ళ *Los Olivos Cafe, 2879 Grand Avenue, Los Olivos 93441; (805) 688–7265. Open 11:00 A.M.–10:00 P.M. daily. Beer and wine. Visa, MasterCard, Discover. Wheelchair accessible.*

Lin Rich Antiques shares the cafe's front porch and specializes in collectibles and bright Hawaiian shirts.

Don't miss the SIDE STREET CAFE on side street Alamo Pintado Avenue, a cafe/art gallery combo to delight several senses—espresso, fantastic salads and sandwiches, fresh breads, and local wines by glass or bottle with a great garden. Extremely popular local hangout.

*ళ *Side Street Cafe, 2375 Alamo Pintado Avenue, Los Olivos 93441; (805) 688–8455, fax (805) 688–9912. Open 8:00 A.M.–9:00 P.M. Beer and wine. Visa and MasterCard. Wheelchair accessible.*

CHAPTER 4

TOURING
SANTA BARBARA
COUNTY WINERIES

*W*e first visit Santa Barbara's downtown winery before heading to the Santa Ynez Valley and the Foxen Canyon Wine Trail, where most of Santa Barbara County's outstanding wineries are located.

SANTA BARBARA WINERY is in urban Santa Barbara, not far from the beach. While it's on Anacapa Street, do not try to take Anacapa down to it. There's a freeway in the way, called Highway 101. Do take State Street all the way down and under Highway 101. Turn left (south) on Yanonali Street, named for a Chumash Indian chief. Although the winery's address is on Anacapa, the winery and tasting room actually face Yanonali. Park at the winery and walk across Yanonali to the tasting room, where'll you find picnic tables and umbrellas—in case you brought along a picnic.

Entrepreneur Pierre Lafond established Santa Barbara Winery in 1962. It was the first commercial winery in Santa Barbara County since Prohibition, and it is now the oldest in the county in continuous operation.

Along with some friends known as the "mountain drivers," a community of home winemakers famous for their bacchanalian harvest festivals (!), Pierre bought grapes from others to make wine and sell it in his shop in the old El Paseo on State Street. A French-Canadian by birth and an architect by training, Lafond began by making fruit wines. He has cafes and boutiques on State Street and in Montecito.

Beginning in 1970, Pierre invested in vineyard land along the Santa Ynez River, and he has kept his winemaking operation right here in downtown Santa Barbara. When the Lafond Vineyard matured, Pierre brought in Bruce McGuire to take over winemaking operations.

This tasting room is part of the fermentation facility, so you are right in the middle of the action. Here you can indulge in all sorts of taste pleasers, including chocolate zinfandel sauce, chocolate hazelnut cabernet fudge, breads and

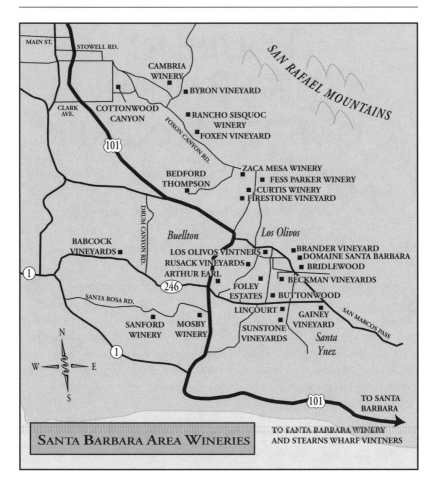

SANTA BARBARA AREA WINERIES

dipping oils, and bread spreads. To indulge a different sort of taste you'll also find winery tote bags, fun miniature French scenery prints, and one of the best collections of cookbooks we have seen in a winery tasting room. Be sure to wander around to the right behind the tasting bar to see the photo gallery that leads to the tank room.

Members of the Santa Barbara Winery Gourmet Club receive quarterly shipments of delightful gourmet goods paired with wines, suggested menus, and recipe ideas for an average shipment cost of $35. This is a one-of-a-kind opportunity for food and wine fans.

Santa Barbara Winery sponsors the Santa Barbara Winery 10 Mile Run with Gold's Gym 5K Fun Run the fourth Saturday in April. The event includes a gourmet food and wine tasting after the early morning race.

Fine points: Featured wines: Chardonnay, Sauvignon Blanc, Johannisberg Riesling, White Zinfandel, Pinot Noir Vin Gris, Paradis Riesling, Cabernet Franc, Cabernet Sauvignon, Pinot Noir, Beaujour (Zinfandel), Syrah, Zinfandel, Late Harvest Sauvignon Blanc. Owner: Pierre Lafond. Winemaker: Bruce McGuire. Cases: 30,000. Acres: 100.

❧ *Santa Barbara Winery, 202 Anacapa Street, Santa Barbara 93101; (805) 963–3633 or (800) 225–3633, fax (800) 411–9463; e-mail: wine@sbwinery.com; Web site: www.sbwinery.com. Open 10:00 A.M.–5:00 P.M. daily. Tasting fee: $3.00 (includes logo glass). Visa, MasterCard, American Express. Wheelchair accessible.*

SANTA YNEZ VALLEY

The Santa Ynez Valley gets its name from the Santa Ynez River, which runs east to west, south of Highway 246, under Highway 101, and out to the Pacific Ocean. West of Highway 101, Highway 246 roughly parallels Santa Rosa Road, and, more accurately, Santa Rosa Road roughly parallels the river. Sanford and Mosby wineries, where we take you first, are both off Santa Rosa Road west of Buellton.

To get to them both, take Highway 246 west from Highway 101, and turn left on Santa Rosa Road. Mosby comes first on your left, but we suggest you go all the way to Sanford (5 miles west of Buellton) and then come back to Mosby on the same (south) side of beautiful Santa Rosa Road.

Vineyardists Richard and Thekla Sanford established SANFORD WINERY in 1981 in what had been a dairy farm. They remodeled the original dairy building into their offices and tasting room, so enjoy the rural feeling. This is a great place to picnic, undisturbed just south of the Santa Ynez River.

Fine points: Featured wines: Chardonnay, Sauvignon Blanc, Pinot Noir Vin Gris, Pinot Noir. Owners: Richard and Thekla Sanford. Winemaker: Bruno D'Alfonso. Cases: 45,000. Acres: 12 and buy from Santa Barbara County.

❧ *Sanford Winery, 7250 Santa Rosa Road, Buellton 93427; (805) 688–3300, fax (805) 688–7381. Open 11:00 A.M.–4:00 P.M. daily. Tasting fee: none. Visa, MasterCard, American Express. Wheelchair accessible via back door.*

The property on which the MOSBY WINERY stands was originally the de la Cuesta land grant (until the 1950s) and was then owned by Hollywood playwright Vince Evans. Bill and Jeri Mosby bought the property in 1979.

In 1999 Bill retired after forty-two years as a dentist in Lompoc. A native of Klamath Falls, Oregon, he was high school state wrestling champion and at

Oregon State University twice prevailed as Pacific Coast wrestling champion before going to dental school. Jeri says Bill's winemaking fascination "began as a hobby but by the early eighties our wine was winning serious awards and Bill was expanding the vineyards to include more of the Italian varietals."

Many locals discouraged Bill from trying to grow Italian varietals here, but fortunately he ignored them. Now he is adding two Rhone varietals, Syrah and Mourvedre, from son Mike's Monterey County vineyards and Chimere Winery in Santa Maria.

You'll recognize Gary out in the vineyard by his worn red beret.

Fine points: Featured wines: Chardonnay, Pinot Grigio, Moscato di Fior D'Arancio, Traminer Aromatico, Gewürztraminer, Moscato di Santa Barbara sparkling wine, Rosato di Sangiovese, Sangiovese, Nebbiolo, Dolcetto, Teroldego, Roso di Santa Barbara, Grappa di Traminer. Owners: Bill and Jeri Mosby. Winemaker: Bill Mosby. Cases: 10,000. Acres: 40.

❧ *Mosby Winery, 9496 Santa Rosa Road, PO Box 1849, Buellton 93427; (805) 688–2415 or (800) 70–MOSBY, fax (805) 686–4288; e-mail: kryspro@yahoo.com; Web site: www.mosbywines.com. Open 10:00 A.M.–4:00 P.M. Monday–Friday, 10:00 A.M.–5:00 P.M. Saturday–Sunday. Tasting fee: $2.50 including glass. Visa, MasterCard, American Express, Discover. Wheelchair accessible.*

Just 0.7 mile east of the Chumash Indian Casino on Highway 246, turn right (south) on Refugio Road to LinCourt and Sunstone wineries. Sunstone is 1.4 miles south of Highway 246.

SUNSTONE VINEYARDS & WINERY is just before the bridge over the Santa Ynez River. Turn a sharp right onto the dirt road and park to the left.

EASY CHILI
from Mosby Winery, Buellton

1 lb. lean stew beef cut in ¾ inch cubes

1 lb. very lean pork cut in small pieces

2 large onions, minced

6 cloves garlic, minced

3 slices bacon

16 oz. can tomatillo or tomato

2 tsp. salt

1 Tbs. corn starch or corn meal

1 ½ tsp. black pepper

¼ tsp. each of dried oregano, sage, and cumin

1 or more Tbs. Mexican cocoa

1 cup coffee (decaf OK)

hot peppers

red wine for thinning

Sauté onions. Combine onions and all other ingredients except wine in large pot and cook till meat is done. Add wine for desired consistency. Simmer 1 hour or more. Great for large gatherings. Serve with warm bread and Mosby Nebbiolo wine. Enjoy!

SUNSTONE VINEYARDS &
WINERY'S EXTERIOR WALL

Designed to create the ambience of a French country winery, and succeeding, Sunstone is one of the most charming wineries you will find anywhere. When you drive onto the grounds, be sure to notice the fabulous multimaterial wall on the eastern end of the building, visible especially when the climbing vines are leafless. The feeling continues in the elegant patio rimmed in rosemary and lavender, in the tasting room, and in the historically accurate Provençal kitchen, complete with wood-burning oven, where elegant meals are prepared and cooking classes are given.

Although grape growing was in Fred Rice's blood (his great-grandfather grew for Inglenook Winery), Fred and Linda had farmed in the Coachella Valley and lived in Santa Barbara before finding this fifty-five-acre property in 1988 to organically farm Merlot, Cabernet Sauvignon, Syrah, Viognier, and Mourvedre varietals. Having only planned to sell grapes to others, they borrowed equipment from friends Marcy and Fess Parker and made their first wines in 1992. The Rices still hand-harvest, hand-sort, and gently crush their fruit.

The Rices' son Bion believes that tasting the wines here at the winery helps the taster experience the *terroir* (soil makeup and surroundings) of this unusual place. Don't miss a chance to explore the 120-foot stone cave dug into the hillside, where wines rest in French oak barrels and elegant dinners are served occasionally. The tasting room offers wines, of course, as well as pasta sauces, grapeseed oils, grape-shape pastas, Merlot wine jelly, Pinot Noir chocolate cherries, and their Eros poster of *The Kiss* by James-Paul Brown.

SUNSTONE VINEYARDS &
WINERY'S KITCHEN AT END
OF TASTING ROOM

Fine points: Featured wines: Chardonnay, Merlot, Cabernet Sauvignon, Eros, Syrah, Muscat Canelli. Owners: The Rice Family. Winemaker: Fred Rice. Cases: 10,000. Acres: 54.

❧ *Sunstone Vineyards and Winery, 125 North Refugio Road, Santa Ynez 93460; (805) 688–9463 or (800) 688–WINE, fax (805) 686–1881. Tasting fee: $3.00. Open 10:00 A.M.–4:00 P.M. daily. Visa, MasterCard, American Express. Wheelchair accessible.*

Halfway between Sunstone and Highway 246 east is LinCourt Vineyards, formerly known as Santa Ynez Winery, in a gray bat-and-board building with a wooden deck with picnic tables, affording great views of the valley. Originally part of the 36,000-acre Mexican land grant where El Colegio de Nuestra del Refugio was in the mid-1880s, the land was bought in 1923 by the Hunt family, which operated a dairy ranch here for fifty years. The colegio's chapel became part of the farmhouse; Claire Hunt Bettencourt still lives there.

Claire's late in-laws planted grapes and converted the dairy building to Santa Ynez Winery with neighbors named Davidge, using milk tanks as wine fermenting tanks. Fred Brander was the original winemaker in 1976, well awarded for his Sauvignon Blanc and Blanc de Cabernet.

The tasting room was built in 1982. Doug and Candy Scott owned the works from 1988 to 1996, when William P. Foley II, CEO of Karl Karcher Enterprises, whose holdings include Fidelity National Title and American Title companies, bought Santa Ynez Winery. Foley, who also owns Foley Estates Vineyard and Winery, has brought in new plantings of Chardonnay and Pinot Noir grapes and renamed the winery LinCourt Vineyards.

Fine points: Featured wines: Chenin Blanc, Pinot Blanc, Chardonnay, Trousseau Gris, Cotillion white table wine, Pinot Noir, Cabernet Sauvignon. Owner: William P. Foley II. Winemaker: Alan Phillips. Cases: 15,000. Acres: 32 plus.

❧ *LinCourt Vineyards, 343 North Refugio Road, Santa Ynez 93460; (805) 688–8381, fax (805) 688–3764. Open 10:00 A.M.–5:00 P.M. daily. Tasting fee: $3.00 includes logo glass. Visa, MasterCard, American Express, Discover. Not wheelchair accessible.*

Turn right (south) from Highway 246 into the Gainey Vineyard road 2.3 miles east of the Refugio Road intersection and continue 0.2 mile on Gainey's excellent paved driveway, which circles a grassy, tree-shaded central court, which seats 700 guests at concerts, at the winery's entrance. Joan Baez and her son Gabriel, the Presentation Hall Jazz Band, and Rita Coolidge exemplify the range of entertainers who perform here.

GAINEY VINEYARD'S PICNIC AND PERFORMANCE CIRCLE,
SANTA YNEZ

Designed to be an educational forum as well as a lovely place to enjoy wines, the tasting room has white walls (lined with stars' photos), wood-beamed ceilings with skylights, and Mexican tile floors. *Wine Spectator* has called Gainey the "best tasting spot on the Central Coast," and *Los Angeles Times'* Robert Lawrence Balzer says "Gainey Vineyard is one of the most beautiful wineries in the world." Kathleen likes the side table loaded with free recipes and tasting note information.

Unlike other wineries that usually have vineyards close to their winery, Gainey has them both here and in the cooler Santa Barbara zone west of Highway 101 off Santa Barbara Road. Gainey's Chardonnay has received 98s in a *Wine Spectator* California Chardonnay vs. white Burgundy wines blind tasting. Stephen Tanzer calls Gainey's Pinot Noir "sexy juice,"

POTATO-GARLIC SOUP WITH ROSEMARY BUTTER
from Gainey Vineyard, Santa Ynez

3 cups chicken broth

1 lb. russet potatoes, diced

20 cloves garlic, peeled

½ cup milk

½ cup heavy cream

2 Tbs. butter

1 ½ tsp. fresh rosemary, chopped

Bring chicken broth, garlic, and potatoes to a boil and simmer until tender, about 15–20 minutes. Remove from heat and puree in a blender or processor. Return to a saucepan, add milk and heavy cream, and heat through. Season with salt and pepper. Mix together the butter and rosemary and drop a teaspoonful into each bowl of soup. Serves four. Serve with Gainey Vineyard Chardonnay.

PENNE WITH VODKA AND TOMATO CREAM SAUCE
from Gainey Vineyard, Santa Ynez

1 Tbs. butter	¼ cup vodka
1 Tbs. olive oil	¼ tsp. crushed red peppers
1 medium yellow onion, chopped	1 lb. penne (mostaciolli) pasta
1-28 oz. can plum tomatoes, drained, seeded, and chopped	fresh grated Parmesan cheese
1 cup whipping cream	chives

Sauté onion in oil and butter until translucent. Add tomatoes and simmer until the juice from the tomatoes is reduced by half, stirring frequently. Add cream, vodka, and peppers, and simmer until thickened. Season with salt and pepper. Toss with cooked pasta and top with Parmesan cheese and chives. Serves four. Serve with Gainey Vineyard Cabernet Sauvignon.

---

and the winery won a four-star gold medal for its 1997 Riesling at the Orange County Fair.

Unusual in winery tasting rooms, Gainey sells biscotti for $1.00 to go with your wine. What a pleasure! You can also enjoy Snapple, Gallo salami, cheeses, and Marcel & Henri's fine pâtés or your own picnic in the garden. Ask about cooking classes, winemaker's dinners, concerts, and their unusual harvest crush party, a real hoot and learning experience.

Fine points: Featured wines: Chardonnay, Sauvignon Blanc, Riesling, Merlot, Pinot Noir, Cabernet Sauvignon, and Cabernet Franc. Owners: father and son Dan J. Gainey and Dan H. Gainey. Winemaker: Dan H. Gainey. Cases: 20,000. Acres 120.

Gainey Vineyard, 3950 East Highway 246, Santa Ynez 93460; (805) 688–0558, fax (805) 688–5864. Open 10:00 A.M.–4:45 or 5:00 P.M. daily; tours at 11:00 A.M. and 1:00, 2:00, and 3:00 P.M. Tasting fee: $3.00 (keep the glass). Visa, MasterCard, American Express. Wheelchair accessible.

As you come out of Gainey, turn right (east) on Highway 246 east, and then take a careful left (north) on Highway 154 to visit Domaine Santa Barbara and Brander Vineyard.

About 3 miles north on Highway 154, turn right (east) on Roblar Avenue, and turn immediately left on the frontage road to Domaine Santa Barbara and Brander wineries, both of whose wines are available at Brander. Brander is the

BRANDER VINEYARD'S CHATEAU
TASTING ROOM, LOS OLIVOS

only winery we have seen that is designed to look like a pink French chateau with turrets. (The chateau is on Brander's labels.)

BRANDER VINEYARD is the baby of Fred Brander, who won his first gold medal in 1978 as winemaker at the old Santa Ynez Valley Winery (now LinCourt) and thereby became the first Santa Barbara winemaker to win a gold medal anywhere. Fred fell in love with high school chemistry, went to Harvey Mudd College, imported European wines, and then studied enology at UC/Davis. Now Brander mixes great wines with great foods at special events throughout the year.

HARVESTERS' STEW
from Fred Brander, Brander Vineyard, Los Olivos

(NOTE: SINCE FRED'S RECIPE SERVES EIGHTY HARVESTERS, AND WE HAVEN'T HAD EIGHTY GUESTS LATELY, I HAVE ADAPTED HIS RECIPE TO SERVE TEN TO TWELVE GENEROUSLY.—KATHLEEN HILL)

2 lbs. beef, preferably chuck or bottom round cut into 2-inch cubes

5 small white onions

6 cloves garlic

4 cloves

16 carrots cut in 1-inch pieces

2 celery stalks

1 clove, ground

4 tomatoes, sliced

1 tsp. salt

large pinch pepper

mustard

thick country bread

Lard the beef with the garlic and cloves and place it in a stewing pot filled with cold water to which the salt has been added. When water comes to a boil, remove foam with a spoon. While the water is still boiling, add all the vegetables and ground clove and simmer for 3 hours. Salt and pepper to taste. Cut thick slices of country bread, spread with mustard, and pour the very hot soup over it. Serve with Brander Merlot.

CHRISTMAS GOOSE
from Fred Brander, Brander Vineyard, Los Olivos

---

8 lb. goose

salt and freshly ground pepper

1 ½ lb. Golden Delicious apples

15 Tbs. unsalted butter

1 ½ lb. pork sausage

12 oz. chestnuts, canned

pinch cinnamon

1 medium carrot, quartered

1 stalk celery, cut into thirds

1 medium onion, quartered

1 cup white wine

Rinse goose with cool water inside and out. Remove wing tips, neck, and gizzard. Sprinkle inside and out with salt and pepper.

For stuffing: Peel, core, and quarter apples. Heat 4 Tbs. butter in frying pan and sauté apples until tender. In separate pan sauté sausage until lightly brown. Remove both apples and sausage with slotted spoon, roughly chop, and combine in bowl. Crumble in chestnuts, season with salt, pepper, and pinch of cinnamon. Mix carefully. Stuff goose and truss.

Preheat oven to 425° F.

Heat 4 Tbs. butter in roasting pan, add goose and brown on all sides. Add carrot, onion, celery, neck, and gizzard. Roast until juices run clear when thigh is pierced. When cooked, transfer goose to a platter, cover with foil, and let stand for 15 minutes. For sauce, deglaze roasting pan with wine and strain. Serve sauce in gravy boat on the side. Serves four to six. Serve with either Brander Cuvee Natalie or Domaine Santa Barbara Pinot Noir.

Enjoy copies of Paul Gauguin's paintings (from $900) on the tasting room walls or picnic under the poplar and cottonwood trees. Tasting room manager Theresa Stanton is extremely helpful and shares her personal flair and enthusiasm. Flowers and London plane trees combine to create a colorful ambience. Do not miss the Santa Barbara Bouillabaisse Festival, held at Brander the third Sunday in May, at which twenty-five local restaurants compete in a seafood cook-off to showcase dry rosé wines and benefit local charities.

DOMAINE SANTA BARBARA is a sister winery to Brander and focuses on Burgundian varietal wines from grapes purchased in Santa Barbara County.

Fine points: Featured wines: Brander label Chardonnay, Sauvignon Blanc (four styles), Semillon, Merlot, Cabernet Sauvignon, Bouchet Tête de Cuvee; Domaine Santa Barbara label Chardonnay, Pinot Gris, Pinot Noir. Owner: Fred Brander. Winemaker: Brander, Fred Brander; Domaine Santa Barbara, Steve Clifton.

DOMAINE SANTA BARBARA, LOS OLIVOS

Cases: Brander 10,000, Domaine Santa Barbara 7,000. Acres: 45.
🍃 *Brander Vineyard and Domaine Santa Barbara, Highway 154 at Roblar Road (frontage road), PO Box 92, Los Olivos 93441; (805) 688–2455, fax (805) 688–8010; Web site: www.brander.com. Open 10:00 A.M.–5:00 P.M. daily summer, 10:00 A.M.–4:00 P.M. daily winter. Tasting fee: $2.50 which goes toward bottle purchase. Visa, MasterCard, American Express. Wheelchair accessible.*

As you leave Brander and Domaine Santa Barbara, turn south on the frontage road, then turn left (east) onto Roblar Avenue to visit brand-new and spectacular Bridlewood.

BRIDLEWOOD WINERY is possibly the most spectacular winery on the central coast. Cory Holbrook sold his wholesale flower business in Medford, Oregon, to fulfill his twenty-year dream of owning his own winery and of using his successful flower-growing techniques in wine growing.

Stressing a team approach, Cory retained respected Daniel Gehrs from Zaca Mesa (an independent-thinking political science major from UC/Santa Cruz) as consulting winemaker. Bridlewood also hired Randy Pace, an MBA, from Stag's Leap Cellars as business manager.

Cory bought this fabulous property, a former Arabian horse ranch complete with horses, racetrack, ponds, and swans. The new mission-style building and

BRIDLEWOOD WINERY'S BRAND-NEW FACILITY,
SANTA YNEZ

visitor center is surrounded by lush lawns, oak trees, rose gardens, croquet courts, and ponds, with wrought-iron tables and chairs for picnicking.

In its first year, Bridlewood won six medals at the San Diego National Wine Competition, quite a shot out of the starting gate. Stop just to experience the splendor.

Fine points: Featured wines: Chardonnay, Viognier, Viognier Reserve, Pinot Blanc, Riesling, Saddlesore Rosé, Syrah, Pinot Noir, and Sangiovese. Owner: Mr. and Mrs. Cory Holbrook. Cases: 15,000. Acres: 105.

❧ *Bridlewood Winery, 3555 Roblar Avenue, Santa Ynez 93460, (805) 688–9000, fax (805) 688–2443; Web site: www.bridlewoodwinery.com. Open 10:00 A.M.–5:00 P.M. daily. Visa, MasterCard, American Express. Wheelchair accessible.*

After you have lunch in Los Olivos (See Chapter 3), simply take Alamo Pintado Road off Grand Avenue to Foley, Rideau, and Buttonwood wineries. If you have lunch in Ballard, Baseline Avenue will take you to Alamo Pintado, where you turn left.

On the west side of Alamo Pintado just south of Baseline Avenue is the driveway to FOLEY ESTATES VINEYARD AND WINERY. Wind up the road to the charming yellow-and-white 1900s dairy farmhouse that now serves as Foley's tasting room. Drive past the house and turn right before the redwood dairy barn, now the functioning winery, into the parking lot. Stroll around the lawn and peacefully take a deep breath and view your surroundings.

The tasting room (in what were the living and dining rooms) has pine floors, ceiling fans, and a brass rail at the bar.

William P. Foley II bought the estate from the Firestone family in April 1997 to fulfill his lifelong dream of developing a world-class wine estate. Foley winemaker Alan Phillips has a notable background, beginning with his studies in enology at UC/Davis in 1976, during which time he worked under the amazing André Tchelistcheff at S. Anderson Vineyards in Yountville on weekends and evenings. In 1981 he and Jay Corley formed Monticello Cellars in the Napa Valley, and after ten years helped with start-ups of several wineries, including Vine Cliff Cellars, V & L Eisele Vineyards, and Kates Vineyard & Winery. Then he consulted in New Zealand, Germany, France, Spain, and Portugal. Most recently he served as winemaker at Byington Winery in the Santa Cruz Mountains.

Fine points: Featured wines: Chardonnay, Sauvignon Blanc, Pinot Noir, Syrah. Owner: William P. Foley II. General manager and winemaker: Alan Phillips. Cases: 15,000. Acres: 12.5

❧ *Foley Estates Vineyard and Winery, 1711 Alamo Pintado Road, Solvang 93463; (805) 688–8554, fax (805) 688–9327. Open 10:00 A.M.–5:00 P.M. daily. Visa, MasterCard, American Express. Not wheelchair accessible.*

A half mile south on Alamo Pintado you will find both Rideau and Buttonwood wineries on the left side of the road. Rideau closes at 4:30 P.M., so be sure to visit it before Buttonwood if you want to get to both.

Nestled in huge oak trees, RIDEAU VINEYARD's tasting room occupies the historic 1884 Alamo Pintado adobe, now beautifully restored. Enjoy the picnic tables on the adobe's porch as well as the tranquil scene. You'll never want to leave.

New Orleans native Iris Rideau used to live up the hill and for ten years drove past the old adobe that had been the Alamo Pintado Stage Coach Inn, which thrived on the overflow from Mattei's Tavern and Inn. Iris just wanted to restore the building, once part of the de la Cuesta land grant, but ended up creating a winery as well in her spare time from her work as a financial planner in Los Angeles.

Now you can visit her delightful project and sample her Creole jambalaya, gumbo, and dips, as well as her fine wines. Kathryn Kepler hosts the tasting room and delightful gift shop. Check out the French wine tasting glasses. Or picnic at the tables under huge ancient oaks.

James Rutherford, formerly at Gainey and Brander wineries, replaced Richard Longoria as Rideau winemaker in 1999.

Fine points: Featured wines: Rhones Syrah, Viognier, Merlot. Owner: Iris Rideau. Winemaker: James Rutherford. Cases: 3,000. Acres: 15.

❧ *Rideau Vineyard, 1562 Alamo Pintado Road, Solvang 93463;*

(805) 688–0717, fax (805) 688–8048. Open 11:00 A.M.–4:30 P.M. daily. Tasting fee: $4.00 includes French glass. Visa, MasterCard, American Express, Discover. Wheelchair accessible.

Another 0.8 mile south of Rideau is homey BUTTONWOOD FARM WINERY & VINEYARD, a rare spot in any wine country. At Buttonwood there is no pretense, no snootiness, and there is lots of friendliness, interesting artwork, herb and vegetable gardens, and women.

Buttonwood is another name for sycamore, which surround the winery. This is a winery property of character and characters. Eighty-something Buttonwood founder and owner Betty Williams works and walks her farm, tall, straight, hat on head, Mexican or Indian jewelry around her neck, walking stick in hand and dog Katie at her heel. You might chat with her while she arranges her precious flowers in the tasting room.

BUTTONWOOD FARM
WINERY & VINEYARD
TASTING ROOM, SOLVANG

Betty grew up in Louisiana in the Huey Long era with the superb cooking of her mother Miss Delphine, whose cookbook you can buy in the tasting room. She graduated from Sarah Lawrence College, did postgraduate work at Tulane University, moved to Southern California, raised three children, got a law degree from the University of Southern California, and taught school. And by that time she was only fifty.

In 1968 Betty bought this property and developed it into a Thoroughbred horse breeding facility, devoting her "spare time" to community activities, including being cofounder of the land trust for Santa Barbara County. In 1983 she began to plant grapes on the mesa portion of Buttonwood. Twelve acres of organic farm replaced the horses (my, it must be fertile!), and now what is left of that effort is right behind the tasting room.

Betty moved on to reading fiction and nonfiction, investigating the Internet, becoming an e-mail junkie, writing poetry, and caring for her dog.

Don't miss the Japanese (Sumi) pen-and-ink drawings of Seyburn Zorthian, Betty's daughter and partner, which also grace the winery's labels. Originals, prints, and posters are available in the tasting room, as is Betty's charmingly written and photographed book, *The Third Leaf* ($10), on the development of a vineyard.

SEYBURN'S SUMPTUOUS SPREAD (WITH A TOMATO TWIST)
from Seyburn Zorthian, Buttonwood Farm, Solvang

---

1 cup ricotta cheese	*1 jar Buttonwood Farm sun-dried tomatoes*
¾ cup cream cheese	*Jane's Crazy Mixed-up salt, to taste*
¼ cup lemon juice	*fresh oregano*
2 cloves garlic	*olive oil*

Blend first 6 ingredients in a food processor. [*Spread on baguette slices, toasted or not.*—Kathleen Hill.] Garnish with fresh oregano and olive oil.

Fine points: Featured wines: Marsanne, Semillon, Sauvignon Blanc, Merlot, Cabernet Sauvignon, Cabernet Franc, Trevin (Cabernet blend), and Kalyra's Black Muscat, Vintage Port, Tawny Port. Owners: Betty Williams, Seyburn Zorthian, and Bret C. Davenport. Winemaker: Michael Brown. Cases: 6,000. Acres: 160.

❧ *Buttonwood Farm Winery & Vineyard, 1500 Alamo Pintado Road, PO Box 1007, Solvang 93464; (805) 688–3032, fax (805) 688–6168; e-mail: info@buttonwoodwinery.com. Open 11:00 A.M.–5:00 P.M. daily. Tasting fee: $3.50 includes glass. Visa, MasterCard, American Express. Wheelchair accessible.*

While it is not in this natural travel pattern, we don't want you to miss RUSACK VINEYARDS on Ballard Canyon Road. You can get to it two ways: From Solvang, take either Ballard Canyon Road just east of Highway 101 or Chalk Hill Road northward. When Chalk Hill intersects with Ballard Canyon Road, follow Ballard Canyon north to Rusack, which will be on the left (west) side of the road.

Nestled in the Ballard Canyon amid lush, wild west green or golden rolling hills, depending on the season, Rusack is the perfect place for a quiet picnic on its redwood deck built around four huge, elegant oak trees.

Alison and Geoff Rusack bought Ballard Canyon Winery in 1992 after successful careers as a Hollywood scriptwriter (Alison) and Santa Monica attorney (Geoff). You can't blame them for choosing this sublime life over Los Angeles traffic.

Rusack is a small, personal winery that produces excellent handcrafted wines and sells only the best in winery gifts. Be sure to notice the beautiful teardrop Citation wine glasses.

Fine points: Featured wines: Chardonnay, Anacapa (Cabernet Sauvignon, Merlot, and Cabernet Franc blend), Muscat Canelli, Soul of the Vine Viognier dessert wine. Owners: Alison and Geoff Rusack. Winemaker: Geoff Rusack. Cases: 3,500. Acres: 40.

❧ *Rusack Vineyards, 1819 Ballard Canyon Road, Solvang 93463; (805) 688–1278; e-mail: rusackvin@aol.com. Open summer 11:00 A.M.–5:00 P.M. daily, winter 11:00 A.M.–5:00 P.M. Friday–Sunday. Tasting fee: $3.75 includes teardrop Citation glass. Visa and MasterCard. Wheelchair accessible.*

FOXEN CANYON WINE TRAIL

The Foxen Canyon Wine Trail basically covers the eleven wineries you can get to via Foxen Canyon Road, which runs from Los Olivos in the Santa Ynez Valley, up the mesa that runs northwestward along the base of the San Rafael Mountains, through the little Santa Maria Valley, and into the city of Santa Maria itself.

You can also start in Santa Maria and get to Foxen Canyon Road by taking the Betteravia Road (east) exit from Highway 101, following it eastward until it turns right (south). At a fork, take Dominion Road to the right for Cottonwood Canyon Vineyard & Winery, or ease to the left on Foxen Canyon Road, and then leftish again to Cambria, and Byron wineries. Tepusquet Road between Byron Winery and Foxen Canyon Road has been washed out, so you should either retrace your tracks to Foxen Canyon Road, or approach the rest of the wineries from Los Olivos.

So here we go. Since there are no restaurants or delis on the Foxen Canyon Wine Trail, we recommend that you either load up with picnic supplies in Los Olivos or Ballard, or make sure that you have had enough to eat before you leave. A few wineries offer some snacks and soft drinks, but nothing very substantial.

We recommend that instead of following Foxen Canyon Road, known on the Ballard side of Highway 154 as Ballard Canyon Road, you go north on Highway 154 or Highway 101 and turn east on Zaca Station Road up this gorgeous valley and into the hills so you won't miss Firestone Vineyard or Curtis Winery.

As you wind your way through these gorgeous Western movie backdrops, you come to the actual Pacific Gas & Electric Zaca Station. This really does look like Fess Parker (Davy Crockett) country! After 2.6 miles turn left up the hill 0.6 mile to FIRESTONE VINEYARD, a real treat to visit. The view from this oak-studded knoll overlooking the estate vineyards is truly breathtaking Wild West.

The stories of the Firestone family and fortune and of the life of their winemaker, Alison Green Doran, are worth reading. The Firestone family fortune came from tires and rubber, which is why most of us know the name. In the

VIEW FROM FIRESTONE VINEYARD, LOS OLIVOS

early 1970s Leonard Firestone purchased a parcel of Santa Ynez Valley, and with his son, Brooks, planted 260 acres of grapes. In 1972 Brooks, his wife Kate, and his father began the winery. Eventually Suntory Ltd. of Japan, the huge wine and spirits company, bought 31 percent of the winery, and in 1994 the Firestones bought out Suntory, returning the entire winery to a family operation. In 1996 Firestone added its Prosperity label, inexpensive table wines, to their list, starting at $6.00 up to a blend with Chilean Merlot at $12 for 1.5 liter.

This highly active and connected political (Republican) family has produced Late Harvest Rieslings served by four U. S. presidents: Reagan, Ford, Bush, and Clinton. A framed handwritten note says "Dear Brooks—Thanks so much for the treat of treats—That Riesling was superb—George Bush."

In 1987 the Firestones purchased Carey Cellars, renamed it Curtis, sold it in 1997, and opened a new must-see small facility just up the road. Following Brooks Firestone's election to the California state assembly, his older son Adam left his law practice to become president of Firestone. Since then Firestone continues to be a "multigenerational project," says Brooks Firestone. Hayley Firestone Jessup runs the retail operations, Kate C. Anderson (Adam's wife) works with distributors in the Northwest, Polly Firestone Walker works in public relations, and Andrew conducts tours and makes beer.

Be sure to check out the second room of this elegant redwood and stone masonry tasting room. Here you can purchase a wide range of condiments (try the Zinfandel orange mustard or the garlic mayonnaise with Sauvignon Blanc), pasta sauces (including artichoke and Zinfandel Bar B Que Sauce),

ORZO WITH MINT AND TOMATOES
from Kate Firestone, Firestone Vineyard, Los Olivos

(NOTE: YOU CAN SAUTÉ THE ONIONS AND COOK THE PASTA UP TO ONE DAY AHEAD, BUT CHOP THE MINT AT THE LAST MINUTE BECAUSE IT OFTEN TURNS BLACK IF IT SITS AROUND.)

2 onions (1 lb.) chopped

2 Tbs. olive oil

3 cups orzo pasta, uncooked

2 qts. water

½ cup chicken broth

⅓ cup lemon juice

¼ cup parsley, minced

2 tomatoes (1 lb.), cored, seeded, and chopped

½ cup minced fresh mint leaves, plus mint sprigs for garnish

salt and pepper

Combine onions and oil in a 10- to 12-inch frying pan over medium-high heat. Stir often until onions are browned and taste sweet, about 15 minutes.

Meanwhile, cook the orzo in 2 quarts boiling water until tender to bite, 6–8 minutes. Drain, rinse with cold water until pasta is cool, then drain again.

In a large bowl, mix together cool cooked orzo, chopped onions, ½ cup broth, lemon juice, and minced parsley. (If making ahead, chill mixture, airtight, up to 1 day.) Add tomatoes and mint just before serving. Garnish with mint sprigs and season to taste with salt and pepper. Serves ten. (*This recipe goes well with all Firestone wines, particularly the Sauvignon Blanc.* —Kathleen Hill)

grapeseed oils, and chocolate sauces with coffee and Merlot or raspberry and Pinot Noir.

Winemaker Alison Green Doran began working as a wine lab technician at the age of fourteen when her parents bought Simi Winery in Sonoma County. André Tchelistcheff, her father's consulting winemaker, discovered Alison's abilities. "You are gifted, you can do this!" he told her, and eventually talked her into switching her major to fermentation science at UC/Davis and to use her "very sensitive nose and palate."

Alison worked for five months at L'Institute National des Recherches Agronomiques in Alsace, France, and returned to the Hoffman Mountain Ranch in 1976 where André Tchelistcheff was also consultant. She came to Firestone as enologist under winemaker Tony Austin while completing her degree at Davis, and then became winemaker at Firestone in 1981 under the guidance of her mentor Tchelistcheff, who remained consultant to the winery until 1989. Married and the mother of Matthew, Alison is also a master chef and enjoys tennis, gardening, opera, and travel.

Fine points: Featured wines: Chardonnay, Sauvignon Blanc, Gewürztraminer, Chenin Blanc, Riesling, Muscat Canelli, Gemstone Rosé, Zinfandel Old Vines, Merlot, Cabernet Sauvignon, Latitude 34.5 Merlot, a 50-50 blend of Santa Ynez and Chilean, Reserve blend reds; Prosperity Red, White, Merlot (Chile). Owner: Brooks Firestone. Winemaker and master chef: Alison Green Doran. Cases: 200,000. Acres: 600.

❧ *Firestone Vineyard, 5017 Zaca Station Road, PO Box 244, Los Olivos 93441; (805) 688–3940, fax (805) 686–1256; Web site: www.firestonevineyard.com. Open 10:00 A.M.–5:00 P.M. daily. Tasting fee: none, $2.00 each for large groups by reservation. Visa, MasterCard, American Express, Discover. Wheelchair accessible including tours.*

ENTRANCE TO CURTIS WINERY, LOS OLIVOS

As you leave Firestone, turn left (east) up Zaca Station Road. Almost immediately you see oil wells, and in 0.6 miles turn left up to Curtis Winery. You can also enter or exit from the entrance near Zaca Station's intersection with Foxen Canyon Road.

In contrast to its sister winery, Firestone, CURTIS WINERY is much more rustic, nestled in huge oak trees, with charmingly rough paths to the winery building and interesting old farm machinery and implements displayed under the trees. Curtis is a gravity-flow winery, so be sure to tour the premises to see nature at work.

Winemaker Chuck Carlson, who serves as assistant winemaker at Firestone, created Firestone's Chilean wine program, including its Prosperity

Merlot blend called Latitude 34.5. Chuck graduated from California State University at Fresno, first went to work for Zaca Mesa up the road in 1981 as a lab technician, and soon became assistant winemaker. He joined Firestone Vineyard's winemaking team in 1992 as assistant winemaker and has worked to develop a Rhone program for Curtis beginning with the 1995 vintage. Chuck has the rare advantage of having worked close to the Foxen Canyon earth for nearly twenty years.

Curtis was Brooks Firestone's mother's maiden name. Appropriately Curtis' Rhone program began with release of the 1995 Curtis Ambassador's Vineyard Syrah. Chuck and his wife Kathleen (good name) have two beautiful children, Chas and Emily, and Chuck also enjoys getting his feet wet fly-fishing, spreading his wings and flying, and ruining a good walk by playing golf.

Fine points: Featured wines: Chardonnay, Sauvignon Blanc, Viognier, Muscat, Syrah, Syrah Rosé, Carignane, Cabernet Sauvignon, Cabernet Franc, Merlot. Owners: The Firestone family. Winemaker: Chuck E. Carlson. Cases: 5,000 (goal 40,000). Acres: Firestone's 600 plus buy from Santa Barbara County.

❧ *Curtis Winery, 5249 Foxen Canyon Road, Los Olivos 93441; (805) 686–8999. Open 10:00 A.M.–5:00 P.M. daily. Tasting fee: $2.50, or $5.00 with Curtis Bohemia crystal glass. Visa, MasterCard, American Express. Wheelchair accessible.*

As you turn left up Zaca Station Road toward Fess Parker's fun winery and vineyard, be sure to enjoy the daffodils along the road (if your timing is right) at the edge of Douglas Vineyards. A mile and a half up Zaca Station, turn right

FESS PARKER WINERY & VINEYARD, LOS OLIVOS

FISH CHOWDER
from Marcy Parker, Fess Parker Winery & Vineyard, Los Olivos

1½ lbs. halibut

8 potatoes, thinly sliced

28-oz. can of tomatoes, whole or chopped

2 medium onions, chopped

1 ½ cup water

salt and pepper

1 ½ cubes butter

1 scant qt. half-and-half

Skin (butcher can do this part for you), bone, and cut the fish into 1-inch squares and place in stockpot. Add potatoes, tomatoes (chopped), onions, salt, pepper, and water and bring to a boil. Stir frequently so that the fish does not stick. Cook on low heat until ingredients are soft. Remove from heat before fish begins to fall apart. Add butter and half-and-half. Season to taste. Reheat when ready to serve. Serve with Fess Parker 1997 Chardonnay "Santa Barbara County."

(south) into FESS PARKER WINERY & VINEYARD, paying attention to the speed jumps. . .er, bumps. Notice when you park in the lot, it is rimmed with marguerites, lavender, and herbs. Divine! And to think Michael Jackson's Neverland is nearby.

Enormous oak trees frame this setting-appropriate winery made of local stone and stucco. Its stone floors, heavy wood and beams, walk-in (who would want to) fireplace, soft pink carpet, and antique furniture make visitors never want to go home. Fess' wife Marcy created the decor and did an excellent job of making a large facility feel like home. You might enjoy gourmet lunches on Marcella's Veranda, named for Marcy, from April to October. Fess Parker also encourages visitors to visit Fess Parker's Wine Country Inn & Spa in Los Olivos and its Vintage Room restaurant featuring American-Mediterranean style food.

Davy Crockett and Daniel Boone fans can pick up Daniel Boone and Disney character memorabilia and videos; Davy Crocket videos, magazines, and CDs; coonskin cork toppers; and even the *Cowboy Cookbook,* in which Fess has a recipe. This gift shop has some of the best and most subtle winery clothing we have seen, and it is definitely the only winery where we have seen Daniel Boone coonskin caps for sale! You will also find Fess Parker foods, caviar, cheese sticks, a wide selection of candles, table linens, and a Fess Parker tile clock. If you're lucky, the onetime "King of the Wild Frontier" will wander through and autograph your wine bottle.

However, the picnic grounds are for use by reservation only, and signs at the grounds entrance also warn "winery beverages only, no smoking, no dogs." July Fourth is always a fun (and crowded) time to visit when Western American history is reenacted on the vast lawn in full costume. You may also want to inquire about the many Santa Barbara area charity events held at Fess Parker.

Since Fess Parker trademarked the phrase "American Tradition" many years ago, he uses it on some of his labels. His definition of the phrase is: "Any business can succeed with the foundation of hard work, integrity, and a goal of excellence." Eli (Fess Jr.) Parker and his wife Laureen were married at the winery in 1995; they have five daughters between them and one son together.

Fine points: Featured wines: Sauvignon Blanc, Chenin Blanc, Chardonnay, Pinot Blanc, Viognier, Mélange (Marsanne and Viognier blend), Pinot Noir, Merlot, Gamay Napa, Zin Gris Mendocino County, Johannisberg Riesling, Muscat Canelli. Owner: The Fess Parker family. Winemaker: Eli (Fess Jr.) Parker. Cases: 45,000. Acres: 736.

❧ *Fess Parker Winery & Vineyard, 6200 Foxen Canyon Road, PO Box 908, Los Olivos 93441; (805) 688–1545, fax (805) 686–1130; Web site: www. FessParker.com. Open 10:00 A.M.–5:00 P.M. daily. Tasting fee: $3.00 includes Fess Parker glass. Visa, MasterCard, American Express. Wheelchair access is at right end of tasting room building.*

ZACA MESA'S GIANT CHESSBOARD OUTSIDE THE TASTING ROOM, LOS OLIVOS

To continue on our Foxen Canyon Wine Trail tour, turn right up Foxen Canyon Road as you come out of Fess Parker. (As if created for a Western movie set but actually the real thing, your surroundings include tumbleweeds and enormous oak trees with lichen hanging limp from their branches.) For the next 3 miles you wander up and down and around the lower San Rafael Mountains, et voilà you come down into a surprisingly peaceful hidden valley up on the Zaca Mesa, 1,500-feet high and above the fog line. In the Chumash Indian language, *zaca* means restful place. And guess what. This is where Zaca Mesa Winery is! This is truly the old California we read about.

Exactly 3.2 miles up Foxen Canyon Road from Fess Parker, turn left at the windmill between two stone posts to ZACA MESA WINERY, a place where you can hike on their well-maintained nature trails winding through native plants and wildflowers (as long as you hike responsibly), camp, and picnic on their lawn with Zack the dog. Play Zaca Mesa's "outdoor sport" of chess on their patio's life-size, 10-by-10-foot chessboard with 3-foot chess pieces and take a nap with Zack.

If you visit in autumn, you can witness the arrival of the winery's gypsy band of dancing scarecrows in the vineyards wearing its usual mix of baseball caps, long underwear, and hospital gowns.

For 2,000 years the Chumash Indians and then Spanish settlers revered Zaca Mesa's bounties and beauty. More recently, Zaca Mesa was the first winery in Santa Barbara county to plant the now-famous Syrah grape, and they now are almost sold out instantly of their Rhone-style varietals and blends. In 1995 Zaca Mesa's 1993 Syrah placed sixth in the world in *Wine Spectator*'s "Top 100 Wines of 1995."

Even if you don't like wine, make the trip to Zaca Mesa to enjoy the air and the natural beauty, as well as the delightfully friendly people and the art in the tasting room. You can't miss the masterly huge photo of Zaca Mesa on the wall. One of the most fun events of the year is Zaca Mesa's Dixie Chicken Barn Dance on Friday night of vintners' weekend in August. Gates open at 5:30 with a BBQ chicken dinner from 6:00 to 7:00 P.M. Willie Martinez of Ono BBQ caters the all-you-can-eat feast, which includes a salad bar and a banana split bar. Tickets are $55 and include Zaca Mesa wines.

Fine points: Featured wines: Chardonnay, Z Gris, Syrah, Z Cuvee, Roussanne, Mourvedre, Crenach, Viognier. Owners: Twin brothers John C. Cushman III and Louis B. Cushman. Winemaker: Benjamin Silver with Kathy Joseph, consulting winemaker. Cases: 50,000. Acres: 246.

🍇 *Zaca Mesa Winery, 6905 Foxen Canyon Road, Los Olivos 93441; (805) 688–9339 or (800) 350–7972; Web site: www.zacamesa.com. Open 10:00 A.M.–4:00 P.M. daily. Tasting fee: none. Visa, MasterCard, American Express. Wheelchair accessible.*

As you leave Zaca Mesa, turn left on Foxen Canyon Road for an exquisite 6.5 mile drive to FOXEN VINEYARD, the pride and joy of Bill Wathen and Richard Dore, great-great-grandson of early Santa Barbara County pioneer Benjamin Foxen (see Chapter 8). Today the winery and tasting room occupy

FOXEN VINEYARD,
SANTA MARIA

the reconstructed 200-year-old, no-frills, big-charm wood buildings of Rancho Tinaquaic. Foxen Canyon is also 2 miles south of Rancho Sisquoc.

Sixth-generation Santa Barbara County resident Dick Dore was born and raised on the family-owned Rancho Tinaquaic right here in Foxen Canyon. Having graduated from UC/Santa Barbara, Dick worked as a banker from the late sixties into the seventies and then gave up his nine-to-five job and moved his family to Europe. For a year and a half, he traveled the back roads of France, Spain, and Italy, a sojourn that led him to his love of great wines.

When Dick and his family moved back to the family ranch in the late seventies, the grape business was just emerging here. He worked odd jobs, including work in local vineyards. His path crossed that of Bill Wathen when he was working as a field hand training grapes and driving a tractor for Bill at what is now part of Cambria Winery's Tepusquet Vineyard. In 1985 Dick and Bill made a hobby wine of Cabernet Sauvignon grapes purchased from Rancho Sisquoc Vineyard, which led to a bonded winery in 1987.

Bill Wathen was born and raised in San Luis Obispo and graduated in 1975 from California Polytechnic with a degree in fruit science. He then worked with local viticultural pioneers Dale Hampton and Louie Lucas in managing Tepusquet Mesa Vineyard, now part of Cambria's estate vineyard, and at Nielsen Vineyard, now part of Byron (Mondavi). In 1978 he went north to manage vineyards at Chalone Vineyards south of Salinas, where Chalone owner Dick Graff became his mentor. Today Bill and his family live nearby. In his spare time Bill coaches Little League baseball.

Dick and Bill make limited production wines and do an excellent job of it. *Fine points:* Featured wines: Chardonnay, Chenin Blanc, Viognier, Pinot Noir, Syrah, Merlot, Cabernet Franc, Cabernet Sauvignon. Owners/winemakers: Richard Dore & Bill Wathen. Cases: 12,000. Acres: 10.

🍇 *Foxen Vineyard, 7200 Foxen Canyon Road, Santa Maria 93454; (805) 937–4251. Open noon–4:00 P.M. Friday–Sunday. Tasting fee: $3.00 per glass. Visa and MasterCard. Wheelchair accessible.*

As you follow Foxen Canyon Road northward toward Santa Maria, your next wine tasting stop is RANCHO SISQUOC WINERY, 18 miles east of Santa Maria. Rancho Sisquoc, part of an old Mexican land grant, shows its historic connections with its unpretentious, environmentally sensitive facilities. The surroundings of this excellent winery on the Sisquoc River include 37,000 acres of green pastures, cattle, and farm purchased in 1952 by San Franciscan James Flood.

Nestled above the Sisquoc River, Rancho Sisquoc's is the only vineyard in the Santa Maria Valley that is frost free. Harold Pfeiffer first made wine here in 1972 for private consumption and as a marketing tool to convince other winer-

RANCHO SISQUOC WINERY, SANTA MARIA

ies that quality fruit could be grown in the Santa Maria Valley. The winery opened to the public in 1977 and has won many awards in the 1990s. The tasting room is built of heavy, dark, barn siding wood. Terracotta pots of colorful flowers are tastefully placed among shade trees. Bring a picnic.

The historic San Ramon Chapel overlooks the entrance to the ranch and adorns every wine label of Rancho Sisquoc. We highly recommend a trek to Rancho Sisquoc, but there's just one problem: you won't want to leave.

 Fine points: Featured wines: Chardonnay, Sauvignon Blanc, Sylvaner, Riesling, Merlot, Cabernet Sauvignon, Cellar Select Red, Select Riesling. Owner: James Flood. Winemaker: Alec Frank. Cases: 10,000. Acres: 208 acres planted of 37,000.

Rancho Sisquoc Winery, 6600 Foxen Canyon Road, Santa Maria 93454; (805) 937–3616, fax (805) 937–6601. Open 10:00 A.M.–4:00 P.M. daily. Tasting fee: none. Visa, MasterCard, American Express. Wheelchair accessible.

As you leave Foxen or Rancho Sisquoc, you have to return to Foxen Canyon Road and head north on it all the way to Santa Maria Mesa Road (Tepusquet Road is washed out). When you get to the intersection, turn sharply back on Santa Maria Mesa Road to Cambria and Byron wineries. If you are approaching from Santa Maria, take the Batteravia Road exit east from Highway 101, follow it around to the right, and visit Cottonwood Canyon before you arrive at the Santa Maria Mesa Road turnoff.

As we continue northward, turn right onto Santa Maria Mesa Road to Cambria, and then Byron. Turn left up Chardonnay Lane when you see the Cambria signs.

CAMBRIA WINERY & VINEYARDS, the hugely advertised and publicized winery, is open only on weekends, so plan accordingly. This part of the Santa Maria Valley was named by native Indians for the natural copper deposits found nearby. Originally called *tepuztli* (later changed accidentally to *tepuzque,* meaning copper coin), the area was renamed Cambria, the Roman word for Wales, by nineteenth-century English and Welsh settlers.

Part of an 1838 Mexican land grant, Rancho Tepusquet raised cattle and row crops through the 1900s. Pioneer grape farmers planted vines here in the 1970s, and Chardonnays from the unique soils of the Santa Maria Bench produced exceptionally flavorful wines. Buyers included Ridge, Acacia, ZD, Beringer, and Kendall-Jackson. In 1987 Jess Jackson of Kendall-Jackson and other wine ventures bought Tepusquet Vineyard, now known as the Cambria Estate Vineyard. Cambria boasts "the longest, coldest wine grape growing season in California, which enables our fruit to develop rich, intense character."

Cambria tasting room manager Tiffany Pelletier worked previously at Santa Barbara Winery in downtown Santa Barbara and is founder of the Santa Barbara County chapter of Women for Winesense.

Fine points: Featured wines: Chardonnay, Viognier, Pinot Noir, Syrah, Sangiovese. Owner: Jess Jackson. Winemaker: Dave Guffy. Cases: 97,000 9-liter cases. Acres: 1,232.

🍇 *Cambria Winery & Vineyards, 5475 Chardonnay Lane, Santa Maria 93454; (805) 937–8091, fax (805) 934–3589. Open 10:00 A.M.–5:00 P.M. Saturday–Sunday. Visa, MasterCard, American Express. Wheelchair accessible.*

We strongly encourage you to venture a little farther south on Santa Maria Mesa Road to BYRON VINEYARD & WINERY. As Santa Maria Mesa Road turns to the left, goes down a little hill, and stops, it runs into Tepusquet Road. Turn leftish onto Tepusquet, and Byron will be on your right.

Immediately you will notice the exquisitely environmentally appropriate design of Byron. The sweeping curved roof resembles the surrounding hills, as do the zinc roofing, cedar planks, iron windows, and free-form panels of the earthy colors of the surrounding brush and hills.

Founder, winemaker, and vice president Byron Kent Brown, known as just plain Ken, worked in sales for IBM and in real estate development, gave it all

BYRON VINEYARD & WINERY FROM ITS
DEMONSTRATION VINEYARD, SANTA MARIA

up, and followed his wine passion to graduate from the Fresno State University enology program in 1974. He became winemaker at Zaca Mesa in 1977, and was the first to introduce Rhone-style grapes to this region with Pinot Noir and Chardonnay, later also the first to plant Pinot Gris and an authentic Pinot Blanc clone in the Santa Maria Valley.

Remaining at Zaca Mesa until 1986, Ken and his wife Deborah Kenly Brown and several partners founded Byron Vineyards & Winery in 1984 and made a great and quick national reputation for its Pinot Noir and Chardonnay. In 1990 Robert Mondavi invested heavily in Byron, the ultimate compliment. Hence this fabulous lodge-style winery was designed by architect Scott Johnson, who also designed the TransAmerica Pyramid and Opus One (Mondavi's Napa Valley joint venture with the Rothschilds).

The winery itself is a multilevel gravity-flow design with four cavelike barrel chais, a VIP tasting area, wine library, and professional kitchen for your not very private party.

Be sure to walk around the redwood deck that rims the tasting room and enjoy the solitude of Tepusquet Creek. Sonoma artist Claudia Wagar's vineyard prints are available in the tasting room for around $30 unframed. Enjoy a picnic on the green lawn and respect the surroundings.

Fine points: Featured wines: Lineage (white blend), Pinot Gris, Pinot Blanc, Chardonnay, Pinot Noir. Owner: Robert Mondavi. Winemaker: Byron Kent Brown. Cases: 70,000. Acres: 641.

Byron Vineyard & Winery, 5230 Tepusquet Road, Santa Maria 93454; (805)

937–7288, fax (805) 937–1246, Web site: www.byronwines.com. Open 10:00 A.M.–4:00 P.M. daily. Tasting fee: none. Visa, MasterCard, American Express, Diners/Carte Blanche, JCB. Wheelchair accessible.

To get to COTTONWOOD CANYON VINEYARD & WINERY from Byron and Cambria wineries, go back on Santa Maria Mesa Road to Foxen Canyon Road and turn right. Then turn a doubling back left on a little fork onto Dominion Road, and signs will lead you to Cottonwood Canyon's green metal building and 5,600 square feet of caves.

Former computer graphics executive Norman Beko bought this property in 1988 and developed its interesting Burgundy-style wines in the tradition of Montrachet, specializing in Pinot Noir and Chardonnay. Norman likens his winemaking to raising children: "nourishing individual characteristics and developing the natural (but different) qualities of each separately."

Unfortunately the babies have grown up and Cottonwood Canyon is for sale. But stop by and enjoy the wine and bright and cheerful artwork.

Fine points: Featured wines: Chardonnay, Pinot Noir. Owner and winemaker: Norman Beko. Cases: 4,000. Acres: 50.

🍇 *Cottonwood Canyon Vineyard & Winery, 3940 Dominion Road, Santa Maria 93454; (805) 937–9063, fax (805) 937–8418, Web site: www.cottonwoodcanyon.com. Open 10:30 A.M.–5:30 P.M. daily. Tasting fee $2.50 current releases, $5.00 reserves. Visa, MasterCard, American Express. Wheelchair accessible.*

SANTA MARIA

One of the main things to do in Santa Maria is eat, particularly if you are here on a weekend. Famous for its tri-tip barbecues, Santa Maria takes its tradition from the Old West days when the rancheros and cowboys would gather under the towering oak trees for Spanish barbecues. The tradition has become a pleasant obsession and weekend ritual. Every Saturday and Sunday, charity volunteers, vendors, and restaurants pull out their barbecues from hibachis to gas barbies on wheels to huge movable pits and sizzle succulent tri-tip or top sirloin to join the pinquito beans and salsa, tossed fresh green salad, and toasted sweet French bread to create a mouth-watering festival. The whole town smells like barbecue.

Although it is difficult to find the center of Santa Maria because shopping centers have created several subcenters, you don't have to worry on barbecue days. All the shopping center parking lots along Broadway are full of barbecues and barbecuers.

Santa Maria barbecue consists of prime top sirloin, about 3 inches thick, cooked over a fire of coals from Santa Maria Valley red oak wood. Salt, pepper, and garlic salt are the only seasonings used, but they are used lots. The steaks are strung on flat steel rods, which are gradually lowered over a bed of red-hot coals for about forty-five minutes. The meat is sliced at the pit and served in large stainless steel pans by waiters. You get to choose your preferred doneness. The bread is used to "dip up" the juice from the serving pan. This may be heaven, carnivores!

We thank the Santa Maria Chamber of Commerce Visitor & Convention Bureau for sharing the secret recipe for Santa Maria barbecue beans.

Santa Maria is also well known for its strawberry and flower fields. Plan to attend the annual strawberry festival the fourth weekend in April to enjoy music, carnival, entertainment, and, of course, strawberries in every presentation imaginable (at the Santa Maria Fairgrounds; 805–925–8824). Another worthwhile annual event is the Obon Festival featuring Santa Maria's diverse populations with Japanese foods, arts and traditions, also at the fairgrounds.

According to our good friend Gordon Phillips, acting city attorney for Santa Maria, the absolute best place in Santa Maria for coffee, salads, and sandwiches is CAFE MONET, which duplicates itself in Lompoc.

SANTA MARIA BARBECUE BEANS
from Santa Maria Valley Chamber of Commerce Visitor & Convention Bureau

---

1 lb. small pink beans (pinquito)

1 strip bacon, diced

½ cup diced ham

1 small clove garlic, minced

¾ cup tomato puree

¼ cup red chili sauce (Las Palmas)

1 Tbs. sugar

1 tsp. salt

1 tsp. dry mustard

Pick over beans to remove dirt and small stones. Cover with water and let soak overnight in a large container. Drain, cover with fresh water, and simmer 2 hours, or until tender.

Sauté bacon and ham until lightly browned; add garlic and sauté a minute or two longer, then add tomato puree, chili sauce, sugar, mustard, and salt. Drain most of liquid off beans and stir in sauce. Keep hot over low heat until ready to serve. Serves eight.

The menu is simple and good. Lots of espresso drinks for every taste, Chai, and passion fruit iced tea, along with very special sandwiches available by whole

($4.85) or half ($2.95). They range from the San Pedro Costa Rica with smoked turkey, ham, red onions, tomato, Swiss and cheddar cheese, and sprouts on wheat bread to tri-tip with Swiss cheese, veggie, garlic chicken breast, pastrami, and basil or almond chicken salad. You can also indulge in bagels, cold burrito wraps, and heated filled croissants, plus great soups or soup and half sandwich ($5.85).

❧ Cafe Monet, 1555 South Broadway, Santa Maria 93454; (805) 928–1912. Open 6:30 A.M.–7:30 P.M. Monday–Friday, 6:30 A.M.–5:00 P.M. Saturday, 7:00 A.M.–5:00 P.M. Sunday. Beer and wine. Visa, MasterCard, American Express. Wheelchair accessible.

The fine Pacific Conservatory of the Performing Arts, which also performs in Solvang, plays here year-round at the Santa Maria Civic Theater in Building D of Alan Hancock College, 800 South College Drive, on the Bradley road side of campus. Call (805) 922–8313 for schedules and reservations.

At the SANTA MARIA HISTORICAL SOCIETY MUSEUM you can enjoy Chumash Indian culture and artifacts of the Mission Rancho and Pioneer periods, and even the Barbecue Hall of Fame!

❧ Santa Maria Historical Society Museum, 616 South Broadway, Santa Maria 93454; (805) 922–3130. Open noon–5:00 P.M. Tuesday–Saturday. Admission free. Wheelchair accessible.

Farmers' markets: Tuesday morning at Oak Knoll South in Orcutt, Wednesday afternoon at Heritage Walk at Town Center West shopping center.

Military and air buffs might enjoy visits to the Santa Maria Museum of Flight at the Santa Maria Airport (805–922–8758) or to Vandenberg Air Force Base (805–734–8232, ext. 63595).

CHAPTER 5

SAN LUIS OBISPO COUNTY: THE INTERIOR

irst of all, let's get the pronunciation straight: San lou-WISS Obispo, **not** *San lou-EE Obispo. Locals get goose bumps and peg visitors as tourists when they hear the latter. Heaven forbid!*

San Luis Obispo County runs east from the Pacific Ocean between Los Padres National Forest and Santa Barbara County to the south and the Santa Lucia Mountain range and Monterey County to the north. It has 80 miles of pristine beaches and coastline to die for. The county's northern border is 190 miles south of San Francisco, and its southern border is 190 miles north of Los Angeles, so it is truly the central coast of California.

Its major city is San Luis Obispo, followed by Paso Robles, Templeton, Atascadero, and the coastal towns of Pismo Beach, Morro Bay, Cambria, and San Simeon, near which is Hearst Castle. (We visit the coastal towns in Chapter 6.)

San Luis Obispo County is generally much more laid-back and much less Hollywood than Santa Barbara County, and you are much less likely to run into movie stars or glitz here. Dress is always casual. Both the city and county of San Luis Obispo take their name from the 1772 Mission San Luis Obispo de Tolosa, named by the missionaries in honor of fourteenth-century Saint Louis, bishop of Toulouse in France.

Most of San Luis Obispo County's wineries are in the Paso Robles area, although there are excellent ones in the Edna Valley south of San Luis Obispo. In Chapter 7 we take you to all those that are open to the public for tasting.

To get to San Luis Obispo, take Highway 1 or 101 from the north or south, and Highways 46, 41, or 166 from the east. Our travel pattern was from north to south. If you are arriving from south of here, just reverse our order.

As you come from the north, you first see the Camp Roberts California National Guard complex of light green buildings that actually straddle the Monterey/San Luis Obispo county lines.

MISSION SAN MIGUEL ARCANGEL, SAN MIGUEL

Be sure to follow the Highway 101 exit signs for a brief visit to San Miguel, a ghost town 7 miles north of Paso Robles whose main claim to fame is the well-preserved **MISSION SAN MIGUEL ARCANGEL**. You can enter San Miguel at one end of "town" and get back on 101 at the other end, so just make a sweep and stop at the mission most people miss.

Mission San Miguel was founded in 1797 by Father Fermin de Lasuen, father presidente of all the missions of Alta California; Father Buenaventura Sitjar of the Mission San Antonio de Padua; and eight soldiers in the Indian village called Vahca, whose original settlers slaved and sweated to build the mission buildings.

In August 1806 a huge fire destroyed two rows of buildings and part of the church roof, originally built of straw and rebuilt with tile. The mission's baptismal register shows 2,892 baptisms (of Indians) and 2,249 deaths of those "sleeping in the crowded little cemetery." The stone foundation of the church you see today was laid in 1816, and the interior decorations were designed by Esteban Munras. The mission was secularized in 1836, the Indians ran away, and Governor Pio Pico sold it for $600 to Petronillo Rios and Englishman William Reed, who had married Maria Antonia Vallejo. Eventually the mission was confiscated, and after the Civil War it was returned to the Catholic Church.

Since 1928 Mission San Miguel has been run by the founding Franciscan padres, who still run a parish church, novitiate, and retreat house. It stands as one of the best preserved California missions. Great loaded gift shop.

※ Mission San Miguel Arcangel,
775 Mission Street, San Miguel
93451; (805) 467–3256. Open 9:30
A.M.–4:30 P.M. (tour closes 4:15 P.M.).
Admission: fifty cents, $1.00 for a fam-
ily. Visa and MasterCard. Mostly
wheelchair accessible.

Now get back on Highway 101
and take the Twenty-fourth Street
exit to Paso Robles. (The Twenty-
fourth   Street   exit   becomes
Nacimiento Lake Road to, you
guessed it, LAKE NACIMIENTO, the
county's top water sports center for
waterskiing, boating, fishing, swimming, camping, and hiking. Call
805–238–3256 for information.)

FATHER JUNIPERO SERRA,
MISSION SAN MIGUEL
ARCANGEL, SAN MIGUEL

PASO ROBLES

Paso Robles is much like it used to be when it was a Wild West hot-and-
dusty farming town, except now a few fabulous restaurants have sprung up on
the east side of City Park.

The average temperature here in the summer is 94°, which means that
there are many days over 100°—in fact several in the 110° range, with an average of 315 sunny days a year. Unless you really thrive on the heat or have excellent air conditioning in your car, we suggest you visit this interior part of San
Luis Obispo County in any season but summer. Late February and March are
ideal: the temperature is 70° and the speed limit is 70. The rolling hills are even
green briefly.

Paso Robles truly looks like a Main Street city, with wide dusty streets, and
just the basics and a few frills available, a central park plaza, and lots of fast
foods. But there are some treasures, both historic and culinary. Stick with us.
We were surprised at the developments.

First of all, the news about the food, not because we are obsessed, but
because good restaurants are what attracted us to Paso Robles, which many
Californians will find hard to believe. Things have changed.

GOOD OL' BURGERS, PASO ROBLES

If you get off Highway 101 at Twenty-fourth Street, you first come to GOOD OL' BURGERS, a local fixture and hangout for everyone from vintners to mayors to highway patrolmen. As you walk inside to order, you see a glass refrigerator with large round meatball-like ovals that get squished into being your juicy delicious hamburger, called colorfully the Coyote, Ranch Hand, or Roundup. The last includes three ball/patties, causing it to cost a whopping "5 bucks," the most expensive thing on the menu. Kathleen prefers the Yardbird, a tasty grilled chicken breast on a wheat bun at "3¾ bucks." You must, absolutely must, indulge in the "tator strips" (fries) and "wagon wheels," huge, hand-dipped onion rings (small of each is plenty to share). The shakes are thick, real, and simple— vanilla, chocolate, and strawberry ("2¾ bucks"). Great for kids, too.

Every winemaker or worker whose dining opinion we asked said, "You gotta try Good Ol' Burgers and Busi's." We agree. One of our favorites.

❧ *Good Ol' Burgers, 1145 Twenty-fourth Street, Paso Robles 93446; (805) 238–0655. Open 10:00 A.M.–9:00 P.M. Monday–Thursday, 10:00 A.M.–10:00 P.M. Friday and Saturday. No credit cards. Tables are wheelchair accessible, inside and ordering are not.*

The WINE VAULT AND HOT SPRINGS DELI is a fun place for food and wine as well as a rare "educational" experience for members of S.O.U.S.E.S., their

Society of Unbelievably Serious Enological Students. Here you can buy all sorts of wine accessories and goodies, gourmet delicacies, ports, sherries, and dessert wines as well as Veuve Cliquot and Charles Krug, and a wide range of local wines. This popular gathering place derives its name from the old Hot Springs Hotel, which once also housed the Paso Robles Police Department and burned down under questionable circumstances. The Hot Springs' bar was so lively that local lore claims that the soused would walk out the door and into the police station to turn themselves in for public intoxication, earning a ride home in the paddy wagon.

✤ *The Wine Vault and Hot Springs Deli, 1314 Spring Street, Paso Robles 93446; (805) 239–9463 or (877) PRWINES. Open 10:00 A.M.–6:00 P.M. Visa, MasterCard, American Express. Wheelchair accessible.*

Arabian horse ranches and vineyards now surround Paso Robles, replacing the cattle with more lucrative "crops." Every spring acres of almond orchards in whitish-pink blossoms explode around the town, once the "Almond Capital of the World" and still a true farming center where farmers come into town for supplies. The town center is City Park, even though it is no longer in the center of town. A new multiplex movie theater assures the downtown will survive, and we have a few favorite restaurants nearby whose secrets we will share with you. Vine Street is loaded with gorgeous Victorian-era homes worth checking out. Antiques stores show up on every little side street, and there aren't many.

Back to the east side of the park on Pine Street. Here you find Busi's on the Park, Bistro Laurent, and Villa Creek restaurants, with Odyssey Culinary Provisions Cafe & Marketplace in the next block.

Our favorite is BUSI'S ON THE PARK, which you enter through the bar and what was the old version of Busi's, whose founder, John Busi, died in 1995. This part looks like a Manhattan cocktail and Kent cigarette place of the 1940s and '50s, which it was. Toward the rear of the bar is an old jukebox and a doorway around to the right that leads to the casually elegant dining room where John Bermudez hosts while his business partner Patricia M. Crawford chefs.

Everything here is outstanding, and portions are generous. The menu changes by season, but you may get a chance to try Thai specialties such as shrimp, beef, and shrimp salad, all elegant and ranging from $7.95 to $14.95. We like the Dungeness crab cakes served with lemon butter, roasted red bell pepper, and sherry aioli ($9.95), and the polenta and pumpkin ravioli are mouth-watering ($16.95), as are the pan-roasted fillet of Atlantic salmon and local (Pacific) whitefish ($18.95) and the mahogany duck Chinese crispy-style served over soba noodles with bok choy ($19.95). Jerry favors the perfect lamb shank braised with Barbera and served with saffron basmati rice ($18.95). The

✤

martinis and Pat's "infamous" bread pudding are better than perfect. Cheesecake fans should try the Alsatian-style cheesecake with a mixed berry coulis ($5.00). One of our favorites.

❧ *Busi's on the Park, 1122 Pine Street, Paso Robles 93446; (805) 238–1390. Open for dinner 5:00–9:00 P.M. Tuesday–Sunday, breakfast and lunch 10:00 A.M.–2:00 P.M. Saturday–Sunday. Full bar. Visa, MasterCard, American Express. Wheelchair accessible.*

Another favorite of ours and most winery people is ODYSSEY CULINARY PROVISIONS CAFE & MARKETPLACE at Pine and Twelfth Streets on the northeast corner of the park. This is definitely the best place to pick up picnic supplies in Paso Robles if you plan to enjoy a picnic at a winery or enjoy the cafe ambience right here.

Odyssey prepares deliciously healthy rotisserie take-home chickens by the half ($4.99) or whole ($6.99) with salads by the pound ($4.99) and focaccia bread by the pound ($3.50). Marvelous sandwiches include roasted eggplant, peppers, artichoke hearts, and chèvre on baguette ($5.95), baked Brie or raclette and artichoke on pane pugliese ($5.95), and roast Brie with chèvre and pesto on Parmesan sourdough ($5.95). All of these come with soup or salad—Greek, Caesar, balsamic potato, penne pasta, Thai pasta, mixed greens, or tabbouleh! Unbelievable! Wrap fans will enjoy choices from Indian curried chicken to Mediterranean veggie ($4.95).

To top it off, have a Ciao Bella gelato or Ben & Jerry's ice cream with excellent espresso drinks, iced frappes, and fruit smoothies. House wine is Pesenti Burgundy or Chablis at $2.50 a glass or $4.00 a half liter.

❧ *Odyssey Culinary Provisions Cafe & Marketplace, 1214 Pine Street, Paso Robles 93466; (805) 237–7516, fax (805) 237–7514. Open 8:00 A.M.–7:30 P.M. Sunday–Thursday, 8:00 A.M.–9:30 P.M. Friday–Saturday. Beer and wine. Visa, MasterCard, American Express. Wheelchair accessible.*

Microbrew fans will enjoy the new outpost of San Luis Obispo's SLO BREWING CO. right here in the center of Paso Robles' wine country. Visit Michael Hoffman's 15,000-square-foot brewery site and sample SLO's national award-winning brews (including Brickhouse Pale, Garden Alley Amber, Cole Porter, and the brewmeister's seasonal special ales) in the taproom and gift shop.

To get to SLO Brewing Co., 1 mile south of Paso Robles, take the Highway 46 west exit right off Highway 101, et voilà!

❧ *SLO Brewing Co., 1400 Ramada Drive, Paso Robles 93446; (805) 239–BEER; Web site: www.slobrew.com. Open 11:00 A.M.–6:00 P.M. daily. Visa and MasterCard. Wheelchair accessible.*

Significant historic buildings in Paso Robles include the newly restored PASO ROBLES INN on the west side of City Park at 1103 Spring Street. The first hotel at this site was built in 1864 and had a wide reputation, attracting movie stars; pianist and Polish Premier Ignace Jan Paderewski, who lived in Paso Robles; and even the Pittsburgh Pirates baseball team. That hotel burned down in 1940. The newest incarnation is worth either a stay or a walk-through.

The PASO ROBLES CARNEGIE HISTORY LIBRARY MUSEUM was designed by W. H. Weeks and completed in 1908 with Andrew Carnegie's $10,000 gift. It now houses a historical museum with rotating exhibits of local and natural history.

❧ *Paso Robles Carnegie History Library Museum, 1000 Spring Street, Paso Robles 93446; (805) 238–4996. Open 1:00–4:00 P.M. Wednesday–Sunday. Admission free. Not wheelchair accessible.*

The GRANARY at 1111 Riverside was built in 1890 and sold to the Sperry Milling Company for flour production and storage. Its steam generator served as Paso Robles' first electric power plant. The Granary later served to store grain and in 1992 it was restored and developed by Newlin Hastings as a collection of retail shops, restaurants, and offices.

EL PASO DE ROBLES AREA PIONEER MUSEUM features displays of farm equipment, carriages, Paderewski memorabilia, Indian artifacts, and unusual household wares depicting life in mid-1880s Paso Robles.

❧ *El Paso de Robles Area Pioneer Museum, 2010 Riverside Avenue, Paso Robles 93446; (805) 239–4556. Open 1:00–4:00 P.M. Thursday–Sunday. Wheelchair accessible.*

ESTRELLA WAR BIRDS MUSEUM displays historic aircraft, vehicles, and memorabilia from World Wars I and II at Paso Robles Municipal Airport. It is also known as the Estrella Squadron of the Confederate Air Force Museum!

❧ *Estrella War Birds Museum, 4251 Dry Creek Road, Paso Robles 93446; (805) 227–0440. Open 2:00–4:00 P.M. Wednesday, 8:00 A.M.–5:00 P.M. Saturday, noon–2:00 P.M. Sunday. Admission free. Wheelchair accessible.*

A FARMERS' MARKET is held twice weekly: Tuesday, at Fourteenth and ParkStreets, 9:30 A.M.–12:30 P.M.; and Friday evenings at Twelfth and Park Streets 4:00–7:00 P.M.

TEMPLETON

We strongly encourage you to take the Main Street exit off Highway 101 just south of Paso Robles to Templeton, a marvelous little relic of the Wild West towns. The current center of activity is across from the granary at McPhee's Grill, the baby of Ian McPhee, creator of Ian's in Cambria, and Dr. Stan Hoffman. A room honors wine guru André Tchelistcheff, the late and revered wine-making consultant to Hoffman's winery.

Ian came to San Luis Obispo County on a football scholarship to California Polytechnic and basically never left. He went home for his first college Thanksgiving and Christmas and then started pleading that his "car broke down" every year after that. Now he is firmly planted in his popular eatery that no one should miss, if only for the fun experience.

Once an 1860s general store, the restaurant still conveys respect for that colorful history, with unique photos toward the back near the rest rooms. You can't miss them as you go to the back patio to enjoy your meal at the wrought-iron chairs and tables. The booths have black-and-white checked upholstery, and dark-flowered virgin vinyl tablecloths cover the tables.

The food is exciting, creative, and hearty—vintners, ranchers, and local gossips and historians pack the place every day. We happened in for the Sunday brunch, an ideal way to sample McPhee's wide array of expertise. The antique bar, which serves as a buffet table at brunch, is laden with the finest smoked-here salmon ever, pastas, potatoes, beans green and brown, baby asparagus, and gorgeous salads. After you make however many trips you choose for the salad and appetizer course, you go to the kitchen window to make your selection of hot entree. We enjoyed roasted lamb and even waker-upper chorizo and eggs. All of this with champagne or softer drinks and your choice(s) from the dessert tray for $18. Drop by for lunch or dinner during the week.

McPhee's Grill, 416 Main Street, Templeton 93465; (805) 434–3204. Open for lunch 11:30 A.M.–2:00 P.M. daily (buffet brunch Sunday), dinner from 4:30 P.M. Beer and wine. Visa and MasterCard. Wheelchair accessible via back patio and door.

Be sure to walk next door to Hermann's Chocolate Lab for amazing handmade candies, truffles, and other sweets. We got to sample the new banana split morsel! Down at the corner is A. J. Spurs Saloon & Dining Hall, voted Best North County Restaurant for seven years. Indeed it is popular Wild West, with good drinks, those famous BBQ steaks, ribs, seafood, and pasta, and what they call "fine Western dining." Go ahead and ride up on your Harley, and stride right in, boots, spurs, and all.

❧ *A. J. Spurs Saloon & Dining Hall, 508 Main Street, Templeton 93465; (805) 434–2700. Open 4:00–9:30 P.M. daily (also in Buellton at 350 Highway 246 east). Full bar (in both meanings). Visa and MasterCard. Wheelchair accessible.*

Both of these restaurants are convenient to wine tasting and are closest to Creston and Wild Horse. We will eventually bring you back here on our wine tasting loop.

ATASCADERO

Best known to the outside world for its state prison, Atascadero is an up-and-coming city attracting loads of Californians because of reasonable real estate prices, good climate, and good shopping at the new Atascadero factory outlet stores.

Visitors also enjoy the forty-year-old Charles Paddock Zoo, the only zoo in San Luis Obispo County. Just 1½ miles west of Highway 101 on Highway 41, one hundred animals dwell on five acres near Atascadero Lake, where you can hike, bike, picnic, paddleboat, fish, or just feed the ducks and geese. Every Tuesday evening in summer locals and visitors enjoy free concerts at Lakeside Pavilion.

Just south of Atascadero near the top of Cuesta Grade is the tiny town of Santa Margarita, an antiques devotee's heaven, with loads of shops and a twice-monthly auction at the Santa Margarita Antique Auction Barn.

There's a FARMERS' MARKET Wednesdays, 3:00–6:00 P.M., in the Rite-Aid parking lot at Highway 41 and El Camino Real.

DOWNTOWN SAN LUIS OBISPO

If we were to move to the central coast, it would probably be to San Luis Obispo. We love it. It seems to have a perfect mix for us: smallish-town atmosphere, big-city conveniences (Gap and Starbucks?), an excellent, highly reputed university with all the cultural benefits that go with it, a diverse community, a real feeling of community, contained growth, environmental sensitivity, fabulous climate, and good, creative restaurants. When do we go?!

The city of San Luis Obispo began when Father Junipero Serra founded Mission San Luis Obispo de Tolosa in 1772, halfway between what are now Los

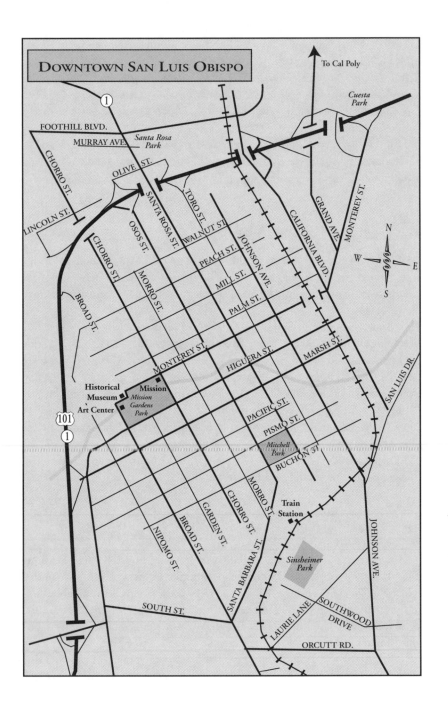

DOWNTOWN SAN LUIS OBISPO

Angeles and San Francisco. The community evolved into a farming and cattle-raising center in the 1840s, a dairy-farming center in the 1870s, an educational center from 1901, and a military and wine center later. The city began to boom in 1894 with the arrival of the Southern Pacific Railroad. In 1901 a vocational school was established and it grew into the highly respected California Polytechnic State University (Cal Poly). The green lines in the streets guide you to historical points of interest on the Path of History.

Today the mission is still the center of town, surrounded by the San Luis Obispo Art Center, the San Luis Obispo County Historical Museum in the former Carnegie Library, cafes and restaurants, and San Luis Obispo's primary downtown shopping area.

The mission, restored between 1930 and 1934, houses an extensive collection of photos, artifacts, tools, clothes, artwork, and other displays, as well as newspaper clippings about the area's pioneers. The gift shop sells loads of religious and mission history memorabilia and books.

MISSION SAN LUIS OBISPO DE TOLOSA was the fifth built in the chain of twenty-one California missions. Built of adobe bricks made by local Chumash Indians, the mission still functions as a Catholic church at the base of Monterey Street at Chorro Street. Mission Plaza, which is bordered by the San Luis Obispo County Historical Museum and the Murray Adobe, functions as a true community gathering place, with festivals throughout the year and footbridges to adjoining cafes and shops.
Rest room alert! There are excellent clean public rest rooms right here in

FATHER JUNIPERO SERRA STATUE AT MISSION SAN LUIS OBISPO DE TOLOSA, SAN LUIS OBISPO

Mission Plaza between the mission and the art center, across from the historical museum. Treat them well.

❧ *Mission San Luis Obispo de Tolosa, 751 Palm Street at Monterey Street, San Luis Obispo 93401; (805) 543–6850. Open 9:00 A.M.–4:00 P.M. winter, 9:00 A.M.–4:30 P.M. summer. Mostly wheelchair accessible.*

Right behind the mission at Monterey and Broad Streets is the SAN LUIS OBISPO ART CENTER, a true community art center where you can view the best of the area's local amateur and professional artists' work. Be sure to drop by for rotating exhibits and class and lecture schedules.

❧ *San Luis Obispo Art Center, 1010 Broad Street, PO Box 813, San Luis Obispo 93401; (805) 543–8562, fax (805) 543–4518; e-mail: ArtCntr@slonet.org; Web site: www.slonet.org/~artcntr. Open 11:00 A.M.–5:00 P.M. Tuesday–Sunday. Admission free. Wheelchair accessible.*

The SAN LUIS OBISPO COUNTY HISTORICAL MUSEUM tells local colorful history through changing displays of old photographs and artifacts. The impressive collection displayed in the former Carnegie Library (1904) ranges from Chumash and Salinan Indian artifacts and mission and ranch artifacts from the eighteenth and nineteenth centuries to a Victorian-era parlor, the lens from the lighthouse at Port San Luis, and a postal delivery wagon. We also found more fascinating local history books and booklets here than in any other store.

The building itself was designed by Watsonville, California, architect W. H. Weeks, and built by locals Stephens and Maino with a $10,000 grant from steel tycoon Andrew Carnegie. It is the only building in the county built with local sandstone and granite.

❧ *San Luis Obispo County Historical Museum, 696 Monterey Street, PO Box 1391, San Luis Obispo 93401; (805) 543–0638. Open 10:00 A.M.–4:00 P.M. Wednesday–Sunday. Admission free. Visa and MasterCard. Not wheelchair accessible.*

If the kids are along, skip right over to the unusual SAN LUIS OBISPO CHILDREN'S MUSEUM a block west and a block south of Mission Plaza at Monterey and Nipomo Streets. This is a hands-on, please-touch place for kids of all ages, with special family fun days Tuesdays. Kids can race to the scene of a fire on the back of a fire engine, watch themselves on television, or career down a dinosaur slide. Children under sixteen must be accompanied by an adult. Great shop!

❧ *San Luis Obispo Children's Museum, 1010 Nipomo Street, San Luis Obispo 93401; (805) 544–KIDS; Web site: www.kids.fix.net. Open 11:00 A.M.–5:00 P.M. Wednesday–Monday. Admission $4.50, children under two free, Sundays $3.75. Visa and MasterCard. Mostly wheelchair accessible.*

One of San Luis Obispo's most unifying and exciting community events is its somewhat famous FARMERS' MARKET every Thursday, catapulting the town into the weekend one day early! Four blocks of farmers and barbecue pits on wheels stir up delicious experiences and a way to experience San Luis Obispo's culture.

Massive barbecues crank out grilled ribs, chicken, and even oysters. Local flower growers and cider pressers offer their specialties, along with jugglers, dancers, a one-man puppet show, musical performers, and other variously varied entertainers. Helium balloons appear to tie down booths selling everything from pizza to warm-from-the-oven aromatic cookies. Mascot Downtown Brown, a 7-foot pretend bear, mingles with the crowd, passing out bear hugs everywhere.

Just make your way to Higuera Street (pronounced here hig-ARE-ah) downtown. The street is closed off for 4 blocks, so park and walk or roll. Shops stay open until 9:00 P.M., and of course restaurants do too.

➴ *Farmers' Market, 4 blocks of Higuera Street, Business Improvement Association, PO Box 1402, San Luis Obispo 93406; (805) 541–0286. Wheelchair accessible.*

We begin our own streetwalking tour right at the mission, as we think you should and will. If you want to walk up the hill (north) 1 block to Palm Street, we encourage you to do so just to see the AH LOUIS STORE, California State Historical Landmark No. 802. If you don't want to hike up there, just join us below.

Ah Louis (Chinese name Wong On) was the best-known merchant of San Luis Obispo's Chinatown, basically the 800 block of Palm Street. He served as unofficial mayor, postmaster, banker, and community center for the city's 2,000 Chinese laborers who built the railroad and its tunnels around

AH LOUIS STORE, SAN LUIS OBISPO

here. Having arrived about 1870 to help his asthma, he first worked as a cook in the French Hotel, then as the foreman and employment agent of all the Chinese who worked for the Pacific Coast Railroad, as well as agent for Chinese quicksilver miners near Cambria. He then sold them all imported and local groceries and everything else they could need.

The Ah Louis store sold pharmaceuticals, rice, peanut oil, sugar cane, hom don (salted duck eggs), hoy tom (sea cucumber), lop op (dried duck), hom yee (salted fish), dried abalone, oysters, canned fish, and a favorite cooling dessert, leong fun. The store's walls were lined with seventy-two drawers of Chinese herbal remedies, which Ah Louis dispensed after taking his customer's pulse to determine what was wrong. His son Howard continued the operation for many years, and the store is now a gift shop.

➳ *Ah Louis Store, 800 Palm Street, San Luis Obispo 93401; (805) 543–4332. Open "irregular hours." Visa and MasterCard. Not wheelchair accessible.*

If you do not want to make the trek up to Ah Louis, just continue with us from here in front of the mission. We begin by heading south from the mission on the same (west) side of Chorro Street.

As you walk or roll, you will enjoy SLO Swim, if you're in the market for small bathing suits and big boards, and Unique Beads, which has great nostalgic beaded curtains and little booths in which to take your selections and create your own necklace. Next comes one of our favorites, and that of many locals, the Cowboy Cookie & Grub Co. for burritos, quiche, hot dogs, and, yes, cookies. Bali Isle Imports is a small emporium of extraordinary exotica including imported clothes, capes, curtains, incense, and home and personal accessories. The nearby San Luis Obispo Chamber of Commerce has loads of specialized information and can tell you what's playing at the new spectacular Performing Arts Center San Luis Obispo, a joint university/city/foundation endeavor at Cal Poly.

The other (eastern) side of Chorro has Johnson's for Children, and the tiny Go Cafe with espresso, smoothies, reference books, and Internet connections. If you're desperate, stop in at Bill's Tavern right next door to Rubber Stamps Unlimited.

Now we are at Chorro and Higuera, the latter being San Luis Obispo's primary shopping street. At the corner turn right (west) down the north side of Higuera toward Broad Street. Browse in Bath & Body, Avanti (for advanced women's clothing), and Tails pet store, and be sure to stop in at Foghorn's Cartoonatorium for a little fun. The Network is a small mall of shops and cafes, including Koffee Klatsch, Sunglass Hut, Ciscos for sandwiches, salads and subs, and Pasta Tazzo. There's a great deck with tables looking across the creek and a bridge to the mission. Everyone stops at Hungry Bear cookies, unfortunately. Mission Mall is an open-air, small mall with upscale shops, including Country Culture yogurt, Just Looking Gallery (caught us!), Up Your Alley women's discount clothing, Wild Women leather outfits and bags from $49.99, and Mr. Michael's furs and fine clothing. The Gold Concept is right next to the Fog & Peach Pub (decent pub grub). Kevin Main's Jewelry Design Studio neighbors with Straight Down Clothing and Ottoman's casual men's clothing. **Rest room alert!** There's a public rest room downstairs at the back of this little mall.

At the corner of Higuera and Broad is a wine lover's mecca, CENTRAL COAST WINES, which knowledgeable Marc Jaeger manages for owner Vaughn Taus. If you don't have time to visit the wineries yourself, this is the place where you can taste and purchase the very best produced on the central coast, as well as some significant imports. We know of visitors who load up by selecting and ordering cases of wine and having them shipped home, which works if you live in states that don't prohibit such pleasures.

If you are around for farmers' market Thursday evening, be sure to stop in for the weekly winemakers' pouring and tasting from 6:00 to 9:00 P.M.

❧ *Central Coast Wines, 712 Higuera Street, San Luis Obispo 93401; (805) 784–9463, fax (805) 544–8761; Web site: www.ccwines.com. Open 10:30 A.M.–7:00 P.M. Friday–Wednesday, 10:30 A.M.–9:00 P.M. Thursday. Tasting fee: $3.00. Visa and MasterCard. Wheelchair accessible.*

In the block of Higuera below Broad on the north side is Vieni Vai Trattoria with sidewalk tables, and across the street is the China Bowl/Kyoto Buffet, a popular economical ($6.75) all-you-can-eat multicultural pile-it-on Asian food experience.

Now that we're on the south side of Higuera, we come to BEAU'S RUSSIA HOUSE CAFE & TEA ROOM, a classically old-fashioned dining room and tearoom. The St. Petersburg full tea with sandwiches and scones is $15.75, light tea is $11.75, the Czars afternoon tea is $21.75 and a meal, while you can also just have finger sandwiches for $6.75. A harpist plays during tea, and you can sip your-own-creation martini at the special martini bar.

This very Russian house serves authentic Russian fare at lunch and dinner with borscht or house salad accompanying lunch entrees, with a choice of salads, roasted red potatoes, kasha, fresh vegetable, and eggplant oriental. Feast on oysters and caviar, bliny and salmon ($7.75), tomatoes filled with crab ($10.95), or cucumber and sour cream salad ($6.95). Lunch entrees include beef stroganoff ($17.95), eggplant caviar-stuffed salmon ($17.95), chopped chicken and veal patties ($9.95), and chicken Kiev ($12.95), plus a selection of "buterbrody" (tea sandwiches).

Dinner offerings might include veal sautéed in caviar sauce ($22.95), marinated rack of lamb ($24.95), poached and baked chicken in walnut sauce

($19.95), stuffed pork loin ($19.95), or fish casserole Moscow style—whitefish baked in casserole with mushrooms, onions, and sour cream and topped with Parmesan cheese ($19.95).

❧ *Beau's Russia House Cafe & Tea Room, 699 Higuera Street, San Luis Obispo 93401; (805) 784–0172. Open 11:00 A.M.–9:00 P.M. Monday–Thursday, 11:00 A.M.–10:00 P.M. or midnight Friday–Sunday. Full bar. Visa, MasterCard, American Express. Not wheelchair accessible.*

Be sure to go around the corner on Broad Street to a sort of gourmet ghetto, the first of which is extremely artery-clearing compared to Beau's. Our favorite comes first, Big Sky Cafe, followed by Boston Bagel and Tio Alberto's, a great little place to stop in for gourmet Mexican food.

The *New York Times* calls BIG SKY CAFE "San Luis Obispo's Best Restaurant" and *Zagat* rates it as "excellent." To say nothing of us: Big Sky is definitely our favorite restaurant in SLO. But don't tell.

As you might not expect, Big Sky's ceiling is painted like a night sky complete with shining stars. A Gazelle ladies' bike hangs over the bar, and fake Mexican arches make niches with tile roofing, leftovers from the place's previous incarnation as a Mexican restaurant. Bloody Marys are made with sake, and Mark Freear's bold bike paintings decorate the walls. You sit on heavy wooden chairs at heavy wooden tables.

Charles Myers cites a Chinese proverb that says roughly, "Let us consider that one big sky covers us all equally." Big Sky serves environmentally sound "modern food," tasty but considerate of your life span. For instance, the mixed grill with three kinds of chicken sausages (from the

---

BIG SKY KILLER CORNBREAD
from Chef Greg Holt, Big Sky Cafe, San Luis Obispo

½ cup butter
1 cup sugar
4 eggs
1 (7 oz.) can diced, roasted green chilies
1 ¼ cup creamed corn
1 cup grated cheddar cheese
1 ½ cup flour
1 cup yellow cornmeal
4 tsp. baking powder
¼ tsp. salt

With electric mixer, cream together butter and sugar. When smooth, beat in the eggs, green chilies, creamed corn, and grated cheese. Sift the dry ingredients together and stir into the wet mixture. Bake in a greased cake pan or muffin tins at 350° F for about 25 minutes. [*These are the absolute best cornbread muffins in the world.—KTH*]

SLO Sausage Company), sautéed beets, fresh green beans, and hush puppies had only seven grams of fat ($8.95). The penne pasta with langoustines in a cilantro lime sauce was unbelievably better than perfect ($13.95). When—not if—you go, do not leave without trying the beignets, fried bread with cinnamon and sugar ($1.95), blueberry ($3.50), or chocolate drizzle and filling ($2.50). One order is plenty for two people who have already eaten too much. Very local wines and brews by the glass. There's an excellent free-at-night parking lot across Broad Street.

Do not miss the "killer cornbread" with any meal. Our breakfast is the Red Flannel turkey hash with basil-Parmesan glazed eggs ($6.50) or the Maytag blue cheese, bacon, and apple omelette ($6.95). And then there's the black bean cakes and eggs ($5.95), smoked salmon and onion scramble ($7.95), and fabulous buttermilk pancakes or three-grain journey cakes ($4.25/$5.25) with choice of banana and toasted walnuts, cranberries and orange zest, or Swiss cheese fillings!

Sandwiches are available at lunch and dinner, as are bowls including gumbo yaya or High Plains turkey chili ($3.25/$5.25), and the Big Sky noodle bowl with buckwheat soba noodles and semolina pasta in clear veggie broth with add-ons of chicken or seafood. Our favorite.

❧ *Big Sky Cafe, 1121 Broad Street, San Luis Obispo 93401; (805) 545–5401. Open 7:00 A.M.–10:00 P.M. Monday–Saturday, 8:00 A.M.–9:00 P.M. Sunday. Beer and wine. Visa, MasterCard, American Express. Wheelchair accessible.*

Back to Higuera working our way up the south side from Broad, we come to Penelope's cards and stuffed animals, the Art of the Sandwich Deli, the Library bar (perfect alibi, Mom), and Mother's Tavern, a new old-looking grill/restaurant with lots of charm and a long dark wood bar with green vinyl stool and chair covers (right next door to the Library, of course). Cloud Nine carries children's apparel, and Edgeware Cutlery & Gifts sells money clips and Swiss Army knives, among other things.

Bubblegum Alley is a major attraction for some people, a narrow walkway from Higuera Street to a parking lot where thousands of people have stuck their gum wads and turned stickiness into an art form, uncensored poetics included.

Atmospheres majors in interior design, and Posies sells Yankee candles, Crabtree & Evelyn products, and Tiffany lamp replicas. Next up the street is a Nannette Kella factory outlet, and the dramatic, gated, white stucco edifice on the corner of Garden Street houses Marshalls Jewelers.

For many people the main attraction on Garden Street is **SLO BREWING CO.**, one of the most popular establishments on the central coast. A sign informs visitors on entering that "This is an unreinforced masonry building. Unreinforced masonry buildings may be unsafe in the event of an earthquake." Duh!

Upstairs is an excellent pub restaurant, loaded with locals at lunchtime, and serving everything from salads to burgers and healthy chicken with huge fries and, guess what, beer. Lots of SLO made-here beer, such as Brickhouse Extra Pale Ale, Cole Porter, Garden Alley Amber Ale, and Earthquake Relief Wheat Beer. A gallery overlooks the tanks and there's a whole explanation of the brewing process. At least look into the turn-of-the-century classic billiard room.

SLO Brewing Co., 1119 Garden Street, San Luis Obispo 93401; (805) 543–1843. Open 11:30 A.M.–10:00 P.M. Monday–Wednesday, 11:30 A.M.–1:30 A.M. Thursday–Saturday, 11:30 A.M.–9:00 P.M. Sunday. Visa and MasterCard. Not wheelchair accessible.

Off Higuera at Morro Street, Gap, Ross, Victoria's Secret, and Starbucks fans will all find their fixes. Jerry likes Nemo Comics nearby. Fans of Cambria's Linn's Main Binn and Restaurant will melt at Linn's Bakery's pastries and goodies (at Chorro and Marsh).

East of Chorro on Higuera near Osos Street, you will run into Woodstock Pizza, a local mainstay, Firestone Grill in an old service station, and Mo's Steakhouse.

Significant Others

Right downtown in San Luis Obispo food lovers must check into MUZIO'S GROCERY, David Muzio's ever-popular, truly European delicatessen specializing in imported gourmet foods, cheeses, salads, hard-to-get mustards, and heaping fabulous sandwiches. One of our favorites.

Muzio's Grocery, 870 Monterey Street, San Luis Obispo 93401; (805) 543–0800. Open 9:00 A.M.–6:00 P.M. Monday–Saturday. Beer and wine. Visa and MasterCard. Wheelchair accessible.

BUONA TAVOLA is a terrific little Italian restaurant right next to the classic Fremont Theatre. Chef/owner Antonio Varia prepares everything from antipasti to pasta, seafood, and Italian desserts. Garden seating and an excellent local wine list. A favorite of many locals.

Buona Tavola, 1037 Monterey Street, San Luis Obispo 93401; (805) 545–8000. Open for lunch 11:30 A.M.–2:30 P.M. Monday–Friday, dinner 5:30–10:00 P.M. Monday–Saturday. Beer and wine. Visa, MasterCard, American Express, Discover. Wheelchair accessible.

APPLE FARM, an actual working gristmill with waterfalls and a waterwheel grinding wheat, producing apple cider, and churning ice cream, is an all-American, mom's-apple-pie comfort center featuring local agricultural products and a large restaurant with hot apple dumplings, fresh-baked cornbread and honey butter, soups, pies, and a salad bar. Seriously hungry folks might enjoy the roast turkey and dressing ($12.95), Santa Maria-style tri-tip ($12.95), country pot roast ($12.95), or pan-fried trout ($13.95). Lunch offers loads of burgers and sandwiches, including a hot meat loaf sandwich to die for ($7.95), open-faced hot turkey sandwich with mashed potatoes and gravy ($7.95), and even a Philly cheesesteak or garden burger ($6.95). Breakfast cooks up apple sausage and almost anything, omelettes, potato pancakes, and enormous country breakfasts.

Be sure to visit the inn, bakery, and cute gift shop where many people get lost enjoying the trinkets.

❧ *Apple Farm, Highway 101 at Monterey exit, 2015 Monterey Street, San Luis Obispo 93401; (805) 544–6100 or (800) 374–3705. Open 7:00 A.M.–10:00 P.M. daily. Beer and wine. Visa, MasterCard, American Express, Discover. Wheelchair accessible.*

The pink and white goopily romantic MADONNA INN spells heavenly romance to some people. Alex and Phyllis Madonna put millions into this 2,000-acre resort and created their personal expression of genuine visitor hospitality, with a different fantasy theme in every bedroom, heart-shaped pillows, and lots of red velvet and textured wallpapers. There's even a Caveman Room carved out of solid rock. Are you ready? If you weren't, this might help. You can just visit and have a look, and men must not miss the famous men's room and its more famous waterfall urinal. If you didn't have to go . . . .

Walk around and stop in at the MADONNA INN COFFEE SHOP & BAKERY for excellent full breakfasts of eggs, meats, pancakes and waffles, fruits including a baked Roman Beauty apple ($3.45), Swiss sausages, a Madonna frittata ($8.45), turkey and broccoli omelette ($8.25), and corned beef hash with eggs ($8.95). A full range of sandwiches hot and cold, salads, healthy meals, and espresso drinks are served at lunch and dinner.

The bakery features French pastries, fruit and cream pies, and their famous Black Forest cakes. Drop in on the ladies' boutique and the men's clothing store.

The Gold Rush dining room glows with thousands of tiny lights to illuminate your steak, seafood, lamb, or chicken cooked over an oak pit barbecue, with great results and ranging from $15 to $22.

Madonna Inn's house wine is bottled by Castoro, and you can buy many local wines in the Madonna Inn Gourmet Gift Shop, which is a fun place to explore anyway. Enjoy!

Madonna Inn, 100 Madonna Road right off Highway 101, San Luis Obispo 93401; (805) 543–3000 or (800) 543–9666.

Shoppers, you may want to continue down Madonna Road a wee bit to the Madonna Mall and outlet shopping centers.

CHAPTER 6

SAN LUIS OBISPO COUNTY: THE COAST

his part of central California contains some of the most dramatic coastline of the western United States, beginning at Ragged Point just below Big Sur (Monterey County), where the ocean waves crash into vertical cliffs.

Average temperatures here are much lower than you'll find in the inland wine country, with year-round highs ranging from 61° to 71° and lows from 40° to 54°. Bring a sweater or jacket and be prepared for spectacular scenery, great walks, and lots of browsing.

SAN SIMEON AND HEARST CASTLE

Once an exciting whaling village, San Simeon is now primarily the historic landmark Sebastian's General Store and San Simeon Pier, built in 1878 by George Hearst, father of William Randolph Hearst, who brought his opulent interior decorations across this pier.

You can get here via Highway 1, Highway 101, and Highway 46 west, or by taking Central Coast Area Transit (805–541–CCAT or 805–781–4467), which connects San Simeon, Cambria, Cayucos, Morro Bay, Los Osos, Cuesta College, California Polytechnic, and San Luis Obispo.

Hearst Castle (officially Hearst San Simeon State Historical Monument) is about 245 miles south from San Francisco via Highway 101 and Highway 46 west, and 205 miles via Highway 1 (six to six and one-half hours). From Monterey it's about 165 miles on Highway 101 and 94 miles on Highway 1, and a little over three hours both routes. From Los Angeles it's 254 miles and six hours either way.

HEARST CASTLE, or La Cuesta Encantada (the Enchanted Hill), is the magnificently opulent dream estate built by William Randolph Hearst north of San Simeon. As a child, Hearst visited San Simeon with his family. After he became an extremely wealthy publisher, he chose this dramatic site on the western slope of the Santa Lucia Mountains to develop his enchanted heaven over nearly thirty years. Hearst's estate was the movie star party mecca in Hollywood's golden age, and today it is a California historical monument visited by nearly a million people each year.

If you choose to join the crowd, it is wise to make reservations, particularly if you want to go on one of the several tours offered. You can explore the castle only on a tour, so we advise booking to see the 165 rooms and 127 acres of gardens, terraces, mosaic pools, and walkways. The whole "house" is furnished with an unusually impressive collection of splendor: Spanish and Italian antiques and art.

From his laborer/miner father Hearst gained his respect and love for the land, and from his mother, Phoebe Apperson Hearst, he acquired his love for European art, Mediterranean architecture, ornamental craftsmanship, and antiques. He built the castle, which he referred to as "the ranch," as a monument to his mother.

Remarkably advanced for its 1919 construction, La Cuesta Encantada was designed by famed architect Julia Morgan and built as a summer home with steel beams and concrete to assure that California earthquakes could not destroy Hearst's dream. The spectacular Neptune pool was enlarged and rebuilt twice. (Kathleen has a mosaic bench her mother made with tiles given her by one of the original pool mosaicists.) Hearst spared no expense importing European antiques, hand-carved ceilings, marble sculptures, and full-grown cypress trees via the San Simeon pier. The Casa Grande has 115 rooms, and several luxurious guest houses surround the main house.

Something like the famous rambling-forever Winchester House in San Jose in which the creative process became almost more important than the result, the castle still was not finished when Hearst died in 1951, thirty-two years after it was begun.

All tours of the Hearst Castle include a half-mile walk and from 150 to 400 stairs (wheelchair tours available by reservation), as well as visits to the Greco-Roman–style outdoor pool, and to an indoor pool lined with Venetian glass and gold. Daytime tours take about one hour and forty-five minutes, including bus tours to and from the visitor center where you park.

First-time visitors will probably enjoy Tour 1 (the only tour available to wheelchairs) for an overall view. Strollers are not permitted on tours. Tours leave the visitor center by bus at the time printed on the ticket, so plan ahead. During the 5-mile, fifteen-minute bus ride to the castle you can listen to an audiotape giving background information, so you can hit the ground running or rolling.

Tours usually sell out in advance, so be sure to call (800) 444–4445 for reservations.

Tour 1 covers La Casa del Sol, an eighteen-room guest cottage, with esplanade and gardens; and La Casa Grande (of which five rooms are shown: the assembly room, the refectory dining room, the morning room, billiard room, and theater).

Tour 2 takes in the upper floors of La Casa Grande, including the doge suite (Italian), the cloister rooms for guests, the library and its 5,000 books and Greek vases, the Gothic suite and Gothic study, and the pantry and kitchen.

Tour 3 includes La Casa del Monte, north wing of La Casa Grande, north terrace and grand entrance, and the video room of photographs and film from the 1920s and 1930s.

Tour 4 (April–October) takes you to the hidden terrace, an overview of the gardens and grounds, La Casa del Mar, Neptune pool dressing rooms, and the wine cellar of La Casa Grande with its 3,000 bottles of rare European vintages and California wines.

The evening tour (spring and fall) takes two hours and ten minutes, including bus trips to and from the visitor center, and covers the living history program, illuminated pools and gardens, highlights of La Casa Grande, and La Casa del Mar.

A fun sidelight is the five-story National Geographic Theater showing of "Hearst Castle™: Building the Dream," which follows the story of the castle from Hearst's inspiration to realization. Enjoy forty minutes of seven-channel surround sound and wild aerial scenery. Admission: adults $7.00, children $5.00.

& *Hearst San Simeon State Historical Monument, Highway 1, San Simeon 93452; reservations (800) 444–4445, recorded information (805) 927–2000. Open 8:00 A.M.–4:00 P.M. daily. Visa, MasterCard, American Express, Discover. Partly wheelchair accessible.*

Besides its historic attractions related to Hearst endeavors, San Simeon has some delightful art galleries, small restaurants, and shops worth exploring. If you are starving for lunch after your castle tour, take a chance on local fare or make your way south to Cambria.

If you visit Hearst Castle, you will probably want to stay in Cambria, which is south on Highway 1, about twenty minutes or 6 miles.

CAMBRIA

Its residents like to boast that Cambria is "where the pines meet the sea," and they are right. A true seaside village once called San Simeon and Santa Rosa, Cambria today is a well-touristed artists' colony where artists can afford to live (in contrast to Carmel, where few true artists can live or rent a studio). In Cambria you will find local artists' work exhibited everywhere.

The primary business of this once farming community now seems to be tourism. Cambria's residents are artists and craftspeople, active retirees, professionals, ranchers, and farmers. Locals and visitors alike indulge in beachcombing, surfing, hiking, biking, fishing, and kayaking, as well as spotting gray whales, seals, sea otters, and elephant seals along the beaches. San Simeon State Beach is just 5 miles north, and Moonstone Beach is right in Cambria. A full range of accommodations faces the beaches in West Cambria. And there's a free Otter Trolley that transports people, not otters, from Moonstone Beach to Cambria's "east and west villages," known to outsiders as East Cambria and West Cambria.

Cambria really has three parts: the restaurants, motels, and inns along Moonstone Drive and beach (great boardwalk); West Cambria; and the older East Cambria.

Cambria is an art and history fan's delight with a load of "cute" shops thrown in. While it has become a little touristy, it also is a very comfortable place in which to be a tourist. So, as Confucius is so often misquoted, just lie back and enjoy it.

Beginning at the north end of West Cambria's Main Street is the Exxon Station, which we wouldn't even mention except that it sells an exceptional collection of Beanie Babies for those of you who care, as well as diesel fuel, about which we do care. Right next to the Exxon station (remember the spill, folks) is the Main Street Grill featuring hopefully local seafood cooked over the huge barbecue, to eat here or take out, followed by the popular Old Stone Station, which serves fish and chips, prime rib, steaks, and seafood at lunch and dinner.

Caren's Corner, just before the Cambria Fine Arts Gallery, offers an eclectic mix that includes stained glass and crafts, ice cream, and espresso (two plastic tables and a few chairs on the sidewalk too). The Coffee Den right next to the Chamber of Commerce on Main Street has good coffee and pastries to enjoy here or take away, as well as Van Ryn watercolors.

Artifacts gallery features the work of Bev Doolittle, Charles Wysocki, and Bob Byerly, while the ever-present painting magnate Thomas Kinkaide, Animation Art, and Yankee Candles all have outlets in the same building. Simply Angels features everything spiritual and doll-like about angels, New Moon offers personal and home accessories, and the Soldier Factory is a truly rare and interesting emporium of miniatures of all sorts, particularly soldiers and model warplanes. If you are into war, go for it.

On the south side of Main Street in Cambria's west village you will find one of our favorites, the Pewter Plough Playhouse, presenting fabulous local productions and an excellent piano bar facing Main Street for before-, during-, and after-performance stops. Safe at Home majors in collectibles and sports miniatures, Paws on Main specializes in rubber stamps, and Sergio's Restaurant & Wine Shop is a primarily Italianate restaurant with Alaskan halibut, Tuscan chicken, crab cakes, sandwiches, and salads, all under $15.

Wearable Images features cotton and natural fabric resort wear for men and women, and the Cargo Company has leather goods, umbrellas, Hawaiian music, knives, cigars, binoculars, and watches. You figure!

Cat lovers will die over the Cat's Corner, with everything imaginable for your kitty, and just in time comes the locally popular WEST END BAR & GRILL for lunch or even late dinner with full bar, live music, kids' menu, and food to go, including burgers, fajitas, salads, and tiger shrimp scampi ($8.25).

Maison de Marie, next to La Crema Espresso Bar, has an interesting combination of old-world gifts and antiques, and a lovely courtyard full of roses to enjoy while indulging in that coffee and pastry.

In Cambria's east village, the west end of Main Street begins with the favorite Harmony Pasta Factory in the Cambria Village Square shopping center, and Bistro Solé featuring international cuisine at lunch, dinner, or Sunday brunch.

Important to most of us is an excellent set of clean public rest rooms in the parking lot on Center Street, accessible from Burton Drive and right off Main Street.

Our favorite street in Cambria is Burton Drive, loaded with excellent restaurants, history, art, and wine. We begin with ROBIN'S at the corner of Burton and Center. Robin's really does what it says: present "a melting pot of excellent ethnic cuisine prepared with the freshest of natural ingredients." Lunch includes a soup and burrito or taco combo ($7.50), grilled fish tostaditas ($7.95), hot sandwiches under $8.00, and salads. Dinner offers a fresh goat cheese and artichoke salad ($7.95); tandoori prawns with mint and fruit chutneys, chapati, and basmati rice ($15.95); North Indian lamb (roghan josh) with yogurt, ground almonds, and toasted coconut ($14.75); Thai green curry ($9.95); or tofu and tempeh ($9.50).

Weekday dinner features the same daily special on the same day, like grilled fresh salmon on Tuesdays, pork loin with port wine on Wednesdays, or Catalan chicken and shrimp on Thursdays for only $9.95. Be tempted by the fabulous salad deli as you enter the front door.

🌿 *Robin's, 4095 Burton Drive, Cambria 93428; (805) 927–5007; Web site: www.robinsrestaurant.com. Open for lunch 11:00 A.M.–2:30 P.M., late lunch 2:30–5:00 P.M., dinner from 5:00 P.M. Full bar. Visa, MasterCard, American Express. Not wheelchair accessible.*

SQUIBB HOUSE, CAMBRIA

Don't miss the SQUIBB HOUSE just down Burton Drive and its Squibb House SHOP NEXT DOOR, a heavenly home to antique primitives, the best of antique kitchen implements, crockery, ceramics, and handcrafted furnishings— all in an 1885 carpentry shop.

Bruce Black has lovingly and accurately restored Squibb House, an 1877 home whose downstairs was used as a classroom while an addition was built to the Cambria school where owner Fred Darke was principal. Darke later served as School Superintendent and County Recorder of San Luis Obispo County. In 1889 Alexander Paterson bought the house, set up his carpentry business next door, and passed the house along to his son Alexander Jr., whose wife Amy became Cambria's Postmaster.

Earl Van Gordon bought the house in 1919 and operated a general store here, then served as postmaster, school trustee, and justice of the peace, eventually leaving the house vacant. Paul and Louise Squibb took over in 1953 and retired here after founding Midland School in Santa Ynez Valley. The Squibbs began a practice later called "squibbing," in which locals pick litter up off the streets and sidewalks.

Bruce Black now operates the fully restored bed-and-breakfast, as well as the Shop Next Door. Both are among our favorites.

❧ Squibb House and *Shop Next Door,* 4063 Burton Drive, Cambria 93428; (805) 927–9600. Visa, MasterCard, American Express. Wheelchair accessible.

Just down this side of Burton from Squibb House is another local institution, BRAMBLES DINNER HOUSE, which has received a *Wine Spectator* award of excellence (1997) and an International Award of Excellence (1999). Rotary meets here Friday at noon, locals come in regularly, and early bird dinners are served from 4:00 to 5:30 or 6:00 P.M.

Try the salmon cooked over seasoned oak wood ($16.95) or prime rib with Yorkshire pudding ($17.95–$19.95) or the Greek and vegetarian specialties. All dinner entrees include soup or salad. Brunch goes slightly Danish with their famous aebleskiver (apple pancakes) with ham or sausage, corned beef hash, omelettes, or shrimp Louie ($10.95–$14.95 with champagne). Excellent central coast and California wine list.

Brambles Dinner House, 4005 Burton Drive, Cambria 93428; (805) 927–4716. Open from 4:00 P.M. nightly, Sunday brunch 9:30 A.M.–2:00 P.M. Full bar. Visa, MasterCard, American Express, Diners, Carte Blanche. Wheelchair accessible.

Across Burton have a look in Sylvia's Burton Drive Inn and then stroll to FERMENTATIONS, a wonderful wine shop with gourmet delicacies and oils and loads of local wines. Tastes of lemon and citrus grapeseed oils and wines are available. Corkscrew collectors will love the rare L'Esprit and Levin historic corkscrew replicas ranging from $70 to $110.

Fermentations, 4056 Burton Drive, Cambria 94328; (805) 927–7141, fax (805) 927–2289. Open 10:00 A.M.–10:00 P.M. daily. Tasting fee: $4.00 and keep lovely glass. Visa, MasterCard, Discover. Wheelchair accessible.

Kids will enjoy the Rumpelstilzchen Children's Book Gallery and the What Iz Art gallery featuring the art of Dr. Seuss next door to Fermentations.

INDIAN RAITA SALAD
from Fermentations, Cambria

2 medium cucumbers

2 Tbs. salt

1 cup plain yogurt

¼ tsp. ground cumin

1 Tbs. fresh mint leaves, finely chopped

1 head butter lettuce, keeping leaves whole

Peel, core, and slice the cucumbers very thin. Put them in a colander or sieve and sprinkle with the salt. Set to one side for at least 1 hour. Rinse well under plenty of cold water.

Place the sliced cucumbers in a bowl with the yogurt, cumin, and fresh-chopped mint, and mix well. Serve the salad on the butter lettuce leaf, using it as a bowl.

This salad goes well with hot and spicy dishes. Serves four.

Walk or roll and explore the abundance of wide-open shops along Main Street, including the Sow's Ear's Cafe just east of Burton Drive, featuring contemporary and American cuisine from chicken-fried steak and chicken and dumplings to salmon wrapped in parchment—often voted a favorite.

LINN'S MAIN BINN is probably the most popular all-around restaurant and bakery in Cambria. San Luis Obispo locals have voted it Best Desserts in the county. This is where people who come to town to socialize over a cup of coffee and a piece of pie gather. While obsessing over breakfast pastries or fruit pies, be sure to try the potpies for lunch or dinner—some of the best we've had in this country—or the hearty soups and salads. You can also indulge in Linn's pies and gourmet packaged foods at their farm store on Santa Rosa Creek Road. Fun gift shops at both locations.

❧ *Linn's Main Binn, 2277 Main Street, Cambria 94328; (805) 927–0371. Open: restaurant: 7:00 A.M.–10:00 P.M. daily, Sunday champagne brunch from 10:30 A.M.; farm store: 10:00 A.M.–4:00 P.M. daily. Beer and wine. Visa, MasterCard, American Express. Wheelchair accessible.*

Worth a trip or perfectly located for motel and inn guests along Moonstone Beach Drive is the SEA CHEST OYSTER BAR AND SEAFOOD RESTAURANT. If you want to go, reservations are absolutely mandatory for this teensy restaurant with great seafaring decor and lines out into the parking lot.

The Sea Chest is right on Moonstone Beach Drive, right across, yes, from the beach and Pacific Ocean. Everything here is good, if you get in. Specialties include broiled halibut ($18.95), Steve's cioppino ($18.95), and calamari ($15.95), as well as fresh oysters at the oyster bar (six for $10), mahimahi, and Boston clam chowder. Too bad it isn't open for lunch!

SEA CHEST OYSTER BAR AND
SEAFOOD RESTAURANT, CAMBRIA

SANTA ROSA EGGS
from Peter Irsfeld, Olallieberry Inn, Cambria

12 eggs

1 ½ cups half-and-half

6 cups grated cheddar cheese

4 ½ oz. diced green chilies

2 cups cottage cheese

1 ½ cups Bisquick

¾ cube melted butter

1 tsp. salt

½ tsp. pepper

Beat eggs and half-and-half together. Add all other ingredients and mix well. Spray cooking spray in two 9-by-9-by-2 baking dishes and divide mixture between the two pans. Bake uncovered in a preheated 350° F oven for about 45 minutes. Top will be slightly browned and a knife should pierce cleanly. Let sit 10 minutes before serving. Serves twelve.

Sea Chest Oyster Bar and Seafood Restaurant, 6216 Moonstone Beach Drive, Cambria 94328; (805) 927–4514; Web site: www.CentralCoast.com. Open from 5:30 P.M. Wednesday–Sunday. Beer and wine. No credit cards. Not wheelchair accessible.

PENNY'S POTATO BUD COOKIES
from Peter Irsfeld, Olallieberry Inn, Cambria

1 cup butter (softened at room temperature)

2 cups sugar

1–2 tsp. coconut extract (to taste)

2 eggs

2 ⅔ cup Betty Crocker potato buds

2 ⅔ cup Bisquick

Cream together softened butter and sugar. Add coconut extract and eggs and blend well. Add potato buds and Bisquick. Blend until all the buds are incorporated into mixture. Mixture will be slightly dry and crumbly. Drop by teaspoonful onto lightly greased cookie sheet. Bake at 350° F for 13–15 minutes. Makes two dozen.

Other restaurants to try here are the Moonstone Beach Bar & Grill, which is conveniently open for breakfast, lunch, dinner, and Sunday brunch (the only restaurant on the beach open for all those hearty meals), or Moonstone Gardens' hamlet restaurant, which serves lunch and dinner from 11:00 A.M. and has three acres of gardens and the Van Gogh's Ear gallery, featuring the work of local and national artists.

Even if you aren't staying there, we encourage you to drop in to visit the OLALLIEBERRY INN right on Main Street, "where time stands still." It's a classic bed-and-breakfast known widely for its fabulous food. Owners Carol Ann

and Chef Peter Irsfeld have put together a cookbook of his best recipes, so that you can reproduce their hors d'oeuvres, breakfasts, hash browns, biscuits, soups, and dinner entrees. If you buy the cookbook, you get a coupon entitling you to two nights for the price of one midweek during off-season months.
🌿 *Olallieberry Inn, 2476 Main Street, Cambria 94328; (805) 927–3222. Visa and MasterCard. Partly wheelchair accessible.*

Cambria's FARMERS' MARKET is held Fridays, 2:30–5:30 P.M., on Main Street next to Veterans Hall.

HARMONY AND CAYUCOS

The grand metropolis of HARMONY (population eighteen) is barely a block long and boasts a post office, wedding chapel, shops and galleries, and the Central Coast Wine Room, an excellent and casual place to taste and select the best of central coast wines, cigars, and gifts. Moving right along we come to . . .

The tiny beach town and fishing village of CAYUCOS is about 14 miles south of Cambria and 19 miles north of San Luis Obispo. It's heaven for surfers and fishers, who can actually fish off the Cayucos Pier without a license. Antiques fans will find plenty of browsing, and the town's murals depicting local and Old West history entertain everyone. If you're either really tough or really stupid, show up for the annual polar bear dip into the Pacific Ocean's 50° waters on New Year's Day. At least join the throngs cheering on the troops.

MORRO BAY

Morro Bay is only 14 miles northwest of San Luis Obispo, which makes it a perfect quick jaunt to curl your toes in the sand or sample some fresh abalone dripping with lemon butter. If you happen to enter Morro Bay on Highway 1 from the southeast, you can follow the Boulevard for 10 blocks of delightful shops and small restaurants. Morro Bay's longest street, Main Street, begins at Morro Bay State Park and runs north to Morro Strand State Beach. You will find loads of antiques shops, art galleries, and edible goodies on Main Street.

One of the first things you notice in this bird sanctuary and fishing village is the 576-foot high Morro Rock right off the water's edge. Named "El Moro" for its domelike shape and discovered by Portuguese explorer Juan Rodriguez Cabrillo in 1542, this first of the so-called Nine Sisters volcanic peaks is about 21 million years old. The peaks separate the Los Osos and Chorro Valleys and run in a straight line for 12 miles. Original resident Chumash Indians camped at the base of these peaks and ate the berries and roots found growing on the Nine Sisters' slopes. There is an active movement to have the peaks designated historical landmarks to prevent further development in their vicinity.

You can't miss the rock unless the fog's in really badly. Follow Embarcadero north to Coleman Drive, near where the peregrine falcons nest and you can occasionally see otters rafting down the channel on passing logs and boards. During the summer there are lifeguards on duty at the beach just north of the rock, with public rest rooms available.

As a bird sanctuary, Morro Bay provides a nourishing habitat to two dozen threatened and endangered species, including peregrine falcon, brant, brown pelican, black rail, blue heron, and snowy plover. More than 195 migratory bird species make their winter homes at Morro Bay, the last estuary of its kind between Mexico and northern California.

The California Fish and Game Commission designated Morro Rock as an ecological reserve for protection of a peregrine falcon aerie, making access to the rock prohibited and trespassing illegal. Since environmental contamination has made the falcons incapable of producing eggshells thick and durable enough to protect a growing embryo, they are now dependent on men and women to help coddle and raise their young. Pity. So the peregrine fund at Cornell University provides nestlings that Morro Bay adult falcons raise as their own. And this is what we humans have wrought!

Morro Bay is also a major West Coast fishing center, so enjoy the multitude of right-off-the-boat fish markets and restaurants along the Embarcadero. Everyone's local favorites are Hoppe's at Marina Square and Hoppe's Hip Pocket Bistro at 901 Embarcadero.

Windsurfing and sailing are big-time pastimes here, and you can rent kayaks, canoes, and boats along the waterfront or bring your own to the free boat launch ramp and fish-cleaning facilities! Chess lovers should not miss the giant chessboard in Centennial Park 3 blocks from Highway 1 on the Embarcadero. It measures 16 feet square and features giant redwood chess pieces weighing from eighteen to twenty pounds each. Call (805) 772–6278 weekdays for reservations. Use fees range from around $10 for residents to $20 for nonresidents to use the whole board per day, with no hourly time limits.

If your interest in sea ventures is deeper, visit the MORRO BAY AQUARIUM & MARINE REHABILITATION CENTER for a cozy and enlightening experience for kids of all ages.

❧ *Morro Bay Aquarium & Marine Rehabilitation Center, 595 Embarcadero, Morro Bay 93442; (805) 772-7647. Open winter 10:00 A.M.–6:00 P.M. Monday–Friday, 9:00 A.M.–7:00 P.M. holidays and Saturday Sunday, summer*

9:00 A.M.–8:00 P.M. daily. Admission: $1.00 adults, fifty cents children five to fifteen, under five free. Wheelchair accessible.

Also be sure to explore the **MORRO BAY NATURAL HISTORY MUSEUM** and the heron rookery at Morro Bay State Park for a slightly more subdued and educational experience covering flora, fauna, and sea culture of the whole central coast. Black Hill, the second in the Nine Sisters chain of ancient volcanoes, is also in the park.
Morro Bay Natural History Museum, Morro Bay State Park, Morro Bay 93442; (805) 772–2694. Open 10:00 A.M.–5:00 P.M. daily. Admission $2.00 adults, $1.00 ages six to seventeen, under six free. Wheelchair accessible.

Within Morro Bay State Park are an excellent golf course and a marina, the latter on State Park Road and open 9:00 A.M.–5:00 P.M. daily, (805) 772–8796. Adventurers and whale fans might also enjoy whale watching (from December 26 until mid-March). Virg's Fish'n (800–762–5263) runs tours daily, weather permitting, which it doesn't always. Virg's will also take you out fishing, or you can take yourself fishing off the pier.

Nearby Cañada de Los Osos (Valley of the Bears), now called Los Osos, is a charming little town worth exploring. It serves as the gateway to Montana de Oro State Park (Mountain of Gold), probably so-named because of the wild mustard growing on its slopes. Legend suggests that Junipero Serra, a Franciscan padre and founder of California's missions, scattered mustard seed so he and his pals could find their way back and forth between the missions along El Camino Real. The park itself encompasses more than 8,000 acres of breathtakingly rugged wilderness and dramatically jagged coastline, making it attractive to hikers, cyclists, campers, and surfers.

Check out Elfin Forest for miniature oaks at the end of Fifteenth Street in Los Osos, with tours every third Saturday. Call (805) 528–5279. Kids will also enjoy Tidelands Children's Park on the Embarcadero while parents gaze out at the boats in the marina.

FARMERS' MARKET is Thursdays, 3:00–5:00 P.M., at Young's Giant Food, 2650 Main Street, Morro Bay.

PISMO BEACH

Pismo Beach is between Avila and Shell beaches on the north and Grover Beach and Oceano on the south, in a 23-mile stretch of glorious, sparkling central coastline. We are not overstating the fact. The water and sky both exhilarate visitors here, at least when the fog isn't in.

If you are coming from the north, Pismo Beach's city hall and the extremely (cannot say that enough) popular McClintock's Saloon & Dining House are on the left (up/east side) of Highway 1. The town's business district stretches northward parallel to the highway, as do new huge stucco house developments on both sides of the highway, and loads of motels of many price ranges, all emphasizing the ocean view.

Dolliver is Pismo Beach's main street, although its two best local restaurants, Giuseppe's Cucina Italiana and Rosa's Ristorante Italiano, are 1 block up (away from ocean) on Price Street. Other local food hangouts include the Burger Factory Drive-In, Nick's Place, and Brad's Fish and Chips. And then there are the more touristy spots down closer to the water.

Pismo Beach is best known for its Pismo clam and Pismo Beach Clam Festival, its wide-open (in a couple of ways) sandy beaches, and its 1,200-foot-long pier lined by local and visiting fishers. The beach itself is perfect for crunching through pebbled coves, riding horseback along the waterline (call 805–489–8100), exploring tide pools (do not disturb), and watching migrating butterflies clustered in the eucalyptus grove at the southern entrance to town on Highway 1. Pismo is a low-key place where dress is casual, as is life in general. (Movie folks are discovering it's a good place to hide out.)

Biking and in-line skating are popular, as are surfing, boogie boarding, and ATV riding year-round on the sand dunes, which are used for many movies and television shows. Rent ATV stuff at BJ's ATV (805–481–5411).

If you arrive hungry, or even if you don't, we suggest you try GIUSEPPE'S CUCINA ITALIANA, which really ought to be a destination restaurant. You will not experience delicately piled nouvelle cuisine of what our friend M.F.K. Fisher used to call "the puddle school" of cooking. Instead, you are in for some of the best Italian food we have ever enjoyed, well served in a fun dining room with white linen tablecloths, elegant Italian ceramics, green walls and pink rose carpets, chairs and upholstered booths, an old copper espresso machine, and a striking copper-and-tile, wood-burning pizza oven right at the back of the room. Then there are the green outdoor tables and even a takeout window, serving every part of the community.

Giuseppe's will also deliver to your door anywhere in Pismo Beach or adjoining Shell Beach, a real plus in the right circumstance!

Bottles of olive oil and balsamic vinegar remain on the table for you to use at any time. We shared the best Caesar salad on God's little earth, full of house-made croutons, garlic, and anchovy dressing, as well as one of their imaginative, perfect pizzas. Ours was the daily special pizza with freshly sliced pepperoni, Canadian bacon, tomatoes, and artichokes, along with a Heineken beer and iced tea for a total of $20.22!

Salads may include grilled portobello mushrooms with chopped arugula, tomato, and shaved Parmigiano cheese ($6.95); Belgian endive, radicchio, sun-dried tomatoes and Gorgonzola ($6.95); vine-ripe tomatoes with basil and fresh mozzarella ($6.95); or sea scallops with lemon, pepper, and virgin olive oil ($8.95).

The pasta offerings are perfect and include soup, Caesar salad, or butter lettuce with Gorgonzola dressing. Try the tortellini Giuseppe with pancetta, mushrooms, tomatoes, and peas ($12.95); the butternut squash ravioli in a grana Parmigiana cream sauce ($13.95); the rigatoni with prosciutto, mascarpone cheese, and portobello mushrooms ($13.95); or the spaghettini with ahi tuna, tomatoes, and capers in a black olive sauce ($14.95). Loads of seafood, eggplant, free-range chicken, veal, scampi, and osso buco are available, as well as filet mignon and rack of lamb. Most entrees are in the $15 range, with the lamb and steak at $21.95.

Pizzas are excellent and begin at $8.39 (12-inch) and $10.25 (16 inch)—plus toppings if you create your own concoction. Their specialties top out at about $16. Calamari lovers, do not miss the sautéed Monterey squid appetizer ($6.52)!

❧ *Giuseppe's Cucina Italiana, 891 Price Street, Pismo Beach 93449; (805) 773–2873 or 773–2870, fax (805) 773–6768. Open from 11:00 A.M. daily, deliveries 4:30–10:00 P.M. daily. Full bar. Visa, MasterCard, American Express, Discover. Wheelchair accessible.*

NIPOMO

Between Pismo Beach and Santa Maria off Highway 101 is the town of Nipomo, and you must make a special trip there to JOCKO'S, a wonderful funky old-fashioned steak house with a historic, Wild West role in the history of the Santa Maria area. Take the Nipomo exit off Highway 101 and go east on Tefft Street to Thompson Avenue. Jocko's is right around the corner on Thompson just north of Tefft. While Santa Maria is known for its barbecue, Jocko's is the restaurant where you can try it at its best any day of the week.

In 1886 Emery Knotts opened a saloon on Tefft Street, but after a fire burned most of the block in 1888, the saloon was moved to the Thompson Street block, just south of the present Jocko's restaurant. Emery had eight sons who helped run the saloon or tend bar, including Ralph "Jocko" Knotts, who was the second licensed driver and a justice of the peace in Nipomo. Jocko's wife, Millie, was the first telephone operator and a local postmaster.

During Prohibition (1920–1933), Jocko ran a garage and service station here, selling car parts and even a little booze—white lightning and homemade brew—out of the trunk of a car. In 1926 Jocko and "Bull" Tognazzini opened a saloon and watering hole called Jocko's Cage at one end of the garage. During the forties, slot machines, poker games, and card rooms appeared and disappeared quickly in sync with the arrivals and departures of authorities.

Jocko's sons Fred and George ran Jocko's Cage through the fifties and started serving barbecue on Saturdays and Sundays, with horseshoe pits under the surrounding pepper trees. To expand their seating they took over a lunch counter in a renovated streetcar next door.

In 1962 George and Fred opened this "new" restaurant and saloon across the street at Tefft and Thompson. The walls are "branded" with the cattle brands of Nipomo ranches, including that of Captain William C. Dana, original owner of the 38,000-acre Nipomo rancho land grant and distant relative of the Knotts family.

Fans really do drive hundreds of miles to experience the best steak dinner they ever had and it is well worth a slight deviation from an almost vegetarian regime just for the taste. The steaks are about 3 inches thick and coated with that salty, garlicky mixture famous in the area. All dinners come with here-baked beans, salad, potato of choice, and ice cream. The spare ribs, chops, chicken, deep-fried rainbow trout, pastas, sandwiches, and salads are equally good. The bar between the two dining rooms is so much fun that you won't mind waiting for your table, which you should plan to do. The martini/old-fashioned glass is part of their logo for good reason. Unless you have a place to take your leftovers or have a huge appetite, we suggest you share a steak.

❧ *Jocko's, 125 North Thompson Avenue, Nipomo 93444; (805) 929–3686 or 929–3565. Open 8:00 A.M.–10:00 P.M. Sunday–Thursday, 8:00 A.M.–11:00 P.M. Friday–Saturday. Full bar. Visa, MasterCard, American Express. Wheelchair accessible.*

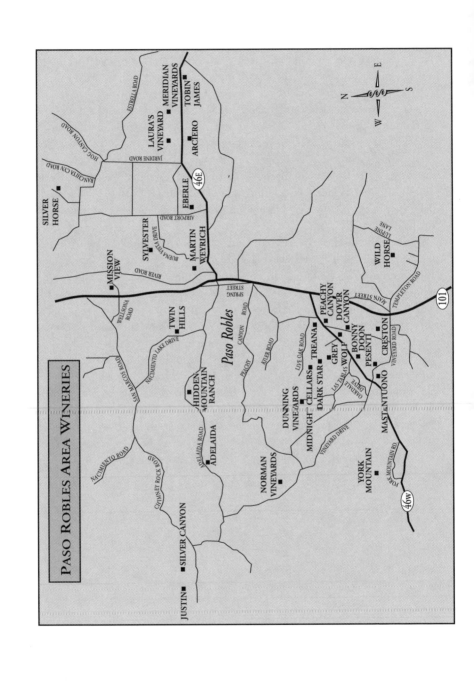

PASO ROBLES AREA WINERIES

CHAPTER 7

TOURING SAN LUIS OBISPO COUNTY WINERIES

M̄ost of San Luis Obispo County's wineries are in the Paso Robles area, which is where we will start and which will take up most of this chapter. But there are also excellent ones in the Edna Valley south of San Luis Obispo, so we go there too. We take you to all the wineries that are open to the public for tasting.

PASO ROBLES AREA

Paso Robles area wineries cluster on and off Highway 46 east and Highway 46 west and some of the latter's side roads. (Please note that Highway 46 west is not the western extension of Highway 46 east. Highway 46 east is Twenty-fourth Street on the west side of Highway 101, and becomes Nacimiento Lake Drive.) Mission View Estate winery in San Miguel is the exception to the rule (there has to be one, right?). So we take you to it first, particularly convenient if you are approaching Paso Robles from the north.

Whether you drive from north or south, you'll be coming via Highway 101, which divides east from west.

In the summer of 1999, Joey Leviste moved his MISSION VIEW ESTATE VINEYARD & WINERY tasting room from right on Highway 101 to his winery in San Miguel. To get here, take the Mission exit in San Miguel to Fourteenth Street, take a right on Fourteenth, cross the railroad tracks, and turn right (south) on River Road to the winery.

Mission View is a small, friendly boutique winery where the enthusiastic staff does a little of everything. Here you can easily see the whole operation. Be sure to ask questions. While visiting Mission View, take the opportunity to walk through Mission San Miguel and its shop. (See p. 132 for Mission San Miguel.)

Fine points: Featured wines: Chardonnay, Fumé Blanc, Merlot, Zinfandel, Cabernet Sauvignon. Owner: Joey Leviste. Winemaker: David Kahn. Cases: 6,000. Acres: 40.

ᵗᵛ *Mission View Estate Vineyard & Winery, 13350 North River Road, San Miguel 93451; (805) 467–3104, fax (805) 457–3719. Open 10:00 A.M.–5:00 P.M. daily. Tasting fee: none. Visa, MasterCard, American Express. Wheelchair accessible.*

WINERIES EAST OF HIGHWAY 101

Now we take you to the wineries out Highway 46 east, and then bring you back on the same road. We do it this way so that you don't crisscross the highway and kill yourself or others. If you don't want to go the whole way, just pick up our tour where you happen to be.

About 5 miles east of Highway 101 are two wineries across the road from each other that seem to exemplify the big and little of the entire wine business: the dramatic, super-financed, and super-designed EOS at Arciero on the south side, and Laura's Vineyard, a homey winery in a nice-looking mobile home on the north side. (It is possible to gun it straight across the highway from one to the other, but it's not worth risking your life. We made it but do not recommend the experience.)

The European feeling you sense looking at the buildings of **EOS ESTATE WINERY** at **ARCIERO ESTATE WINERY** comes from its model, Monte Cassino, a

EOS AND ARCIERO ESTATE WINERIES, PASO ROBLES

one-time Benedictine monastery built centuries ago near the Arciero family home in Santa Elia Fiumerapido. The Arciero brothers' construction company built the winery. Convenient and smart!

Local wind blows the scent of rose gardens through the air. The 6,000-square-foot tasting room and visitors' center has the most comprehensive and elegant gift shop we have seen anywhere. But the real surprise and treat is right around the corner to the right just inside the front door. Even if you aren't a race car fan, you will enjoy the chance to be this close to famous miraculously fast cars, such as cars driven by Arciero Racing Team members Scott Pruett and Cristiano da Matta.

A whole deck of tables facing the vast winery building welcomes you to picnic, and the staff here is extremely well informed and helpful.

EOS ESTATE WINERY and ARCIERO ESTATE WINERY are the creations and dreams of former Indianapolis 500 race car driver Frank Arciero Sr., who more recently has sponsored drivers Phil Hill, Dan Gurney, Al and Bobby Unser, and Michael Andretti.

In 1939 Frank (then fourteen) and his brother Phil (ten) came from Italy, where they had stomped grapes and crushed olives, to join their father and older brother in New York. Neither of them spoke English. The young brothers became ditchdiggers and learned enough to start a paving business. Visiting his Army son at Fort Ord, Frank attended car races at Monterey's Laguna Seca Raceway and fell in love. And he was off to the races! Phil now runs Arciero Brothers concrete construction empire. Now Frank Arciero Jr. (Butch) and his wife Betty help with sales and marketing, Butch having worked in his father's construction business and succeeding as Driver of the Year in the Mickey Thompson Off Road Grand Prix Series Unlimited Super 1600 class. Oh yes, you can buy loads of Arciero racing team paraphernalia, from hats to coffee mugs.

And by the way, the Arcieros are making some excellent wines, too. Their 1995 Zinfandel rates equally with several from Napa Valley and costs about half the price. Got your interest now?

Arciero's EOS series, named for the Greek goddess of dawn, focuses on classic, old-world methods and quality. Eos is pictured on labels near the constellation Orion, with whom she supposedly had a dalliance. At EOS the grapes are harvested as near dawn as possible to keep the fruit cool and help retain flavors. According to mythology, Eos gave birth to the four winds—Boreas, Eurusm, Zephyrus, and Notus—after which EOS' four vineyard blocks have been named.

The Vernon Underwood Family, majority owners of Young's Markets, are now partners in EOS Estate Winery.

Fine points: Featured wines: EOS Chardonnay, Sauvignon Blanc, Zinfandel, Cabernet Sauvignon, Moscato; Arciero Arpeggio, Nebbiolo, Sangiovese, Chardonnay, Chenin Blanc, White Zinfandel, Merlot, Cabernet Sauvignon, Petite Syrah, Zinfandel, Merlot, Muscat Canelli. Owners: EOS: Arciero and Underwood families; Arciero: Arciero family and Kerry Vix. Winemakers: EOS: Napa consultant Tom Eddy; Arciero: Stephen Felten. Cases: 200,000 plus. Acres: 700 plus.

🍇 *EOS and Arciero Estate Wineries, 5625 Highway 46 east, PO Box 1179, Paso Robles 93447; (800) 249–WINE. Open 10:00 A.M.–5:00 P.M. daily.* Visa, MasterCard, American Express, Discover. Wheelchair accessible.

When you leave EOS and Arciero, turn right (east) and go another few miles to TOBIN JAMES CELLARS, the most hilariously fun winery anywhere. While it's a bit out there—12 miles east of Paso Robles—and in ambience, too—it is actually the first winery you come to if you are coming from Fresno or Bakersfield on Highway 246 east.

As you approach Tobin James on Union Road and Highway 246 east, you first see the peak-roofed, yellow-with-purple-trim Victorian that is Tobin James' little bed-and-doughnut or bed-and-Danish. As you drive into the winery parking lot, you see the two-story wood winery with wagon wheels, palm trees, and all sorts of cowboy and old farm paraphernalia, with the B&D just beyond. Sunbursts are the theme here—they appear on all of Tobin James' labels.

Tobin James Shumrick, unearned Southern accent and all, founded Tobin James after working in a wine shop in Cincinnati, Ohio; as assistant winemaker at Eberle Winery; and as founding winemaker at Peachy Canyon, which duties he performed for free on the condition that he could make his own wine there as well. You will find him outrageous, brilliant, and funny, as we did.

At that Cincinnati wine shop, Gary Eberle walked in one day to promote Estrella River Winery, in which he was then a partner. Toby said he would love to come out to Paso Robles to learn to make wine and would work a harvest crush for free just for the chance. Following his stint as a cellar rat and barrel room manager, and later in marketing positions at Estrella, Toby followed Eberle to his own winery, where Eberle offered him the position of assistant winemaker.

One day at Eberle, a vineyard manager brought six tons of grapes that had been rejected by another winery as well as by Gary Eberle, and Toby said. "I'll take 'em." He talked Eberle into letting him make some wine out of them, and as Toby says, "The medals just started rockin' in." The experience gave him the courage to go out on his own, and Tobin James is the Wild West result. This is a guy who knew at age eighteen that he would have his own winery, and it

IN FRONT OF THE TASTING ROOM OF
TOBIN JAMES CELLARS, PASO ROBLES

shows. He's very honest in saying that his Chateau Le Cacheflo (not a French wine, but a blend of Syrah, Mourvedre, Grenache and a splash of Zinfandel) is a "pool, patio, and BBQ wine."

The tasting room is loaded with funk and junque, including a heavy, long wooden tasting bar Jesse James shot two bullets through and Tobin James brought here from Missouri, a kids' jail play corner, free video games, and great music in the background, all of which adds up to feeling like you're in a saloon and bordello—precisely Toby's goal. Toby also welcomed investor/partner Lance Silver, who migrated to Paso Robles from Los Angeles (where he developed and sold an extremely successful clothing company) and now lives over the tasting room with his family.

The B&D is terrific. We stayed in what's dubbed the penthouse apartment, which felt like the perfect self-sufficient studio to live in for awhile and write a few good (of course) books. The complete kitchen and washer/dryer combination along with the plush feather bed and views make this place heaven. It really is a B&D&W, since it comes with a bottle of wine. Van Halen and Heather Locklear were the next scheduled guests. Unfortunately we had to rouse Lance because we were too dumb to work the high-tech television control and couldn't get it to turn off. But then that's our problem.

Fine points: Featured wines: Chardonnay, Chardonnay Afterglow, Zinfandel, Cabernet Sauvignon, James Gang Merlot and Muscat, Chateau Le Cacheflo blend, Syrah Bulls Eye, Muscat Dream Catcher, Charisma Dessert Zinfandel, Dessert Sauvignon Blanc Jubilation, Sparkling Wine Dream Weaver. Owners: Tobin James Shumrick and

Lance Silver. Winemaker: Tobin James Shumrick. Cases: 15,000. Acres: none, buy locally.

❧ *Tobin James Cellars, 8950 Union Road, Paso Robles 93446; (805) 239–2204, fax (805) 239–2204. Open 10:00 A.M.–6:00 P.M. daily. Visa and MasterCard. Wheelchair accessible.*

As you leave Tobin James, turn left out of the driveway onto Union, and then left extremely carefully (west) back onto Highway 246 east. Watch out for cars coming around the bend from the right (east). All the wineries we take you to between here and Paso Robles will now be on the right (north) side of the highway.

In 1.2 miles you come to MERIDIAN VINEYARDS' roller-coaster driveway, which leads you to one of the most beautiful French-like wineries on the central coast, with young tasting room staffers to match. As you get out of the car and follow the path lined with a tastefully labeled herb garden shaded by 200-year-old oak trees to the natural stone winery, signs announce "Caution: Rattlesnakes. Please stay on path." Believe them. Don't miss the view of Meridian's home vineyards.

You are welcome to enjoy a picnic at Meridian's green umbrellaed tables. If you didn't bring supplies, Meridian is one of the few wineries in the area that has a full and exquisite deli case with goodies such as Dutch and Vermont cheeses, waters, and chocolates, with plenty of crackers available nearby. Be sure to check out the work of Chicago artist Thomas Gathman, who designed the jazzy Meridian labels and whose deal includes Meridian continuing to buy his creations. Hence you get to see a private show whenever you visit. Enjoy!

Winemaker Chuck Ortman is the story at Meridian. Ortman majored in graphic arts at the California College of Arts and Crafts in Oakland, but when a

friend gave him some wine he had made in his mother's basement (much better than bombs!), he was hooked. To his parents' chagrin, in 1968 he got a job dragging hoses (about as low as you can go) in the Napa Valley for Joe Heitz and moved his wife Sue and their daughter there.

MERIDIAN VINEYARDS'
TASTING ROOM

LAMB CHOPS WITH ROAST ASPARAGUS AND PEARL ONIONS
from Meridian Vineyards, Paso Robles

8 double lamb chops

8 oz. peeled pearl onions

1 lb. asparagus, white part of stalks trimmed off

olive oil

2 tsp. fresh rosemary, minced (save 4 sprigs for garnish)

1 cup Merlot

1 Tbs. minced shallots

2 cloves garlic

salt

1 qt. veal stock (or other stock or broth) reduced to 1 cup

Marinate lamb chops in minced rosemary, olive oil, and garlic.

Brown the pearl onions in olive oil and cover. Roast in 375° F oven for 15–20 minutes, tossing every 5 minutes.

Season the lamb with salt and pepper and brown in large sauté pan. Reserve pan drippings for sauce preparation to follow. Place the chops on a cooling rack on a sheet pan. Roast the chops at 425° F. for 10–12 minutes or until they reach 120° F internal temperature.

Lay the asparagus in one layer in a baking dish, toss in olive oil, salt, and pepper. Roast the asparagus for 7–8 minutes at 425° F.

Using the pan the lamb was browned in, lightly sauté the shallots and minced rosemary. Add the Merlot and reduce to 2 Tbs. Add the reduced lamb stock. Season with a pinch of salt and pepper and pour into a bowl.

Presentation: Place 2 chops at the bottom of each plate. Fan out 5 spears of asparagus in between and top the asparagus with roasted onions. Spoon the sauce over each chop and garnish with a rosemary sprig. Serves four. Serve with Meridian Vineyards California Merlot.

In the next twenty years Ortman worked or consulted for Heitz, Spring Mountain, St. Clement, Fisher, Far Niente, St. Andrew's, Shafer, Cain Cellars, and Keenan, during which an Ortman style developed, being one of the first California winemakers to explore barrel fermentation instead of using stainless steel tanks.

Ortman first bottled an Edna Valley Chardonnay under his own label in 1979, and changed the name to Meridian at Sue's suggestion to show his love for sailing and because it "means the achievement of an idea." In 1988 Wine World Estates (now Beringer Wine Estates) invested in Meridian and bought this winery (then Estrella River Winery), for Ortman and Meridian to develop. Now Meridian taps its vast vineyard resources here at its home vineyard in Paso Robles in the Edna Valley, and in Santa Barbara County's Santa Maria Valley. This is a delightful place to visit.

Beringer also owns Los Hermanos, Stag's Leap, Beringer, Chateau St. Jean, Chateau Souverain, and Napa Ridge wineries.

Fine points: Featured wines: Chardonnay, Sauvignon Blanc, Gewürztraminer, Cabernet Blanc, Pinot Noir, Merlot, Syrah, Cabernet Sauvignon, Zinfandel. Owner: Beringer Wine Estates. Winemaker: Chuck Ortman. Cases: won't reveal. Acres: 3,534 of their own, buy from 1,397 of others.

🍇 *Meridian Vineyards, 7000 Highway 46 east, PO Box 3289, Paso Robles 93447; (805) 237–6000; Web site: www.meridianvineyards.com. Open 10:00 A.M.–5:00 P.M. daily. Tasting fee: none. Visa, MasterCard, American Express, Discover. Wheelchair accessible.*

As you come out of Meridian, turn right (west) on Highway 246 east, and in 3 miles make a hard right and then an immediate right through the white

LAURA'S VINEYARD,
PASO ROBLES

gate into Laura's Vineyard, right across the highway from EOS and Arciero. Laura was the mother of founder Cliff Giacobine and Gary Eberle. She helped found Estrella River Winery just up the road, where Meridian is now.

LAURA'S VINEYARD, with its white and baby blue mobile home with a metal porch and overhang for outdoor tasting and picnics,
offers a stark contrast to Arciero. Inside, George and Betty Cazaly host the small, cozy tasting room, full of more blue and white and lots of wine-oriented gifts. New owners (1996) Paso Robles Estates, headed by president Patrick O'Dell (who also owns Turnbull Vineyards in the Napa Valley), plans to build a new winery with big-time landscaping, eventually. For now, the lawn and porch will do just fine, thank you.

Fine points: Featured wines: Chardonnay, Semillon, White Zinfandel, Gamay Beaujolais, Cabernet Franc, Zinfandel, Cabernet Sauvignon, Syrah. Owners: Paso Robles Estates. Winemaker: Jon Engleskirger. Cases: 5,000. Acres: 432.

❧ *Laura's Vineyard, 5620 Highway 246 east, Paso Robles 93447; (805) 238–6300. Open 10:00 A.M.–6:00 P.M. daily. Tasting fee: none. Visa and MasterCard. Wheelchair accessible, although portable rest room is not.*

Wiggle your way back to Highway 246 east and turn right (west) and go 2.4 miles to EBERLE WINERY, which you approach through the high overhead entry gate. The redwood winery, surrounded by poplar trees and flowers, overlooks Eberle's estate vineyards.

Just walking into Eberle is a blood-pressure-lowering experience. Chants waft through the air, guests look as if they're hanging out in a friend's living room, there are loads of known and unusual Jewish and other cookbooks on the shelves, and the staff are grown-ups. Be sure to walk out the door on the left wall of the tasting room to a platform to view the tanks and smell and hear the winemaking process— a rare experience for visiting tasters.

A native of Pittsburgh, Pennsylvania, Eberle founder Gary Eberle studied biology at Penn State on scholarship while playing defensive lineman on the football team and meeting and marrying Jeanie. After graduation the Eberles moved to Louisiana, where Gary excelled at the study of cellular genetics at Louisiana State

EBERLE WINERY ENTRANCE, PASO ROBLES

University. There he befriended a professor who introduced him to food and fine wines, particularly Bordeaux, and he quickly became fascinated with the Cabernet Sauvignon grape that is the basis of many Bordeaux. Breaking off his genetics studies, Gary visited UC/Davis, where he told the enology department chair that he wanted to be a winemaker, and the chair let him in the program without even requiring him to take the qualifying exam! He ended up with a doctorate in fermentation and enology, rare indeed.

On returning to Louisiana, Gary and Jeanie conferred for "seconds" and decided to move to California. Gary's goal at Davis was to make the best Cabernet Sauvignon possible. He studied the Paso Robles region, saw huge potential, and in 1974 planted 500 acres of vineyards on the Estrella River plains, naming the winery Estrella River and developing it to producing 200,000 cases a year. Estrella River was eventually sold to Wine World Estates, now Beringer Wine Estates, whose Meridian Vineyards now occupies the former Estrella River site. At Eberle Gary focuses on handcrafted limited quantity wines.

Be sure to ask to see the 15,863 square feet of caves where you can look in on the Wild Boar Room, a 100-seat underground dining facility where guest chef dinners are held regularly. This is one mailing list to get on! Loads of gold medals for Chardonnays and Cabernets.

Fine points: Featured wines: Chardonnay, Grenache, Syrah, Zinfandel, Cabernet Sauvignon, Cabernet Sauvignon/Syrah blend, Counoise Rosé, Muscat Canelli, and Côtes du Robles, a red blend. Owner and enologist: Gary Eberle. Winemaker: Bill Sheffer. Cases: 19,500. Acres: 38 and buy locally.

> ### BREADED PORK CHOPS WITH CAPER SAUCE
> *from Eberle Winery, Paso Robles*
>
> *4 pork chops, cut ¾ inch thick*
> *1 egg, beaten*
> *1 tsp. salt*
> *¼ tsp. freshly ground black pepper*
> *½ cup dry bread crumbs*
> *¼ cup vegetable oil*
> *2 Tbs. butter*
> *2 Tbs. chopped capers*
> *⅓ cup beef broth*
>
> Trim the fat off the chops. Dip chops in the egg beaten with salt and pepper, then coat with the bread crumbs. Heat the oil in a skillet. Cook the chops in the oil 15 minutes on each side. Pour off the oil and add the butter, capers, and broth. Cook 10 minutes longer, and spoon sauce over chops on plate. Serves four. Serve with Eberle Grenache.

❧ *Eberle Winery, 3½ miles east of Paso Robles on Highway 46 east, PO Box 2459, Paso Robles 93447; (805) 238–9607. Open 10:00 A.M.–5:00 P.M. daily,*

10:00 A.M.–6:00 P.M. summer. Tasting fee: none. Visa, MasterCard, American Express, Discover. Wheelchair accessible.

When you come out of Eberle's driveway, turn right (west) again and go another 2.8 miles back toward Paso Robles to the newly remodeled **MARTIN-WEYRICH WINERY.** This puts you just 0.8 miles east of Highway 101.

We visited the winery, formerly known as Martin Winery, while construction of a new tasting room that will look like an Italian villa was going on. We stepped on and over the tasting room boxes being moved to a trailer for the duration, with loud pleadings from the staff not to call them "trailer trash." In 1998 daughter Mary Martin (no relation to the late actress) and her husband, Dave Weyrich, bought the winery from her brothers, all of whom benefit from the family's Martin Outdoor billboard sign company.

Martin-Weyrich considers itself to be the premier producer of Italian varietals in the United States, attributing many firsts to itself: the only American winery exhibiting at the Italian VinItaly of Verona; first grower and producer of Nebbiolo in the United States in modern times; the largest plantation of Nebbiolo in the United States; first U.S. winery to focus solely on Cal-Italia

---

STUFFED RIB EYE WITH GORGONZOLA CHEESE
from Cynthia Reed's Kitchen,
Martin-Weyrich Winery, Paso Robles

4 10-oz. rib-eye steaks	*1 tsp. fresh rosemary*
6 garlic bulbs (⅓ cup roasted garlic)	*½ cup olive oil*
10 oz. Gorgonzola cheese	*pepper to taste*

Cut the tops off 6 garlic bulbs and place in a shallow baking dish. Cover with olive oil and roast in a 200° F oven for 1½ hours. Cool for 10 minutes. Squeeze paste from each bulb.

Place garlic paste, cheese, and rosemary in a food processor and mix until creamy. Chill for 30 minutes.

Make pockets in each steak with a small, sharp knife. Make the cuts ½ inch long and 1 inch deep, slicing into the lean side of the meat. Place chilled mixture in a pastry bag and pipe mixture into steaks. Use a toothpick to close end. Sprinkle pepper on both sides of steak. Grill or barbecue to desired temperature. Absolutely to die for! Serves four. Serve with Martin-Weyrich Cabernet Etrusco. Open wine 1 hour before serving.

varietals; first and only U.S. producer to age and ferment Chardonnay in chestnut barrels; first U.S. producer to blend Sangiovese with Cabernet Sauvignon; first and only producer to use a "vino di ripasso"; first and only U.S. producer to make traditional Vin Santo from straw-dried Malvasia grapes, then aged in barrels; and first U.S. producer to import all of its glass directly from Italy.

We also happen to like the Italian pottery collection they have for sale. The staff are nice, too! Watch for their "Italian style bed-and-breakfast" and seasonal concerts in their amphitheater. You can also get cheese and lunch nibbles here for your picnic.

Fine points: Featured wines: Chardonnay in Botti, Pinot Grigio, Sangiovese Il Palio, Nebbiolo, Nebbiolo Vecchio, Cabernet Etrusco, Zinfandel La Primitiva, Insieme blend, Moscato Allegro, Grappa di Aleatico, Grappa di Nebbiolo. Owners: Dave and Mary Martin Weyrich. Winemaker: Craig Reed. Cases: 25,000; 50,000 by 2000. Acres: 350 plus.

❧ *Martin-Weyrich Winery, 2610 Buena Vista, PO Box 2599, Paso Robles 93447; (805) 238–2520, fax (805) 238–0887. Open 10:00 A.M.–5:00 P.M. Tasting fee: none. Visa, MasterCard, American Express, Discover. Wheelchair accessible.*

A little way up Buena Vista Drive from Martin-Weyrich and Highway 246 east is SYLVESTER WINERY, the newish baby of Sylvester Feichtinger. You can get here more directly by turning north from Highway 246 east onto Airport Road and left again onto Buena Vista Drive.

Sylvester bought the ranch in 1962 (a wise move indeed), growing pistachios and grapes since 1989. After his grapes turned into such good wine for others, he decided to make his own wine, with substantial success. Sylvester brought in former Grgich winemaker Craig Effman. (Grgich recently won a gold at the Western Wine Competition for its 1997 Chardonnay.)

Enjoy the small deli in Sylvester's spacious tasting room, where you can purchase imported meats and cheeses and crackers to snack on around the winery. Don't miss Sylvester's three vintage Rock Island Line train cars.

Fine points: Featured wines: Chardonnay, Cabernet Sauvignon, Merlot, Sangiovese, Syrah. Owner: Sylvester Feichtinger. Winemaker: Craig Effman. Cases: 20,000. Acres: 150 vineyard.

❧ *Sylvester Winery, 5115 Buena Vista Drive, Paso Robles 93446; (805) 227–4000, fax (805) 227–6128; Web site: www.sylvesterwinery.com. Open 11:00 A.M.–5:00 P.M. Monday–Friday, 10:00 A.M.–5:00 P.M. Saturday–Sunday. Tasting fee: none. Visa, MasterCard, American Express. Wheelchair accessible.*

PASO ROBLES WINERIES WEST OF HIGHWAY 101

On the west side of Highway 101 you have to make some choices, and those may depend on the time you have to tour and taste. Or perhaps you want to head for specific wineries. We offer a 50-mile Big Circle Tour (with options) and a 15-mile Little Circle Tour. You could spend a day or two sampling on the Big Circle Tour and make the Little Circle Tour in an afternoon, if you hurry. Of course you can just do part of either tour.

Big Circle Tour

Less than a mile off Highway 101, Twenty-fourth Street becomes Nacimiento Lake Drive. As you wind through the hills and almond groves, do not miss Jardine Ranch's COUNTRY NUT HOUSE, where you can purchase locally grown nuts and fruits (these are not people). If the place looks closed, "which it never is," ring the doorbell and Mary or Bill Jardine will come serve you. Bill's family homesteaded this place in 1889 and has been a real pioneer in nut ranching in these parts.

Just taste the crunchy almonds, fruits, nuts, and candies, and it's easy to convince yourself of the health benefits in the gift packs, including the fat.

❧ *Country Nut House at Jardine Ranch, 910 Nacimiento Lake Drive, Paso Robles 93446; (805) 238–2365. Visa, MasterCard, American Express, Discover. Wheelchair accessible.*

Twin Hills Ranch Winery, farther up the road, has been closed for months. It was recently purchased by Peachy Canyon Winery.

Take Adelaida Road west off Nacimiento Lake Drive to visit Hidden Mountain Ranch and Adelaida wineries. Don't let a sign proclaiming PARK ENTRANCE 600 FEET get you excited and dreaming of walking in wilderness. It's a mobile home park. You also pass signs for Hidden Mountain Ranch, a spectacular view down to the right if you dare look, and then you turn left into Hidden Mountain Road 4.5 miles from where you left Nacimiento Lake Drive. The road's a bit rough, lined with eucalyptus trees, and uphill. In about a half mile you turn right at the top of the hill and start your descent. Obey the 10 MILES PER HOUR sign, please, particularly past the house. The tasting room is straight ahead.

HIDDEN MOUNTAIN RANCH, known as the Hoffman Mountain Ranch in the late sixties, is a must stop if you are interested in the fine wine history of the central coast. Stanley Hoffman, a Beverly Hills cardiologist who opened a small practice in Templeton, bought 1,200 acres that reminded him of Burgundy, France, approached and analyzed the land as a scientist, planted vineyards, and retained legendary wine guru André Tchelistcheff to serve as consulting winemaker. Local lore includes tales of Dr. Hoffman hanging IV bottles from vines to give them nutrients the soil lacked.

In 1976 the Hoffman family, including Mrs. Terresa Hoffman and sons David and Michael, built a 70,000-gallon winery to keep up with the demand created by Tchelistcheff's genius. Michael now has the extremely popular SLO Brewery in Paso Robles, and Dr. Hoffman is Ian McPhee's partner in McPhee's Grill in Templeton.

In the mid-eighties Dr. Hoffman sold the winery to a large Japanese corporation that made bulk wine to sell to others. In 1997 three families of engineers who escaped the San Francisco Bay area bought Hoffman Mountain Ranch and renamed it Hidden Mountain Ranch. Those families include Heidi and Jean Changala (he worked at Meridian Vineyards for ten years), Audrey and winemaker Dave McHenry, and Georgia and Randy Vignola, who own and operate a mechanical contracting business that specializes in winery refrigeration and processing systems. (His name must have led him to wine).

The rustic tasting room is the original dark wood winery. You stand on the winery's original cement floor, but ferns have been added to soften the ambience. The tasting bar is a simple wood plank connecting two wine barrels. Tchelistcheff first lived in the house with the Hoffman family but the situation became uncomfortable, so the Hoffmans built him his own tree house to live in. Remember, this mountain has 110° temperatures in the summer, and snow in the winter.

Fine points: Featured wines: Chardonnay, Merlot, Zinfandel, Syrah, Petite Syrah, Cabernet Sauvignon, Muscat Canelli, Late Harvest Muscat Canelli. Owners: Jean and Heidi Changala, Dave and Audrey McHenry, Randy and Georgia Vignola. Winemaker: Dave McHenry. Cases: 3,500. Acres: 115.

Hidden Mountain Ranch, 2750 Hidden Mountain Road, Paso Robles 93446; (805) 238–7143, fax (805) 238–4997. Tasting fee: $2.00 and keep the glass. Visa and MasterCard. Wheelchair accessible.

As you come out of Hidden Mountain Ranch, turn left on Adelaida Road for about ½ mile, then turn into ADELAIDA CELLARS' road, through Andrew's Curve, and arrive at the winery and tasting room parking lot a mile farther. Adelaida's bold sign on a winery stucco wall is in stark contrast to other winery facades in the neighborhood, and you are indeed in for a different experience. You are just 18 miles east of Hearst Castle and the Pacific Ocean.

FROM HIDDEN MOUNTAIN
RANCH TO EVERYWHERE...

As you walk in the door, you will be greeted by owner/partner Elizabeth Van Steenwyk or another happy and usually funny person who serves elegant organic sausages and other hors d'oeuvres to prospective wine purchasers along with tastes of wine. Kids of all ages will enjoy the paper and crayons, and the apples, bananas, and grapes in a basket at the far end of the tasting bar. The winery's warehouse is to your right, and the barrel room dresses up marvelously for elegant celebration dinners. We also like Adelaida's campaign buttons for designated drivers that proclaim "I'll drink mine later."

Just as many coffee lovers believe in mountain-grown beans, Adelaida believes in mountain-grown grapes, planting the vines close together in the rocky, chalky soil to make them work harder. More than 85 percent of the area's grape harvest is sold to Napa and Sonoma wineries.

It was this legendary fruit and the peaceful lifestyle that first drew John Munch and his wife, Andree, to the west side region, where they purchased ten acres and named the property Adelaida after the old Adelaida schoolhouse built in the 1880s to serve the original mountain community. John made his first bottle of wine under the Adelaida label in 1981, and that Cabernet Sauvignon ranked as one of the top ten Cabs in the country.

In 1990 John met Don and Elizabeth Van Steenwyk and their son Matt at a local wine tasting. With a long family history of walnut and almond growing in the Paso Robles area, the Van Steenwyks were interested in diversifying into wine grapes. So John and the Van Steenwyks got together, combined their talents and what they had to give, and created a 500-acre vineyard and winery on the Van Steenwyks' spectacular 1,700-acre ranch. In 1994 the Van Steenwyks purchased sixty acres of vineyards from the neighboring Hoffman Mountain Ranch, originally developed by Dr. Stanley Hoffman with the help of winemaker André Tchelistcheff.

Today John has been joined by winemaker Steven Glossner and assistant winemaker Phil Curnow. Curnow grew up in England and needed to find the perfect place where he could surf and work in the wine business. So he found Adelaida. Elizabeth Van Steenwyk serves as president and CEO of the winery, and John Munch continues as winemaker extraordinaire, vineyard honcho, newsletter scrivener, and raconteur, challenged in the last only slightly by Phil. Don Van Steenwyk oversees his company Applied Technology and its main manufacturing plant in Paso Robles.

 Fine points: Featured wines: Chardonnay, Chenin Blanc, Zinfandel, Cabernet Sauvignon, Sangiovese, Pinot Noir, Blanc de Blancs Sparkling wine. Owners: Don and Elizabeth Van Steenwyk. Winemaker extraordinaire: John Munch. Winemaker Steven Glossner. Cases: 6,000 plus. Acres: 500.

❧ *Adelaida Cellars, 5805 Adelaida Road, Paso Robles 93446; (805) 239-8980 or (800) 676–1232, fax (805) 239–4671. Tasting fee: $3.00 and keep the glass. Open 11:00 A.M.–5:00 P.M. daily. Visa and MasterCard. Wheelchair accessible.*

As you get back onto Adelaida Road, turn left (west) and enjoy 5 miles of gorgeous rolling hills, pistachio and almond trees, and lichen hanging from large oak trees. Most of the road is about 1½ lanes with no center line, so careful!

If you have time, venture a little farther westward to Carmody McKnight Estate Wines, known until 1999 as Silver Canyon Estate Wines. If you don't have time and wish to go directly to Norman Vineyards, about 3.8 miles along Adelaida Road from Adelaida Cellars, turn left (south) on Vineyard Drive. Then follow the directions below (after the section on Carmody McKnight).

To get to Carmody McKnight, follow Adelaida Road past its intersection with Vineyard Drive and turn right (north) on Klau Mine Road to Chimney Rock Road. Turn left on Chimney Rock to Carmody McKnight, which will be on your right, just 17 miles west of Highway 101.

CARMODY MCKNIGHT ESTATE WINES is well worth the extra time to visit two characters in a marvelous 133-year-old house. Gary Carmody, an accomplished artist (aka Gary Conway) who uses his own landscape paintings on his labels, starred in the television series *Burke's Law* as a sidekick of Gene Barry, and played the part of the commander in *The Land of the Giants* series. As a screenwriter, Gary wrote *American Ninja* and *Woman's Story.*

Marian McKnight, a former Miss America from South Carolina, works in the winery with her husband, so they decided to rename Silver Canyon, which she and Gary have owned for thirty-six years, with their own names and not have to explain the relationship any more.

Gary found the broken-down ranch by looking at it with his realtor from a helicopter that promptly crashed on the 320-acre property. Gary and the realtor stumbled out of the whirlybird and Gary said, "I'll take it!"

Daughter Kathleen Conway, who grew up on what became Conway Vineyards, makes a fabulous Cabernet Franc and manages the day-to-day business of the vineyard and winery.

Kristin Ball, formerly with the highly esteemed Elaine Bell Catering in Sonoma, runs the tasting room and is extremely knowledgeable about pairing food and wine. Music of the four great tenors—if you count Andrea Bocelli—wafts throughout the tasting room.

Do not miss the art gallery overlooking a lotus pond and Gary's fabulous watercolors, which he blends with his belief in the "art of the vineyard" to make great art and wine. His book *Art of the Vineyard* includes over a hundred of his brilliant landscapes, which some critics liken to Richard Diebenkorn's work, although Gary uses much brighter colors. Most of Gary's current work is inspired by the surrounding Cambrian hills and Santa Lucia back country.

 Fine points: Featured wines: Chardonnay, Cadenza Meritage blend, Cabernet Sauvignon, Merlot, Cabernet Franc, and a special late harvest wine called Kathleen Cabernet Franc. Owners: Gary Carmody aka Gary Conway, Marian McKnight Conway, Kathleen Conway. Winemaker: Greg Cropper. Cases: 3,500. Acres: 130.

❧ *Carmody McKnight Estate Wines (Silver Canyon), 11240 Chimney Rock Road, Paso Robles 93446; (805) 238–9392, fax (805) 238–3975. Open 10:00 A.M.–5:00 P.M. daily. Tasting fee: $3.00 including glass. Visa, MasterCard, American Express. Wheelchair accessible.*

To visit Norman Vineyards after Carmody McKnight, go back (east) on Chimney Rock Road and turn right (south) on Klau Mine Road, and left on Vineyard Drive to Norman.

For about 4 miles the road curves through lovely woods and an oak-tree tunnel before breaking out into the sunlight and vineyard. Just past Jensen Road is NORMAN VINEYARDS' large stucco building and parking lot. Climb the wooden stairs into the tasting room,

VINEYARD VIEW FROM NORMAN
VINEYARDS, PASO ROBLES

complete with piano and oriental rugs on Spanish tile floors. If it feels like some-one's living room, that's because it has been. Sitting on the sofa in front of the iron wood stove is yummy in winter; the rest of the year, the French doors lead you to a deck, tile patio, lawn, and then vineyard. Remember, summer temperatures here often reach 115° during the day, and drop as low as 50° the same night.

Native Californians Art and Lei Norman actually have lived here—that is, until their new house was finished at the eastern end of the vineyard. We love the attitude here, from the Zinners Wanted T-shirts, hats, and corkscrews, to the Pepsi and Sprite soft drinks available free to designated drivers and only fifty cents to others. And then there's Art's No Nonsense Wine Club and "Rules for a No Nonsense Bar-B-Que" (see sidebar, p. 185).

Art's grandfather's family made wine in Switzerland as far back as the six-teenth century and in the Santa Cruz Mountains in the 1880s. Art accepted his first glass of wine from his grandfather when Art was three years old. His grand-father and father made six barrels of Zinfandel a year from Livermore Valley grapes, and his "grandmother doled it out whenever we had enough people around to use up a whole barrel." Or the wine was bottled in gallon jugs, which friends and family were expected to return for refills.

ART'S POACHED SALMON
from Art Norman, Norman Vineyards, Paso Robles

2 lb. Pacific salmon fillet	½ tsp. tarragon, dry
1 yellow onion, sliced	½ tsp. basil, dry
1 large tomato, sliced	1 tsp. garlic, chopped fine
1 cup Chardonnay	fresh parsley sprigs
1 tsp. white wine Worcestershire sauce	

Marinate salmon fillets in Chardonnay for 1 hour. Drain and save ½ cup mari-nade. Add white wine Worcestershire sauce.

Place fillets on sheet of aluminum foil. Sprinkle with tarragon and basil. Top with sliced onion and tomatoes. Fold up foil and pour marinade over fillets. Pleat-fold foil, sealing completely.

Cook over medium coals on barbecue for 5–7 minutes, or in oven at 400° F for 5–7 minutes. Drain juice into saucepan. Continue cooking salmon an additional 5–7 minutes at reduced heat (350° F in oven). Reduce juice in saucepan to about ¼ cup.

To serve, place salmon fillets on platter and pour reduced juice over salmon. Garnish with fresh parsley. Serves eight. Serve with Norman Vineyards' Pinot Noir.

By the time he was seventeen, Art was fermenting wine, too. He collected leftover grapes from local produce wholesalers to make wine for his grandmother, who in turn distilled it into brandy. Art fermented his wine in "a huge number" of five- and ten-gallon pottery crocks. "Grandmother's still and laboratory was her laundry room." Eventually he worked for free on weekends for Louis M. Martini, hosting visitors in the cellar and giving tours and then going waterskiing on Lake Berryessa. When Art and Lei got married, Julio Martini took them into the cellar and toasted their marriage with several old vintages!

Having grown grapes for others since 1971, Art and Lei left their hectic careers as engineer and accountant in southern California's Northridge and now make wine and merry to fabulous kudos from Jerry Mead and Robert Parker for their Zinfandel and Cabernet Sauvignon.

Art tells a great story about the nearby William Cain Vineyard where he gets his Pinot Noir grapes. Emergency room surgeon Bill Cain planted his vineyard about twenty years ago with cuttings from the old Hoffman Mountain Ranch Vineyard. Dr. Stanley Hoffman told Art that his vineyard began with cuttings propagated from mother vines (over eighty years old) from the

RULES FOR A NO NONSENSE BAR-B-QUE

1. *Open one bottle of Norman Vineyards' No Nonsense Red and prepare fire.*

2. *Pour half a glass in proper stemware and light fire.*

3. *Sip wine while tending fire and seasoning meat.*

4. *Pour another half glass and wait for a good bed of coals to develop while continuously checking the appropriateness of the wine.*

5. *When coals are ready, pour another half glass and put meat on to cook, checking frequently for tenderness of meat and richness of wine.*

6. *Pour rest of the wine in the glass, drizzle some onto meat until ready to turn over, then continue to drizzle onto the meat while sipping the wine until cooked (both the meat and you).*

7. *Open another bottle of No Nonsense Red and serve with dinner.*

Paul Masson Vineyard above Saratoga, cuttings taken by Paul Masson himself from the famous Louis Latour and Romanée Conti Vineyards near Beaune, France. Art says, "Stan was told by the elderly vineyard manager that the sailing ship on which the cuttings were shipped became becalmed shortly after rounding the Horn. In addition to the cuttings and Paul Masson, the cargo consisted of a load of potatoes. Being afraid the cuttings would dry out, Paul bought the cargo and inserted the cuttings into the potatoes, thus saving them for planting in California. At least it's a good story."

Now that he has a new winemaker, Robert Nadeau, Art can spend more time in the vineyards. Nadeau comes from Eberle Winery on the east side, where he made Barbera from Norman-grown grapes. Now you can actually taste Norman's own Barbera made here by Nadeau. Both Norman and Nadeau are strongly into dispelling wine myths. How refreshing!

Fine points: Featured wines: Chardonnay, Sauvignon Blanc, White Zinfandel, Pinot Noir (Cain), Zinfandel, Cabernet Franc, No Nonsense Red, Cabernet Sauvignon, Barbera, Late Harvest Zinfandel. Owners: Art and Lei Norman. Winemaker: Robert F. Nadeau. Cases: 8,000. Acres: 70.

Norman Vineyards, 7450 Vineyard Drive, Paso Robles 93446; (805) 237–0138. Open 10:00 A.M.–5:00 P.M. daily. Tasting fee: none. Visa, MasterCard, American Express, Discover. Wheelchair accessible at hill side of building.

Those of you who have followed us on our Big Circle Tour will arrive at Vineyard Drive and Highway 46 west right across from Mastantuono, which is on our Little Circle tour. You can either cross Highway 46 west directly to Mastantuono and pick up the Little Circle Tour, or you can turn right (west) to York Mountain Winery, 9 miles west of Highway 101. Follow York Mountain's signs and turn onto York Mountain Road, which loops off and back onto Highway 46 west.

YORK MOUNTAIN WINERY is a must-see because it is the oldest winery between San Francisco and Santa Barbara and it has its own appellation, the smallest in California and one of the smallest in the United States. During Prohibition wine fans could still bring in a jug and get it filled with wine.

Established in 1882 as Ascension Winery by Andrew York on land originally deeded by President Ulysses S. Grant, York Mountain grows its grapes on non-irrigated hillsides up to 1,500 feet. Andrew York and his sons produced about 80,000 gallons of wine annually, shipping it in barrels to San Francisco and the San Joaquin Valley by horse-drawn wagons. Later, when York sons Walter and Silas operated the winery, world renowned Paso Robles resident, statesman, and pianist Ignace Paderewski brought grapes from his Adelaida Rancho San Ignacio to the Yorks to have them make his personal wine. In 1944 third-generation Yorks, Wilfrid and Howard, took over the oldest continuously producing winery.

Whittier College chemistry and physics graduate Max Goldman bought York Mountain Winery in 1970. Goldman had worked as chemist for Lodi's Roma Wine Company, as vice president of production at Great Western

YORK MOUNTAIN WINERY, TEMPLETON

Champagne in Hammondsport, New York, and as vice president of production at Bohemian Distilling Company in Los Angeles. Both Max and his winemaker son Steve have been widely awarded for contributions to winemaking and education. Steve has also served as director of the Central Coast Wine Grape Growers Association and of the California Wine Institute, and as vice president of the Paso Robles Vintners and Growers Association. The Goldmans have won hundreds of medals for their wines, averaging eight to ten a year. Goldman's daughter Suzanne Redberg serves as tasting room manager, and we love the jovial, casual ambience she has created.

Built with local stone and brick formed on-site, the winery tasting room has two roaring fireplaces (in winter) and some of the best deli foods available in Paso Robles area wineries. Here you can get boxed Brie and Camembert cheeses, smoked clams and mussels, New York Deli beer mustard, cheese sticks, and Stonewall Kitchen sauces and jams, as well as a great selection of gifts.

 Fine points: Featured wines: Chardonnay, Pinot Noir, Cabernet Sauvignon, Zinfandel, Dry Sherry, Black Muscat. Owner: Max Goldman. Winemaker: Steve Goldman. Cases: 4,000. Acres: 7 and buy from other York Mountain vineyards.

❧ *York Mountain Winery, 7505 York Mountain Road, Templeton 93465; (805) 238–3925, fax (805) 238–0428. Open 10:00 A.M.–5:00 P.M. daily. Tasting fee: $1.00. Visa, MasterCard, Diners. Wheelchair accessible.*

Now you can continue west on Highway 46 west 13 miles to Cambria, or turn left (east) back to continue your wine tour by picking up our Little Circle Tour at Mastantuono (see below).

Little Circle Tour

If your time is limited, you can take this loop beginning at Highway 101 and visit Treana, Midnight Cellars, Dark Star, Grey Wolf, Mastantuono, Pesenti, Creston, Wild Horse, Cider Creek cider mill, Bonny Doon and Sycamore Herb Farms, Peachy Canyon, Castoro, and Dover Canyon wineries.

You can begin the Little Circle Tour at its southern end on Vineyard Drive of Highway 101 in Templeton, or at its northern end, where Highway 46 west heads west from Highway 101 south of the city of Paso Robles. Whew!

The entire Little Circle Tour is thought of as the Templeton area, although the one-street city of Templeton is on the east side of Highway 101. Be sure to go there.

We begin at the northern end by taking Highway 46 west off Highway 101. Since we believe in sticking to one side of any highway and then coming back on the other side, the first winery we come to on the right is Treana Winery, about 1.5 miles west of 101. Turn right (north) onto Arbor Road and there you are, with the winery on the west side and the bed-and-breakfast on the east side of Arbor.

The pride of long-time Paso Robles farmers, the Hope family, Treana has two enterprises here in Templeton Gap, TREANA WINERY and ARBOR INN BED AND BREAKFAST. The buildings themselves are large and feel like modern French in style. The winery is an excellent place to pick up deli goodies such as Laura Chenel goat cheeses, Bries, and sausages for a winery picnic or to enjoy here on these wide-open-spaces and lushly manicured grounds. You will also find exquisite glassware, a great selection of books, and even fine cigars.

TREANA WINERY, PASO ROBLES

Winemaker Chris Phelps trained in Bordeaux, studied at UC/Davis, and served as winemaker at Dominus Winery in the Napa Valley for twelve years. He has been joined in winemaking tasks by Austin Hope of the well-known owner-family. Treana makes Treana Proprietary Red Table Wine and white Rhone, a blend of Viognier and Marsanne varietals, in addition to its line of family wines under the Treana and Liberty School labels.

Rooms at the Arbor Inn are all decorated in elegantly comfortable wine varietal themes, with coffee served in the living room at 7:00 A.M., a full breakfast served in the dining room from 8:30 to 10:00 A.M., and wine, hors d'oeuvres, and conversation served from 5:00 to 6:00 every evening. All of Treana is a most pleasant experience.

Fine points: Featured wines: Chardonnay, Viognier/Marsanne, Rosato, Cabernet Sauvignon, Treana Red (praised hugely by *Wine Spectator* and *Wine Enthusiast*), Late Harvest Merlot, Liberty School Cabernet Sauvignon. Owners: The Hope Family. Winemakers: Chris Phelps and Austin Hope. Cases: 50,000. Acres: 200 and buy from others.

✒ *Treana Winery, 2175 Arbor Road, PO Box 3260, Paso Robles 93447; winery (805) 238–6979, Arbor Inn (805) 227–4673, fax (805) 238–4063. Open 10:00 A.M.–5:00 P.M. daily. Tasting fee: none except for groups larger than 8. Visa and MasterCard. Wheelchair accessible.*

Next we come to Dark Star and Midnight Cellars, both slightly up Anderson Road from Highway 46 west. Dark Star is 0.3 mile up Anderson Road (2.2 miles from Highway 101), and Midnight Cellars is right next door. Dark star and midnight? Hmmmm.

Yes, the old barn at DARK STAR CELLARS houses one of the funniest winery experiences around. You have to see the off-the-wall International Tacky Wall Clock Hall of Fame behind the tasting bar, which is right in the winery just inside the barn door. If you bring in a clock that's tacky enough to hang, you get one bottle of

INTERNATIONAL TACKY WALL-CLOCK HALL OF FAME, DARK STAR CELLARS, PASO ROBLES

Dark Star wine. If you bring in a really bad clock, you get two bottles of wine! It's OK, your mother will never miss it.

Hilariously irreverent Dark Star owner Norm Benson left Hollywood to make the best wine possible. For fun he writes his "Star News" for friends of the winery, and the newsletter alone is worth getting on the mailing list.

Since Norm often runs out of his small-lot wines quickly, this is one winery where it really pays to join his club and be sure to get some of his best. The "Normego (Norm's ego) Notes" in the two-sided, one-page newsletter allow him to repeat himself, as well as a few specials, with the admonition: "If you need more wine . . . make it snappy."

 Fine points: Featured wines: Chardonnay, Merlot, Cabernet Sauvignon, Ricordati (Bordeaux blend), Zinfandel. Owner, winemaker, gardener, and electrician: Norm Benson. Cases: 3,000. Acres: none; buys locally.

❧ *Dark Star Cellars, 2985 Anderson Road, Paso Robles 93447; (805) 237–2389, fax (805) 237–2589; e-mail: DarkStarCellars@msn.com. Open 11:00 A.M.–5:00 P.M. Friday–Monday. Tasting fee: none. Visa, MasterCard, American Express. Wheelchair accessible.*

MIDNIGHT CELLARS is a small and elegant winery owned and run by a bunch of characters who all happen to be related to each other. The Hartenberger family's winery idea began with an offhand remark made in jest on a vacation and somehow it became their family reality. They bought 150 acres, converted the barn to a winery, and retained winemaker consultant Nick Martin, enabling them to hit the ground running.

What a group! Robert Hartenberger is president, vineyard manager, and legal counsel for the winery, having begun his life in Chicago and continued it as a corporate attorney in Glendale, California, in 1990. In 1995 he left the corporate world to chase his dream and now he chases gophers and drives his little blue tractor through his vineyard.

Mary Jane Hartenberger is treasurer, head chef, and matriarch of Midnight Cellars. She spends the school year as librarian at Loyola High School in Los Angeles, commuting to the winery on weekends. Bob and Mary Jane's youngest son, Rich, is now winemaker and marketing director and spends his free time "hacking up area golf courses" with anyone he can find. Rich's wife Michele manages the tasting room and does the bookkeeping since she and Rich moved here from Chicago, "giving up corporate jobs for the more laid-back lifestyle and sheer ease of filling out tax returns" (i.e., earn no money, pay no taxes). Bob and Mary Jane's oldest son, Mike, helps Bob in the vineyard and with market-

Turkey Tetrazzini
from Midnight Cellars, Paso Robles

8 oz. angel hair pasta	*salt and cayenne pepper*
5 Tbs. butter or margarine	*1 can (8 oz.) water chestnuts,*
2 onions, chopped	*sliced and drained*
1 clove garlic, finely chopped	*2 cups cooked turkey, chopped*
1 cup mushrooms, sliced	*2 Tbs. dry sherry*
¼ cup flour	*½ cup grated Parmesan cheese*
2 ½ cups milk	*paprika*

In a large pot of boiling, salted water, cook pasta until al dente, about 10 minutes. Drain and set aside.

Meanwhile, melt 1 Tbs. butter in a large frying pan over medium-low heat. Add onion, garlic, and mushrooms. Cook until tender, about 3 minutes. Remove from pan and set aside.

Melt remaining 4 Tbs. butter in pan. Using a whisk, blend in flour and cook, stirring for 2–3 minutes without browning. Whisk in the milk and season to taste with salt and cayenne pepper. Cook until slightly thickened. Add sautéed mushroom mixture, water chestnuts, turkey, and sherry.

Preheat oven to 400° F. In a greased 2-qt. baking dish, arrange a layer of pasta, then a layer of creamed turkey. Sprinkle with grated cheese and paprika. Repeat layering procedure until dish is full. Bake 30 minutes. Serves four. Serve with Midnight Cellars Zinfandel.

ing duties, a far cry from his former Chicago job in electronic components sales. What hurt the most was giving up his Bulls season tickets, so do not even try to reach him during Bulls play-off games. And if you are lucky, you will get to meet Hannah, youngest of the clan, in one of her rare tasting room appearances.

Cool bottled water is available, as is lots of Midnight Cellars logo stuff, including handsome shirts, "grapey" ceramics, candles, pins, earrings, pewter sun catchers, and wine-bottle stoppers.

Midnight Cellars has won an amazingly huge number of important awards and high ratings for such a new winery. Connoisseurs should be sure to check it out.

Fine points: Featured wines: Chardonnay, Sauvignon Blanc, White Zinfandel, Cabernet Franc, Merlot, Cabernet Sauvignon, Zinfandel. Owners: Robert, Mary Jane, Michael, Richard, and Michele Hartenberger. Winemaker: Rich Hartenberger. Cases: 4,000. Acres: 26 of 150.

❦ *Midnight Cellars, 2867 Township Road, Paso Robles 93446; (805) 237–9601, tasting room (805) 239–8904, fax (805) 237–0383; e-mail: DeadGopher@aol.com. Open 10:00 A.M.–5:30 daily. Tasting fee: none. Visa, MasterCard, American Express. Wheelchair accessible.*

Also right along Highway 46 west is GREY WOLF CELLARS, in a sixty-year-old gray farmhouse converted to a small tasting room with the winery in the back in the converted outbuilding. Approach this short driveway carefully because of the deep crevices on this dusty knoll. The American flag signals that the winery is open.

After successful careers in construction development in California's central valley, Joe and Shirlene Barton ran a restaurant in Steamboat Springs, Colorado, where they caught the wine bug, and then came west to look for the wine dream. After visiting and looking in the Napa Valley, they settled on the less expensive, more friendly, more community-oriented Paso Robles area, as have many wine folks in these parts.

Grey Wolf Cellars began in August 1994; Joe and Shirlene became partners shortly thereafter, and they purchased full control in January 1996. Their son Joe Jr., who has studied fruit science and viticulture at California Polytechnic in San Luis Obispo, plays a strong role in the vineyard planting and care. Although Joe Sr. studied enology at Fresno State, he credits his success to other local wine-makers for generously sharing support and advice on how to make quality wine. Quite a community!

Every year local Western artist Larry Bees, who has done commissioned portraits of John Wayne and others exhibited in the Cowboy Hall of Fame, draws a new wolf for Grey Wolf wine labels. You can see the full series in the quaint, fun tasting room.

Fine points: Featured wines: Chardonnay, Fumé Blanc, Cabernet Sauvignon, Zinfandel, Merlot, Red Table Wine, Muscat Canelli. Owners: Shirlene and Joe Barton Sr. Winemaker: Joe Barton Sr. Cases: 3,000. Acres: buy from Paso Robles area until vineyard matures.

❦ *Grey Wolf Cellars, 2174 Highway 46 west, Paso Robles 93446; (805) 237–0771. Open 11:00 A.M.–5:00 P.M. daily. Tasting fee: none. Visa, MasterCard, American Express. One step into doorway, will help wheelchairs.*

While we know the next stop is completely against our stay-on-one-side-of-the-road principles, we will tell you that Santa Cruz's Bonny Doon winery has a tasting room across Highway 46 west, next door to the Sycamore Farms Natural Herb Farm & Vineyard. Bonny Doon is a fun place whose best-known wine is Original Zin, but it is really a Santa Cruz establishment, so see our *Hill Guides: Monterey and Carmel* for details.

SYCAMORE FARMS NATURAL HERB FARM & VINEYARD is a food lover's and professional and home cook's paradise. Walk between the winery tasting room and the Sycamore salesroom to the herb farm and garden in the back for a trip directly to heaven. Sycamore Farms' hundreds of herbs are grown organically, and just visiting this place is a motivational education.

You can buy everything you need to grow herbs yourself, whether you live in an apartment building or in a suburban sprawl with lots of dirt. Classes and work-shops, held at least monthly, range from herb growing, wheat weaving, and vegetarian pizza making to using soy foods and tofu, sushi platter preparation, and aromatherapy with herbs.

You must pick up a copy of the *Sycamore Gazette* for loads of recipes, planting advice, class schedules, and herb listings. Don't miss the Annual Basil Festival, the first Saturday in August, where the best local chefs concoct basil delicacies. Even Mike Hoffman, brewmeister and owner of SLO Brewing Company, serves his special Basil Rathbone Ale. Lots of music, face painting, and general frivolity prevail.

❧ *Sycamore Farms Natural Herb Farm & Vineyard, 2485 Highway 46 west, Paso Robles 93446; (805) 238–5288 or (800) 576–5288. Open 10:00 A.M.–5:00 P.M. Tasting fee at Bonny Doon: $2.00. Visa, MasterCard, American Express, Discover. Wheelchair accessible.*

SYCAMORE FARMS NATURAL HERB FARM & VINEYARD, PASO ROBLES

If you have violated our principle and followed us across the highway, turn left (west) across the traffic to our next stop on Highway 46 west, CIDER CREEK BAKERY & CIDER TASTING ROOM. The bright green "barn" is a refreshing distraction from wine tasting for little and big kids. Make no mistake, this is a gourmet cider-making establishment and bakery. What a treat! You are now 4.5 miles west of Highway 101.

Umbrellaed tables welcome sweet tooths to stick around awhile, and inside the red-and-white tile decor makes you smile immediately. But smell the fresh caramel apples, steaming apple pastries from strudel to pies to turnovers, cinnamon flips, apple cinnamon bread, and cookies! Even the kids can belly up to the bar to taste three kinds of ciders, all made from apples grown on Ken and Susie Jevec's surrounding property—with no added sugar, water, or preservatives. They also sell dried fruits and coffee, along with fruit and apple butters, preserves, jellies, cider vinegar, honey mustard dip/dressing, apple barbecue glaze, baking mixes, syrups, lots of olives and salsas, Vidalia onion products, Fortunes teas, and the most complete selection of apple cookbooks you will ever see. One of our favorites.

❧ *Cider Creek Bakery & Cider Tasting Room, 3760 Highway 46 west, Templeton 93465; (805) 238–5634. Open 10:30 A.M.–5:00 P.M. daily. Visa and MasterCard. Wheelchair accessible.*

Practically across the road from Cider Creek is MASTANTUONO WINERY at the junction of Vineyard Drive and Highway 46 west. Turn south on Vineyard Drive and immediately left on Oakview Road.

Formerly in the furniture business at his factory in West Los Angeles, Pasquale Mastantuono started a home winemaking club in Woodland Hills and won prizes for his amateur wine made from Paso Robles grapes. He moved here in 1976.

When we visited, Jerry found jack-of-all-trades Pasquale in the basement fixing machinery. He also designed his winery building with rough wood floors. He collects all sorts of things from early airplane upholstery material to

MASTANTUONO WINERY, TEMPLETON

corkscrews, the latter of which are displayed on the tasting room walls, along with hunting trophies. T-shirts appealing to the catholic in us all read "Forgive Me For I Have Zinned." You might want to try the Cuisine Perel vinegars and grapeseed oils, Armstrong olives, Green Mountain cheeses, Rapelli's salami, sauces, vinaigrettes, dressings and mustards made with wine, chips, and soft drinks. They're all here.

Enjoy the bocci ball court and great picnic lawns where you can also sip Pasquale's Italian varietals. The rest room is the outhouse off the parking lot, complete with crescent moon cutout.

BABKA CZEKOLADOWA-POLISH CHOCOLATE CAKE
from Mastantuono Winery, Templeton

FOR THE CAKE:
  5 eggs
  1 cup sugar
  1 cup plus 2 Tbs. melted butter
  5 oz. semisweet chocolate, melted
  juice of ½ lemon
  lemon peel, freshly grated
  1½ cups cake flour
  1 tsp. baking soda
  ½ tsp. salt

FOR THE CHOCOLATE FROSTING
  2 tsp. butter
  3 oz. semisweet chocolate
  1 Tbs. water
  1 tsp. lemon juice
  1 tsp. vanilla extract
  1 cup sifted powdered sugar

Preheat oven to 350° F. Grease and flour a 9-inch tube pan.

In a large bowl, beat eggs and sugar until pale and creamy. Add butter, chocolate, lemon juice, and lemon peel. Beat 5 minutes or until smooth. In a small bowl, sift together cake flour, baking powder, baking soda, and salt. Gradually add dry ingredients to egg mixture, beating constantly. Beat until smooth.

Pour batter into prepared pan. Bake 45 minutes or until a wooden pick inserted in center comes out clean. Cool cake in pan 2–3 minutes on a rack. Turn out of pan. Cool completely on rack. Prepare chocolate frosting. Drizzle or spread warm frosting over cooked cake. Let stand at room temperature until frosting sets. Makes one 9-inch cake.

CHOCOLATE FROSTING: Melt butter and chocolate in a small saucepan over low heat. Remove from heat. Stir in water, lemon juice, and vanilla. Stir in 1 cup powdered sugar into chocolate mixture. If frosting is too thin, add more sifted powdered sugar. If too thick, add a little hot water. Perfect with Mastantuono's Champagne.

Watch for Mastantuono's Boar and Chicken BBQ during the Paso Robles Wine Festival in mid-May. For $10 you get your choice of boar or chicken, beans, salad, freshly baked breads, sodas, and a "guaranteed good time," including dancing on the huge lawn and a bocci ball tournament. If you bring a coupon from the Mastantuono *Zin Man* newsletter, you get a free glass of Mastantuono wine.

Fine points: Featured wines: Pinot Grigio, White Zinfandel, Fumé Sauvignon Blanc, Nebbiolo, Barbera, Sangiovese, Champagne, California Port, San Luis Tequila Wine. Owner and winemaker: Pasquale Mastantuono. Cases: 11,000. Acres: none but buys locally.

❧ *Mastantuono Winery, 2720 Oak View Road, Templeton 93465; (805) 238–0676. Open 10:00 A.M.–5:00 P.M. daily. Tasting fee: none. Visa, MasterCard, Diners. Wheelchair accessible, but outhouse is not.*

As you leave Mastantuono, turn right (east) onto Vineyard Drive. In about half a mile and just around a curve is PESENTI WINERY AND VINEYARDS.

Pesenti is a great old Italian winery that looks like just that, complete with stucco residence at one side of the parking lot. The Pesentis were the originals around here, planting their first Zinfandel vineyard in 1923 during Prohibition after clearing the property of oak trees. Frank and Caterina Pesenti raised five children right here and he built the house and winery himself.

The first winery building was completed in 1934 after Prohibition's repeal, and still follows "the founder's no-frill approach: to offer well-made, award-winning wines at reasonable prices." In the early 1940s Frank and Caterina's son Victor and son-in-law Al Nerelli joined the winery and oversaw additional Zinfandel plantings in 1947 and 1965, all dry-farmed (not irrigated). The third generation of the local Pesentis, Al's son Frank Nerelli, joined the winery in the 1970s and now serves as winemaker. Frank Nerelli truly thinks that the quality of local fruit is phenomenal and says, "Everyone is willing to help each other. I believe that's why the central coast has been able to gain so much recognition in such a short time."

Behind the great dark wood bar, you will find glass shelves of other people's wines, including Honeywood (Salem, Oregon) fruit wines, Chaucer wines (Monterey), and wine-based Mexican coffees. Pesenti also sells unusual hand-painted wine glasses.

Fine points: Featured wines: Chardonnay, Fumé Blanc, Sauvignon Blanc, French Colombard, White Table, Chablis, White Burgundy, Grey Riesling, Gewürztraminer, Johannisberg Riesling, Muscat Canelli, Chateau D'Oro, White Zinfandel, Rosé Table Wine,

Cabernet Sauvignon, Zinfandel, Burgundy, Red Table Wine, Zinfandel Port, Sherry, Cream Sherry, Muscatel, Champagne, and Honeywood's fruit and berry wines, Kalana, Amore di Verona, Southern Mist, Los Cabos. Owners: Al Nerelli and Victor Pesenti. Winemaker: Frank Nerelli. Cases; 15,000. Acres: 78.

🌺 *Pesenti Winery and Vineyards, 2900 Vineyard Drive, Templeton 93465; (805) 434–1030 (phone and fax). Open 8:00 A.M.–6:00 P.M. daily. Tasting fee: none. No credit cards. Wheelchair accessible.*

As you leave Pesenti, make an extremely careful left turn onto Vineyard Drive, with special caution because the curves blind your vision of oncoming cars. In 2.7 miles you will come to CRESTON VINEYARDS just west of Highway 101. You can also get to Creston simply by taking the Vineyard Drive exit off 101—it comes up immediately.

In a low-ceilinged small house with picnic tables under huge trees, you will immediately notice the collection of stuffed bears and dolls, quite unusual in your everyday winery. But this is not your everyday winery. Its principal owner is *Jeopardy* host Alex Trebek, who invested with founding partners Stephanie and Larry Rosenbloom.

The Rosenblooms transformed the old Indian Creek Ranch from a

POTATO GNOCCHI
from Silvia Pesenti Nerelli of Pesenti Winery, Templeton

8 medium potatoes
5 Tbs. butter, room temperature
4 large eggs
2 tsp. baking powder
6 cups all-purpose flour
spaghetti sauce
Parmesan cheese, grated
salt and pepper to taste

Boil potatoes until done. Drain, and while still hot, mash potatoes until free of lumps. Beat in butter and eggs, salt and pepper, and baking powder. Add flour until dough is stiff. Work and knead dough until it is smooth. Take a small amount of dough at a time and shape into a long roll about the size of a finger and cut into 1-inch pieces. Roll each piece over the back of a fork and place on a cookie sheet and freeze. When frozen, gnocchi may be put into a freezer bag to use when needed. "I find they are much easier to handle when frozen."

TO COOK: Put into a large pot of boiling water and carefully with slotted spoon gently stir to keep them from sticking to the bottom of the pot. When they come to the top, gently remove them to a heated serving dish.

"You may use your favorite spaghetti sauce and sprinkle generously with grated Parmesan cheese. Also delicious with Alfredo sauce. Or simply lightly brown butter with finely chopped garlic and pour over cooked gnocchi and sprinkle with cheese"—Silvia Pesenti Nerelli

trampled mud and ramshackle place in 1980 into an operating vineyard, winery, and scenic recreational outpost. Creston's goal is to "blend the best of French philosophy, tradition, and finesse with state-of-the-art California technology." The winery's first winemaker and general manager, Victor Hugo Roberts, was with the winery from the first crush in 1982 until 1997. Current winemaker Tim Spear joined Creston in August 1996 after extensive experience in wineries in Paso Robles, New Zealand, and Bordeaux.

Presidential portrait artist James-Paul Brown paints special works for each Creston varietal label, which coincides with Creston's wines being served at the inaugurations of Presidents Reagan, Bush, and Clinton.

You can even get Sonoma Cheese Factory cheeses here, along with soft drinks, cold bottled water, and crackers.

Fine points: Featured wines: Chardonnay, Sauvignon Blanc, Semillon, Merlot, Zinfandel, Cabernet Sauvignon, Pinot Noir. Owners: Majority partner Alex Trebek and founding partners Stephanie and Larry Rosenbloom. Winemaker: Tim Spear. Cases: 50,000. Acres: 550.

᠅ *Creston Vineyards, Highway 101 and Vineyard Drive, Templeton 93465; (805) 434-1399, fax (805) 434-2426; Web site: www.wines.com/creston.html. Open 10:00 A.M.–5:00 P.M. Monday–Thursday, 10:00 A.M.–6:00 P.M. Friday–Sunday. Tasting fee: none. Visa, MasterCard, American Express. Wheelchair accessible.*

SOPA DE ALMENDRAS (ALMOND SOUP)
from Alex Trebek and his Alex Trebek's International Dinner Party Book

---

2 Tbs. butter

3 cups beef bouillon

⅛ tsp. each nutmeg, thyme, and mace

1 cup blanched ground almonds

2 Tbs. flour

1 whole clove

salt and pepper to taste

2½ cup light cream

¼ cup toasted slivered almonds

Melt butter in a saucepan; blend in the flour. Gradually add bouillon and bring to a boil, stirring constantly. Add nutmeg, thyme, mace, clove, and ground almonds. Reduce heat, simmer 30 minutes. Strain into a clean saucepan. Add cream and heat to serving temperature. Season with salt and pepper, and sprinkle with toasted almonds. Serves six to eight. Serve with Creston Vineyards Pinot Noir or Zinfandel.

Before you go back on Vineyard Drive to Bethel Road and Dover Canyon, Castoro, and Peachy Canyon wineries, we suggest you cross Highway 101 and continue east on Templeton Drive to WILD HORSE WINERY & VINEYARDS,

WILD HORSE WINERY & VINEYARDS, TEMPLETON

thrice voted Best San Luis Obispo County Winery by *New Times* readers. Go out Templeton Road about 2.5 miles from Templeton and Main Street in Templeton and turn left (north) on Wild Horse Winery Court, et voilà!

Wild Horse resides in an elegant-but-casual-feeling, two-story building on a mesa above the Salinas River. White wrought-iron picnic tables with blue umbrellas dot the lush gardens. Its name comes from the wild mustangs that roam east of the estate, descendants of the first Spanish horses brought to California. The mustangs' free and unbridled spirit has been adopted as Wild Horse's approach to winemaking exploration and techniques.

The tasting room building, which is surrounded by white ranch fencing, has soft, warm beige walls, Spanish tile floors, Wild Horse tie-dyed kids' shirts, and elegant shirts and caps for grownups.

Wild Horse Winery founder, director of winemaking, and president for life Kenneth Q. Volk III is a great guy and third-generation California native from San Marino. Ken first got an associate's degree from Orange Coast Community College, then transferred to Cal Poly in San Luis Obispo, where he graduated in fruit science, intending to manage citrus or avocado groves. The wine bug bit him, though. He made some good wine in his "wine garage" and then got hired to work the 1981 crush at nearby Edna Valley Vineyard. He began to plant Wild Horse Estate vineyards in 1982.

In 1983 Wild Horse Winery & Vineyards launched itself with a Pinot Noir from Santa Maria's Sierra Madre Vineyard and a Cabernet Sauvignon from Paso Robles. March 23, 1986, was a very-big-deal date for Ken: Wild Horse released its first wines, 125 cases of Pinot Noir and 450 cases of Cabernet, and he and

Tricia Tartaglione, a Cordon Bleu-trained chef and cooking instructor, were married. Note the order of events on that auspicious day! Now Ken and Tricia live in San Luis Obispo with their two children, Kenny and Valentina.

Ken has been lauded as Central Coast Winemaker of the Year by the KCBX Wine Classic (1990), Winemaker of the Year by Central Coast Winegrowers Association (1992), Agriculturist of the Year by Cal Poly (1994), and Central Coast Winemaker of the Year by the California Mid-State Fair (1998). In addition, Wild Horse was named Winery of the Year by *Wine & Spirits* magazine (1990).

 Fine points: Featured wines: Chardonnay, Pinot Grigio, Trousseau Gris, Tocai Friulano, Orange Muscat, Roussanne, Pinot Noir, Merlot, Cabernet Sauvignon, Syrah, Valdiguie, Dolcetto, Old Vine Field Blend Red Wine, Grenache, Mourvedre, Negrette, Late Harvest Roussanne. Owners: Ken and Tricia Volk. Winemaker: Jon Priest. Cases: 100,000. Acres: 49 and buy locally.

🍇 *Wild Horse Winery & Vineyards, 1437 Wild Horse Winery Court, Templeton 93465; (805) 434–2541, fax (805) 434–3516. Open 11:00 A.M.–5:00 P.M. daily. Tasting fee: none. Visa, MasterCard, American Express. Wheelchair accessible.*

If you're hungry for lunch, wander into "downtown" Templeton by turning right (west) as you leave Wild Horse and following Templeton Road back to Main Street. Turn right (north) on Main Street and drop into McPhee's Grill (across from the granary) for your restorative. (See "Templeton" in Chapter 5.)

Back on the winery trail, cross Highway 101 once again heading west, and keep going to Bethel Road. Turn right up (north) Bethel Road for a couple of miles to DOVER CANYON WINERY.

DOVER CANYON WINERY, TEMPLETON

Located on the Jan & Kris Vineyard and Horse Ranch property, Dover Canyon specializes in Rhone varietals and tries to emulate those of Europe's Rhone River Valley region, which stretches from the Alps south of Zurich, Switzerland, along the Italian-French border, and into the Mediterranean near Marseilles.

Fine points: Featured wines: Rhone Reserve (Viognier/Roussanne blend), Cougar Ridge Chardonnay, Merlot, Ménage, Zinfandel, Zinfandel Port, Renegade Red, Viognier, Roussanne, Syrah, Cabernet Syrah, Sangiovese. Owner and winemaker: Dan Panico. Cases: 3,000. Acres: none, buy locally.

᧔ *Dover Canyon Winery, Bethel Road, Templeton 93465; (805) 434–0319, fax (805) 434–0509. Open 11:00 A.M.–5:30 P.M. Thursday–Monday. Tasting fee: $2.00, one fee waived per bottle purchase. Glasses $3.00 additional. Visa and MasterCard. Not wheelchair accessible.*

As you leave Dover Canyon, turn right (north) on Bethel Road to Castoro and Peachy Canyon across the road from each other and both near the intersection of Bethel Road and Highway 46 west. Castoro is quite visible from Highway 46 west.

BASIL TENDERLOIN CARNITAS
from Dover Canyon Winery, Templeton

6–8 flour tortillas
pork tenderloin
½ cup olive oil
½ cup Dover Canyon Renegade Red wine
¼ cup white Worcestershire sauce
fresh garlic chives, bay leaves, thyme, and oregano
2–3 cups fresh basil leaves
2–3 vine-ripened tomatoes, chopped
1 white onion, chopped
1 yellow bell pepper, chopped
salsa

Place the pork tenderloin in a 1-gallon sealable plastic bag with the olive oil, wine, white Worcestershire sauce, and plenty of chopped fresh herbs. (Strip the tiny leaves off the thyme stems, and gently crush the bay leaves.) Marinate for 2–3 hours or longer.

Grill or roast the tenderloin at medium temperature until faintly pink, about 1 hour. Slice tenderloin into bite-size pieces and serve on warmed (but still soft) flour tortillas with fresh basil leaves, chopped tomatoes, chopped onion and peppers, and salsa.

If you are in the vicinity, you can get all your fresh herbs at Sycamore Farms 1 ½ miles west of Dover Canyon on Highway 46 west.

CASTORO CELLARS is a place of beauty, humor, art, and good wine. Niels Udsen, a native of Ventura, California, graduated from Cal Poly in agricultural business management, aiming at the wine business. After getting married, Niels and his wife, Bimmer, looked for winery work in Oregon and Washington to no avail, coming back to the Paso Robles area to work the harvest at Estrella River Winery (now Meridian). Niels worked from the cellar floor up at Estrella River over the next five years while creating Castoro Cellars (1983), with Niels making the wine and Bimmer selling it.

Castoro is Italian for beaver, which was Niels' nickname most of his life. Hence, the Beaver makes "dam fine wine," of course! Even wine critic Dan Berger says "Inside this charming country tasting room, you'll find some of the best wines in the state."

When you drive into Castoro's parking lot, park between the youngish trees that someday will shade the parking places, a most thoughtful gesture. Walk or roll up the 100-foot-long sloping walkway covered with misty vines and planted with colorful seasonal posies, including hundreds of crocus. Newish cork trees will offer their own cork harvest in "only twenty years." Don't miss Castoro's animal menageries, including Harley the pot-bellied pig, Pepper the pygmy goat, Duke the English setter, and the just ducky ducks.

Castoro's tasting room and patio feel like a great restaurant and cafe, with soft yellow walls, Mexican tile floors, and a side room featuring regional art shows, a real service to the arts community. We especially enjoy the word block games on the tasting bar, particularly the "Politics of Words." The tasting room offers Ghirardelli chocolate bars for just $1.00 (great with Zin-fandel), canned beaver to "open only with adult supervision," and mouse pads that suggest you "Wine a little. You'll feel better."

CASTORO CELLARS' PATIO,
TEMPLETON

Castoro stresses the team approach to winemaking, the team consisting of Niels, winemaker Tom Myers (who taught Niels at Estrella River), and assistant winemaker Mikel Olsten. Their two vineyards are called Hog Heaven after the wild hogs that inhabit the area, and Blind Faith, on which Niels and his wife bought it while she was in her native Denmark.

As a result of Castoro's characteristic innovative thinking, Castoro now does a 70,000-case, custom-crush service for other wineries that includes bottling, labeling, pressing, and fermentation. A great place to visit.

 Fine points: Featured wines: Fumé Blanc, Chardonnay, Chenin Blanc, Gamay Nouveau, Tempranillo (Spanish varietal), Quindici Anni 1996 Anniversary Reserve, Cabernet Sauvignon, Zinfandel, Late Harvest Zinfandel Port, White Zinfandel, Muscat Canelli, Zinfandel grape juice for kids and designated drivers. Owners: Niels and Bimmer Udsen. Winemakers: Niels Udsen, Tom Myers, Mikel Olsten. Cases: 20,000 of their own. Acres: 381.

Castoro Cellars, 1315 North Bethel Road, Templeton 93465; (888) DAM–FINE, fax (805) 238–2602; e-mail: Castoro@thegrid.net. Open 11:00 A.M.–5:30 P.M. daily. Tasting fee: $2.00 for seven tastes and logo glass. Visa, MasterCard, American Express. Wheelchair accessible.

PEACHY CANYON WINERY,
TEMPLETON

Near the intersection of Highway 46 west and Bethel Road is PEACHY CANYON WINERY, nestled amid giant trees in the white, over-one-hundred-years-old Old Schoolhouse Ranch building, which has its original floors. Walk out back to the lush sprawling lawn with picnic tables and caged roosters right next to the vineyards. Enjoy the jukebox, paintings, and the house cat sleeping in a basket atop the upright piano just to the left of the door.

Former southern California schoolteachers Doug and Nancy Beckett moved to Paso Robles in 1981 with their sons Joshua and Jacob. Doug had also worked in the construction industry, leased shopping centers in San Diego, and co-owned a chain of liquor stores.

The Peachy Canyon Winery building was completed in 1987 and opened in 1988 to house the Tobias Vineyards project with Doug and his then partner, Pat Wheeler. Tobias produced a highly regarded local hearty Zinfandel from the Benito Dusi Ranch, and when that partnership dissolved, Doug and Nancy decided to create their own distinct label. Since then their Zinfandel has ranked in the *Wine Spectator's* Top 100 list (1992).

The Becketts always take lots of their wine with them when they travel, finding it opens all sorts of doors, such as those of the government in China and a chance to pick grapes at a Czechoslovakian castle. As we have heard from many Paso Robles area vintners, Doug always mentions the "unique camaraderie here in Paso Robles that you just don't find any other place," working with other winemakers such as Niels Udsen of Castoro Cellars, Toby Shumrick of Tobin James Winery, Chris Johnson of HMR Vineyard, and Robert Nadeau of Norman Vineyards. Actually, we have also witnessed this sharing community feeling in Oregon, Washington, and British Columbia, but rarely anywhere else in California. Peachy Canyon recently purchased Twin Hills Winery, so stay tuned.

Doug is generally credited with inventing the concept of west side and east side (of the Salinas River) for subcultures of Paso Robles grapes.

Fine points: Featured wines: Chardonnay, Zinfandel, Cabernet Sauvignon, Merlot, Red Blend, Late Harvest Zinfandel. Owners: Doug and Nancy Beckett. Winemakers: Doug Beckett and Tom Westberg. Cases: 20,000. Acres: 120 plus buy locally.

❧ *Peachy Canyon Winery, 1480 North Bethel Road, Templeton 93465; (805) 237–1577, fax (805) 237–2248; e-mail: peachy@tcsn.net; Web site: www.peachy-canyonwinery.com. Open 11:00 A.M.–5:00 P.M. daily. Tasting fee: none for seven tastes, $1.00 for reserves. Visa and MasterCard. Wheelchair accessible.*

EDNA VALLEY AND ARROYO GRANDE VALLEY AREA

The Edna Valley and Arroyo Grande Valley and their special wine regions run inland south of the city of San Luis Obispo, parallel with Pismo Beach and east of Highway 101, which at this point heads west to Pismo Beach. Highway 227 cuts right through the appellation and connects to Highway 101 at both ends.

Here you will find lots of very personal wineries, and a couple of larger corporate ones with extremely local passion and management. We take you from San Luis Obispo southward to Cottonwood Canyon, Laverne Vineyards, Windemere, Seven Peaks, Edna Valley Vineyard, Claiborne & Churchill, Talley Vineyards and Saucelito Canyon, and Laetitia Vineyards and Winery, then back on Highway 101.

From downtown San Luis Obispo, follow Higuera Street south and turn left (east) on Tank Farm Road. From Highway 101, take the Los Osos or Higuera Street exit and turn north on Higuera on the west side of Highway 101, work your way back parallel to the highway north and turn right (east) on Tank Farm Road.

To get to the COTTONWOOD CANYON WINERY's local tasting room, take Tank Farm Road east and soon turn right (south) on Santa Fe Road to Cottonwood Canyon on the right. This used to be Cottonwood Canyon's wine production facility for Chardonnay, Pinot Noir, Cabernet Sauvignon, and Merlot, but all of their wine is now made at their winery in the Santa Maria Valley, where they also have a tasting room. (See Chapter 4.)

❧ *Cottonwood Canyon Winery, 4330 Santa Fe Road, San Luis Obispo 93401; (805) 549–9463; Web site: www.cottonwoodcanyon.com. Open 11:00 A.M.–5:00 P.M. Saturday–Sunday. Visa, MasterCard, American Express. Wheelchair accessible.*

Leaving Cottonwood Canyon, return to Tank Farm Road and turn right (east) and then turn left (north) on Highway 227 to get to Laverne and Windemere. Turn right (east) on Capitolio Way, and then left on Sacramento Drive. Or just take Broad Street from downtown San Luis Obispo, turn left (east) on Capitolio, and left on Sacramento. The two wineries share a garage door that they roll up to open both wineries.

LAVERNE VINEYARDS co-owner Peter Cron calls his winery's decor "basically a garage gone bad" and "early American auto," and is he right! Laverne is truly a small, family-owned-and-operated winery that only makes handcrafted Chardonnay and Cabernet Sauvignon. Peter worked at Estrella River Winery in the 1980s and opened here in 1998. Stop by for fun and a chat with the winemaker/owner.

Fine points: Featured wines: Chardonnay and Cabernet Sauvignon. Owners: Peter and Therese Cron. Winemaker: Peter Cron. Cases: 1,200. Acres: none yet, buys from others.

❧ *Laverne Vineyards, 3490 Sacramento Drive, Suite E, San Luis Obispo 93401; (805) 547–0616, fax (805) 743–8772. Open noon–4:00 P.M. Saturday–Sunday. Tasting fee: none. Visa and MasterCard. Wheelchair accessible.*

WINDEMERE WINERY owner and winemaker Cathy MacGregor really means her invitation to "stop by and say hi to the winemaker. That's me." She does everything and ends up winning medals for her limited edition wines. All her grapes come from the family-owned MacGregor Vineyard, which her father, retired aerospace engineer Andy MacGregor, bought here in the Edna Valley in the 1980s. Andy, the third wine grower here in the Edna Valley, also got the Edna Valley appellation established.

Cathy studied evaluation of food at UC/Davis and worked at the highly respected Grgich winery in the Napa Valley. She runs the whole Windemere operation herself. She also shares the "garage" with the Crons at Laverne. Lots of fun and good wines here, and you'll find out what it's like to start out making wine on your own at both of these wineries.

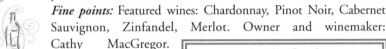

Fine points: Featured wines: Chardonnay, Pinot Noir, Cabernet Sauvignon, Zinfandel, Merlot. Owner and winemaker: Cathy MacGregor. Cases: 2,400. Acres: 61.

Windemere Winery, 3482 Sacramento Drive, Suite E, San Luis Obispo 93401; (805) 542–0133, fax (805) 473–3836; Web site: www.windemerewinery.com. Open 11:30 A.M.–5:00 P.M. Thursday–Sunday. Tasting fee: $2.00 and keep the glass or take $2.00 off wine purchase. Visa, MasterCard, American Express. Wheelchair accessible.

As you leave Laverne and Windemere, turn left (south) on Sacramento Drive, right (west) on Capitolio Way, and then left (south) again on Highway 227, and then turn left again onto Tank Farm Road, passing through a large new housing subdivision.

As Tank Farm turns into Orcutt and turns south, turn with it and continue for about 3 miles to SEVEN PEAKS WINERY in the charming 1907 yellow, one-room Independence School building. The little building was dedicated as a school in 1909, and remained one until 1954, when the Righetti family took it over.

The charming little tasting room has soft creamy-yellow walls,

---

"I'M NOT A SHRIMP CHOWDER"
from Cathy MacGregor, Windemere Winery, San Luis Obispo

¼ *lb. butter (not margarine)*
1 cup red onion, diced
1 cup celery, diced
1 cup flour
4 cups hot chicken stock (ideally shrimp stock but I have never made it)
2 cups cubed potatoes
1 qt. heavy whipping cream
4 cup salad shrimp
salt and white pepper

Sauté red onion and celery in butter until onion and celery are clear, not brown. Add flour to above mixture and make a roux. Cook flour. Add stock slowly and bring to a boil. If stock is added too quickly, you will get lumps. Add potatoes and cook until tender.

Add cream and shrimp and bring to a simmer. Adjust final taste with salt and white pepper. Serves six to eight. Serve with Windemere Chardonnay.

---

with everything elegantly displayed, from the finest cookbooks to the finest quality blue work shirts. You can also get Calistoga sodas, Elena's pastas and sauces, and Cuisine Perel's sauces. Don't miss artist Lorri Trogdon's unusual hand-painted wine glasses.

Named for the seven volcanic peaks (morros) formed here 25 million years ago by movement of the Pacific and North American plates, the seven peaks are the eastern sisters of Morro Rock in Morro Bay and the most distinctive features of the local landscape. From Seven Peaks' little knoll you can see five of the seven peaks on a clear day.

Seven Peaks is a partnership between Australia's Southcorp Wines, producer of Penfolds and Linemans and Australia's largest winemaker and exporter, and James Niven's Paragon Vineyard Company, which farms and manages more than 2,000 acres of Edna Valley vineyards. James Niven's father, Jack, founded Paragon Vineyards as well as Edna Valley Vineyard winery, which the Niven family now co-owns with the Chalone Wine Group. Southcorp farms 14,000 acres of vineyards throughout Australia.

Winemaker Ian Shepherd has a colorful international wine résumé, beginning as a cellar hand at McLaren Vale winery in South Australia and graduating from Roeworthy Agricultural College in 1982. Ian then became technical assistant for Saltram Wine Estates in the Barossa Valley and in 1983 served as assistant winemaker with Kanonkop Estate in South Africa. The same year he worked at Domaine Ropiteau, a Burgundian producer based in Meursault.

In 1985 he went back to Saltram in Australia and joined Seppelt's, a Southcorp Wines company, where he became winemaker. A year later he received a graduate degree in enology. Back to Seppelt's Great Western winery

SEVEN PEAKS WINERY TASTING ROOM IN OLD
INDEPENDENCE SCHOOL, SAN LUIS OBISPO

BACON-WRAPPED MONKFISH WITH A FAVA BEAN CREAM
from Chef Bill Hoppe, Hoppe's Marina Square, Morro Bay
for Seven Peaks Winery, San Luis Obispo

FOR THE MONKFISH:
  12 slices bacon, partially cooked
  12 monkfish medallions
  ¼ bunch fresh thyme, stemmed
    and minced
  salt and pepper to taste

FOR THE FAVA BEAN CREAM:
  2 cups heavy cream
  2 lbs. fava beans, cooked and shucked
  salt and pepper to taste

FOR THE FAVA BEANS:
  2 Tbs. bacon fat
  2 lbs. fava beans cooked and shucked
  Garnish:
  chives, sprigs, and flowers

Lay the slices of bacon on a flat work surface. Sprinkle each monkfish medallion with thyme, salt, and pepper. Wrap each piece of monkfish with bacon and set aside. In a large nonstick sauté pan, add wrapped monkfish medallions bacon side down, and sauté until the monkfish is medium rare and the bacon is crisp. Keep warm.

FOR THE FAVA BEAN CREAM, bring the cream to a boil in a medium-size saucepan, then remove from the heat. Carefully add the hot cream and the fava beans to a blender and puree until smooth. Strain the puree through a fine mesh sieve. Season to taste with salt and pepper.

FOR THE FAVA BEANS, in a large sauté pan, melt bacon fat over medium-high heat. Add fava beans and sauté until heated through. Season with salt and pepper.

TO SERVE, spoon the fava bean cream onto the center of each plate. Arrange monkfish medallions, 3 per plate, and finally add the fava beans. Garnish with chive sprigs and flowers. Serves four. Serve with Seven Peaks Reserve Chardonnay.

---

in Victoria, Australia, and then the move to California to make the wines for Seven Peaks. He now heads Southcorp's California wine operations.

Fine points: Featured wines: Chardonnay, Cabernet Sauvignon, Cabernet Shiraz, Shiraz, Pinot Noir, Merlot. Owners: Paragon Vineyards & Southcorp Wines of Australia. Winemaker: Ian Shepherd. Cases: 68,000. Acres: 2,000.

❧ *Seven Peaks Winery, 5828 Orcutt Road, San Luis Obispo 93401; (805) 781–0777, fax (805) 543–2600; Web site: www.7peaks.com. Open 10:00 A.M.–5:00 P.M. daily. Tasting fee: none. Visa and MasterCard. Tasting room is wheelchair accessible, outhouse rest room is not.*

As you leave Seven Peaks, turn left (south) very carefully on Orcutt Road, and continue along this gorgeous terrain at the base of the foothills. If you want to go to Edna Valley Vineyard next, turn right (west) on Biddle Ranch Road. If you prefer to continue south on Orcutt past lovely vineyards and wineries not open to the public, go ahead and visit Talley Vineyards & Saucelito Canyon near Lopez Lake Recreational Area.

When you approach EDNA VALLEY VINEYARD and its tasting room, you might find it difficult to understand what the unusual angular building is doing out here in this blissfully beautiful region. And that is the whole point. Once inside, you see that the nearly 180-degree windows afford spectacular views of Islay Mountain and some of the seven peaks, of Meridian and Paragon vineyards, and of Seven Peaks' Independence School building against the hills to the east. Breathtaking!

Edna Valley Vineyard is now a joint venture between Paragon Vineyards and Chalone Wine Group, since the latter bought into the winery founded by Jack Niven, whose son James Niven now runs Paragon. The Niven family owned and sold Purity Stores.

VIEW NORTHWARD FROM EDNA VALLEY VINEYARD,
SAN LUIS OBISPO

Once inside the Jack Niven Hospitality Center tasting room and gift boutique, you will gasp at the view and want to move right in. Forever. Check out the outstanding book selection, aprons, pot holders, corkscrews, and other gadgetry for wine aficionados. Edna Valley hosts the most stunning cooking classes and guest chef series in central California, ranging from cooking with tofu to sausages, from traditional English dinner to vegetarian sushi, and including Provençal cuisine, baking bread, and low-fat grains. Then there's the summer bluegrass concert, an annual barbecue, wine seminars, New Year's Eve Explosion for sixty people, and even Julia Child book signings.

Winemaker Clay Brock employs a "minimalist, hands-off" approach to winemaking, allowing Pinot Noir to ferment in one-ton bins instead of pouring it into a fermentation tank. His credentials are superb: a degree from Cal Poly in agricultural business and stints at Byron (now owned by Robert Mondavi), Robert Sinsky in the Napa Valley, Corbett Canyon Winery nearby, and at the elbow of his father, a Napa Valley vineyard manager.

Edna Valley offers terrific hourly behind-the-scenes tours of its production facility, where you can see the whole winemaking process in action from beginning to end, including their demonstration vineyard. Also on the tour is the only truly underground cellar in the Edna Valley, which holds 2,000 cases. These are some of the friendliest tours you will experience, and guides happily explain terms to guests, so please don't be embarrassed to ask.

If you are in the vicinity on a Friday evening and feel frisky, see if you luck into their Friday Evening Wine Down happy hour from 5:00 to 8:00. These treats became so popular with locals that they only hold them occasionally. If you come during the rest of the week, you will get a much better look at the surroundings.

Fine points: Featured wines: Chardonnay, Pinot Noir Vin Gris, Sauvignon Blanc, Viognier, Pinot Noir Vin Rouge, Pinot Noir, Cabernet Sauvignon, Syrah, Muscat Canelli. Owners: Paragon Vineyards and Chalone Wine Group. Winemaker: Clay Brock. Cases: 100,000. Acres: 1,000 producing.

☙ *Edna Valley Vineyard, 2585 Biddle Ranch Road, San Luis Obispo 93401; (805) 544–5855, fax (805) 544–7292; e-mail: info@ednavalley.com; Web site: www.ednavalley.com. Open 10:00 A.M.–5:00 P.M. daily, tours hourly 11:00 A.M.–4:00 P.M. daily. Tasting fee: none. Visa, MasterCard, American Express. Wheelchair accessible.*

Come back down Edna Valley's driveway and turn left (west) on Biddle Ranch Road to Highway 227. Note that it is called Edna Valley Road here (and going into San Luis Obispo it becomes Broad Street; south of south of Price Canyon Road it is called Carpenter Canyon Road).

Our next must-stop is tiny CLAIBORNE & CHURCHILL, possibly

ENTRANCE TO
CLAIBORNE & CHURCHILL,
SAN LUIS OBISPO

the most environmentally sound winery building in the country. To get here from Edna Valley, turn left (southwest) on Edna Valley Road. Turn left (south) on Biddle Ranch Road, which north of this intersection is called Edna Road, and in San Luis Obispo is called Broad Street. Just past Price Canyon Road turn quickly into Claiborne & Churchill, right at the corner (this is where Broad Street/Highway 227/Edna Road becomes Carpenter Canyon Road). Coming from the south, you must alertly make a sharp left into the winery driveway.

Claiborne (Clay) Thompson and Fredericka Churchill met while teaching at the University of Michigan. Clay, who holds a doctorate in Scandinavian studies from Harvard, was widely recognized as the world's foremost authority on medieval Scandinavian literature, while Fredericka was a lecturer in German language. Seeking a huge change in their lives, the newlyweds moved here in 1981, and Clay soon landed a $6.00-an-hour cellar rat job at Edna Valley Vineyard.

Since the staff was small at that time, Clay got to learn all aspects of the winemaking process, and realized he wanted passionately to make his own fine wine. And he was smart enough to want to do something no one else was doing but something that would work in this environment. Hence, his emphasis on Alsatian wines such as dry Gewürztraminer, dry Riesling, and some late harvest wines.

Claiborne & Churchill's building is interesting in itself. Friends helped erect the winery, the first commercial straw bale building in California. Its 16-inch walls are made of rice straw bales sealed with stucco, resulting in a building that supposedly can't be destroyed by fire or water and whose wine cellar requires no heating or cooling. Be sure to check out the "truth window" inside the tasting room, through which you can see some of the straw, and to look at the collection of photos recording the actual building of architect Marilyn Farmer's design.

PEARS POACHED IN
PORTOBISPO
from Claiborne & Churchill

3 ripe but firm Bartlett pears
1 375 ml bottle of PortObispo
1 cup water
½ cup sugar
1 stick cinnamon
7 whole cloves
2 Tbs. orange juice
2 Tbs. brandy

Peel, halve, and core the pears. Blend the port and water with the sugar, cinnamon, cloves, and orange juice in a saucepan and bring to a boil, stirring to dissolve sugar. Reduce heat, add the pears, and simmer covered for about 30 minutes. Add the brandy and let cool.

Place each half-pear (chilled or at room temperature) in a dessert dish and spoon a little of the port liquid over it. Finish with a dollop of whipped cream on top. *Voilà!* Serves three to four.

Fine points: Featured wines: Dry Riesling, Dry Gewürztraminer, Chardonnay, Pinot Noir, Sweet Orange Muscat (excellent), Dry Muscat, PortObispo California Port. Owners: Claiborne Thompson and Fredericka Churchill-Thompson. Winemaker: Claiborne Thompson. Cases: 5,000. Acres: buy from Edna Valley, Monterey, and San Luis Obispo and Santa Barbara counties.

❦ *Claiborne & Churchill, 2649 Carpenter Canyon Road, San Luis Obispo 93401; (805) 544–4066. Open 11:00 A.M.–5:00 P.M. daily. Tasting fee: none, but $2.00 each for groups of ten or more. Visa, MasterCard, American Express. Wheelchair accessible.*

From here we take you back into the foothills to Talley Vineyards & Saucelito Canyon (in the same tasting room). Then we head south to rejoin Highway 101 to visit Laetitia and travel on southward to Santa Maria and Santa Barbara.

As you come out of Claiborne & Churchill's driveway, turn right, and then almost immediately turn leftish onto Corbett Canyon Road, passing elegant ranches, estates, and vineyards, and, you guessed it, the much advertised Corbett Canyon Vineyards, which is not open to the public. Turn left onto Tiffany Ranch Road, appropriately named for the exquisite neighborhood. When you reach Orcutt Road, turn right and wind your way for a couple of miles to Lopez Valley Lake Road and turn left. In 1 mile turn left again onto Talley/Saucelito Canyon Road. You are now on the northern edge of the Arroyo Grande Valley.

TALLEY VINEYARDS and SAUCELITO CANYON VINE-YARD & WINERY share the Talley family's beautiful historic adobe tasting room on a knoll overlooking Talley's cilantro field. (Saucelito Canyon is much farther up in the hills and isn't open to the public unless you call way ahead.) El Rincon Adobe was built beginning in 1837 and grew into a New England-style adobe house where, eventually, Ramón Branch and his bride,

TALLEY VINEYARDS AND SAUCELITO CANYON TASTING ROOM IN EL RINCON ADOBE, ARROYO GRANDE

Maria Isabella Robbins (a member of the Carillo family), raised eleven children. The Branches were well-known for their entertaining and huge barbecues, during which two Chinese cooks helped Isabella. The farm was worked by Chumash Indians, Spaniards, and buccaneers.

The Talley story began in 1948 when Oliver Talley started growing specialty vegetables in the Arroyo Grande Valley. While helping to grow great veggies at Talley Farms, Oliver's son Don grew an interest in the viticulture developing nearby in the Edna Valley and Santa Barbara County. Don convinced himself that Chardonnay and Pinot Noir grapes would do well on the steep loam and clay hillsides, similar to the Côte de Nuits region, and above the produce farm land. So in 1982 he planted a small test plot of five varietals.

Talley produced its first wine in 1986, in a small winery adjacent to a vegetable cooler. Currently Talley uses its 8,500-square-foot, state-of-the-art facility featuring a total gravity system for crushing to make sure grapes are handled in the most gentle manner possible. Now Don and Rosemary Talley and their son Brian and his wife Jonine all oversee day-to-day operations with winemaker Steve Rasmussen.

 Fine points: Featured wines: Chardonnay, Sauvignon Blanc, Cuvée, White Riesling, Pinot Noir, Late Harvest Sauvignon Blanc, Late Harvest White Riesling. Owners: Don and Rosemary Talley. Winemaker: Steve Rasmussen. Cases: 12,000. Acres: 118.

Saucelito Canyon has an interesting history. Englishman Henry Ditmas first planted French and Spanish vines on Rancho Saucelito (willows ranch) in 1879, after he, his wife Rosa, and their son Cecil homesteaded the property in 1878. Henry and Rosa divorced in 1886, and he took off for San Francisco and Boston, where he died in 1892 at age forty-seven. Meanwhile, back at the ranch, Rosa married neighbor A. B. Hasbrouck and moved onto his 4,437-acre St. Remy Ranch, formerly the Rancho Arroyo Grande.

Hasbrouck died in 1915 in the midst of a devastating *phylloxera* infestation of the vineyards, but Rosa Ditmas Hasbrouck kept the St. Remy Winery going with grapes grown on Rancho Saucelito. Clever lady! Although she officially closed St. Remy, tenants continued to make wine through Prohibition, the wines made here gaining a finer and finer reputation for quality.

Rosa died in 1927 and left it all to her son Cecil, who managed to lose St. Remy due to financial difficulties, but hung on to Saucelito, leaving it to his daughters Margaret Ditmas Coyner and Barbara Ditmas Tanis. The two daughters sold the property to Santa Barbara native William Greenough in 1974.

When Bill bought the property, the wines had been abandoned for more than thirty years and the vines were grossly overgrown. Bill discovered that although the vine tops were dead, the roots were still alive, so he "picked out one shoot from each root crown, then cut off the rest to create a new trunk . . . . The intense fruit from those three acres of century-old, nonirrigated vines provide a compact central structure for our Zinfandel."

Fine Points: Featured wines: Zinfandel. Owners: Nancy and Bill Greenough. Winemaker: Bill Greenough. Cases: 3,000. Acres: 8.

Talley Vineyards and Saucelito Canyon Vineyard and Winery, *3031 Lopez Drive, Arroyo Grande 93420; Talley: (805) 489–0446,* *fax (805) 489–0996; Saucelito Canyon (805) 489–0446, (805) 489–8762 or (805) 543–2111. Open 10:30 A.M.–4:30 P.M. daily June–September; 10:30 A.M.–4:30 P.M. Thursday–Monday October–May. Tasting fee: none. Visa and MasterCard. Wheelchair accessible.*

From here we take you on another scenic but somewhat direct route to Highway 101 and Laetitia Vineyard and Winery. As you leave Talley Vineyards and Saucelito Canyon, turn right on Lopez Road and continue southwest as its name changes to Branch Road. Do not be tempted to turn north on Highway 227 unless you want to stop in Arroyo Grande for lunch. Many winery workers recommend the Back Door Deli or the Branch Street Deli in Arroyo Grande. Otherwise, keep going to Highway 101 and head south toward Santa Barbara.

Watch very carefully for the sign for LAETITIA VINEYARD & WINERY on the east side of Highway 101. If you are approaching from the north, get in the left lane and turn into the center strip, get your bearings as traffic races by, watch carefully for a traffic break, and gun it across two lanes of northbound traffic and up Laetitia's driveway.

A visit to Laetitia (lay TEE shia), 12 miles south of San Luis Obispo and just 2 ½ miles from the Pacific Ocean, can be one of the most pleasant and restful stops on your wine exploration tour. We felt as if we had walked into a friend's bright, sunny kitchen and breakfast room to say hi and have a look at their new books and oils, to say nothing of the wines. We met Julie Fellion, a Rutherford (Napa Valley) native whose mother, Carol, we met at the fabulous Steves' Hardware in St. Helena. We also met San Franciscans who make a couple of trips to Laetitia annually just to visit and pick up their wine.

Formerly Maison Deutz, a proud producer of sparkling wines, Laetitia has joined with Barnwood Vineyards of Santa Barbara County. In 1998 Laetitia began to focus on still wine production, receiving high ratings and gold medals for its Pinot Noir, Chardonnay, and Pinot Blanc.

Nebil "Bilo" Zarif founded Barnwood Vineyards in 1994, having spent much of his life in France as a collector of Bordeaux wines. He partnered with his longtime friend Selim Zilkha and now Barnwood is a 2,000-acre estate in the Santa Barbara Highlands (3,200 feet elevation). The new staff will continue to produce handcrafted, Barnwood estate-bottled wines as well as Laetitia's premium still and sparkling wines. Since Mssrs. Zarif and Zilkha are dedicated to investing in the ultimate team approach to winemaking and management, we suggest we all watch for great wines to come. Soon you can even tour the caves they're building into the clay and limestone hillside.

In the meantime, enjoy the elegant sparklers and other fine wines, as well as fig vinegar and a wide range of salad oils. If you call in the morning, Nathan Carlson or Julie will order a picnic basket delivered for lunch to enjoy on the patio. What a nice touch!

 Fine points: Featured wines: Laetitia Chardonnay, Pinot Blanc, Vin Gris (100 percent Pinot Noir), Rosé, Viognier, Pinot Noir, Syrah, Brut Select, Cremant de Noir, Elegance Reserve; Barnwood Sauvignon Blanc, Merlot, Cabernet Sauvignon, Muscat Canelli. Owners: Bilo Zarif and Selim Zilkha. Winemakers: Laetitia: Christian Roguenant; Barnwood: Jon Clark. Cases: Laetitia 15,000; Barnwood 30,000. Acres: 2,000.

🍂 *Laetitia Vineyard & Winery and Barnwood Vineyards, 453 Deutz Drive, Arroyo Grande 93420; (805) 481–1763 or (805) 481–1772, fax (805) 481–6920; Web site: www.laetitia@thegrid.net. Open 11:00 A.M.–5:00 P.M. daily. Tasting fee: $2.00. Visa, MasterCard, American Express. Wheelchair accessible.*

From here you can easily go to San Luis Obispo, Pismo Beach, or south to Santa Maria and Santa Barbara.

CHAPTER 8

HISTORY OF CALIFORNIA'S CENTRAL COAST

uan Rodriguez Cabrillo was an intrepid explorer and a courageous commander, but he was unlucky. Although Portuguese, he had been an aide to Spaniard Hernando Cortez in the conquest of Mexico since 1520. On June 27, 1542, the viceroy of New Spain sent him north from the west coast of Mexico to explore the unknown coast of mythical California in two small ships, San Salvador and Victoria.

TWO CENTURIES OF NEGLECT

Hugging the coast, he discovered San Diego Bay (he named it San Miguel) and San Pedro Bay. In the middle of October, he steered his little flotilla into Santa Barbara Bay. Anchoring off the beach, he was greeted by curious natives who had paddled out in their canoes. Cabrillo was rowed to shore and proclaimed that this land belonged to the king of Spain. He and his men visited the Indian village, where presents were exchanged.

Then Cabrillo sailed away to explore the Channel Islands before again heading north. He spotted and named Morro Bay and Morro Rock. Just as he came in sight of the southern cape to Monterey Bay, the winds drove his ships out to sea. Cabrillo made it to the latitude of San Francisco Bay, but once again the weather forced him away. The storm became so violent that it knocked him down in his ship and broke his arm. He turned back, hoping to spend the winter on one of the Channel Islands. His injured arm did not heal, the break festered, and gangrene set in. By the time he made it to San Miguel Island, he was failing. On January 3, 1543, he died and was buried on the island in a now lost grave. His ships eventually limped back to Central America.

It would be more than fifty years before the Spanish made another serious attempt to explore the west coast north of Baja California. Instead they concentrated on developing trade with the Philippine Islands and other Far East ports, bringing gold, spices, and jewels across the Pacific to Acapulco in scurvy-ridden galleons.

Sir Francis Drake, the English privateer, sailed around Cape Horn into the Pacific in 1577. He pirated Spanish treasure ships and claimed for England the land at Drake's Bay, north of the undiscovered Golden Gate. There is evidence that in 1579 Drake also stopped at Goleta Beach just west of Santa Barbara to repair his leaky *Golden Hind* and to take on fresh water. In 1891 a sixteenth-century anchor was found in a wooded area near the slough. Then in 1981 five encrusted muzzle-loading cannons were discovered in the water just east of Goleta. British records state that Drake's ship finished his round-the-world trip short one anchor and five cannons.

Two Spanish crews did touch land on the central coast before the end of the sixteenth century, but really by accident. Under Captain Pedro de Unamumo a galleon returning from Manila took shelter in Morro Bay, which de Unamumo claimed for Spain. He sent a landing party inland to explore as far as present-day San Luis Obispo. They were attacked by Indians, two crewmen were killed, and Unamumo lifted anchor. Eight years later Captain Sebastian Rodriguez Cermeño foolishly attempted to explore the California coast with a loaded treasure ship, the *San Agustin*, on his way back from the Philippines. His ship was smashed on the rocks trying to enter Drake's Bay. In a longboat his crew rowed and sailed back to Mexico, landing for a rest and trade with the natives at San Luis Obispo Bay, where the Indians called them "Christianos"—a word apparently learned from Unamumo's men before they were chased off.

In 1602 the Spanish organized a serious expedition to explore the California coast. Under the command of Sebastian Vizcaino, a Spanish Basque, three ships— *San Diego, Santa Tomas,* and *Tres Reyes*—sailed from Acapulco on May 5, 1602. Among the 200 in his command were three Carmelite friars and a cartographer.

The little fleet struggled up the Mexican coast for a half year until November when it reached Cabrillo's San Miguel Bay, renamed San Diego by Vizcaino. The expedition was in trouble from head winds, leaking water barrels, and the first signs of scurvy. After a rest they picked up speed, and eventually anchored at Santa Catalina Island.

On December 4, 1602, Vizcaino steered his ships around a point on the mainland into a sweeping bay with a wide beach. Carmelite Friar Antonio de la Ascension was in charge of naming new landmarks, and since the date was the anniversary of the death of Santa Barbara, he named the place for that saint. Barbara was an early Roman Christian who had been beheaded by her father, infuriated because she refused to renounce her religion. Immediately thereafter her father was struck dead by a lightning bolt.

Vizcaino did not land, but invited aboard canoes full of chanting natives, including the local chief. The meetings were friendly, with the chief offering several wives per sailor if they would come ashore, but Vizcaino turned down the offer. What the crew wanted is not known. The Spaniards sailed farther north, anchoring briefly in San Luis Obispo Bay, where they traded with natives who paddled out to the ships.

Vizcaino did land at the broad bay that Cabrillo had only seen before being driven away by a storm. He named it Monterey for the count of Monterey, viceroy of New Spain—a politically correct decision—and a nearby river, Rio de Carmelo for the Carmelites—a religiously correct choice.

Scurvy, the mariner's disease caused by deficiencies of vitamins and other nutrients on long voyages, racked Vizcaino's crew. He put the worst thirty-four cases onto the *Santo Tomas* headed back to Acapulco, after the priests gave many of them last rites. Only nine men survived the return trip. The other two ships made it back to Mexico by late February, but more than forty of their crewmen had died.

Viceroy Monterey was enthusiastic about Vizcaino's discoveries, but was replaced in 1603. The new viceroy fired Vizcaino and shelved a 1606 order from the king of Spain that he send Vizcaino back to Monterey with colonists. Charges of embezzlement were brought against Vizcaino's able cartographer, Captain Geronimo Martin de Palacios, who was tried and hanged. The reports of the expedition were ignored. It was more than 160 years before the California coast would be visited again by Europeans.

During the seventeenth century, the Spanish military and religious established only small settlements in Sonora, Mexico, and present-day Arizona. The Jesuits founded five missions in Baja California.

PORTOLA AND SERRA ON THE COAST

In 1765 King Carlos III appointed bright, energetic, and mentally unstable Jose de Galvez as visitor general of New Spain. Exploration and settlement of Alta California (San Diego and north) was high on his list of priorities. He established a port at San Blas, north of Acapulco on the west coast of Mexico, as a shipping base to California. At the same time the king expelled the Jesuits from all Spanish possessions in reaction to the Jesuit habit of assuming governmental and diplomatic functions. This left the Franciscans as the principal religious order in the Spanish territories.

Galvez named veteran army officer Captain Gaspar de Portola military governor of Baja California, and also gave Portola authority as governor of Alta

California, with no constituents, except for Indians. Portola and Galvez met at San Blas to plan an expedition to find Vizcaino's Monterey Bay. Portola would march up the coast, shadowed by two ships to support and supply the marchers at San Diego and Monterey Bay.

Appointed to create and manage an anticipated chain of missions was Father Junipero Serra, a 5-foot-2 Franciscan friar, who combined administrative talent with unrelenting religious fervor. He scourged himself to a point of painful ecstasy and limped through life with an ulcer on his leg from an old infected insect bite.

The expedition did not go well. After leaving in late March 1769, the first leg of the trip to San Diego was late, because one of the ships went too far out to sea and delayed everyone. Serra was ill with his sporadic leg infection, so he was lifted onto a mule in Baja and managed to make it to San Diego Bay but could go no farther. He agreed to stay there to direct construction of a mission.

Departing San Diego on July 14, Portola's party included Friar Juan Crespi and another Carmelite priest, twenty-seven soldiers, fifteen Christian Indians, mule drivers, an engineer, and a dozen others, plus cattle for food. They passed through modern-day Los Angeles, San Fernando Valley, Ventura, Santa Barbara, and San Luis Obispo, hacking out a trail as they went. On the narrow plain between today's Ventura and Santa Barbara, Portola counted twenty-one Indian villages, each centered around a large round council house. One of these native towns specialized in making canoes, so Portola's soldiers ignored the saint's name given it by Father Crespi and insisted on calling it Carpinteria— carpenter's shop.

The party slogged through the sand at Pismo Beach, traded with Indians near Price Canyon, and spotted numerous giant bears in what they called Cañada de los Osos ("Valley of the Bears"), a name that lives on. Proceeding past Morro Bay, present-day Cambria, and San Simeon Bay, they prepared to tackle the climb over the Santa Lucia Mountains in search of Monterey Bay.

Eighty-three days after leaving San Diego, Portola and his men reached Punta de los Pinos, at the southern cape of Monterey Bay. Based on Vizcaino's description of Monterey Bay as a sheltered port and not a sweeping crescent of beach, Portola's party did not recognize it. They pushed onward and when they came to the Salinas River they reckoned it was the Rio Carmelo. Geographically confused, cold, and near starvation, Portola's men pressed on until they discovered San Francisco Bay, unknown until that moment. Portola turned around and led his worn-out troops back the way they had come. Eating the mules one by one, the starving expedition managed to crawl back to San Diego by late January 1770.

Buoyed by the arrival at San Diego of the *San Antonio* with fresh supplies and men from Mexico in late March, the indefatigable Portola organized another expedition to locate Monterey. While Captain Juan Perez Hernandez sailed up the coast with Father Serra, supplies, and some of the men, Portola retraced his land route northward, again passing through the future Santa Barbara and San Luis Obispo. He made it to Monterey Bay in only thirty-seven days. This time he was convinced this was the "noble harbor" described by Vizcaino. A few days later the ships arrived.

Leaving Father Serra and Pedro Fages as the commandant, Portola boarded the ship *San Antonio* and never returned to Alta California, but governed from Loreto in Baja. Within a year Serra moved the Monterey Mission to a bluff above the nearby Rio Carmelo, which he named San Carlos Borromeo de Carmelo (Carmel Mission) and where he made his headquarters. In 1771 he inaugurated missions San Antonio de Padua in the Santa Lucia Mountains southwest of King City and San Gabriel Arcangel in the Los Angeles basin.

THE CROSS COMES TO THE VALLEY OF THE BEARS

When the crops failed and a supply ship did not show up, Fages organized a grizzly bear hunt in the Valley of the Bears. More than 9,000 pounds of bear meat were carted over the hills to save the starving Monterey settlers. This hunt also introduced the soldiers to the attractive and friendly Chumash Indian girls. Known for their good looks, above-average height, artistry, and smarts, the Chumash occupied most of the land from south of Santa Barbara north to the San Luis Obispo Valley. The mutual attraction between soldiers and maidens resulted in numerous assignations and some of the first marriages between natives and settlers.

Determined to force regular supply ship deliveries from San Diego, in August 1772 Father Serra began a mule ride south with Fages. Near the site of the recent bear hunt, Serra halted the pack train beside a flowing creek. There he had the men raise a cross, sang a mass, and left Padre Jose Cavaller to build the mission Serra had christened San Luis Obispo de Tolusa for Saint Louis, bishop of Toulouse (son of the king of Naples). The Chumash name for the place was Tixlini.

Indian labor built a mission chapel and a house, both made of logs and adobe with a roof of dried reeds, and planted crops for the padres and Christianized Indians. On several occasions Indians from non-Chumash tribes shot flaming arrows onto the dry roof, setting the buildings on fire, and eventually partially destroying them. In response the mission fathers developed a form to bend clay into interlocking roof tiles, which were dried and fired in a kiln. The fire- and waterproof tiles soon became standard at all California missions.

Four years would pass before Serra would be able to dedicate another mission, much to his almost non-Christian anger. He was in a running feud with three appointed governors of California, Pedro Fages, Fernando Rivera, and Felipe de Neve, and in 1782, Fages again. At the core of the argument was whether the church or the military would control the direction of the colony. Specifically, all of the governors as military men felt that presidios should be built to protect the settlers before money and labor were expended on establishing missions.

Captain Juan Bautista de Anza appeared in Monterey on May 1, 1774, after an amazing trek across the southwest desert to Mission San Gabriel (east of present-day Los Angeles), and then up the old Portola route to Monterey, having stopped at Mission San Luis Obispo. A week later Father Serra followed, having walked from San Diego in the last leg of a trip back from Mexico City.

Arriving at Monterey Serra performed weddings for three soldiers and their native brides. Some Indians felt these intermarriages showed Spanish respect for the indigenous people and encouraged natives to become baptized. Serra intended to bring Christianity to the Indians, teach them agriculture and light manufacturing (like making adobe bricks), educate the young women in European-style crafts such as weaving and domestic service, fight the evil of polygamy (actually a privilege of taking three wives accorded only to chiefs of some tribes), and use their labor.

The natives were impressed by the Spaniards' equipment, guns, clothes, glass beads, ships, and other objects, as well as the apparent ability of the priests to commune with their god. Therefore, many Indians came forward to be baptized in this new religion. Soon many of them were working in serflike peonage, their daughters separated from their families, and the rhythm of their lives, so necessary to hunting, fishing and gathering, was interrupted forever.

Viceroy Antonio de Bucarelli was very much pro-California and felt Alta California was more attractive than the blistering hot, rock-hard peninsula of Baja California. Bucarelli ordered the provincial capital of the Californias transferred from Loreto in Baja to Monterey. This was accomplished in February 1777. He also OK'd the governor giving deserving soldiers small plots of land.

De Anza came through San Luis Obispo from Arizona again in 1776. This time he led forty soldiers, their wives, children, muleteers, horsemen, and two officers, for a total of 240 headed for Monterey. They had no wagons, but drove herds of horses, mules, and cattle.

SERRA AND THE GOVERNORS CLASH

After a four-year hiatus, Serra was permitted to found missions at San Francisco, San Juan Capistrano, and Santa Clara. But in February 1777, Felipe de Neve was named governor of the Californias. When Serra and de Neve met at Monterey, the governor said he agreed that Spanish colonization of the areas of Buenaventura and Santa Barbara was essential to guarantee Spanish domination of Alta California. In February 1782 the governor asked Serra to come south with two padres to head the new missions at both locations. Serra decided he would move to Santa Barbara himself and close out his career there. After dedicating a mission at Buenaventura on March 31, 1782, Serra joined de Neve on the trail to the future Santa Barbara. There the governor was able to convince Yanunali, the local chief, that it would be beneficial to Chumash people if a Spanish settlement were to move in near the village of 500 indigenous folk and a dozen other rancherias that looked to the chief for leadership.

For three weeks de Neve let Father Serra cool his heels while Portola's old scout, Lieutenant Jose Francisco de Ortega, started construction of the presidio. Only then did de Neve tell Serra that the founding of the mission would have to wait until the presidio was completed. A dejected Serra took the next passing ship back to Monterey. He returned twice by ship to conduct masses and confirmations at the presidio chapel the following year, but found the presidio in a constant state of expansion.

While founding the mission was on hold, in 1782 the Spanish government granted 17,826 acres to the pueblo of Santa Barbara. Ranchers, retired military, and other favorites of the governors received "concessions" that allowed them the "use" of large tracts of land, but title to the property technically remained in the government. Neither consulted nor reimbursed were the Indians, who had lived in harmony on the land for several millennia without titles.

Pedro Fages returned for a second stint as governor in 1784 and agreed to let the establishment of the Santa Barbara mission proceed. Fages informed Serra of that decision by letter, but Serra died of cancer within a month. It was two years before a specific Santa Barbara Mission site was chosen, after Goleta and Montecito were considered and rejected. Finally Father Fermin Lasuen, the new presidente general of the missions, dedicated the Santa Barbara mission on December 4, 1786.

FOUR NEW MISSIONS

Construction began in the spring of 1787 at the present location west and uphill from the presidio—exactly 1 mile, the distance Serra had prescribed to keep the sex-starved Spanish soldiers away from the Indian maidens living under the protection of the church. The original small structure was soon succeeded by a larger four-room adobe. An even more spacious and sturdy mission building was completed in 1794. Meanwhile the presidio was expanded and reconstructed of stone, lumber shipped from Monterey, and adobe bricks and tiles made by Indian laborers.

That same year construction of the present mission at San Luis Obispo began. Its arcade was supported by classic Greco-Roman round columns instead of the arches usual in the Spanish-style structures or the frontier post-beam method employed in later missions.

While the mission fathers brought Christian teachings and some training to the natives in various trades, in the long run the mission system destroyed the Indian culture, family life, and self-reliance. European diseases, against which the natives had no immunity, finished the destruction by wiping out entire tribes. Unfortunately the padres believed that baptism and conversion meant signing up for life as wards of the mission. Sending soldiers to chase after "runaways" and the use of the whip, the stocks, and other punishments to keep them in line were standard procedures.

Spain's position as a world power began to shrink in the late 1700s. The British and Spanish came close to war in a dispute over rival outposts on Vancouver Island on the north coast, and Spain had to agree to keep only what it already occupied in the Western Hemisphere. Fearful of British and Russian probes in the north Pacific, the Spanish became desperate to reinforce their control of California.

There followed a period when the missionaries and the military—the cross and the sword—worked in concert to expand colonization. A year after Santa Barbara Mission opened, Padre Lasuen founded La Purisima Concepcion Mission on December 8, 1787, at what is now downtown Lompoc. Santa Cruz and Soledad were established in 1791, but for six years the governors would not authorize new missions without the means to protect them. Eventually, believing the Indians were subdued, three more missions were inaugurated in a four-month period in 1797. One was San Miguel Arcangel, north of San Luis Obispo, at the juncture of the Salinas and Nacimiento Rivers. On dedication day, hundreds of natives showed up, primarily Salinnans, but also some Tulares who came from over the mountains.

Father Esteven Tapis, the latest presidente of the California mission system, wanted to establish a stop north of Santa Barbara that could be reached in a day's walk and could become an agricultural producer. Tapis chose a site in the Santa Ynez Valley at today's Solvang, dedicated the new mission, the nineteenth in California, on September 17, 1804, from an altar under a brushwood shelter. He gave it the name Santa Ines for Saint Agnes, a beautiful and wealthy thirteen-year-old Christian nun of the fourth century who refused to renounce her religion despite horrible threats (from burning to mass rape) by Roman officials, and was beheaded.

MISSIONS PROSPER ON INDIAN LABOR

An adobe mission building was quickly built at Santa Ines, and within two years there were 570 native converts, but as a harbinger of what was to come, 118 of them had died, primarily of European diseases. Even such illnesses as measles proved deadly. However, the cattle and sheep reached 13,000 head, and there were substantial crops of wheat, corn, and other agricultural products. Initially there was a shortage of water, which prevented the natives from taking their traditional steam baths.

The same year as the founding of Santa Ines there were 2,074 baptisms of Indians at San Luis Obispo, but also 1,091 deaths. The mission at San Luis Obispo operated seven sheep ranches, ran tens of thousands head of cattle, had bumper wheat crops, and raised chickens and vegetables. San Miguel followed suit on almost the same scale. All of this success was due to efforts of the mission Indians, who worked in return for basic foods, blankets, some clothing, and primitive housing.

Since there were no native grapes in California suitable for winemaking, Father Serra had root stock shipped in so that the missions could make their own sacramental wine. The so-called Mission grapes resulted in a sweetish wine that was passable. Before the close of the eighteenth century all of the missions on the central coast planted vineyards, as did Santa Barbara Presidio Commandante Felipe de Goycoehea next to what is now De la Vina Street.

La Purisima had two vineyards near the coast, while Santa Ines was successful with three vineyards, but grapes planted next to the mission itself did poorly. None of them matched the production of San Gabriel in the Los Angeles area, which remained the viticulture center of the territory until after statehood. In the early days the crush was performed by barefoot Indians stomping grapes on a steer hide. The juice was fermented in wooden vats.

Santa Barbara's population in the first years scarcely reached more than 250, with almost half of pure Spanish blood, mostly born in Mexico. They were followed in number by mestizos of Spanish-Indian mix, and then variations of mulatto and mestizo combinations. Santa Barbara grew as retired soldiers settled nearby with their families.

RULE OF THE *GENTE DE RAZON*

The social division between those of solely Spanish descent (who modestly called themselves *gente de razon*—people of reason) and those of mixed blood was clear, sharp, and generally immutable. Marriages between one of the *gente de razon* and a mestizo, an Indian, or a person of other mixed blood, were virtually nonexistent. The government jobs, the priesthood, the large land grants, the business opportunities, and the marriages to others of the aristocracy were all their monopoly. Even corporals and sergeants could rise to prominence and wealth in frontier society as long as they were of pure Spanish blood.

British explorer Captain George Vancouver had negotiated with Spanish Admiral Juan Francisco de la Bodega y Quadra for return of British property on Vancouver Island seized by the Spanish. The two men became instant friends, even agreeing the island would be named Vancouver and Quadra (which it remained until the 1840s). The admiral invited the Englishman to visit him in California. When Vancouver landed at Monterey, a four-week fiesta was thrown in his honor. Sailing on to Santa Barbara, Vancouver anchored offshore, and the wary commandante was polite, but restricted Vancouver's men to the area within sight of the presidio (except for an English botanist, who could explore freely) and insisted they return to their ship at night.

Vancouver sailed away with gifts, sheep, vegetables, water, and lots of information, for he wanted to assess the strength of the Spanish hold on California for possible future expansion by the British. He reported that "Santa Barbara presidio bore the appearance of a far more civilized place than any of the other Spanish settlements in California."

Alta California was officially separated from Baja in 1804, along the line approximately where the American-Mexican border lies today. Monterey remained the capital of Alta. Within a few years cattle ranches around Santa Barbara and Monterey and other coastal valleys were producing thousands of hides, which became the underpinning of the wealth of Alta California. Hide was used for shoes, clothing, saddles, and thongs to bind rafters to posts in construction.

In the early 1800s American ships out of Boston began making regular stops on the California coast to buy hides at docks piled high with the leather. The

Yankees called the hides "Spanish dollars." Otter skins were being taken and shipped to China at the rate of 2,000 a year. However, the king of Spain arrogantly declared the hunting of otter a Spanish monopoly, so they had to be smuggled. High tariffs on importing goods to trade for hides led to further smuggling. American ships would stop at a channel island or in small coves on the coast, unload, and then report only a small cargo to import. Sometimes they would load up away from the main harbor to avoid export taxes. However, California officials, more anxious for trade than taxes (which went to the home country) often winked at such practices and ignored official restrictions on allowing foreign vessels to land.

Fandangos, bullfights, horse races, bearbaiting, music, extravagant weddings, Chinese fireworks, romance, and easy living made this the golden age for the Californio ranchers and their extended families clustered around each central ranch house. Father Lasuen died in 1803, leaving the mission system without a strong leader. The Catalan Volunteers, the seventy-man infantry company at the Monterey presidio, were shipped back to Mexico in 1803 and 1804, as no longer necessary for the protection of the pueblo and mission. In 1804 the commandante of the Santa Barbara presidio, Ramundo Carrillo, outlawed the carrying of knives, which had been commonly tucked in sashes and too often pulled out during arguments.

CHAOS, EARTHQUAKE, AND TIDAL WAVE

In 1806 what started as a roof fire at Mission San Miguel burned down the mission and its large supply of crops, wool, hides, and cloth. It took twelve years to complete construction of a new, larger, and tile-roofed (fireproofed) mission. Most wonderful was the vivid artistry of Esteban Munras, a wealthy ranchero with great design talents, who finished his work in 1821. His murals and decorations have been preserved without being retouched—unique among all California missions.

The home country of Spain was in chaos due to the rampages of Napoleon Bonaparte, who invaded Spain in 1808 and put his brother Joseph on the throne. In the turmoil liberators arose in South America to lead revolts that freed most of the continent. Attempting to emulate their efforts, a Mexican priest, Miguel Hidalgo y Costilla, declared Mexico independent of Spain in 1810. After raising a large army of peasants led by ex-army officers, and meeting early successes, the rebels were defeated when they attacked Mexico City. Hunted down by the Spanish army and betrayed by traitors in his ranks, Father Hidalgo and his top generals were shot in 1811. The result was that Alta California was pretty much on its own.

After a summer of nerve-wracking tremors along the Santa Barbara coast, on December 21, 1812, all hell broke loose. Centered under the ocean just off Lompoc, an earthquake equal to the seismic power of the 1906 San Francisco quake occurred. It destroyed the missions at Santa Barbara and Lompoc, and substantially damaged the one at Santa Ines. The presidio was left with half standing walls and half rubble. If that were not trouble enough, the quake was followed by a great tsunami triggered by the sudden cleft in the sea bed. Ocean water roared seaward—exposing the ocean floor—and then came back in five gigantic tidal waves every quarter of an hour. The fourth was a 50-foot-high wall of water that tore into the coast, splintering wooden buildings and washing away adobes, until it stopped at the steps of the presidio.

The Boston ship *Mercury* under Captain George Washington Ayres, often suspected of smuggling, was anchored in Refugio Cove. Lifted on the crest of the tidal wave, the ship was carried half a mile inland (to a point just below President Ronald Reagan's Tip Top Ranch) and just as quickly was sucked back to sea in the outflow. In the hills little volcanoes spewing sulfur appeared, and offshore of today's Summerland, oil spouted from the ocean floor. A crack 100 feet wide and a fifth of a mile long ripped open Santa Rosa Island, causing the Indians living there to send word they wanted the soldiers to come get them, while others paddled on their own to shore. Soon everyone had left San Miguel Island, except for a forgotten woman who lived there alone for the next twenty years.

In the wake of the devastation, the missionary fathers at Santa Barbara decided it was best to erect a new church. The present large and architecturally attractive "Queen of the Missions," begun in 1815, was built of sandstone with walls 6 feet thick. In charge of designing and building the new mission was Padre Antonio Ripoli, a student and devotee of Greco-Roman architecture. The basic construction was completed in 1820 but add-ons and improvements, including a water aqueduct from the hills, continued to be built for more than a dozen years. The second tower was not erected until the 1830s.

At Santa Ines reconstruction and some expansion was begun, but even with Indian labor it was slow going. The flattened La Purisima Concepcion (at what is now La Purisima Mission State Park in Lompoc) was abandoned and a new mission was built in 1815 at its present location further inland.

DE LA GUERRA TAKES CHARGE

Appointed commandante of the Santa Barbara presidio that year was thirty-six-year-old Jose de la Guerra y Noriega, a Spaniard who had immigrated to Mexico as a teenager. A career officer, he had been a lieutenant at Santa Barbara since 1806, and was married to Maria Antonia, the daughter of previous commandante Carrillo. As his family expanded, he had Casa de la Guerra built to house them. For the next forty years Captain de la Guerra would be the wealthiest and most influential man in Santa Barbara.

Commandante de la Guerra soon faced a test of nerve. Hippolyte de Bouchard, a French pirate posing as a liberator, sailed down the California coast in 1818 with two ships flying the flag of Buenos Aires, principal province of newly independent Argentina. De Bouchard looted and burned much of Monterey in November and then set sail for Santa Barbara. He anchored at the smugglers' haven, Refugio Cove, but found that the cattle on the Ortega rancho had been herded inland. A squad of Spanish soldiers captured three of his crew by lassoing them like stray horses and took them to Santa Barbara.

On December 8, 1818, a fighting mad pirate captain and his 300 crewmen dropped anchor in Santa Barbara Bay. A message was delivered to de la Guerra: Release the three men or else. He was outnumbered three hundred to fifty, so in full view of the pirate ships de la Guerra marched his scant troops along the beach into a wooded area, where the men changed clothes and marched back. They repeated this maneuver in varied costumes until the buccaneers were convinced he had more men than the invaders. An exchange was arranged, three pirates for one captured Californio, and the pirates sailed away to sack San Juan Capistrano.

While the frustrated pirates were smashing up the deserted Ortega rancho, one of the crew, Joseph Chapman, slipped away. An American sailor who had been shanghaied in Hawaii, Chapman walked to Santa Ines Mission where the friars gave him sanctuary. De la Guerra agreed to a form of probation since Americans (particularly of pirate crews) were illegal aliens under Spanish law. The condition was that Chapman, an accomplished carpenter, mason, and mechanic, would build a grist mill for San Gabriel Mission near Los Angeles.

After two years Chapman returned to Santa Ines, where he built another grist mill to grind wheat and directed reconstruction of the mission. He also converted to Catholicism (he had been a Baptist), and in 1822 he married Guadalupe Ortega (whose uncle owned the Refugio Rancho). Given amnesty by the governor of California, he and his bride moved to San Fernando for a decade and then returned to Santa Barbara. When he died in 1849, he was the first Yankee permitted burial at the Santa Barbara Mission.

MEXICAN INDEPENDENCE AND THE NEW CALIFORNIOS

The struggle for Mexican independence from Spain had not died with Father Hidalgo. Another parish priest, Father Jose Morelos, led a volunteer army that controlled much of southern Mexico, but in 1815 he was captured by Spanish troops and shot. Leadership of the independence movement passed to guerrilla general Vicente Guerrero. When Agustin Iturbe, the commander of the troops fighting the rebels, switched sides, the Spanish viceroy had to agree to Mexican independence, which was granted on August 24, 1821.

Rumors of independence had circulated from ships up from Baja California as early as January 1822. On April 11, 1822, the official announcement was made to a gathering in the plazas of Monterey and San Luis Obispo, and on April 13 de la Guerra declared independence before a lineup of his soldiers and most of the population of Santa Barbara, numbering about a thousand. Then he personally ran down the Spanish flag, but to his embarrassment there was no Mexican flag to be hoisted. No matter, there followed a weeklong fiesta. Almost everyone joined in taking the oath as citizens of the Mexican empire. The Franciscan fathers waited a week to decide to take the oath, thereby missing the festivities.

One of the first changes under an independent Mexico was legalization of trade with foreign citizens. By the summer of 1822, two partners, Englishman William Hartnell and Scotsman Hugh McCulloch, were importing, selling, and buying for export, with a virtual monopoly in trade with the missions, negotiated by the smooth-talking (in both English and Spanish) Hartnell. He paid a Spanish dollar per hide. They were soon followed by William Gale, representing the Boston trading firm of Bryant and Sturgis, who challenged Hartnell's monopoly by offering two dollars a hide. Other Americans and English were soon on the scene, like Alpheus B. Thompson, a Boston sea captain who managed the Santa Barbara office for Bryant and Sturgis, sea captain Daniel Hill, Alfred Robinson, and Louis F. Burton.

Further north William G. Dana, another Boston sea captain, settled outside of San Luis Obispo, turned rancher, and with his wife, Josefa Carrillo from Santa Barbara, raised a large family—twenty-one children, of whom thirteen reached adulthood. The miracle is that Dona Josefa survived. Former British Merchant Marine officer William Benjamin Foxen, who first traded at Santa Barbara in 1818, not only married Eduarda Osuna, daughter of a local official, but endeared himself to Jose de la Guerra by rebuilding the commandante's schooner lying wrecked at Goleta (which means schooner).

The pattern was usually the same. Find an attractive daughter of one of the prominent pure Spanish families, convert to Catholicism, become a Mexican citizen, and then marry the girl. The usual age for marriage by young women among the Californios was between fourteen and sixteen. The first families were few, the daughters numerous, and the Americans and English gentlemen fit well into the frontier elite society of the *gente de razon.*

Almost all prominent Californios were related by marriage. Trade competitors Hartnell and Robinson wed daughters of de la Guerra. Future Californio leader Mariano G. Vallejo, American settler John Wilson, Alpheus Thompson, and Louis Burton all married Carrillo women, as did William G. Dana, San Luis Obispo's leading American immigrant. And, of course, Señora de la Guerra had been a Carrillo. There were Vallejo sisters who became wives of four prominent merchants, and girls from the Pico, Ortega, and Tapia families married new arrivals. Use of large ranchos, exemptions, and trading rights came easily to them. And when the time came for land grants, family connections counted above all else.

REVOLT OF THE CHUMASH

The Indians became increasingly restive working as near serfs while the soldiers were paid, fed, and clothed at government expense. Their resentment came to a flash point at Santa Ines Mission in February 1824 when a Chumash man was severely flogged by a corporal. Armed only with bows and arrows, young Indians chased the guards and mission padre Francisco Xavier Uria into a building back of the mission and set fire to it. Amazingly, when the fire spread to the roof of the mission itself, the natives ran to put out the flames and save the building. Facing reinforcements by soldiers from Santa Barbara, the Indians headed for the hills, returning only after Uria had guaranteed them amnesty. However, the flames of rebellion had spread to the Santa Barbara and La Purisima Concepcion missions.

At Santa Barbara Indians invaded the mission armory, overwhelmed the three guards, and took an elderly priest hostage. De la Guerra, fearing a massacre, called all local citizens to move within the walls of the presidio. At the same time the Indians sent their women and children into the hills. The presidio soldiers attacked the mission, killing two of the natives, but were beaten back. When de la Guerra's men paused for a strategy session during the noontime siesta, the Indians faded away, and kept going until they reached the land of the Tulares in the San Joaquin Valley. De la Guerra sent troops to forcibly bring them back, but the Indians evaded them in a dust storm. The commandante did better by sending a priest carrying a proclamation of amnesty along with the next squad of soldiers. In June 1824 the Indians voluntarily trekked back to Santa Barbara.

The same day as the Santa Barbara takeover, natives seized La Purisima Concepcion. They barricaded the gates and fought off a siege by Mexican troops for four weeks. Finally the mission was surrounded by cavalry and the walls were breached by Mexican cannon fire. In the battle one soldier and sixteen Indians were killed before they were convinced to surrender by the mission's padre. Seven Indian leaders were soon executed by Mexican authorities.

A more subtle form of rebellion was the growing use of graffiti in the form of derogatory pictures and symbols surreptitiously painted and carved, often during prayers, on mission walls and benches. The mission fathers were kept scurrying about with whitewash to cover up the signs of resentment. Mission San Miguel Arcangel was the hardest hit, and some irreligious carving can still be seen there.

COMIC OPERA GOVERNMENT

During the remainder of the 1820s, the governments of Mexico and the two Californias were comic opera. In Mexico City General Iturbide created the empire of Mexico and had himself named Agustin the First (he was also the last). He was ousted by a revolt two years later. A republic followed in 1824 with a revolving door of presidents, either by election or rebellion. For the department of California this meant official neglect, nonpayment of soldiers, and repeated changes of governors and policies.

The Mexican central government adopted an anti-Spanish policy, which precluded those born in Spain from holding office in spite of oaths of allegiance to Mexico. Californios generally ignored this policy since many social leaders and respected citizens, including priests (the particular target of the campaign), had been born in Spain. One of these was Commandante Jose de la Guerra. When he was elected a disputado (congressman) for California, he sailed for Mexico City via Acapulco. The congress had given his place to his alternate and refused to seat him. Some anti-Spanish zealots were prepared to kill him for his audacity in trying to take his elected position. Disguised as a peasant, he escaped in the middle of the night, with nothing but a passport back to California and a cache of gold coins hidden in a false bottom to his attaché case. Reaching the west coast, de la Guerra bought a schooner. But his ship was wrecked as it entered the slough at Goleta, so the commandante and his crew had to wade ashore.

In 1829 all native Spaniards were ordered by government decree to leave California in thirty days. Commandante de la Guerra received an exemption from the governor. Father Ripoli, designer and builder of the Santa Barbara Mission, and Father Jose Altimira, founder of the mission at Sonoma, boarded ships for Spain without fanfare.

In November 1829, unpaid, hungry, and ragged soldiers, led by an ex-convict named Joaquin Solis, revolted at Monterey, seized the presidio there, and began marching south with Santa Barbara as their next target. Governor Jose Maria de Echeandia headed north from San Diego to the Santa Barbara presidio. By the time the governor got there, Solis and his rebels were encamped at Santa Ines Mission. Belatedly the governor sent messages to each mission asking them to send able-bodied men, and dispatched a courier to Solis, requesting his surrender in return for amnesty. The rebel leader replied with a counterdemand that Echeandia hand over Santa Barbara, and began marching toward the town.

The governor sent the older women to safety on a ship in the harbor and urged the rest of the population to seek protection at the presidio. Then he ordered acting Commandante Romualdo Pacheco (de la Guerra was on a trip to Mexico) to take his ninety men and intercept Solis at Rancho Dos Pueblos. When the rebels appeared, Pacheco immediately retreated to the presidio. At what is now Mission and De la Vina Streets, Solis set up a cannon aimed at the presidio 1 mile away, just out of range. For two days the cannons of the presidio and the rebels banged away at each other, doing no damage, and causing no casualties. Thirty of the rebels defected, and then Solis' forces ran out of gunpowder. Solis beat a retreat, eventually getting back to Monterey. There he found that the soldiers he had left in charge had been provided a barrel of rum by the foreign merchants, had gotten falling-down drunk, and had been easily jailed. Solis was transported to Mexico in chains and then deported to his native Chile.

One bit of fallout from the soldiers' rebellion was the charge against Padre Luis Martinez, longtime pastor at Mission San Luis Obispo, that he had aided the rebellion by feeding the soldiers when they passed by the mission on their march south. Governor Echeandia demanded the father's arrest and a trial for disloyalty to the government. Held in Santa Barbara, the trial was a stacked deck, with seven "jurors," including the governor and some officers who disliked Martinez. The padre was convicted by a six-to-one vote, put on a ship, and deported to Spain. The underlying reasons were that he was a Spaniard and he had repeatedly made sarcastic comments about the idleness of the soldiers.

SECULARIZATION OF THE MISSIONS

More land was needed to reward friends and pioneers, and encourage ranches and businesses. The obvious source was the extensive mission land. Thus, in 1834 the Mexican government decreed "secularization," under which the mission properties would be taken by the government. Actually the zenith of mission success and productivity had been reached by 1830; by 1834 the missions were in decline. In most cases the government took control and legal title. It often sold off much of the land, sometimes renting the property back to the Catholic Church for local chapels. The mission system was over, often leaving bewildered mission Indians to their own devices.

The buildings at Santa Barbara Mission were not secularized by the Mexican government in 1834. It was the only California mission excluded. Father Narciso Duran, by then the father presidente of the California missions, moved his headquarters from Carmel to Santa Barbara.

San Luis Obispo, San Miguel, La Purisima, and Santa Ines were all leased back as parish churches. In 1844 Santa Ines became California's first institution of higher learning, a religious seminary called College of Our Lady de Refugio. This temporarily immunized the mission against sale to private interests.

In September 1835 popular Governor Jose Figueroa died of a stroke. The central government replaced him with Mariano Chico, who promptly picked a fight with foreign merchants like Hartnell and flaunted a mistress he called his niece. Then he ordered the arrest and deportation of Santa Barbara's Father Narciso Duran on the grounds that the popular priest was a Spaniard. Actually Chico was angry because the padre would not sing a high mass for the governor because of his mistress/niece. When a squad of soldiers brought Father Duran in a *careta* (a big-wheeled Mexican cart) down to a boat to the departing ship, the women of Santa Barbara linked arms around the *careta,* and set up a mournful howl. The captain of the ship, a friend of Duran's, "protested" this interference, so the women said he would have to take them too. While the soldiers stood by, with the help of two de la Guerra sons, the women "kidnapped" Duran and took him back to the mission as the captive of Santa Barbara's lovelies. Ten days later Governor Chico boarded an outbound ship and never returned. He had been in office only three months.

Nicolas Gutierrez, the next acting governor, was a womanizer who liked to impose himself on young Indian girls. Soon he ordered the arrest of the president of California's house of deputies *(Disputacion),* Juan Bautista Alvarado, because the deputies had recommended that governors be elected by popular vote. Alvarado and his cousin Jose Castro organized a rebellion against Gutierrez. On November 3, 1836, Castro deployed his handful of men on the ridge above Monterey, where they lit several campfires, beat drums, and sounded trumpets as if they had the Monterey presidio surrounded. The governor's troops began to desert and Castro demanded that Gutierrez surrender. The governor refused. One cannon shot through the roof of Gutierrez's house (the rebels' only cannonball), and he decided to resign.

ALVARADO AND THE LAND GRANTS

The *Disputacion* promptly chose Alvarado as governor—the first native Californio to hold that position. Mariano Vallejo was named commandante general of California, although he remained headquartered in Sonoma. While General Castro announced that California was a free state, the rebels settled for a form of autonomy within the Mexican nation.

Richard Henry Dana, a Harvard student from Boston, signed up as a common seaman to recover from eyestrain after a serious bout of measles. In 1835 Dana (a cousin of central coast pioneer William G. Dana) worked loading hides at Santa Barbara as a sailor on the Bryant and Sturgis trading ship *Pilgrim.* In 1840, while a law student, Dana published his story of the trip in his masterfully written *Two Years Before the Mast,* which became a best-seller and is still published. The work stimulated American interest in California.

In bone-chilling detail Dana described how the sailors had to wade into the surf to load hides and leather sacks of tallow at Santa Barbara because there was no dock. Each time there was stormy weather at Santa Barbara the ship had to hoist sails and head out to sea to avoid being dashed on the shore. Dana noted that the hills above the village were denuded of trees due to a recent forest fire. A lumber shortage was always a problem, and when ships brought lumber down from Monterey it had to be floated ashore because there was no pier.

Dana also provided charming details of the wedding reception for Anita de la Guerra and Alfred Robinson, a local agent for Bryant and Sturgis, including flirtatious games of women breaking perfume-filled "eggs" on the heads of the men and the young swains planting their hats on favored girls, who could reject the man by tossing his hat on the floor. However, his Yankee evaluation of the *gente de razon* was that "The Californians are an idle, thriftless people, and can make nothing for themselves. The country abounds in grapes, yet they buy, at a great price, bad wine made in Boston and brought round [the Horn] by us."

During his six years in office, Alvarado distributed twenty-eight land grants. These included large ranchos in Sonoma and Napa Valleys recommended by his cousin, Mariano Vallejo, numerous grants throughout what is now Monterey County, and thousands of acres to Swiss-born John Sutter at the confluence of the Sacramento and American Rivers. In the Santa Barbara area Carrillos and their in-laws were the most favored beneficiaries of grants, including La Purisima Mission property, and a ranch to son-in-law William Hartnell.

The story was much the same in present-day San Luis Obispo County. Carrillo daughter and in-law Dana received 38,000 acres at Nipomo, and Ramona Carrillo, who married sea captain John Wilson, got 49,000 acres. In many cases the grants only confirmed the existing right to use the lands for ranching.

The government named nonclerical administrators of all missions except Santa Barbara, and physical deterioration accelerated. To solve cash flow problems, the padres at Santa Barbara leased out mission buildings (except for the main chapel and cloister) to former American sea captain Daniel Hill and his son-in-law "Doctor" Nicolas A. Den. Den, a Scottish medical school dropout, practiced medicine in Santa Barbara because there were no other physicians. Hill received a grant of Goleta, and Den was given Rancho Dos Pueblos northwest of the city.

In 1840 the pope created a California diocese and named Reverend Francisco Garcia Diego y Moreno of Mexico as bishop. Moreno arrived in January 1842, and the entire town populace, led by Padre Duran, greeted him at the beach and escorted him to the mission as he rode in a carriage pulled by local men. The bishop was so impressed he decided to make Santa Barbara his seat rather than San Diego as originally planned. He had hopes of building a cathedral, but the "pious fund" for such purposes was frozen and used by the government to secularize missions. The bishop died four years later (as did Duran), and was buried at the mission. The seat of church leadership went elsewhere.

Manuel Micheltorena, appointed governor in 1842, tried to maintain control with a company of 300 *cholos*, made up of the dregs released from Mexican prisons. Following a confusing mock war between competing factions, and a revolt by the combined forces of ex-governor Alvarado and southern Californian Pio Pico, Micheltorana resigned in 1844. Pico became governor and moved the capital from Monterey to Los Angeles, leaving General Castro governing as military commander in Monterey. It was all sandbox politics and left California with no coherent government.

POLK COVETS CALIFORNIA

In 1844 James K. Polk, an advocate of western expansion, was elected president of the United States. In 1845 Polk offered Mexico $40 million for California and New Mexico. The proposal was rejected. His appetite for California led him to plan to take the southwest and California one way or another.

U. S. Army Captain John C. Fremont, officially the chief of a party of sixty-two topographical engineers, was sent roaming around the northern Sacramento Valley and southern Oregon. He claimed he was searching out trade routes to the west. On March 1, 1846, Fremont and his buckskin-clad, scraggily-bearded, rifle-toting company camped out near Monterey. Three of his men rode over to the ranch of General Castro's uncle, and "insulted" his daughters. General Castro immediately sent Fremont a written order to leave California or be arrested. The mercurial Fremont responded by flying an American flag atop Mount Gavilan. Castro raised 200 volunteers. American consul Thomas Larkin convinced Fremont to leave, despite the captain's offer to fight to the death.

Unknown to anyone in California, on May 13, 1846, the U.S. Congress had declared war against Mexico, on the pretext that there was a dispute over the Mexico-Texas border. On June 15, the United States and Great Britain agreed to divide "Oregon Country" at the forty-ninth parallel, but the U.S. acquiesced to the British desire to keep Fort Victoria on the southern tip of Vancouver Island. This settlement freed the United States from the threat of British naval intervention in its Mexican War.

Fremont returned to Sutter's Fort and encountered a group of Americans from the Sacramento Valley who wanted to throw off Mexican rule. Fremont urged them to intercept a herd of horses Vallejo was sending to Castro at Santa Clara. With fresh mounts, the Americans rode toward Sonoma. In Napa Valley they added more men, and at dawn on June 14, 1846, thirty-three rough-looking men rode into the Sonoma plaza, arrested Mariano Vallejo, his brother-in-law Jacob Leese, brother Salvador Vallejo, and the general's male secretary. The captives were taken to Sutter's Fort where Fremont insisted they be kept in prison.

At Sonoma the Americans declared the formation of the California Republic, elected a president by acclamation and raised a flag featuring a grizzly bear in the shape of a pig with a red stripe cut from a petticoat and a red star. A few days later Fremont showed up and recruited most of the Bear Flaggers into what he called his California battalion.

SLOAT TAKES MONTEREY

On July 2, three American warships under the command of Commodore John D. Sloat anchored in Monterey harbor. Sloat had orders to seize the ports of California if war had been declared, but he had no official report of war. Learning that Fremont was leading a company of 200 to take control of California, war or no war, Sloat landed 250 marines and sailors on July 7 and seized the custom house. The American flag was raised, the Navy band played, and Sloat made a diplomatic speech in which he promised full citizenship rights to the Californios, announced his men would pay for supplies, and said that church properties would be protected.

The locals cheered, for Sloat was preferable to the rude Bear Flaggers who held Vallejo in prison or to Fremont and his California battalion, which had shot and killed three unarmed Californios when they had attempted to surrender near San Rafael.

Sloat sent naval Lieutenant Joseph Warren Revere, grandson of Paul Revere, to Yerba Buena and Sonoma to raise the Stars and Stripes. On July 9, Revere pulled down the Bear Flag in Sonoma, thus ending the twenty-five-day regime of the California Republic. Fremont marched south to Monterey.

THE MEXICAN WAR: ROUND ONE

Unsure he had acted legally, Sloat transferred his command to Commodore Robert F. Stockton the first week in August. As his last act Sloat ordered Mariano Vallejo and his compatriots freed from prison and allowed to go home. A few days later an official dispatch reported that a state of war did indeed exist.

Governor Pico moved his headquarters to Santa Barbara and issued a call for all Mexican citizens to take up arms against the Americans. General Jose Castro beat a strategic retreat southward to join Pico, who moved into hiding in the hills south of Los Angeles. Fremont's men invested San Luis Obispo without opposition. Then he took a ship to San Diego with his battalion and occupied that pueblo without a fight. Commodore Stockton sailed from Monterey to Santa Barbara, where his marines raised the American flag. Leaving a few men to occupy Santa Barbara, he then marched into Los Angeles which he found undefended and virtually deserted.

Believing the battle for California over, Fremont and Stockton returned to Monterey. However, Californio resistance armies were gathering in the countryside outside the towns. Armed with a single brass cannon, General Jose Maria Flores' 400 Mexican guerrillas drove the American soldiers in Los Angeles out to San Pedro harbor, where they holed up on a U.S. ship. Santa Barbara was soon retaken by Flores' little army, which chased the occupying Americans over the mountains into the San Joaquin Valley. San Luis Obispo was recaptured by volunteer civilians.

Stockton and Fremont now had to fight the war over. Stockton sailed to retake San Diego and Los Angeles. Fremont enlarged his battalion, took on a group of Indian scouts from as far away as Walla Walla, and marched south. His 300 horsemen charged into San Luis Obispo at night in a pelting rainstorm and took the town easily. Fremont's men caught an Indian courier carrying a letter signed by ranchero Jose de Jesus Pico, warning other Californios of Fremont's impending attack. Pico had been taken prisoner when San Luis Obispo had been first occupied, and in exchange for parole had signed a pledge not to take up arms again. Fremont ordered the Indian summarily shot; his stoic bravery facing death becoming the stuff of legend. Then at the mission where his men were drying out, Fremont held a drumhead court martial of Pico and sentenced him to death for violating his parole.

The next morning Fremont was visited by a delegation of Californio women led by beautiful, aristocratic Ramona Carrillo de Wilson. For over an hour she talked, playing on Fremont's vanity, his best instincts, and his future in the hearts of Californios. Most of all she was an attractive woman, a Carrillo, courageous and rational, not unlike his own wife, the fabled Jesse Benton Fremont, daughter of Senator Thomas Hart Benton. The mesmerized Fremont relented and pardoned Pico, who had been scheduled to be shot within the hour.

By December 21, 1846, Fremont's ragtag forces had reached Benjamin Foxen's ranch, northeast of Santa Barbara. Onetime English sea captain Foxen in his twenty-five years around Santa Barbara had converted to Catholicism, become a Mexican citizen, been befriended by the de la Guerras, and married a local girl. He and his family had not fled from their adobe, choosing to protect their property.

The usual route from the north into Santa Barbara was through Gaviota Pass, which could be a death trap since it was a narrow defile between high cliffs. Foxen's wife had heard a rumor that Mexican troops were preparing to ambush the Americans there and push boulders down on them. Fremont was already nervous about trying the pass and asked Foxen if there was another way. Foxen agonized over loyalty to Mexico and the probability that California would become U. S. territory. Eventually Foxen suggested the seldom-used old Indian trail over the Santa Ynez range through the steep San Marcos pass, and asked his son to show Fremont the way.

FREMONT CAPTURES SANTA BARBARA

Fremont's army made it over the pass in a Christmas deluge. Two hundred of his horses and mules slipped on the wet rocks and fell to their deaths. Luckily no men were killed. Thus, Fremont marched into Santa Barbara out of the hills, from a surprise direction. There were no Mexican soldiers to oppose them; they had been sent to the Los Angeles basin to battle the gringos and were not lying in wait in the rocks above Gaviota Pass. Captain Foxen would pay a price: For a long time he was ostracized by many diehard Californios as a traitor and his ranch house was later burned by unknown arsonists. His descendants still own much of his ranch.

Meanwhile in October the California departmental assembly held a special meeting and voted out Governor Pio Pico and replaced General Jose Castro with Manuel Castro, partly because those worthies were south of the border trying to get assistance from the Mexican central government instead of fighting. His removal thwarted Pico's plan to sell the missions.

At the battle of San Pascual (east of San Diego) the Mexicans under General Andres Pico badly bloodied a troop of 175 U.S. Army regulars led by General Stephen Kearny, who had marched from New Mexico. However, the Americans had too great an advantage in numbers, armaments, and military experience. The final victory by Fremont at Cahuenga Pass in San Fernando Valley ended the war in California.

Enter into history another dynamic woman, Bernarda Ruiz, widow of an army officer, owner of the Conejo Ranch, and related by blood or marriage to just about everyone. Fearful that Fremont and Stockton would impose a harsh treaty on the Californios, she asked Jesus Pico (the same man saved by the intervention of Ramona Carrillo) to arrange an interview with Fremont before he left Santa Barbara. He granted her a ceremonial five minutes that turned into two hours. With feminine wiles and playing on his ambitions, she convinced him that "when he became governor" it would be best for him to have thousands of friends gained by a generous and compassionate peace. When the surprisingly generous truce, which gave equality to Californios and Americans, was presented by Fremont, Ramona was present. Andres Pico readily signed on behalf of Mexico.

The Mexican War officially concluded with the Treaty of Guadalupe Hidalgo, signed on February 2, 1848, and soon ratified by both the U.S. Senate and the Mexican government. California, Arizona, New Mexico, and Nevada became American territory, and U.S. citizenship was granted to all Californios. News of ratification by the Mexican government reached Monterey in August 1848.

THE CONSTITUTIONAL CONVENTION

California was neither a territory nor a state and lacked any official government. In June 1849 military governor Brigadier General Bennett Riley ordered an August election of delegates to a constitutional convention in Monterey scheduled for September. Of forty-eight delegates chosen from ten districts, eight were Spanish-speaking Californios, led by General Vallejo, with William Hartnell translating. French-born former *alcalde* Jose Covarrubias was the delegate from Santa Barbara, and Henry A. Tefft, lawyer son-in-law of William G.

Dana, represented San Luis Obispo. Also delegates were Pablo de la Guerra and Jose A. Carrillo, whose proposal that Santa Barbara be the state capital was easily defeated. There was only one mestizo delegate.

The delegates voted to apply to Congress as a state rather than as a mere territory. The proposed constitution prohibited slavery, but gave the vote to white males only, which created a crisis since many Californians were of mixed Indian blood. The result was a compromise: The new legislature when formed could give the vote to all males of Indian blood.

In November 1849 the new constitution was approved by a popular vote of 12,064 to 811. An interim legislature was elected to meet at San Jose. Even before Congress admitted California as a state on September 9, 1850, this legislature created twenty-seven counties, including San Luis Obispo (population 336) and Santa Barbara, which included what is now Ventura County. Santa Barbara incorporated as a city in 1850 and San Luis Obispo in 1856. Ventura County was split off in 1872.

SAN LUIS OBISPO AND SANTA BARBARA LAID OUT

In 1851 one of the first acts of the San Luis Obispo county government was to authorize a survey and development of a street plan for the town of San Luis Obispo. Santa Barbara's city council did the same. The meandering streets and hazy property descriptions would be replaced by fixed lines. However, in the case of Santa Barbara the original survey was full of errors and the wooden survey stakes often broke, rotted, or disappeared. After fences were built these mistakes were obvious. Eventually the council ordered a new survey, which provided grist for decades of real estate litigation.

The American influence on Santa Barbara style was soon evident in the use of wood instead of adobe as the basic building material. Shiploads of lumber from northern California and Oregon Territory were soon being floated onto the beach.

Although the peace treaty had provided for honoring existing rights of Mexican citizens, the great influx of settlers after the discovery of gold in 1848 put the Mexican land grants in jeopardy. The federal Land Claims Commission heard the title disputes, but evidence was hard to produce, since title descriptions were vague and almost never based on surveys. Squatters took over sections of ranches, refused to pay rent, and then challenged the title in court. Often the cases dragged on for years—as many as thirty—and legal costs became prohibitive. Although most grant holders won, the rancheros were ordered to pay for surveys that they usually could not afford.

Many of the Californios were land rich and cash poor. Their wealth had been built on Indian labor, and the new generation could not afford laborers and was neither physically nor temperamentally prepared to work the land. To get cash they mortgaged parcels of their property to those with ready money at usurious rates as high as 2 percent a month. But even hardworking rancheros were faced with low prices for cattle during the 1850s. The drought of 1863–1864 finished off many herds. In Santa Barbara County the number of cattle dropped from 200,000 to 5,000 in that one year. Thus most old rancheros lost their property to foreclosure or distress sales.

Santa Barbara's new government got a scare August 1, 1854, when the Land Claims Commission denied the town's application for confirmation of the Spanish government's 1782 land grant. The decision was appealed to the U.S. Supreme Court and eighteen years later the occupied 17,826 acres were confirmed as city property.

CRIMINAL GANGS AND FRONTIER JUSTICE

A weak government with no trained lawmen was trying to manage endless square miles of rugged territory. Thousands of newcomers had arrived looking for gold or other quick riches. Hundreds of dispossessed young Californians roamed the countryside. Given those circumstances a crime wave in California was a virtual certainty.

Actually the bloodiest crime occurred before statehood was granted. At San Miguel Mission, an Englishman named William Reed and two Californio friends had bought all but the chapel and priests' quarters, and converted the buildings into a home for Reed and his family. Reed was believed to have returned from the goldfields with a stash of gold dust. One day in October 1848 five deserting British sailors stopped by, and then returned at night to murder Reed, his wife (nee Maria Antonia Vallejo), a daughter and son-in-law, three younger children, an elderly black servant, and three guests—a total of eleven victims. The killers then tore apart Reed's home in a futile search for the gold. Ranchers John M. Price and Francisco Branch organized a posse and ran down the murderers on the sands of Pismo Beach. The vigilantes tied up their prisoners and heaved them into the ocean to drown.

Gangs preyed on travelers suspected of carrying money, gold, or jewels, and invaded the homes of the wealthy. Horse and cattle rustling was a favorite occupation, after which the thieves faded into the countryside. The most infamous was Joaquin Murrieta, whose career began in the late 1840s. With accomplices such as "Three Finger" Jack Garcia (who had stabbed to death two captured Bear

Flaggers in 1846), Murrieta often hid in the caves east of Paso Robles after a robbery or a killing. When he was at work near Santa Barbara, he and his gang would hunker down in the hills above the Rincon de la Playa Rancho east of Carpinteria. Years later $13,000 in stolen jewels was found buried there. Although Murrieta was killed in 1853, survivors of his gang were active until the shooting of Abelardo Mendoza while resisting arrest in San Luis Obispo in 1884.

The largest gang was organized by twenty-one-year-old Juan Flores, who had escaped in the mid-fifties from San Quentin's primitive prison, where he was serving a term for horse stealing. He had more than fifty in his organization, which operated from San Luis Obispo to San Juan Capistrano, south of Los Angeles. All too often a robbery or cattle rustling was accompanied by a killing. In a running gun battle in Los Angeles County the sheriff and two deputies were shot dead. A small army under former Mexican General Andres Pico hunted down the Flores gang, shot some in gun battles, and caught and hanged others after brief "trials." Finally Flores and several of his ring were captured and legally arraigned before a judge, who ordered them tried by the county superior court. A mob, ignoring the new sheriff's protests, took Flores from jail and hanged him and a few others. In some cases those hanged were only young Mexicans who had helped Flores evade capture. One was entirely innocent.

Self-help justice got a bad name around Santa Barbara in August 1859, when the bodies of well-known horse thief Francisco Badillo and his son were found hanged in the woods. Badillo was eighty years old and his murdered son was only fourteen. Younger Badillo children identified the perpetrators as prominent citizen John Nidever and his son George. A group of Mexican-Americans spotted George, beat him up, stabbed him, and shot him for good measure. Miraculously he survived. The Nidevers were tried and acquitted, as were those who assaulted young Nidever. Public sentiment demanded a stronger government and appointments to the vacant offices of sheriff and district attorney.

In San Luis Obispo a vigilante committee was organized in May 1858, by community leaders such as William G. Dana and lawyer William Graves. Following the murder of two Frenchmen, the local vigilantes caught the alleged killers, forced them to confess, and then hanged them. After putting a damper on crime in the area, the committee disbanded.

Perhaps this explains that when notorious Jesse James and his brother Frank showed up in Paso Robles while on the lam from Missouri, they were strictly law-abiding. Frank James' signature appears as one of the two surveyors on the first map of Paso Robles.

An unusual bunch of outlaws was the so-called Gang of Five, organized by dashing 6-footer Jack Powers, who had arrived as a nineteen-year-old sergeant in the New York Volunteers when they occupied Santa Barbara in 1847. He had grown up in New York City's Hell's Kitchen, but his smooth manners and glib tongue belied his hard beginnings. He had become a superb horseman in the army and took a job as groom at the de la Guerra stables. At night he was a drinker and gambler, popular with the young town hotshots, and charmer of young women and the Santa Barbara elite. With four old army buddies Powers secretly created the Gang of Five, which virtually ruled the town by intimidation between 1854 and 1858. Even when suspicion fell on Powers that he and his buddies were night riders stealing cattle and ambushing travelers, the local lawmen were afraid to confront him.

One man who was not afraid of Powers and his bully boys was Dr. Nicolas Den. When Powers' gang tried to rustle cattle from a Den ranch in the Santa Ynez Valley, the doctor's cowboys chased them off. In retaliation Powers invaded Den's other ranch at Dos Pueblos. At Den's urging, Sheriff W. W. Twist called up a 200-man posse. A liquored-up Gang of Five rode into Santa Barbara to face the posse in what shaped up to be a California version of the gunfight at the O.K. Corral. At the corner of Carrillo and Anacapa Streets, in front of Twist's house, the first of the gang rode up and ineffectually stabbed the sheriff only to be shot dead while still in his saddle. Another shot and it was the Gang of Three. At this point the rest of the posse arrived and faced three leveled rifles from behind a large sycamore tree. The reluctant posse chickened out and decided to go have a drink. Powers retired from the scene, but his days of intimidation were over. When murder charges were brought against him, he hopped a ship for Mexico. Two years later he was stabbed to death in a fight over a woman.

Tiburcio Vasquez was a bandit from a prominent Monterey family who robbed stages and rustled cattle for several years. After most jobs he would hide out in the hills above Paso Robles, much like Murrieta. An acknowledged hater of gringos, he was a Robin Hood to many younger mestizos. He was caught and tried in San Jose for murder. During the trial no witness could identify him, but he gave himself away by joking to one potential witness: "A fine watch you had. I have often regretted I didn't take it." He was hanged on March 19, 1875.

ROUGH ROADS AND COASTAL SHIPPING

For the first sixty years after statehood, the road system along the coast was primitive at best. El Camino Real (the King's highway) was a trail, which was gradually improved enough to serve as a stagecoach route, bumpy, erratic, often steep, and impassable during heavy rains. An underlying problem was that all roads were under local control, either county or a road district. Often ranchers

would scrape and cut their own roads to use sweat equity for their road tax, usually without a survey or engineering. Sometimes there was oil and gravel, but
most roads were dirt. Although some bridges were of stone, to save money most
counties built them of wood.

A stagecoach line between San Francisco and Los Angeles (following the old
mission trail) was inaugurated in 1861, running three times a week. A year later
it went on a daily schedule with relays of teams of horses stabled along the way.
The entire trip took three-and-a-half days. Five years later once-a-week stages
were galloping between San Luis Obispo and the coastal settlements of Cambria
and San Simeon. A network of stage routes gradually grew to connect smaller
towns with major centers up and down the coast.

Nevertheless, along the coast most farm product delivery and passenger
travel was by ship. An enterprising Santa Barbara businessman, Samuel
Brinkerhoff, built the first wharf on the Santa Barbara waterfront in 1868.
Located at the foot of Chapala Street, the wharf was 500 feet long. It proved a
substantial improvement, but it was not long enough to reach deep water and
accommodate larger vessels, including lumber ships.

A stagecoach road was completed over the San Marcos pass to Santa Ynez
Valley northeast of Santa Barbara that same year, avoiding the roundabout route
via Gaviota Pass—heading west to go northeast. The roads from Los Angeles
and Ventura were incredibly rough.

As Santa Barbara grew, the supply of water barely kept up. Originally much
of the city relied on wells, but the aquifers contained only a finite amount. In
1872 the city made a deal to transfer to the city the mission's right to Mission
Creek water, except for enough to service the mission. Metal pipes were installed
to deliver the creek water to the city cisterns. Not long thereafter artesian wells
were put down to augment the city's water source. In the early 1900s a 4-mile
tunnel was built by the city to tap into the Santa Ynez River, and that was followed by a dam across the river to create a reservoir.

John P. Stearns, attorney and lumberyard owner, was determined to get a
wharf that would be sturdy and long enough to service all sizes of ships. He
obtained a large loan from Colonel William Welles Hollister, who had made a
fortune in sheep raising in San Benito County and had a financial hand in several Santa Barbara enterprises. Armed with the financing, Stearns convinced the
city council to give him a permit to build a 1,900-foot-long wharf at the foot of
State Street, and a twenty-year license to operate it. It was completed by the close
of 1872. The older Chapala Street wharf was destroyed by a storm in 1878.

Stearns Wharf became the principal conduit of farm products out and needed lumber in. It was also an immediate shot in the arm to the tourist business,
particularly from Los Angeles. The problem was that there were not enough

places to stay. Some small hotels used horse blankets to provide sleeping places on the floor during the summer. The *Daily Press* campaigned editorially for more hotels.

To meet the need a group of businessmen, headed by Colonel Hollister, organized the Seaside Hotel Corporation, which changed its name to Santa Barbara Harbor Company when its members decided to build on State Street in the heart of town, away from the water: Their Arlington Hotel opened in 1874 and was the most elegant tourist hotel in southern California. A mule-powered streetcar carried visitors from Stearns Wharf up State Street to the Arlington. Soon State Street was paved—unusual for the time. Other new hotels followed. In the 1870s lot prices skyrocketed from $100 to $5,000 each.

"Dry" Lompoc, Santa Barbara Wineries, and Santa Maria's Gusher

The town of Lompoc was founded at the original site of Mission La Purisima Concepcion and Mexican land grants to brothers Jose and Joaquin Carrillo, totaling nearly 47,000 acres. In 1874 the land was conveyed to the California Immigrant Union of San Francisco, an organization that settled communities willing to covenant by deed that "No vinous, malt, spirituous, or other intoxicating liquors shall ever be sold or manufactured upon any portion of the Lompoc and Mission Vieja Ranchos." Most of the colonists were ardent prohibitionists.

Twice merchants tried to circumvent the antibooze restriction. A druggist who stocked a supply of liquor was invaded by a crowd of women who began breaking bottles. When he waved a pistol in their direction, the ladies were joined by a group of men who made him put the gun away and watch the destruction. Another man tried to set up a quiet bar in a cottage. It was blown up by a charge of dynamite, set off by unknown parties. The *Lompoc Record* suggested the bomber might have been "a nihilist from Russia."

Santa Barbara wineries and vineyards kept a steady position as fourth in the state, after Napa, Sonoma, and Los Angeles Counties, but did not fall victim to *phylloxera* in the north or Anaheim's disease in the south. Before statehood the missions were the principal producers of wine, with a little output by individual vineyards. Albert Packard planted an extensive vineyard on the west end of Santa Barbara in the 1850s and built the first large winery, La Bodega, located on West Carrillo Street, in the late 1860s. By the end of the century there were at least seventeen winemakers in the county, some clustered in the Santa Ynez valley, others close to the sea, plus the large Santa Cruz Island Winery.

Except for the mission fathers, the first serious winemaker in San Luis Obispo County was former French Legionnaire Pierre Dallidet, who came to town in 1853 after trying his hand at gold mining. He built an adobe and planted a sixteen-acre vineyard. Eventually Dallidet had 7,200 vines. His winery continued in operation for a time after his death in 1905. His adobe is now owned by the county historical society.

A notorious Santa Barbara murder occurred in 1880. Clarence Gray was the Republican candidate for district attorney. Noisy and unstable, he had a record of violence, having beaten up an editor and a priest. Theodore Glancey, newly hired editor of the *Press,* wrote an editorial urging "decent Republicans" to vote against Gray. In revenge Gray shot Glancey in the back, killing him. Gray was tried three times: a hung jury in Santa Barbara; a conviction and a twenty-year sentence when the case was transferred to San Mateo County, which was reversed on the claim that the jury had been drinking alcohol; and somehow the third ended in an acquittal. Gray then disappeared.

In 1867 two former Mexican grants in the Santa Maria Valley were voided by court decisions, and the area was opened up for homesteading. Several homesteaders bought land cheap, built houses, and subscribed for a school. In 1875, they laid out the town of Central City on a half square mile set apart by four adjoining landowners. In the early 1880s the name was changed to Santa Maria.

In 1882 the narrow-gauge Pacific Coast Railroad connected Santa Maria with a shipping point at Port Harford to serve local farmers. But it was the discovery of oil in the areas of Los Alamos and Orcutt, followed by the huge Hartnell gusher at Santa Maria in 1904 that stimulated instant growth—tripling Santa Maria's population in the next dozen years. It was soon the second largest city in Santa Barbara County and remains so today.

THE RAILROAD BUILT IN FITS AND STARTS

The settlers of the communities between San Miguel in the north and Carpinteria in the south realized that if they were to prosper and grow they needed a railroad connection with the outside world. They watched from afar as the transcontinental railroad was completed in 1869. Of more immediate interest to the central coast was the San Francisco & San Jose Railroad, which opened in 1864. A group of San Francisco businessmen bought that railway in August 1868 and changed the name to Southern Pacific. Its president announced the railroad would be extended down the coast all the way to San Diego. He was blowing promotional smoke, for San Jose remained the southern terminus. A year later the Central Pacific bought the Southern Pacific, which eventually gave its name to the entire system.

Both the Central Pacific and the Southern Pacific were owned by the so-called Big Four of Leland Stanford, Charles Crocker, Charles P. Huntington, and Mark Hopkins, who had originally been Sacramento businessmen. With a monopoly on transcontinental rail travel, and thousands of acres of excess property along the rights-of-way, they were now fabulously wealthy. It was also beneficial to the group that Stanford was governor of California between 1862 and 1864.

Their first move after completing the transcontinental railroad was to begin construction of a railroad down the San Joaquin Valley toward Los Angeles, hooking up with Sacramento, Oakland, and San Francisco. The Big Four felt the inland route was a much easier engineering job; since most of it was flat, there was great agricultural potential, and their land agents had already acquired a right-of-way. It would reach Bakersfield in 1874 and connect with Los Angeles in 1876.

Meanwhile the Southern Pacific had extended the rails to Soledad in Monterey County in 1874. There was no pressure on the company to get tourist business up and down the coast since it owned the steamship line that was carrying passengers to resorts on the shore like Cambria, Morro Bay, and Pismo Beach, as well as Santa Barbara. The Southern Pacific was more interested in laying rails to Monterey and its massive Del Monte Hotel. When there were complaints from citizens in San Luis Obispo County, the railroad hierarchy hinted that they might just run the line over the mountains at Gilroy or San Miguel, tie in with its San Joaquin route, and forget the rest of the central coast.

Following a decade of inactivity, the Southern Pacific again began to push south along the route of El Camino Real. The rails reached San Miguel in October 1886, Paso Robles in November 1886, Templeton in April 1887, and after a brief hiatus, Santa Margarita on January 3, 1889. Sleepy San Miguel woke up as a center for shipping farm products. A city plan with a grid of streets and a 2-square-block downtown park was laid out for Paso Robles, which was already popular as a resort due to its mineral springs. At an auction in Paso Robles on November 17, 1886, 228 lots were sold. On Spring Street the large Paso Robles Inn, with a fireplace in every room, opened its doors in 1891. Templeton (named for a Big Four son, Templeton Crocker) and Santa Margarita both blossomed as commodity shipping centers.

Then the railroad construction stopped cold just 10 miles north of San Luis Obispo.

Southern Pacific Vice President Charles Huntington faced a mass meeting in San Luis Obispo in April 1889 that demanded to know when the railroad would reach the town. Huntington replied that the land titles were so fouled up that the railroad did not want to take the time and money to find the owners and buy the right-of-way. He challenged the town to take care of the problem. The city established a committee, found the owners, and bought the land for the railroad, but it took three years. In return the railroad sent its crews carving out a route over the San Lucia Range, which required seven tunnels, the famous horseshoe curve (where the front cars would actually parallel the last carriages), cuts, fills, and a long steel trestle in a 10-mile stretch.

A Chinatown arose in downtown San Luis Obispo in the 1880s, primarily of railroad laborers. Its leader was Ah Louis (real name Wong On), a labor contractor who started a grocery store and a brickyard. He provided workers for county roads, for flower farms, and for local narrow- and broad-gauge railroads connecting San Luis Obispo, Arroyo Grande, and Avila Bay, as well as a horse-drawn streetcar line on San Luis Street. His brick store still stands, but the rest of Chinatown was torn down in the 1930s.

On May 5, 1894, the rails reached San Luis Obispo, followed by a county-wide celebration to greet a train full of Southern Pacific officials. Already the railroad had built a luxury hotel, the Ramona, right where the trains would stop. Everything at the Ramona was first class—electric lights, private baths, tennis courts, fire alarms, even a stage connecting to the ocean at Avila Beach. San Luis Obispo also benefited by installing a skillfully engineered system that separated floodwater runoff from sewage, then a modern innovation.

The Southern Pacific finally began extending its railroad from Los Angeles north toward Santa Barbara in the 1880s. In 1887 the rails reached Santa Paula, Ventura, and Carpinteria in three months. On August 19, 1887, the first train from Los Angeles rolled into Santa Barbara, met by a crowd of more than 1,000.

FIRST TRAIN REACHES SANTA BARBARA, AUGUST 19, 1887

(Courtesy of the Santa Barbara Historical Society.)

The city declared a holiday—there was a banquet at the Arlington Hotel and a public picnic laid out near the beach. The train's arrival stimulated a land boom with sales at inflated prices, but it soon deflated when the Southern Pacific halted at Ellwood, a few miles west of Goleta. However, farm and ranch products, including the increasingly popular lemon crop, found the rails to Los Angeles an easy mode of transport to the consuming world.

Slowly the gap between the railheads was closed, as the railroad extended south one town at a time. A national recession following the panic of 1893 halted the construction a tantalizing 50 miles north of Ellwood. The gap was closed on December 29, 1900. The first southbound train arrived at Santa Barbara on April 3, 1901. Six weeks later President William McKinley rode the train, stopping at San Luis Obispo and Santa Barbara on his way to Los Angeles from San Francisco.

Fire was the implacable enemy of hotels built to accommodate the coast's visitors. Santa Barbara's magnificent Arlington went up in smoke in 1909, and a new version replaced it. The beachside Potter Hotel was destroyed by flames in 1921. In San Luis Obispo during two decades some seventeen hotels burned down, mostly old wooden structures, but also the plush 112-room Andrews Hotel. Built by banker J. P. Andrews, it opened October 1885 and burned down

THE SECOND ARLINGTON HOTEL

(Courtesy of the Santa Barbara Historical Society.)

seven months later, unfortunately also setting Andrews' bank ablaze. The Southern Pacific's magnificent Ramona burned in 1905. The original Paso Robles Inn met a fiery fate in 1941.

OF COLLEGES AND MISSION RESTORATION

In 1901 the legislature authorized a college for San Luis Obispo, California Polytechnic. Envisioned by its local sponsors as a regional mechanical trade school, Cal Poly was actually established as a statewide school with home economics and agriculture as well as mechanics. Today it is a major California university with popular majors in business, agricultural business, architecture, and engineering. The Santa Barbara Teachers College opened in 1909 and after many years became first Santa Barbara State College and eventually part of the University of California system as UC/Santa Barbara on a seashore campus at Goleta.

The Catholic Church filed a claim for title to the secularized missions before the federal Land Claims Commission. In 1862 the commission ruled in favor of the church and President Abraham Lincoln agreed that the federal government would not appeal the decision. However, many of the missions were in a state of disrepair, particularly where they had been used for such nonreligious functions as barns, saloons, houses, and stores.

Eventually all the missions on the central coast were restored by the church, through public efforts supported by both small and large donations, or by the government, which was the case with La Purisima Concepcion. Unlike other missions Santa Barbara was not sold by the Mexican government, since an impending sale negotiated by Governor Pio Pico was voided when California became U.S. territory at the end of the Mexican War. For many years it was also a Catholic educational center. While damaged in the 1925 Santa Barbara earthquake, the sturdy old building survived in better shape than much of downtown, and within two years the mission was fully retrofitted, including restoration of a collapsed tower.

Title to La Purisima was returned to the Catholic Church in 1874, but the mission was so dilapidated that the church sold it. In 1935 it was acquired by the state of California and restored by 1937, in part through the efforts of young men of the federal Civilian Conservation Corps, who actually made 110,000 adobe bricks and planted gardens of early California plants.

Santa Ines got its property back in 1862, but the buildings were deteriorating. In 1882 the lands surrounding the mission and the seminary were sold off. Under church management between 1904 and 1930 there was a program of gradual improvement of the mission itself. Murals that had been painted over were uncovered. In March 1911 the bell tower—holding five bells dating from the first two decades of the 1800s—collapsed and was replaced by a temporary structure. A proper tower was built in 1949 thanks to a contribution of $500,000 from the Hearst Foundation.

In 1868 in an unbelievable attempt to modernize the buildings, the adobe San Luis Obispo mission was covered with wooden shiplap. However, between 1930 and 1934 it was restored in the original mission style, once again displaying its inherent beauty. The effect was further enhanced in 1968 when the city council closed Monterey Street in front of the mission.

In the 1860s and 1870s the long arcade of Mission San Miguel became an early day strip mall of shops with a popular saloon. The mission buildings were restored to the Catholic Church in 1878, and a gradual rehabilitation of the structures began. In 1928 the Franciscan order again took charge and accelerated the renovation, which returned the mission to its earliest appearance. The only change was the installation of pews for worshipers, since the chapel serves as a parish church. The mission is the most attractive building in the town of San Miguel, now a ghost of its turn-of-the-century glory days as a railroad hub.

Not far from the crumbling Santa Ines Mission was a giant bean field owned by the Santa Ynez Valley Development Company. The only building on it was the one-room Santa Ynez School, which served the children of the valley farms. Meanwhile the Danish Lutheran Church Convention, meeting in Michigan, voted to develop a Danish colony and a Danish folk school at a suitable location in the west. In 1911 a committee of three Lutheran leaders found Santa Ynez Valley and bought the 9,000-acre bean field for the Danish-American Colony Corporation. They named the colony Solvang (sunny field).

Within a few months the first wave of Danes arrived. Soon there arose the Solvang Hotel, the Bethania Lutheran Church, several homes, a bank, a bakery, and other shops. The folk school, Attedag ("another day") College, was erected in 1914 and classes on Danish culture and trades for young men were given until 1937. After World War II almost spontaneously Solvang became a model Danish village and famous tourist destination.

DEVELOPMENTS: MONTECITO TO HEARST CASTLE

The California legislature decided to do something about the state's patchwork road system, and in 1905 authorized a bond issue to fund a system of state highways. Envisioned were two principal highways, just in time for the age of the automobile. One would become Highway 101, linking cities between San Francisco and Los Angeles on the old El Camino Real route. The other route would be Highway 99, down the center of the state, and also going to Los Angeles. Although it would take about fifteen years to complete the highway system, by the early 1920s California would have one of the best in the country, with a concrete two-lane highway passing through Paso Robles, San Luis Obispo, Santa Maria, Buellton, Santa Barbara, and Carpinteria. In the 1930s scenic Highway 1 would give thousands of tourists easy access to coastline towns not reached directly by Highway 101.

Santa Barbara became a popular destination for the wealthy in the first decades of the 1900s. Montecito, with its oak-studded rolling hills southeast of the center of town, became an enclave of large mansions with views of the ocean. Charlie Chaplin, the nation's number one movie star at the time, built the luxurious Montecito Hotel in 1928. Other stars found Santa Barbara a handy escape from the spotlight. West of the city, the 2,000-acre Hope Ranch was purchased in 1887 by the Pacific Improvement Company, owned by Southern Pacific's Big Four, and subdivided into extra-large lots.

Journalist Thomas Storke bought the failing *Daily News* for $1,500 in 1913. Then he purchased another moribund paper, the *Independent,* for a mere $2,500, merging them as the *Daily News and Independent.* For years he competed with the venerable *Morning Press.* In 1932, in the heart of the Depression, he was able to buy his rival cheap, and in 1937 he combined them as the *News-Press.* His legend and fame went national in 1962 when the *News-Press* won a Pulitzer Prize for its articles on the ultraright John Birch Society. For more than fifty years Storke's views helped shape Santa Barbara. He lived to be ninety-five, dying in 1971. The *News-Press* is now part of the New York Times chain.

In 1919 media mogul William Randolph Hearst began building his castle on the family ranch above the village of San Simeon, which was also Hearst's. Designed by Julia Morgan, California's leading female architect, the palace grew year after year with classic statuary, giant swimming pools indoors and out, a medieval-looking dining hall, tennis courts, apartments, offices, and art galleries, all furnished with antiques from Europe. The most influential newspaper publisher in the country until his death in 1951, Hearst presided over his empire from the castle, sending out directives simply signed "The Chief" and entertaining friends, topflight columnists, and his mistress, movie actress Marion Davies. Eventually the Hearst Foundation conveyed the Hearst Castle to the state of California.

Not only was Santa Barbara a retreat for cinema luminaries, it was also popular as a place to make movies in the silent film era, with its variety of outdoor scenery—hills, canyons, and beaches—with historic buildings as backdrops.

Prohibition (1920–1933) made the manufacture and sale of alcoholic beverages illegal. As a tourist destination and a resort of the prominent who thought that limitations on lifestyle were meant for others, Santa Barbarans tended to find Prohibition unpopular and something of a joke. Throughout the twenties liquor smuggling became a game of cops and robbers. The coves, inlets, and islands that had been smugglers' lairs in Spanish and Mexican times now sheltered high-speed boats and trucks with dimmed lights rumbling through the night. Canadian rumrunners would land on the Channel Islands and deposit their liquid cargo, and then local motorboats would load up and usually evade revenue cutters, local deputies, and federal revenuers. A tank truck filled with liquor painted exactly like a Richfield Oil truck regularly drove through Santa Barbara until a deputy sheriff spotted it where there were no gas stations.

Grape production was not diminished by Prohibition. The law allowed production of 200 gallons a year for "personal use." Grape juice was shipped across the country for home winemakers, often with the warning not to add yeast lest it cause "illegal fermentation." However, professional wineries were history, except for a few elsewhere in California licensed to make wine for "sacramental purposes."

NATURE AND PEARL CHASE SHAKE UP SANTA BARBARA

As Santa Barbarans were waking up on June 29, 1925, the city was rocked by the most violent earthquake since 1812, a 6.3 on the Richter scale. The town had become a hodgepodge of style, intermixed with some old buildings covered

HOTEL CALIFORNIAN AFTER THE 1925 EARTHQUAKE

(Courtesy of the Santa Barbara Historical Society.)

with unfortunate facades. It was what one writer called "a wasteland of western junk." The earthquake splintered the wooden buildings, and the masonry structures collapsed in clouds of powdered plaster. Some 618 buildings were destroyed or substantially damaged. State Street was a total mess. Thirteen people in the area were killed.

After the initial cleanup, a wonderful thing happened. Led by Pearl Chase, a dynamic woman with an indefatigable zeal for civic beauty and public responsibility, Santa Barbarans realized they had a real chance to rebuild the city with harmonious designs. Miss Chase, who had graduated from the University of California at age 19, pushed, reasoned, and intimidated civic leaders for fifty years as chair of the city's Plans and Planting Committee. She also founded the Santa Barbara Trust for Historic Preservation and the California Conservation Council. Pearl was honored as "Woman of the Year" by *The Los Angeles Times* (1952) and the City of Santa Barbara (1956).

PEARL CHASE

(Courtesy of the Santa Barbara Historical Society.)

Height limitations and other controls were adopted by the city government. New stores, office buildings, commercial courtyards, theaters, and even service stations were built in compatible Mediterranean, Colonial Spanish, Mission Revival, and related styles.

The earthquake saved Santa Barbara from mediocrity. Fortunately there was local wealth and money earned from tourism to fund the reconstruction and tasteful development. Years later, after a major oil eruption from offshore wells, the city's response was much the same. Take advantage of disaster: They shut down the wells in the name of good ecological sense valued over taxes and profits.

The highlight of the new Santa Barbara was the courthouse completed in 1929, designed by architect William Moser in Spanish Moorish style. Surviving historic adobes blended in well with the new structures. Two warm, artfully developed State Street commercial courtyards—El Paseo and La Arcada—not only employed quality design, but helped keep business downtown.

BEAUTIFICATION OF SAN LUIS OBISPO

In 1949 San Luis Obispo was an ugly town dominated by train yards. There were no central park and almost no trees lining the streets. Its historical centerpiece, the Mission, faced a line of parking meters along Monterey Street. The first seeds of change were planted in 1949 by three students in the art class of Margaret Maxwell at San Luis Obispo Junior College working on a project to "apply art to the community." They came up with the concept of "Mission Gardens" in front of the Mission, which would require closing Monterey Street. The city council was not interested.

Cal Poly professor of architecture Kenneth Schwartz also had students tackle the problem of developing a downtown park. They too thought the only answer was closing Monterey Street and incorporating the open space across the street into a public park. Agreeing with them were the planning commission, a landscape consultant hired by the city, and the new planning director. But losing parking spaces was anathema to the council.

In 1967 three Cal Poly seniors were given a matching fund grant by the council to suggest ways to beautify downtown, as long as they presented a plan that did not include closing Monterey Street. At a standing-room-only council meeting, the students had the nerve to present two plans, the first of which recommended closing the street. The spectators were enthralled, but the meeting grew raucous when the mayor barked that they had violated their mandate and should pay back their grant.

The result of the uproar was an initiative to adopt a city park plan closing Monterey Street. Drafted by former city attorney George Andre, the measure passed by a popular vote of two to one. A tree planting program was accelerated. Monterey Street was closed. In 1970 architectural professor Schwartz was elected mayor for the first of five two-year terms, along with a pro-planning slate of three council candidates. The park was built, the art museum added, and private citizens planted flowers, shrubs, and trees at no cost. Eventually another block was added to the park. Across the creek business owners granted an access easement in perpetuity and donated brickwork to make a walkway. The park now hosts concerts, the Mozart Festival is held in the Mission, and in September 1999 the "Creek Walk" was completed along the park side of the creek.

The Downtown Association, the Chamber of Commerce, the city council, and the people of San Luis Obispo caught the spirit of the movement. There are sign ordinances prohibiting the garish and glaring, and more and more trees have been planted. San Luis Obispo is ugly no more.

Although UC/Davis enology professors had long contended that the central coast could be a prime wine-producing region, it took two Davis grads, Uriel Nielson and Bill DeMartini, to kick-start the wine renaissance in Santa Barbara County. Their initial success in their 1968 Santa Maria Valley planting evoked a rush of interest and attention to some of the existing wineries. Dozens of new-comers to the wine business were encouraged to establish wineries and plant vines. Paso Robles, San Luis Obispo, and Edna Valley were not far behind. The number of vines, wineries, cases of wine, medals, and higher ratings have grown every year in the past decade.

The history of California's central coast is a story of delayed discovery. The Spanish dallied for two centuries, the Mexican government treated it like a stepchild, many of the first Americans were primarily exploiters, the railroad barons put it at the bottom of their schedule, the wine gurus ignored its obvi-ous potential, and mother nature was often unkind. Tourists hurried past its beauty on the way to somewhere else. In response the people of Santa Barbara and San Luis Obispo Counties have struggled to improve not only image but reality. In great measure they have gotten it right. Now it is up to you to dis-cover the central coast.

CHAPTER 9

LIST OF LISTS

*C**alling ahead is highly recommended for all these events. Dates often change yearly, as do locations. Ticketed events are often sold out early.*

*A*NNUAL EVENTS

Santa Barbara County

January

Blues Festival, second three-day (Friday–Sunday) weekend, Royal Scandinavian Inn, Solvang; (805) 688–8000

February

Whale Festival and Week of the Whale, ten days celebrating gray whale migration, exhibits, live entertainment, arts, crafts, classic cars, at Stearns Wharf; (805) 966–0500; Web site: www. sbnet.com/whales

March

Santa Barbara International Film Festival, ten days starting first Thursday, premieres of American and foreign independent films, workshops, special events with actors, at Arlington Theatre and other venues; (805) 689–4636 or (805) 963–0023

International Orchid Show, second three-day weekend, displays for awards, Earl Warren Showgrounds, Santa Barbara; (805) 967–6331

Taste of Solvang, third three-day weekend, food festival with live entertainment, throughout Solvang; (800) 468–6765 or (805) 688–6144

April

Presidio Days, Friday–Sunday, Santa Barbara's birthday celebrated at the Presidio; (805) 966-9719

Santa Barbara County Vintners' Festival, second three-day weekend, wine tasting from forty wineries, food from local restaurants, Santa Ynez Valley; (800) 218–0881

Spring Arts Festival, arts and crafts, BBQ, chili cook-offs, carnival, entertainment, Lompoc; (805) 735–8511

Vintners' Festival, third Saturday and Sunday, local wines and entertainment, Solvang; advance tickets required, (805) 688–0881 or (800) 218–0881

Santa Maria Valley Strawberry Festival, food and drinks emphasizing strawberries, parade, carnival, entertainment; county fairgrounds; (805) 925–8824

Festival of Performing Arts, music, dance, theater presented by Santa Barbara Dance Alliance; Lobero Theatre, Santa Barbara; (805) 564–7295

Santa Ynez Valley Carriage Classic, carriages and wagons from all over, Solvang; (805) 688–4454

May

Cinco de Mayo, some events May 5 and others at closest weekend, music, dance, performances, poetry, celebrating Mexico's historic day, various locations, Santa Barbara; (805) 965–8581

Arabian Horse Show, three-day weekend, beautiful thoroughbreds; Earl Warren Showgrounds, Santa Barbara; (805) 967–6331

Children's Festival, clowns, pony rides, games, Alameda Park, Santa Barbara; (805) 965–1001

Chinese Festival, Saturday in the middle of the month, 11:00 A.M.–5:00 P.M.; Chinese food, fashion, dance, Oak Park, Santa Barbara; (805) 963–3571

Multicultural Festival, international music, dance, art, food, presented by Santa Barbara Dance Alliance, Las Positas Park, Santa Barbara; (805) 564–7295

Irish Festival, Irish music, dance, food and beer, Oak Park, Santa Barbara; (805) 687–4343

Art About Town, yearly art walk to open studios, Santa Barbara; (805) 966–5373

June

Santa Barbara Dance Festival, three-week dance festival featuring swing, multicultural, tap, at parks and beaches, Santa Barbara; (805) 564–7295

Traditional Jazz Festival, first full three-day weekend, Royal Scandinavian Inn, Solvang; (805) 688–8000 or (800) 624–5572.

Summer Solstice Celebration, starts noon on Saturday closest to June 21, one day, parade, entertainment, food, music, dance, several locations, parade of more than 100 zany non-motorized (and no horses) units starts at Alameda Park on State Street, Santa Barbara; (805) 965–3396

Santa Ynez Valley Historic Timeline, five days in fourth week of month, historic displays, food, entertainment, in Solvang, Los Olivos, Santa Ynez, Ballard, and Buellton; (800) 468–6765

Elks Rodeo and Parade, four-day event, top U.S. rodeo riders, parade, Western music and dancing, BBQ; (805) 922–6006

Lompoc Valley Flower Festival, last weekend in June, carnival, entertainment, parade, Lompoc; (805) 735–3255

July

Santa Barbara County Fair, one week, exhibits, horse shows, food, carnival, music, entertainment, fireworks, Santa Barbara County Fairgrounds, Santa Maria; (805) 925–8824

August

Old Spanish Days, first week in August, grand parade and fiesta, rodeo, Spanish marketplaces, children's parade, carnival, Santa Barbara; (805) 962–8101

Old Mission Santa Ines Fiesta, second three-day (Friday–Sunday) weekend, food, festivities, mariachis, Santa Ines Mission in Solvang; (805) 688–4815

Annual Warbird Roundup, fly-ins and historic planes, Santa Maria Public Airport, Santa Maria; (805) 922–8758

September

Danish Days, third three-day weekend, folk dancing, music, parades, pageants, entertainment, food, Solvang; (805) 688–6144

Santa Barbara International Jazz Festival, three-day weekend, jazz at the beach, top musicians, Santa Barbara; (310) 452–5056

Mexican Independence Day, dance, music, food celebrating Mexican heritage; (805) 925–8824

California Avocado Festival, weekend salute to avocado and exotic fruits from Carpinteria valley, food, games, displays, Carpinteria; (805) 684–5479

October

Fiddlers' Convention, bluegrass and country music competition, Stow House, Goleta; (805) 964–4407

Goleta Lemon Festival, one day, everything in lemons, entertainment, craft show, Stow House, Goleta; (805) 967–4618

November

Dixieland Jazz Festival, three-day weekend, jazz bands at several locations, Solvang; (805) 688–8000

December

Winterfest, monthlong old-world winter celebration, light displays in Danish village, Solvang; (805) 688–6144

San Luis Obispo County

February

Annual Mardi Gras Jazz Festival, Dixieland bands, various venues, Pismo Beach; (805) 773–1661

March

Central Coast Orchid Show, first Friday and Saturday, orchids from central coast displayed, judged, sold, small entrance fee, South County Regional Center, Arroyo Grande; (805) 929–1791

Paderewski Festival, honors famed pianist and Polish President Ignace Paderewski, history, music, food, wine, San Luis Obispo; (805) 238–0506

Zinfandel Weekend, third three-day weekend, more than thirty Paso Robles area wineries present tasting of Zinfandel by glass or from barrel, banquet, auction, open houses, events at Paso Robles Library and Paso Robles Inn, Paso Robles, (805) 239–8463; e-mail: prvga@pasowine.com; Web site: www. pasowine.com

May

Paso Robles Wine Festival, second three-day weekend, wine tasting, food, music, several venues; (805) 239–8463; e-mail and Web site as above in Zinfandel Weekend

Beachfest, beach-type events, including volleyball tournament, surfing, Pismo Beach; (805) 773-4382

June

Custom Car Show, hundreds of classic cars, hot rods, at pier and downtown, Pismo Beach; (805) 489-5456

July

KCBX Central Coast Wine Classic, wine auction, tastings, banquets, Avila Beach; (805) 781–2026

San Luis Obispo Mozart Festival, two weeks starting fourth Friday in July, orchestral and choral performances, jazz, recitals, and "lots of Mozart," at Christopher Cohan Performing Arts Center, Mission San Luis Obispo and other venues, including Laetitia and Martin-Weyrich Wineries, and Atascadero Lake Pavilion, banquets, special events; year 2000 is thirtieth annual festival; PAC Ticket Office, Grand Avenue, San Luis Obispo 93407; (805) 756–2787, fax (805) 756–6088, Web site: www.mozartfestival.com

August

California Mid-State Fair, star-level entertainment, family fun, Paso Robles; (805) 239–0655

September

Western Days, festival of country dancing, food, art, Pismo Beach; (805) 489–2885

October

Clam Festival, half-century-old festival celebrating "Clam Capital of the World," parade, entertainment, surfing contest, sand castles, clam chowder competition, Pismo Beach; (805) 773–4362

Morro Bay Harbor Festival, two-day weekend, wine, seafood, entertainment, ship tours, Morro Bay; (805) 772–1155

San Luis Obispo Film Festival, films from many countries, San Luis Obispo; (805) 781–2777

Paso Robles Harvest Wine Affair, second three-day weekend, wine tasting and events; (805) 239–8463; e-mail: prvga@pasowine.com; Web site: www.pasowine.com

Dixieland Jubilee by the Sea, top Dixieland bands, need presold badge to attend events, various venues, Pismo Beach; (805) 773–4382

November

Rosemary Festival, celebrates rosemary, other herbs, Cambria; (805) 927–3624

December

Decemberfest, all December up to Christmas, holiday celebration, events, activities, downtown San Luis Obispo; (805) 541–0286

*P*LACES TO STAY

(Cities listed south to north)

Carpinteria

Best Western Carpinteria Inn, 4558 Carpinteria Avenue, Carpinteria 93013; (805) 684–0473, fax (805) 684–4015; $105–$135; many patios, small pool, dining room, pets OK with deposit

Motel 6 (two locations), 4200 Via Real, Carpinteria 93013; (805–684–2981) and 5550 Carpinteria Avenue, Carpinteria 93013; (805–684–8602)

Santa Barbara

Montecito area

Coast Village Inn, 1188 Coast Village Road, Santa Barbara 93108; (805) 969–3266, fax (805) 969–7117; $115–$155; pool, smoke free, continental breakfast, children free, no pets

Four Seasons Biltmore, 1260 Channel Drive, Santa Barbara 93108; (805) 969–2261, fax (805) 969–4682; $400–$480; waterfront resort, AAA four diamonds, pool, tennis courts, pets OK

Miramar Resort Hotel, 1555 South Jameson Lane, Santa Barbara 93108; (805) 969–2203, fax (805) 969–3163; $75–$200 plus; pools, tennis courts, sauna, dining room, coffee shop, cocktail lounge, no pets (Warning to light sleepers—railroad runs through)

Montecito Inn, 1295 Coast Village Road, Santa Barbara 93108; (805) 969–7854, fax (805) 969–0623; $185–$225; pool, sauna, some fireplaces, restaurant, cafe, free breakfast, no pets

Cabrillo Boulevard

Beachcomber Inn, 202 West Cabrillo Boulevard, Santa Barbara 93101; (805) 965–4577, fax (805) 965–9937; $115–$250; small pool, continental breakfast, small pets with deposit

Best Western Beachside Inn, 336 West Cabrillo Boulevard, Santa Barbara 93101; (805) 965–6556, fax (805) 966–6626; $109–$189; pool, restaurant, bar, no pets

Fess Parker's Doubletree Resort, 633 East Cabrillo Boulevard, Santa Barbara 93103; (805) 564–4333, fax (805) 564–4964; $229–$269; patios, balconies, grounds, pool, tennis courts, restaurant, coffee shop, bar, pets with deposit

Harbor View Inn, 28 West Cabrillo Boulevard, Santa Barbara, 93101; (805) 963–0780, fax (805) 963–7967; $150–$350; pool, whirlpool, restaurant, on-sale license, AAA four diamonds, no pets

Ocean Palms Beach Resort, 232 West Cabrillo Boulevard, Santa Barbara 93101; (805) 966–9133, fax (805) 965–7882; $115–$250; pool, whirlpool, some fireplaces, continental breakfast, pets OK with small fee

Radisson Hotel Santa Barbara, 1111 East Cabrillo Boulevard, Santa Barbara 93103; (805) 963–0744, fax (805) 962–0985; $169–$199; pool, restaurant, on-sale license, no pets

Santa Barbara Inn, 901 East Cabrillo Boulevard, Santa Barbara 93103; (805) 966–2285, fax (805) 966–6584, $187–$302; pool, whirlpool, sundeck, refrigerators, French restaurant, on-sale license, no pets

West Beach Inn, 306 West Cabrillo Boulevard, Santa Barbara 93101; (805) 963–4277, fax (805) 564–4210; $106–$201; pool, whirlpool, continental breakfast, afternoon wine and cheese, no pets

Close to beach (within 3 blocks)

Country Inn by the Sea, 128 Castillo Street, Santa Barbara 93101; (805) 963–4471, fax (805) 962–2633; $109–$229; patios or balconies, small pool, whirlpool, sauna, continental breakfast, smoke free, no pets

Eagle Inn, 232 Natoma Avenue, Santa Barbara 93101; (805) 965–3586, fax (805) 966–1218; $130–$185; most rooms with kitchen, no pets

Franciscan Inn, 109 Bath Street, Santa Barbara 93101; (805) 963–8845, fax (805) 564–3295; $81–$195; pool, whirlpool, no pets

Holiday Inn Express–Virginia Hotel, 17 West Haley Street, Santa Barbara 93101; (805) 963–9757, fax (805) 963–1747; $79–$205; historic landmark, continental breakfast, no pets

Marina Beach Motel, 21 Bath Street, Santa Barbara 93101; (805) 963–9311, fax (805) 564–4102; $75–$225; whirlpools, continental breakfast, free bike use, no pets

Mason Beach Inn, 324 West Mason Street, Santa Barbara 93101; (805) 962–3203, fax (805) 962–1056; $125–$155; pool, whirlpool, continental breakfast, no pets

Tropicana Inn and Suites, 223 Castillo Street, Santa Barbara 93101; (805) 966–2219, fax (805) 962–9428; $96–$172; pool, whirlpool, smoke free, continental breakfast, no pets

Villa Rosa, 15 Chapala Street, Santa Barbara 93101; (805) 966–0851, fax (805) 962–7159; $110–$250; small pool, whirlpool, no pets

State Street

Best Western Pepper Tree Inn, 3850 State Street, Santa Barbara 93105; (805) 687–551, fax (805) 682–2410; $146–$168; two pools, whirlpools, sauna, restaurant, on-sale license, no pets

Hotel Santa Barbara, 533 State Street, Santa Barbara 93101; (805) 957–9300, fax (805) 962–2412; $179–$219; restored historic hotel in heart of downtown, continental breakfast, valet parking, no pets

Lemon Tree Inn, 2819 State Street, Santa Barbara 93105; (805) 687–6444, fax (805) 687–4432; $85–$250; pool, whirlpool, restaurant, on-sale license, no pets

Mountain View Inn, 3055 De la Vina Street (corner of State), Santa Barbara 93105; (805) 687–6636, fax (805) 682–6750; $90–$169; pool, continental breakfast, no pets

Orange Tree Inn, 1920 State Street, Santa Barbara 93101; (805) 569–1521, fax (805) 682–6854; $75–$220; pool, no pets

Sandman Inn, 3714 State Street, Santa Barbara 93105; (805) 687–2468, fax (805) 687–6581, $80–$150; pool, whirlpool, restaurant, bar, continental breakfast, no pets

Other acceptable accommodations on State Street: Motel 6 (800–466–8356), Plaza Inn (805–687–3217), Sahara Motel (805–687–2500), San Roque Motel (805–687–6611), Sandpiper Lodge (805–687–5326), Sunset Motel (850–687–3813), Travelers Motel (805–687–6009)

Other Santa Barbara Neighborhoods

Best Western Encina Lodge, 2220 Bath Street, Santa Barbara 93105; (805) 682–7277, fax (805) 563–9319; $126–$156; pool, sauna, whirlpool, numerous kitchens, restaurant, on-sale license, no pets

Pacific Suites, 5490 Hollister Avenue, Santa Barbara 93111; (805) 683–6722, fax (805) 683–4121; $120–$180; pool, whirlpool, breakfast cafe, small pets OK

Ramada Limited, 4770 Calle Real, Santa Barbara 93110; (805) 964–3511, fax (805) 964–0075; $75–$145; pool, whirlpool, continental breakfast, no pets

The Upham, 1404 De la Vina Street, Santa Barbara 93101; (805) 962–0058, fax (805) 963–2825; $140–$195; restored historic (founded 1871) Victorian with cottages, antiques, spa, restaurant, beer/wine, complimentary breakfast, no pets

---

$\mathscr{B}$ED AND BREAKFASTS

A surprising number of Santa Barbara bed-and-breakfasts are historic buildings dating back well over a century. Simpson House Inn (805–963–7067), an 1878 Italianate Victorian, has been awarded a remarkable five diamonds by AAA, and has fourteen units. Bath Street Inn (805–682–9680) is an 1890 Queen Anne Victorian, and the Cheshire Cat (805–569–1610) is an 1880 Queen Anne Victorian. The Mary May Inn (805–569–3398) includes a Queen Anne Victorian and a Federal style house, both built in the 1880s. The Parsonage (805–962–9336) is an 1892 Victorian and is smoke free. Tiffany Inn (805–963–2283) is in Colonial Revival style built in 1898, and one house of Blue Dolphin Inn (805–965–2333) dates from 1860, making it one of the city's oldest occupied structures. The Glenborough Inn (805–966–0589) includes a portion built in the 1880s, while Olive House Inn (805–962–4902) is a California Craftsman erected in 1904. Early twentieth-century structures include Old Yacht Club Inn (805–962–1277) and the Secret Garden & Cottages (805–687–2300). Even if you are not a devotee of historic architecture, you can enjoy the hospitality of the hosts and hostesses who have developed the amenities in these grand old buildings.

Goleta

Best Western South Coast Inn, 5620 Calle Real, Goleta 93117; (805) 967–3200, fax (805) 683–4466; $110–$118; pool, whirlpool, free breakfast, no pets

Holiday Inn–Santa Barbara/Goleta, 5650 Calle Real, Goleta 93117; (805) 964–6241, fax (805) 964–8467; $125–$135; pool, pets OK

Solvang

Best Western–King Frederik Motel, 1617 Copenhagen Drive, Solvang 93463; (805) 688–5515, fax (805) 688–2067; $69–$89; pool, whirlpool, free breakfast, no pets

Best Western Kronborg Inn, 1440 Mission Drive, Solvang 93463; (805) 688–2383, fax (805) 688–1821, $45–$100; whirlpool, small pets OK

Chimney Sweep Inn, 1564 Copenhagen Drive, Solvang 93463; (805) 688–2111, fax (805) 688–8824; $75–$275; cottages, lodge, suites, fireplaces, continental breakfast, no pets

Danish Country Inn, 1455 Mission Drive, Solvang 93463; (805) 688–2018, fax (805) 688–1156; $99–$129; some lofts at higher rate, small pool, spa, free breakfast, no pets

Hamlet Motel, 1532 Mission Drive, Solvang 93463; (805) 688–4413, fax (805) 686–1301; $65–$140; continental breakfast, no pets

Petersen Village Inn, 1576 Mission Drive, Solvang 93463; (805) 688–3121, fax (805) 688–5732; $135–$235; villagelike complex of cafes, bakery, conference facilities, AAA four diamonds, buffet breakfast, buffet in piano bar, no pets

Quality Inn of Solvang, 1450 Mission Drive, Solvang 93463; (805) 688–3210, fax (805) 688–0026; $85–$200; indoor pool, game room, free breakfast, no pets

Royal Copenhagen Motel, 1579 Mission Drive, Solvang 93463; (805) 688–5561, fax (805) 688–7029; $79–$109; pool, free breakfast, no pets

Solvang Royal Scandinavian, 400 Alisal Road (mail to PO Box 30), Solvang 93463; (805) 688–8000, fax (805) 688–0761; $101–$160; some patios or balconies, pool, whirlpool, restaurant, on-sale license, continental breakfast, no pets

Svendsgaard's Danish Lodge, 1711 Mission Drive, Solvang 93463; (805) 688–3277, fax (805) 686–5616; $75–$136; many fireplaces, pool, spa, continental breakfast, no pets

Three Crowns Inn, 1518 Mission Drive, Solvang 93463; (805) 688–4702, fax (805) 688–6907; $75–$165; some cottages, continental breakfast, no pets

Viking Motel, 1506 Mission Drive, Solvang 93463; (805) 688–1337; $52–$58; free breakfast, small pets for small fee

Bed-and-breakfast: Story Book Inn (805–688–1703), smoke free

Ballard

Ballard Inn, 2436 Baseline Avenue, Ballard 93463; (805) 688–7770, fax (805) 688–9560; $170–$250; AAA four diamonds, wine tasting afternoon, no pets

Los Olivos

Fess Parker's Wine Country Inn, 2860 Grand Avenue (mail to PO Box 849), Los Olivos 93441; (805) 688–7788, fax (805) 688–1942; $200–$350; some rooms with gas fireplaces, dining, pool, whirlpool, smoke free, no pets

Buellton

Best Western Pea Soup Andersen's Inn, 51 East Highway 246 (mail to PO Box
    197), Buellton 93427; (805) 688–3216, fax (805) 688–9767; $69–$89;
    pool, whirlpool, free breakfast, no pets
Also Rancho Santa Barbara Marriott (805–688–1000), Windmill Motor Inn
    (805–688–8448), EconoLodge (805–688–0022)

Lompoc

Best Western Vandenberg Inn, 940 East Ocean Avenue, Lompoc 93436; (805)
    735–7731, fax (805) 737–0012; $40–$95; pool, sauna, whirlpool, free
    breakfast, small pets OK with fee
Embassy Suites Hotel, 1117 North H Street, Lompoc 93436; (805) 735–8311,
    fax (805) 735–8459; $109; pool, no pets
Holiday Inn Express, 1417 North H Street, Lompoc 93436; (805) 736–2391, fax
    (805) 736–6410; $109-$119; pool, whirlpool, free breakfast, no pets
Inn of Lompoc, 1122 North H Street, Lompoc 93436; (805) 735–7744, fax
    (805) 736–0421; $69–$79; indoor pool, children under twelve free, free
    breakfast, pets OK with fee
Quality Inn and Executive Suites, 1621 North H Street, Lompoc 93436; (805)
    735–8555, fax (805) 735–8566; $79–$109; pool, spa, breakfast buffet, pets
    OK with fee
Tally Ho Motor Inn, 1020 East Ocean Avenue, Lompoc 93436; (805)
    735–6444, fax (805) 735–5558; $49–$54; sauna, whirlpool, free breakfast,
    pets OK with fee

Santa Maria

Best Western Big America, 1725 North Broadway, Santa Maria 93454; (805)
    922–5200, fax (805) 922–9865; $55–$90; pool, whirlpool, restaurant, on-
    sale license, continental breakfast, pets OK
Comfort Inn, 210 South Nicholson Avenue, Santa Maria 93454; (805)
    922–5891, fax (805) 928–9222; $56–$76; pool, spa, continental breakfast,
    small pets with fee
Holiday Inn Hotel and Suites, 2100 North Broadway, Santa Maria 93454;
    (805) 928–6000, fax (805) 928–0356; $78–$158; pool, whirlpool, restau-
    rant, on-sale license, no pets
Santa Maria Hilton, 3455 Skyway Drive, Santa Maria 93454; (805)
    928–8000, fax (805) 928–5251; $69; pool, spa, restaurant, lounge, conti-
    nental breakfast, no pets

Santa Maria Inn, 801 South Broadway, Santa Maria 93454; (805) 928–7777, fax (805) 928–5690; $99–$119; pool, spa, restaurant, lounge, no pets

Arroyo Grande

Best Western Casa Grande Resort and Suites, 850 Oak Park Road, Arroyo Grande 93420; (805) 481–7398, fax (805) 481–4859; $80–$120; pool, sauna, whirlpool, restaurant, lounge, continental breakfast, no pets
Also Crystal Rose Inn (850–481–1854) and EconoLodge (850–489–9300)

Grover Beach

Holiday Inn Express Grover Beach, 775 Oak Park Boulevard, Grover Beach 93433; (805) 481–4448, fax (805) 473–3609; $59–$95; pool, whirlpool, steak house and saloon, continental breakfast, no pets

Pismo Beach

Best Western Shelter Cove Lodge, 2651 Price Street, Pismo Beach 93449; (805) 773–3511, fax (805) 773–3511; $118–$198; pool and spa, free breakfast, no pets
Best Western Shore Cliff Lodge, 2555 Price Street, Pismo Beach 93449; (805) 773–4671, fax (805) 773-2341; $139; pool, sauna, whirlpool, balconies, restaurant, lounge, no pets
Cottage Inn by the Sea, 2351 Price Street, Pismo Beach 93449; (805) 773–4617; $89–$179; pool, spa, continental breakfast, no pets
Kon Tiki Inn, 1621 Price Street, Pismo Beach 93449; (805) 773–4833, fax (805) 773–6541; $86–$100; pool, sauna, whirlpools, racquetball and tennis courts, restaurant, on-sale license, no pets
Oxford Suites Resort, 651 Five Cities Drive, Pismo Beach 93449; (805) 773–3773, fax (805) 773–5177; $89–$129; pool, whirlpool, free breakfast, pets OK
Sand Castle Inn, 100 Stimson Avenue, Pismo Beach 93449; (805) 773–2422, fax (805) 773–0771; $119–$179; whirlpool, sundeck, no pets
Sea Venture Resort, 100 Ocean View Avenue, Pismo Beach 93449; (805) 773–4994, fax (805) 773–0924; $139–$349; pool, continental breakfast, no pets
Spyglass Inn, 2705 Spyglass Drive, Pismo Beach 93449; (805) 773–4855, fax (805) 773–5298; $109–$189; pool, whirlpool, restaurant, on-sale license, no pets
Also, Beachcomber Inn in the center of town (805–773–5505) and modestly priced motels including Edgewater (805–773–4811), Ocean Palms (805–

773–4669), Rose Garden Inn (805–773–1841), Sea Crest Resort
(805–773–4608), Sea Gypsy (805–773–1801), and Shell Beach (805–
773–4373)

Avila Beach

Sycamore Mineral Springs Resort, 1215 Avila Beach Drive, Avila Beach 93405;
    (805) 595–7302, fax (805) 595–2911; $129–$300; pool, spa, restaurant,
    lounge, hot tubs, no pets
Inn at Avila Beach, 256 Front Street, Avila Beach 93405; (805) 595–2300, fax
    (805) 773–8606; $99–$249; pool, spa, no pets
Also San Luis Bay Inn (805–595–2333)

San Luis Obispo

Apple Farm Inn and Apple Farm Trellis Court, 2015 Monterey Street, San
    Luis Obispo 93401; (805) 544–2040, fax (805) 546–9495; Inn:
    $169–$189; AAA four diamonds; Trellis Court: $99-$109; shared pool,
    whirlpool, restaurant, no pets
Best Western Royal Oak Hotel, 214 Madonna Road, San Luis Obispo 93405;
    (805) 544–4410, fax (805) 544–3026; $69–$89; pool, whirlpool, free
    breakfast, small pets OK
Best Western Somerset Manor, 1895 Monterey Street, San Luis Obispo
    93405; (805) 544–0973, fax (805) 541–2805; $79–$112 (includes
    breakfast); pool, whirlpool, coffee shop, children twelve and under free,
    no pets
Days Inn, 2050 Garfield Street, San Luis Obispo 93401; (805) 544–8886, fax
    (850) 546–0734; $49–$135; pool, whirlpool, free breakfast, pets OK
Embassy Suites, 333 Madonna Road, San Luis Obispo 93405; (805)
    549–0800, fax (805) 543–5273; $109–$174; indoor pool, whirlpools,
    restaurant, on-sale license, pets OK
Holiday Inn Express, 1800 Monterey Street, San Luis Obispo 93401; (805)
    544–8600, fax (805) 541–4698, $99–$149; pool, spa, restaurant, on-sale
    license, free breakfast, no pets
La Cuesta Motor Inn, 2074 Monterey Street, San Luis Obispo 93401; (805)
    543–2777, fax (805) 544–0696; $85–$120; pool, whirlpool, continental
    breakfast, no pets
Madonna Inn, 100 Madonna Road, San Luis Obispo 93405; (805)
    543–3000, fax (805) 643–1800; $87–$198; dining room, lounge, shops,
    coffee shop, bakery, smoke free, no pets

Quality Suites, 1631 Monterey Street, San Luis Obispo 93401; (805) 541–5001, fax (805) 546–9475; $109–$159; pool, spa, no pets

Sands Suites and Motel, 1930 Monterey Street, San Luis Obispo 93401; (805) 544–0500, fax (805) 544–3529; $79–$139; pool, whirlpool, on-site deli and liquor store, continental breakfast, pets OK with $5.00 fee

Decent bargains: Campus Motel (805–544–0881), EconoLodge (805–544–8886), Peach Tree Inn (805–543–3170)

Los Osos

Best Western Sea Pines Golf Resort, 1945 Solano Street, Los Osos 93402; (805) 528–5252, fax (805) 528–8231; $89–$129; nine-hole golf course, driving range, restaurant

Morro Bay

Ascot Suites, 260 Morro Bay Boulevard, Morro Bay 93442; (805) 772–4437, fax (805) 772–8860; $110–$295; some rooms with whirlpools, pool, spa, restaurant, continental breakfast, no pets

Best Western San Marcos Inn, 250 Pacific Street, Morro Bay 93442; (805) 772–2248, fax (805) 772–6844; $79–$159; complimentary wine, free breakfast, no pets

Embarcadero Inn, 456 Embarcadero, Morro Bay 93442; (805) 772–2700, fax (805) 772–1060; $95–$135; many balconies and fireplaces, whirlpools, no pets

Inn at Morro Bay, 60 State Park Road, Morro Bay 93442; (805) 772–5651, fax (805) 772–4779; $129–$299; many rooms with fireplaces or balconies, pool, no pets

La Serena Inn, 99 Morro Avenue (mail to PO Box 1711), Morro Bay 93442; (805) 772–5665 (phone and fax); $79–$104; sauna, continental breakfast, no pets

Sunset Travelodge, 1080 Market Avenue, Morro Bay 93442; (805) 772–1259, fax (805) 772–8967; $89–$189; pool, continental breakfast, pets with fee

Other decent lodgings, some with bay views: Ascot Inn (805–772–4437), Bay View Lodge (805–772–2771), Best Western El Rancho (805–772–2212), Best Western Tradewinds (805–772–7376), Blue Sail Inn (805–772–7132), Breakers Motel (805–772–7317), Days Inn (805–772–2711), EconoLodge (805–772–5609), El Morro Lodge (805–772–5633), Keystone Inn (805–772–7503), Morro Crest Inn (805–772–7740), Sundown Motel (805–772–7381), Twin Dolphin (805–772–4483), Villager Motel (805–772–1235)

Cayucos

Beachwalker Inn, 501 South Ocean Avenue, Cayucos 93430; (805) 995–2133, fax (805) 995–3139; $85–$150; continental breakfast, no pets

Also four modest motels: Cypress Tree Motel (805–995–3917), Dolphin Inn (805–995–3810), Estero Bay Motel (805–995–3614), and Shoreline Inn (805–995–3681)

Atascadero

Best Western Colony Inn, 3600 El Camino Real, Atascadero 93422; (805) 466–4449, fax (805) 466–2119; $49–$129; pool, saunas, whirlpool, restaurant, lounge, continental breakfast, no pets

Paso Robles

Adelaide Inn, 1215 Ysabel Avenue, Paso Robles 93446; (805) 238–2770, fax (805) 238–3497; $45–$72; pool, sauna, whirlpool, no pets

Best Western Black Oak Motor Lodge, 1135 Twenty-fourth Street, Paso Robles 93446; (805) 238–4740, fax (805) 238–0726; $58–$76; pool, sauna, whirlpool, playground, coffeeshop, no pets

Holiday Inn Express Hotel and Suites, 2525 Riverside Avenue, Paso Robles 93446; (805) 237–6500; $59–$149; indoor pool, no pets

Paso Robles Inn, 1103 Spring Street, Paso Robles 93446; (805) 238–2660, fax (850) 238–4707; $80; pool, restaurant, lounge, no pets

Travelodge Paso Robles, 2701 Spring Street, Paso Robles 93446; (805) 238–0078, fax (805) 238–0822; $44–$68; pool, pets with $4.00 fee

Bed-and-breakfast: **Arbor Inn B&B,** 2130 Arbor Road, Paso Robles 93446; (805) 227–4673, fax (805) 227–1112; $125–$235; AAA four diamonds, no pets

Cambria

Best Western Fireside Inn by the Sea, 6700 Moonstone Beach Drive, Cambria 93428; (805) 927–8661, fax (805) 927–8584; $99–$169; pool, whirlpool, continental breakfast, no pets

Bluebird Motel, 1880 Main Street, Cambria 93428; (805) 926–4634, fax (805) 927–5215; $64–$150; no pets

Blue Dolphin Inn, 6470 Moonstone Beach Drive, Cambria 93428; (805) 927–3300, fax (805) 927–7311; $95–$220; continental breakfast, no pets

Cambria Landing on Moonstone Beach, 6530 Moonstone Beach Drive, Cambria 93428; (805) 927–1619; $95–$225; some cottages, breakfast in bed, whirlpools, no pets

Cambria's Pelican Suites, 6316 Moonstone Beach Drive, Cambria 93428; (805) 927–1500, fax (805) 927–3249; $100–$250; pool, continental breakfast, no pets

Fog Catcher Inn, 6400 Moonstone Beach Drive, Cambria 93428; (805) 927–1400, fax (805) 927–0204; $115–$170; pool, whirlpool, buffet breakfast, no pets

Moonstone Inn Motel, 6180 Moonstone Beach Drive, Cambria 93428; (805) 927–4815, fax (805) 927–3944; $110–$150; Jacuzzi, breakfast in bed, no pets

San Simeon Seaside Resort, 7200 Moonstone Beach Drive, Cambria 93428 (mail to PO Box 117, San Simeon 93452); (805) 927–4648; $78–$110; nine-hole golf, pool, croquet, cottages, no pets

Sea Otter Inn, 6656 Moonstone Beach Drive, Cambria 93428; (805) 927–5888, fax (805) 927–0204; $100–$130; pool, whirlpool, continental breakfast, no pets

Also (along Moonstone Beach Drive): Sand Pebbles Inn (805–927–5600), Captain's Cove Inn (805–927–8581), White Water Inn (805–927–1066), Cypress Cove Inn (805–927–2600), Cambria Shores Inn (805–927–8644), Castle Inn by the Sea (805–927–8605), Mariners Inn (805–927–4624); (downtown) Creekside Inn (805–927–4624), and Burton Drive Inn (805–927–5125)

Bed-and-breakfasts: Blue Whale Inn B&B (805–927–4647, AAA four diamonds), J. Patrick House (805–927–3812), Olallieberry Inn (805–927–3222), Squibb House (805–927–9600), and Beach House (805–927–9850, not wheelchair accessible)

San Simeon

Best Western Cavalier Ocean Front Resort, 9415 Hearst Drive, San Simeon 93452; (805) 927–4688, fax (805) 927–6472; $89–$149 and up; pools, restaurant, bar, pets OK

California Seacoast Lodge, 9215 Hearst Drive, San Simeon 93452; (805) 927–3878, fax (805) 927–1781; $65–$135; pool, continental breakfast, no pets

El Rey Garden Inn, 9260 Castillo Drive (mail to PO Box 200), San Simeon, 93452; (805) 927–3998, fax (805) 927–8268; $89–$109; small pool, whirlpools, restaurant, free breakfast, no pets

Also Quality Inn (805–927–8659), San Simeon Lodge (805–927–4601), Silver Surf Motel (805–927–4661), Motel 6 Premier (805–927–8691), Sands Motel (805–927–3243)

San Miguel

One small, modestly priced motel: Western States Inn (805–467–3674)

*G*OLF COURSES

(All eighteen-hole, unless otherwise specified)

Santa Barbara County

Santa Barbara

Rancho San Marcos Golf Course, 4600 Highway 154, Santa Barbara; may need one-month reservation; (805) 688–6334

Santa Barbara Golf Club, Las Positas Road and McCaw Avenue, Santa Barbara; par 70; need one-week reservation; (805) 687–7087

Goleta

Glen Annie Golf Course, 405 Glen Annie Road, Goleta; par 71; need one-week reservation; (805) 968–6400

Hidden Oaks Golf Course, 4760 Calle Camarada, Goleta; nine holes, par 3; (805) 967–3493

Ocean Meadows Golf Course, 6925 Whittier Drive, Goleta; nine holes, par 3; (805) 968–6814

Sandpiper Golf Course, 7925 Hollister Avenue, Goleta; par 72; need one-week reservation; (805) 968–1541

Twin Lakes Golf Course, 6034 Hollister Avenue, Goleta; nine holes, par 29; (805) 964–1414

Vandenberg Air Force Base

Marshallia Ranch Golf Course (semiprivate), Vandenberg Air Force Base; par 72; (805) 734–4764

Lompoc

La Purisima Golf Course, 3455 East Highway 246, Lompoc; need one-week reservation; (805) 735–8395

Buellton

Zaca Creek Golf Course, 223 Shadow Mountain Drive, Buellton; nine holes, par 29; (805) 688–2575

Solvang

River Course at the Alisal, 150 Alisal Road, Solvang; par 72; (805) 688–6042

Nipomo

Black Lake Golf Resort, 1490 Golf Course Lane, Nipomo; par 72; (805) 343–1214

Santa Maria

Sunset Ridge Golf Course, 1425 Fairway Avenue, Santa Maria; nine holes, par 29; (805) 347–1070

San Luis Obispo County

Grover Beach

Pismo State Beach Golf Course, 25 Grand Avenue, Grover Beach; nine holes, par 29; (805) 481–5215

Avila Beach

Avila Beach Golf Resort, Avila Beach Drive, Avila Beach; par 71; (805) 595–4000 (ext. 510)

San Luis Obispo

Laguna Lake Golf Course, 11175 Los Osos Valley Road, San Luis Obispo; nine holes, par 31; (805) 781–7309

Los Osos

Sea Pines Golf Resort, 250 Howard Avenue, Los Osos; nine holes, par 28; (805) 528–1788

Morro Bay

Morro Bay Golf Course, 101 State Park Road, Morro Bay; par 71; (805) 772–4560

Paso Robles

Hunter Ranch Golf Course, 4041 Highway 46 east, Paso Robles; par 72; (805) 237–7444

Paso Robles Golf and Country Club (semiprivate), 1600 Country Club Drive, Paso Robles; par 71; (805) 238–4710

Atascadero

Chalk Mountain Golf Course, 10000 El Bordo Avenue, Atascadero; par 72; (805) 466–8848

$\mathcal{M}$ISSIONS OF THE CENTRAL COAST

Five of the chain of twenty-one missions founded in California by the Franciscan fathers were built in what is now Santa Barbara and San Luis Obispo Counties between 1772 and 1804. They are, in order from south to north:

Mission Santa Barbara, 2201 Laguna Street, Santa Barbara 93105, (805) 682–4713

La Purisima Concepcion, in La Purisima Mission State Historic Park, 2295 Purisima Road, Lompoc 93436; (805) 733–3713

Mission Santa Ines, 1760 Mission Drive, Solvang 93463; (805) 688–4815

Mission San Luis Obispo de Tolosa, 751 Palm Street at Monterey Street, San Luis Obispo 93401; (805) 543–6850

Mission San Miguel Arcangel, 775 Mission Street, San Miguel 93451; (805) 467–3256

$\mathcal{M}$USEUMS

Santa Barbara Museum of Art, 1130 State Street, Santa Barbara; (805) 963–4364

Carriage and Western Arts Museum, 129 Castillo Street, Santa Barbara; (805) 962–2353

Karpeles Manuscript Library Museum, 21 West Anapamu Street, Santa Barbara; (805) 962–5322

Santa Barbara Historical Museum, 136 East De la Guerra Street, Santa Barbara; (805) 966–1601

Santa Barbara Museum of Natural History, 2559 Puesta del Sol Road, Santa Barbara; (805) 682–4711

South Coast Railroad Museum, 300 North Los Carneros Road, Goleta; (805) 964–3540

Lompoc Museum, 200 South H Street, Lompoc; (805) 736–3888

Santa Maria Museum of Flight, 3015 Airpark Drive, Santa Maria; (805) 922–8758

Santa Maria Valley Historical Society Museum, 616 South Broadway, Santa Maria; (805) 922–3130

Museum Art Center, near Cook and Pine Streets, Santa Maria; (805) 346–1855

Elverhoj Museum of History and Art, 1624 Elverhoj Way, Solvang; (805) 686–1211

Santa Ynez Valley Historical Museum, 3596 Sagunto Street, Santa Ynez; (805) 688–7889

San Luis Obispo Art Center, 1010 Broad Street, San Luis Obispo; (805) 543–8562

San Luis Obispo County Historical Museum, 696 Monterey Street, San Luis Obispo; (805) 543–0638

San Luis Obispo Children's Museum, 1010 Nipomo Street, San Luis Obispo; (805) 544–5437

Saint-Onge Museum of Natural History, Thirteenth and Spring Streets, Paso Robles; (805) 467–3710

*F*ACTORY STORES

Santa Barbara is known for its factory stores of companies that originated there. Here are the larger ones.

Italian Pottery Outlet, 19 Helena Street, between State and Anacapa Streets, Santa Barbara 93101; (805) 564–7655. Open 10:00 A.M.–6:00 P.M. Monday–Saturday, 10:00 A.M.–5:00 P.M. Sunday. Visa, MasterCard. Wheelchair accessible. The largest selection of Italian ceramics in the West, including seconds and firsts from classics to glass, jewelry and garden fun.

Jandd Mountaineering, 30 Calle Cesar Chavez, Santa Barbara 93103; (805) 882–1195. Open 9:00 A.M.–7:00 P.M. Monday–Saturday, 11:00 A.M.–5:00 P.M. Sunday. Visa, MasterCard, Discover. Wheelchair accessible. Great independent source for outdoor and adventure gear, first and seconds in travel and book packs and luggage, fly-fishing, hiking, mountaineering equipment. Fun place and people.

Magellan's Catalog Retail Outlet Store, 110 West Sola Street, next to the Upham Hotel, Santa Barbara 93101; (805) 568–5400. Open 9:00 A.M.–5:30 P.M. Monday–Saturday. Visa, MasterCard. Partly wheelchair accessible. One of U.S.'s largest mail-order travel stores for hats, clocks, outer wear, bags, walking sticks.

Santa Barbara Ceramic Design Factory Store, 436 East Gutierrez Street, Santa Barbara 93101; (805) 966–3883. Open 10:00 A.M.–5:00 P.M. daily. Visa,

MasterCard. Wheelchair accessible. Irregulars, overstock, discontinued and experimental pottery, as well as seconds from Mary Engelbreit, Nancy Thomas, Classic Pooh, Judy Buswell, Carol Endres, and others.

Teddy Bear Outlet, 4185-1 Carpinteria Avenue, Carpinteria 93013; (805) 566–4883, fax (805) 684–5536. Open 10:00 A.M.–5:00 P.M. Monday–Saturday, 12:00–5:00 P.M. Sunday. Visa, MasterCard, American Express. Wheelchair accessible. More than 50,000 collector Steiff, Gund, Applause, Cooperstown, Raikes, Boyds, Russ Berrie, and artist teddy bears.

Territory Ahead Outlet Store, 419 State Street, Santa Barbara 93101; (805) 962–5558. Open 10:00 A.M.–6:00 P.M. Monday–Saturday, 11:00 A.M.–5:00 P.M. Sunday. Visa, MasterCard, American Express, Discover. Wheelchair accessible. Same great outdoor equipment and clothing as in its retail store one block up State Street, but here everything is maybe one season old and a lot less expensive. Great people both places.

INDEX

ABOUT THE
AUTHORS

*K*athleen and Gerald Hill are native Californians who have lived in Sonoma Valley for more than two decades. As a team the Hills wrote *Sonoma Valley: The Secret Wine Country, Victoria and Vancouver Island: A Personal Tour of an Almost Perfect Eden, The Real Life Dictionary of the Law* (now on law.com), *The Real Life Dictionary of American Politics*, and an international exposé, *The Aquino Assassination*. Kathleen is the author of *Festivals USA* and *Festivals USA—Western States*, and she has written articles for *The Chicago Tribune, San Francisco Magazine, Cook's Magazine, San Francisco Examiner Magazine, James Beard Newsletter* and other periodicals, while Gerald was editor and co-author of *Housing in California*.

The Hills have been active in Sonoma civic and arts organizations, serving on boards of the Sonoma Cultural and Fine Arts Commission, Community Services Commission, and Sonoma Valley Hospital, among others.

Kathleen earned an A.B. at University of California at Berkeley, a Certificat from the Sorbonne in Paris, and an M.A. at Sonoma State University. Gerald holds an A.B. from Stanford University and a Juris Doctor from Hastings College of the Law, University of California.

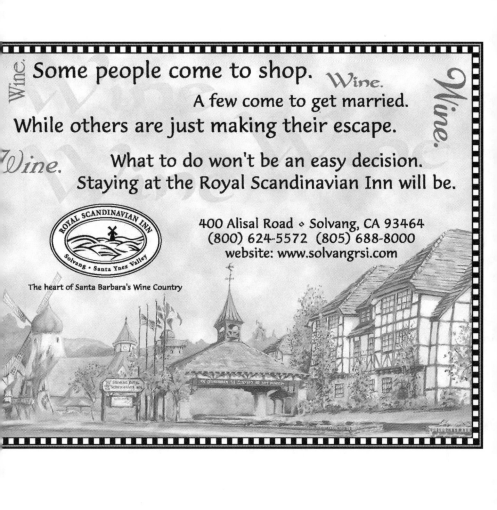

"Spirit of place! It is for this we travel, to surprise its subtlety; and where it is a strong and dominant angel, that place, seen once, abides entire in the memory with all its own accidents, its habits, its breath, its name."

—Alice Mynell, English poet & essayist

Other titles in the Hill Guides *Series:*

Monterey & Carmel: Eden by the Sea
Napa Valley: Land of Golden Vines
Northwest Wine Country: Wine's New Frontier
Sonoma Valley: The Secret Wine Country
Victoria and Vancouver Island: A Personal Tour of an Almost Perfect Eden

To order other titles in the *Hill Guides* Series, contact us at:
The Globe Pequot Press • P.O. Box 480 • Guilford, CT 06437
Ph: 800–243–0495 • www.globe-pequot.com